Yale Language Series

A GRAMMAR OF CLASSICAL ARABIC

WOLFDIETRICH FISCHER

Third Revised Edition

Translated from the German by

JONATHAN RODGERS

YALE UNIVERSITY PRESS
NEW HAVEN & LONDON

Designed by the translator.
Set with EMTEX and ArabTEX in Computer Modern Roman
and Naskh type by the translator.
Printed in the United states of America.

Library of Congress Cataloging-in-Publication Data
Fischer, Wolfdietrich.
[Grammatik des klassischen Arabisch. English]
A Grammar of Classical Arabic / Wolfdietrich Fischer ; translated from German by Jonathan Rodgers. - - 3rd rev. ed.
p. cm. - - (Yale Language Series)
English and Arabic
Includes bibliographical references and index
ISBN 0-300-08437-4 (alk. paper)
1. Arabic language - - Grammar. I. Title II. Series
PJ 6303 .F53 2001

00-048714

A catalogue record for this book is available from the British Library.

The paper in this book meets the guidelines for permanence and durability of the Committee on Production Guidelines for Book Longevity of the Council on Library Resources.

10 9 8 7 6 5 4 3 2 1

Contents

PARADIGMS

Translator's Preface

Wolfdietrich Fischer's *Grammatik des klassischen Arabisch*, Porta Linguarum Orientalium, NS XI, Wiesbaden: Harrassowitz, 1972 (reprinted with additions to the bibliography in 1987) is unquestionably the most useful reference grammar of the classical language for graduate students who have acquired proficiency in German. It is both sufficiently concise for quick reference as the student works on classical texts and rich in content to instill confidence. Although for the English-speaking student, W. Wright's *A Grammar of the Arabic Language* (3rd edition, Cambridge University Press, 1991) contains far more material, its inconvenient arrangement, obsolete English style, and often unhelpful historical and comparative linguistic data make it less than ideal for quick reference and possibly confusing. Of course, as a comprehensive resource for the study of the classical Arabic language, Wright is unsurpassed. For the English-speaking student—or one with inadequate command of German—and, especially, for the student who might be under certain conditions disinclined to invest effort and time in consulting the exhaustive richness of Wright, there has been no suitable reference grammar. This translation of Fischer's *Grammatik* aims to make up for that lack and place into the student's hands a useful and accessible reference tool.

The transliteration of the Arabic examples is based on the system employed by the English *Encyclopædia of Islam*, new edition (Leiden, 1954), with two notable exceptions, namely ق is rendered by *q*, rather than *ḳ*; ج is *j*, rather than *dj*. Thus, ث, خ, ذ, ش, غ are *th*, *kh*, *dh*, *sh*, *gh*. The ل of definite article is assimilated to the following "sun" letters, so that أَلشَّمسُ is rendered *ʾash-shamsu*, rather than *al-shamsu*.

The original bibliography, now more than ten years old, has been updated with significant and major contributions to the field of classical Arabic grammar and linguistics. Since, however, almost all recent books and articles on classical Arabic grammar and its cognate fields are indexed or available in full-text in one or several electronic resources, the translator felt that an exhaustive update in print would be superfluous. Thus, the updated bibliography presented here is expected to serve only as an initial reference tool.

The idea to undertake the translation of Fischer's invaluable resource was conceived long ago when the translator was a graduate student who felt acutely the need for a handy English-language reference resource to aid in working on classical texts. The work was not begun until recently and has progressed unsteadily as time permitted. Originally planned to be completed several years ago, it only now appears thanks to persistent and gentle reminders from the editors at Yale University Press and the forbearance of the translator's employer and spouse.

The translator is pleased to acknowledge the indispensable and patient assistance of the author, who graciously provided changes and additions to the original text for incorporation into this updated English edition. The chapter on syntax, especially, benefits from his numerous additions and improvements.

Well-deserved credit is due Wolfhart Heinrichs, who willingly and patiently read through the translation, spotted numerous errors in translation and style, and contributed valuable and much appreciated suggestions for improvement.

The contribution of Peter T. Daniels, who volunteered to undertake the laborious task of proof-reading the final draft, is gratefully acknowledged. His acute eye eliminated countless misspellings, inconsistencies, and other typographical blunders.

This work was produced with Eberhard Mattes' typesetting program EMTEX, in combination with Klaus Lagally's set of TEX macros, ArabTEX. Their valuable contribution is hereby gratefully recognized. ArabTEX significantly facilitated the typesetting of the text in mixed Arabic and Roman fonts.

This work is dedicated to two towering figures of American scholarship, John Rodgers, geologist and musician, and Franz Rosenthal, Arabist, Islamicist, and Semitist. Their inestimable and unmatched work continues to challenge and inspire us.

Jonathan Rodgers
Ann Arbor, April 2000

Preface

For German readers, Carl Brockelmann's *Arabische Grammatik* has served for more than half a century as the textbook presenting a systematic grammar of classical Arabic. The longevity of his grammar is due to its exactness and precision, as it masterfully limits itself to the essentials. His description of the syntax represents a significant advancement in Arabic grammatical studies. When Otto Harrassowitz invited me to undertake a revision of this tried and proven text, which had already gone through fourteen editions, it immediately became clear that it was really time to begin from the ground up. Reworking the old grammar was out of the question.

Earlier grammars had borrowed their system of description from the Arab grammarians and adapted it to the style of Latin grammars used in schools. When Carl Brockelmann undertook his revision of Socin's *Arabische Grammatik* for *Porta linguarum orientalium* in 1904, he was still working on his *Grundriß der vergleichenden Grammatik der semitischen Sprachen*. In particular, the syntax in this small Arabic grammar benefited from the results of this historical-comparative study. Since then, however, our understanding of this area of Arabic grammar has grown, as basic research in grammatical methodology has progressed. Research begun a few decades ago that has led to a clearer knowledge of Akkadian has thrown into question many of the old principles of Semitics and demands a completely new presentation of the historical-linguistic issues. Modern linguistics justifiably requires that a grammar emphasize the descriptive aspect over historical speculation, which has, indeed, proven to be an inadequacy of previous grammatical descriptions.

A grammar that is intended to be used mostly as a teaching and reference work, and thus is not a linguistic treatise, should not experiment with methodological and terminological innovation. Therefore, traditional terminology and, in general, the traditional arrangement of the grammar have been preserved, although efforts have been made to present a description consistent with current theory. It has avoided, accordingly, a break with tradition.

Those who wish to embark on training in classical Arabic and those who are already well-acquainted with it have an equal need for a systematic grammar that contains not just the bare essentials, but also everything that is necessary for the interpretation of texts. Brockelmann's treatise, despite its excellence, is too terse. Whenever searching for help in interpreting difficult passages, one must resort to Wright's larger and more comprehensive work, *A Grammar of the Arabic Language*, or to the more specialized works on syntax by Hermann Reckendorf. In producing a new grammar of classical Arabic, I took efforts to offer more comprehensively and present as elaborately and completely as possible all the grammatical material required for the interpretation of classical prose as one might encounter under normal circumstances. The material selected is representative of the morphology and syntax of normal classical Arabic. Deviations from the norm, as they occur in pre- and post-classical texts, are pointed out in the notes. The information presented should also be more than sufficient for the understanding of poetical texts.

The examples cited are for the most part borrowed from the standard grammatical treatises (Wright, Nöldeke, Reckendorf, Brockelmann, Wehr, Spitaler) and to a smaller extent are supplemented from my own stock. As is usual in a work intended for instructional purposes, the origin of the examples is not given in detail. Specialists will be able to find out in most cases the sources without too much difficulty. Only citations from the Koran are noted as such. As far as possible, the example phrases in the chapter on syntax are taken from prose texts. Since, however, so much previous research has been based on poetical texts, the goal of drawing examples exclusively from prose sources could not always be fulfilled. Nevertheless, examples from poetry, when they are not explicitly so indicated, are used only if they can illustrate prose usage as well.

Description of the functions of morphological groups (e.g., forms of the verb, state of the nominal forms, elative, etc.), as well as the formal description of word constructions (e.g., genitive constructions, numerical expressions, agreement), can be found in the section on morphology. This arrangement represents a departure from the traditional, in which such grammatical material is usually treated in syntax. Similarly, the function and formal arrangement of the particles within the sentence structure are also presented in morphology. The treatment of the syntax itself then comes in its proper place: It comprises the description of the sentence composed of its parts (Syntax: Parts of the Sentence) and the hierarchical arrangement of the clauses that make up the sentence (Syntax of Clauses). Consistently, I have attempted to underpin the syntactic system with a formal theoretical basis. Such an arrangement of the material is best suited for introducing features of the language with which the beginner is unacquainted. The arrangement according to function can readily offer to users of this grammar the facts about function and meaning of specific linguistic phenomena.

A consistent arrangement with numerous cross-references whenever several principles are involved in one and the same feature, as well as repetition, when necessary, should make it easier for the user to look up and locate specific morphemes and structures. The rules are concisely formulated, and the examples provided are selected to be as representative as possible. The illustrative text and examples provided are intended to supplement one another and to be mutually self-explanatory. References to other sections of the work should not be overlooked. The reference numbers always refer to paragraph numbers (§). Numbers following decimal points refer to the notes: §110.5 means §100, Note 5.

Arabic citations and examples are vocalized only in the phonology and syntax chapters. In morphology, the unvocalized Arabic is provided with transliteration. That offers the advantage of allowing the reader to become accustomed to seeing unvocalized text, as is the normal situation in Arabic texts. Additionally, this manner of representation allows one to see clearly how Arabic forms are correctly transcribed, an important feature, given the increasing significance of transcribed citations in the scholarly literature. Hypothetical forms are noted by a preceding *, and historical development or origin of forms is noted by > or <.

Earlier grammars usually offered the terminology of the Arab grammarians. By design, most of the Arabic technical terms are absent from this treatise. After considerable thought, they were left out and should be reserved for a specialized description of the system of native Arabic grammar. The system used in this grammar does not rely on the Arabic grammatical tradition. The use of Arabic terminology would, if it were employed, inevitably cause misunderstandings. Only occasionally, and only when an Arabic expression has been naturalized in European grammars, has it been employed.

The notorious difficulties of classical Arabic have their origin not only in the language itself and its inadequate and equivocal orthography, but also in the paucity of useful aids available to the student. The lexicon and grammar are still far from the point where the language can be said to be fully probed and understood. This grammar claims only to attempt to gather together in a concise and clear manner the results of previous scholarship and fashion these into a grammatical system that adequately describes the language. In undertaking this endeavor, several Arabists, foremost Prof. Anton Spitaler and Prof. Hans Wehr, have supported me by offering their friendly advice and many valuable ideas. I hereby extend to them my sincere gratitude. The publication of a new edition in English gives me the opportunity to add some corrections and improvements. Finally, I feel bound to say special thanks to Jonathan Rodgers, who spared no effort to translate this book precisely and in an adequate manner.

Erlangen, April 1996
Wolfdietrich Fischer

Introduction

As a result of the conversion of Arabs to Islam and their establishment of the Islamic empire, Arabic, originally a language of poetry and religion, arose as the linguistic medium of learning and literature for the entire Islamic world. Muslims employed this language, known to us as classical Arabic, in government administration, in literature and science. After the revival of modern Persian and the rise of popular literary languages like Turkish began to constrain the far-flung realm of Arabic in later centuries of the empire, classical Arabic continued to serve as the language of learning for the Islamic world, particularly in the area of religious scholarship. Wherever used, Arabic has maintained the status of a language of the learned and cultured. Modern written Arabic is, indeed, a continuation of and the current version of classical Arabic.

From its earliest times to the present, Arabic has remained superficially almost unchanged. Apart from a few details, the morphology of the old poetic language and that of modern written Arabic are identical. Although the language has continued naturally to change and adapt to new circumstances in many aspects of word usage, in choice of syntactic patterns, and in style, the vocabulary and syntax have remained fundamentally similar.

The "classical" period of this learned literary language occurs in the late eighth and ninth centuries, the golden age of the Abbasid Caliphate. In Kufah and Basrah, philologists had begun to impose on the grammar an academic system, assemble the lexicon, and write the works of lexicography. Mastery of classical Arabic became the highest ideal in the education of Muslims. Philology and grammar became the most thoroughly cultivated sciences in the Islamic world.

Vintage texts of pre- and early Islamic poetry served preeminently as the foundation and prototype of the philological discipline that took shape in the 9th century, while the Koran also played a role. These "pre-classical" old Arabic texts, however, frequently exhibit subtle differences from the language of the "classical" period: Among them is a degree of morphological freedom and archaism that did not gain acceptance in prescriptive grammatical circles and therefore vanished from the classical language. It is difficult, however, to draw a precise boundary between the "pre-classical" language of the pre- and early Islamic corpus and the "classical" language of the philologically learned, because the early texts were widely known, learned, and admired. To speakers of Arabic, *belles lettres* means almost exclusively poetry. In poetry, the often celebrated poets of pre- and early

Islamic times have always been invoked, and archaic forms and unusual syntactic constructions recur with equal frequency in the poetry of later generations.

Despite the prescriptive preoccupation of Arab philologists and grammarians and the language's almost definitive stabilization by the 9th century, classical Arabic did not cease to exist as a natural language. There was constant contact with the spoken language alongside the pursuit on the part of scholars of more precise and flexible means of expression. Out of these conditions, new stylistic and syntactic formations soon developed. By the end of the tenth century, the classical period had ended and gave way to a post-classical form whose constructions and expressions, although rejected by prescriptive grammatical norms, became widely accepted. Nevertheless, the demarcation is equivocal. For every writer who faithfully adhered to classical models, there was another who felt little compunction about indulging in innovation.

From the beginning of its tradition, from the pre-classical language of pre- and early Islamic poetry up through modern written Arabic, classical Arabic has been the language of poetry, culture, literature, and science, the language of the school and education, but not the everyday spoken language. Coexisting with the classical tongue has been another Arabic that contrasts in some respects in morphology and syntax and that is exclusively spoken and not written. Command of the cultural language has always been an issue of education and scholarship. Of course, there were writers who had little or no familiarity with grammatical rules and who thus consistently used forms and expressions from the spoken Arabic in the written or incorrectly used classical forms. We call the language of such writers "Middle Arabic", because it occupied an intermediate position between the learned language and the spoken. Examples of this form exist abundantly in documents of Christian or Jewish origin. The maintenance of classical Arabic was the principal concern of Muslims who revered it as the language of the Koran.

Despite some modification, the structure of classical Arabic, which had stabilized in the 9th century, has remained a genuine immutable standard. The description of classical Arabic necessarily focuses on the language of the "classical" period. This grammar treats above all this classical language. Insofar as it is possible from the current state of research, the "pre-classical" and "post-classical" languages are referred to as divergent forms. Deviations from the classical norm, which cannot be unequivocally identified as either pre- or post-classical, are designated "non-classical".

Writing System

The Alphabet

§**1.** In the 3rd century AD, Arab Nabateans, although they had normally used Aramaic as their written language, began writing Arabic. The 22 letters of the Aramaic alphabet, some of which in the course of time had acquired the same shape, could not adequately represent the 28 consonantal phonemes of Arabic. The Arabs had to distinguish the ambiguous letters they had adopted with diacritical marks. The original Aramaic order of the alphabet is preserved when the letters serve as numbers (see table):

ا ب ج د ه و ز ح ط ی ك ل م ن س ع ف ص ق ر ش ت

Various writing styles developed during Islamic times, including, among the most important, the monumental *kūfī* and the cursive *nas<u>kh</u>ī*. A peculiar style, the *ma<u>gh</u>ribī* extended throughout North Africa (*Ma<u>gh</u>rib*) and Muslim Spain. Today, the most frequently encountered printed fonts are based on the *nas<u>kh</u>ī*.

Note 1. Script without diacritical marks is called رسم *rasm*. Diacritical marks are partly or altogether lacking in some manuscripts.

Note 2. In the Maghribi style of writing, ڢ is used in place of ف (*fā'*) and ڧ in place of ق (*qāf*).

Note 3. Today, the order of the letters in the alphabet is for the most part determined by similarity of shape. Instead of the order ه و ی as the last three letters, one sometimes encounters an older order و ه ی. There are also other sequences. In Muslim Spain and North Africa the usual order was:

ا ب ت ث ج ح خ د ذ ر ز ط ظ ك ل م ن ص ض ع غ ف ق س ش ه
و ی

§**2.** Arabic writing runs from right to left. Some letters are joined to each other, while others are separate. The letters ا د ذ ر ز و connect only to the preceding, not to the following, letter. Thus, a letter that follows one of these must assume its initial form: صاحب *ṣāḥib*, أهل *ʾahl*, صديق *ṣadīq*, أذن *ʾu<u>dh</u>un*, فرس *faras*, رأس *raʾs*, منزل *manzil*, موضع *mawḍiʿ*, وفد *wafd*.

Table of the Arabic Writing System

Isolated	From Right	Medial	To Left	Tran-scription	Letter Name	Numeric Value
ا	ـا	—	—	*ʾ, ā*	*ʾalif*	1
ب	ـب	ـبـ	بـ	*b*	*bāʾ*	2
ت	ـت	ـتـ	تـ	*t*	*tāʾ*	400
ث	ـث	ـثـ	ثـ	*t͟h*	*t͟hāʾ*	500
ج	ـج	ـجـ	جـ	*j*	*jīm*	3
ح	ـح	ـحـ	حـ	*ḥ*	*ḥāʾ*	8
خ	ـخ	ـخـ	خـ	*k͟h*	*k͟hāʾ*	600
د	ـد	—	—	*d*	*dāl*	4
ذ	ـذ	—	—	*d͟h*	*d͟hāl*	700
ر	ـر	—	—	*r*	*rāʾ*	200
ز	ـز	—	—	*z*	*zāy*	7
س	ـس	ـسـ	سـ	*s*	*sīn*	60
ش	ـش	ـشـ	شـ	*s͟h*	*s͟hīn*	300
ص	ـص	ـصـ	صـ	*ṣ*	*ṣād*	90
ض	ـض	ـضـ	ضـ	*ḍ*	*ḍād*	800
ط	ـط	ـطـ	طـ	*ṭ*	*ṭāʾ*	9
ظ	ـظ	ـظـ	ظـ	*ẓ, ḏ*	*ẓāʾ*	900
ع	ـع	ـعـ	عـ	*ʿ*	*ʿayn*	70
غ	ـغ	ـغـ	غـ	*g͟h*	*g͟hayn*	1000
ف	ـف	ـفـ	فـ	*f*	*fāʾ*	80
ق	ـق	ـقـ	قـ	*q*	*qāf*	100
ك	ـك	ـكـ	كـ	*k*	*kāf*	20
ل	ـل	ـلـ	لـ	*l*	*lām*	30
م	ـم	ـمـ	مـ	*m*	*mīm*	40
ن	ـن	ـنـ	نـ	*n*	*nūn*	50
ه	ـه	ـهـ	هـ	*h*	*hāʾ*	5
و	ـو	—	—	*w, ū*	*wāw*	6
ى	ـى	ـيـ	يـ	*y, ī*	*yāʾ*	10

For pronunciation, see §§27 ff.

§**3.** Calligraphy prescribes the use of ligatures to join certain letters:

a) Initial forms of ب ت ث ن ی, when joined to ج ح خ and م create the following ligatures, respectively: بج تج ثج نخ, etc., or بحـ تحـ يجـ ثحـ, etc., and بم تم ثم يم, etc., or بمـ نمـ تمـ, etc. Similarly, ف and ق join with ج ح خ to form, respectively: فخ or فخـ, etc.

Note 1. For typographical reasons, certain ligatures containing ج ح خ, such as بج فج تخ لج, etc., are avoided in print. Instead, such combinations as بج فج, etc., are employed.

b) The *lām–alif* ligature is written لا and لا, respectively; *lām-mīm*, لم and لم, respectively; *kāf-alif*, كا; *kāf-lām*, كل; *kāf-lām-alif*, كلا.

Note 2. In the لا *lām-alif* ligature, of Nabatean origin, it appears that the left shaft, *lām*, and the right, *alif*, cross to form لا < *لا .

c) Before final ی, ب ت ث ن ی and ف ق are shortened to: بی تی نی فی قی, etc. Before ی and ر ز, the "teeth" of س ش and ص ض are altered to form the ligatures: سر شز سى صر ضى.

d) In combination with ر ز and final ن, the medial form ـبـ of ب ت ث ن ی is changed as follows: بر تز بن ين, etc.

Note 3. In a sequence of several letters of the basic form of ـبـ or ـر — including the "teeth" of س ش ص ض — alternating higher and lower forms are used to distinguish the letters. The sequence begins with a lower form: تنسب *tanassaba*, يتثبت *yatathabbatu*, شتيت *shatīt*, تصنيف *taṣnīf*.

Note 4. ى is also written ي (with two points under the form, as in, يـ ـيـ). In many countries, ي is employed to express *ī* and *ay*, while ى is used to express *ā* (§10).

Orthography

§**4.** The orthography of classical Arabic was fixed during the 8th–9th century by the Arab grammarians. With few exceptions, classical orthographic conventions have remained valid until the present for the written language. Some archaic, pre-classical spellings have been preserved in the classical orthography (cf. §§7.7; 8; 9; 10.2). These archaic writing conventions originated in a form of Arabic that in several respects deviated from the classical norm, but they were adopted anyway almost without change by classical Arabic. The most important deviations are: ʾ (*hamzah*) was not pronounced within a word or in final position; occasionally, it was replaced by *w* or *y* (§14). The noun case endings *-un*, *-in*, *-an* were lacking. The feminine ending was *-ah* (§13). In adapting the orthography to the phonology of classical Arabic, auxiliary orthographic signs were introduced. These include signs to denote vowels, which were imperfectly represented in a writing system that consisted of consonant signs only. The auxiliary signs are used consistently and fully only in the Koran and frequently in poetry. For the most part, they are employed as needed to assist the reader through difficult texts, or frequently they are completely lacking.

Short Vowels

§**5.** The short vowels *a, i, u* are rendered by diacritical marks placed above or below the consonant that precedes them. (For the romanized pausal forms of the Arabic technical terms, see §57.)

1. ـَـ (فَتْحَةٌ *fatḥah*) *a* (فَتْحٌ *fatḥ*): مَنَعَ *manaʿa*, ذَهَبَ *dhahaba*.
2. ـِـ (كَسْرَةٌ *kasrah*) *i* (كَسْرٌ *kasr*): شَرِبَ *shariba*, قَبِلَ *qabila*.
3. ـُـ (ضَمَّةٌ *ḍammah*) *u* (ضَمٌّ *ḍamm*): عَظُمَ *ʿaẓuma*, عَلُ *ʿalu*.

§**6.** ـْـ (سُكُونٌ *sukūn*) marks the absence of a vowel after a consonant. At the end of a word, this sign is called جَزْمَةٌ *jazmah*: بَلْ *bal*, نِعْمَ *niʿma*, يَكْتُبْ *yaktub*.

> **Note 1.** On the dropping of *sukūn* with *ā, ī, ū*, see §7. For other examples, see §18.

Long Vowels

§**7.** Long vowels are represented by: ا = *ā*, ى = *ī*, و = *ū*, where the preceding letter retains the corresponding short vowel sign (i.e., ـَـ *a*, ـِـ *i*, ـُـ *u*). Usually, however, ـْـ *sukūn* is not placed over ا ى و : قَاتَلَ *qātala*, نُوزِعَ *nūziʿa*, لُومِي *lūmī*, سِيرِي *sīrī*. On the other hand, *sukūn* is written where و and ى represent *aw* and *ay*: لَوْمِي *lawmī*, سَيْرِي *sayrī*.

> **Note 1.** For ي representing *ī*, *ay* and ى, *ā*, see §§3.4; 10.

Note 2. A "silent" ا follows و in the plural verb ending *-ū*, *-aw*: كَتَبُوا *katabū*, يَكْتُبُوا *yaktubū*, رَمَوْا *ramaw*, يَلْقَوْا *yalqaw*.

Note 3. For metre and *tajwīd*, the vowels in the personal pronoun suffixes هُ, هِ usually count as short, if a closed syllable precedes, but long if an open syllable precedes. There is no orthographic distinction made: دَارُهُ *dāru-hū*, رِجْلِهِ *rijli-hī*, رَمَاهُ *ramā-hu*, يَرْمِيهِ *yarmī-hi* (§268).

Note 4. Final *-ī* in ذِهِ *dhihī*, هٰذِهِ *hādhihī*, تِهِ *tihī*, هَاتِهِ *hātihī* 'these' (fem.), is not written. In the Koran, the same kinds of spellings also occur frequently in other words: رَبِّ *rabbī* 'my lord', صَالِ *ṣālī* 'burning'. In poetry, they are often encountered at verse end where all vowels count as long (§56c).

Note 5. Final *-ū* in هُمُ *humū*, كُمُ *-kumū*, تُمُ *-tumū* (§264.2) is not written.

Note 6. For metre in poetry, أَنَا *ʾanā* 'I' usually counts as *ʾana*.

Note 7. Despite their short *u*, the plural demonstratives (§274 f.) are commonly written with و: أُولَى *ʾulā*, أُولَاءِ *ʾulāʾi*, أُولُو *ʾulū*, أُولَاكَ *ʾulāka*, أُولَائِكَ *ʾulāʾika*.

§8. In archaic spellings, for example in the Koran, *ā* is not consistently represented by ا . To distinguish long from short vowels, *alif* is introduced as a vowel sign: قِيٰمَةٌ = قِيَامَةٌ *qiyāmatun* 'rising up', إِلٰهٌ = إِلَاهٌ *ʾilāhun* 'god', سَمٰوٰتٌ = سَمَاوَاتٌ *samāwātun* 'heaven', ثَلٰثٌ = ثَلَاثٌ *thalāthun* 'three', لٰكِنْ = لَاكِنْ *lākin* 'but', etc. In some words, this spelling is consistently used: هٰذَا *hādhā* 'this', أَللّٰهُ *ʾal-lāhu* 'God', أَلرَّحْمٰنُ *ʾar-raḥmānu* 'the merciful', ذٰلِكَ *dhālika* 'that'.

Note 1. For technical reasons, sometimes just ـَ (*fatḥa*) is printed in place of ـٰ : هَذَا, i.e., *hādhā*, إِلَهٌ, i.e., *ʾilāhun*.

§9. Some words ending in *ātun* have preserved a historical spelling with an Aramaic antecedent: صَلٰوةٌ and صَلَاةٌ *ṣalātun* 'prayer', حَيٰوةٌ and حَيَاةٌ *ḥayātun* 'life', زَكٰوةٌ and زَكَاةٌ *zakātun* 'alms', مِشْكٰوةٌ and مِشْكَاةٌ *mishkātun* 'lamp niche'. Similar examples of historical orthography are found in رِبٰو (أَلرِّبٰو) and رِبًا (أَلرِّبَا) *riban* (*ʾar-ribā*) 'usury', تَوْرِيٰةٌ and تَوْرَاةٌ *tawrātun* 'Torah'.

§**10.** At the end of a word, -*ā* is frequently written with ى (§3.4): رَمَى *ramā* 'he threw', ذِكْرَى *dhikrā* 'remembrance', عَلَى *ʿalā* 'on', بَلَى *balā* 'certainly!'. When such an -*ā* occurs within a word, it is written with ا : رَمَاهُ *ramāhu*, ذِكْرَاهَا *dhikrāhā*. The following rules for the writing of *ā* with ى obtain: With verbs, writing with ى is the rule; only in the basic stem (I) of verbs ending in *w* (III-*w* §250) is it written with ا . With nouns, ى figures when *ā* is not part of the stem (§64 b). Stem final -*ā* should be written with ا only in III-*w* roots; see also §12.

Note 1. After ي, ا is always used to represent *ā*: دُنْيَا *dunyā* 'world' (not دُنْيَى), أَحْيَا *ʾaḥyā* 'revived' (not أَحْيَى).

Note 2. In Koranic spelling, ى for *ā* is often retained within a word before an affix. *Alif* is used as a vowel sign to designate *ā* (cf. §8), as it does for final *ā*: رَمَى *ramā*, رَمَيٰهُ *ramāhu*, سِيمَيٰهُمْ *sīmāhum*.

Note 3. The Arab grammarians applied the term أَلِفٌ مَقْصُورَةٌ *alif maqṣūrah* to *ā* written with ى (and ا), in contrast to أَلِفٌ مَمْدُودَةٌ *alif mamdūdah* for -*āʾu*(*n*) written with اء.

Tanwīn (Nunation)

§**11.** The consonantal writing system does not represent the noun endings -*un*, -*in*, -*an* (§147). These must be indicated by diacritical marks ـٌ -*un*, ـٍ-*in*, ـً *an*. The accusative ending, ـً -*an*, is additionally accompanied by ا (*alif*): رَجُلٌ *rajulun*, رَجُلٍ *rajulin*, رَجُلًا *rajulan*. ا does not appear with the accusative diacritic ـً, however, in the feminine ending -*at-an* (§13): مَدِينَةً *madīnatan*, جَمِيلَةً *jamīlatan*, or in words ending in -*āʾ*: سَمَاءً *samāʾan*.

Note 1. An archaic spelling has been preserved in the proper name ʿAmr: Nominative عَمْرٌو *ʿAmrun*, Genitive عَمْرٍو *ʿAmrin*, Accusative عَمْرًا *ʿAmran*. The و serves to distinguish graphically ʿAmr from the otherwise similarly written proper name ʿOmar: Nominative عُمَرُ *ʿUmaru*, Genitive, Accusative عُمَرَ *ʿUmara*.

Note 2. The writing ـًا occurs both in إِذًا *ʾidhan*, alongside إِذَنْ *ʾidhan*, 'then, therefore', and in the energetic ending -*an* (§215): يَنْفَعًا *yanfaʿan* or يَنْفَعَنْ *yanfaʿan*, 'may it be useful'.

§**12.** In nouns whose stem final *-ā* is written with ى (§10), when the *-n* ending is added, the spelling with ى is retained and the final *-an* is written ـًى: هُدًى *hudan*, فَتًى *fatan* (compare أَلْهُدَى *ʾal-hudā*, أَلْفَتَى *ʾal-fatā*). The spelling with ى *ā* is the rule, if *y* is the final root letter; however, if it is *w*, ا is written: عَصًا *ʿaṣan* (compare أَلْعَصَا *al-ʿaṣā*).

Note 1. Spellings with ى and ا alternate frequently in nouns: عَصًا *ʿaṣan* or عَصًى *ʿaṣan* (root *ʿ-ṣ-w*), حَشًا *ḥashan* or حَشًى *ḥashan* (root *ḥ-sh-w*).

Tāʾ marbūṭah

§**13.** The origin of the orthography of the feminine singular ending *-at(un)*, *-āt(un)* is non-classical *-ah*, *-āh* (§4). To produce the classical pronunciation, the two points of the ت are placed on the ه: كَلِمَةٌ *kalimatun*, كَلِمَةٍ *kalimatin*, كَلِمَةً *kalimatan* (§11), فَتَاةٌ *fatātun*, فَتَاةٍ *fatātin*, فَتَاةً *fatātan*.

Hamzah

§**14.** The glottal stop, ʾ, which in classical Arabic is a phoneme, was preserved only at the beginning of a word in the non-classical language, according to the consonantal writing system. In initial position, it was indicated by ا: امر *ʾamr* 'order', ابل *ʾibil*, 'camel', اخت *ʾukht* 'sister'. In all other positions, since it was no longer pronounced, ʾ was not written. In syllable-final position, the disappearance of ʾ caused the lengthening of the preceding sound: راس *rās* 'head' in place of classical رَأْسٌ *raʾsun*, بير *bīr* 'well' for classical بِئْرٌ *biʾrun*, بوس *būs* 'misery' for classical بُؤْسٌ *buʾsun*. Vowels of like quality were contracted after the disappearance of ʾ: روس *rūs* 'heads' for رُءُوسٌ *ruʾūsun*, سال *sāla* 'ask' for سَأَلَ *saʾala*; between vowels of different quality, *w* or *y* developed: سوال *suwāl* 'question' for سُؤَالٌ *suʾālun*, قايم *qāyim* 'standing' for قَائِمٌ *qāʾimun*, خطيه *khaṭīyah* 'sin' for خَطِيئَةٌ *khaṭīʾatun*. After consonants, ʾ was completely dropped or replaced by *y* or *w* for morphological reasons: بد *bad* 'beginning' for بَدْءٌ *badʾun*, مسله *masalah* 'question' for مَسْأَلَةٌ *masʾalatun*, سوه *sawwah* 'disgrace' for سَوْءَةٌ *sawʾatun*.

At the end of a word, ʾ disappeared after long vowels: سما *samā* 'heaven' for سَمَاءٌ *samāʾun*, بري *barī* 'innocent' for بَرِيءٌ *barīʾun*, سو *sū* 'evil' for سُوءٌ *sūʾun*.

§**15.** In classical Arabic orthography, ʾ (هَمْزٌ *hamz*) is represented by ء (هَمْزَةٌ *hamzah*), where, depending on the spelling convention, ا و ى serve as carriers (or 'seats'), or, if none of these letters is available, ء has no seat. If *hamzah* falls on ئـ or ـئ, the letter loses its diacritical points. The following rules for the writing of *hamzah* obtain as a result of historical orthography:

a) At the beginning of a word, ا carries *hamzah*: أَمْرٌ *ʾamrun*, إِبِلٌ *ʾibilun*, أُخْتٌ *ʾukhtun*.

b) Before and after *a*, ا carries *hamzah*, if *i* or *u* is not in contact: رَأْسٌ *raʾsun*, أَرْأَسُ *ʾarʾasu*, سَأَلَ *saʾala*, قَرَأَ *qaraʾa*.

c) Before and after *u*, و carries *hamzah*, if *i* is not in contact: بُؤْسٌ *buʾsun*, أَبْؤُسٌ *ʾabʾusun*, رَؤُفَ *raʾufa*, رُؤَسَاءُ *ruʾasāʾu*.

d) Before and after *i*, ى carries *hamzah*: بِئْرٌ *biʾrun*, اَسْئِلَةٌ *asʾilatun*, كَئِبَ *kaʾiba*, قَائِمٌ *qāʾimun*, رِئَاسَةٌ *riʾāsatun*, سُئِلَ *suʾila*.

e) At the end of a syllable, *hamzah* is written without a seat following a consonant or long vowel: سَمَاءٌ *samāʾun*, بَرِيءٌ *barīʾun*, سُوءٌ *sūʾun*, بَدْءٌ *badʾun*, شَيْءٌ *shayʾun*, شَيْئًا *shayʾan*.

f) Within a word, ء is written without a seat after a consonant or long vowel in the classical orthography: سَاءَلَ *sāʾala*, مَسْءَلَةٌ *masʾalatun*, سَوْءَةٌ *sawʾatun*, خَطِيءَةٌ *khaṭīʾatun*. Today, however, one usually encounters these spellings: مَسْأَلَةٌ or مَسْئَلَةٌ, سَوْأَةٌ, خَطِيئَةٌ.

Note 1. The ء sign derives from ع (ع).

Note 2. After stem final *-āʾ*, the accusative ending *-an* is not marked by ا: سَمَاءً *samāʾan* (not سَمَاءًا); see §11.

Note 3. Today, the sound sequences *ʾī* and *ʾū* within a word are usually written ئي and ؤو. Older spellings avoid the sequence of two ى's or و's and prefer ءِي and ءُو : رُؤُوسٌ = رُءُوسٌ *ruʾūsun*, كَئِيبٌ = كَئِيبٌ *kaʾībun*.

Note 4. An isolated historical spelling occurs in مِائَةٌ *miʾatun* 'hundred'.

Maddah

§**16.** Rather than أا for ʾā, to avoid two successive ا's, one writes: آ (مَدَّةٌ *maddah*): آكِلٌ ʾ*ākilun*, قُرْآنٌ *qurʾānun*, رَآهُ *raʾāhu*.

Note 1. In archaic spelling, for example in the Koran, *madda* identifies the sound sequences *āʾ*, *īʾ*, *ūʾ* (long vowel + ʾ): أَصْدِقَآؤُهُ ʾ*aṣdiqāʾuhū*, يَجِيٓءُ *yajīʾu*, سُوٓئِلَ *sūʾila*.

Shaddah

§**17.** Doubling of a consonant is indicated by ـّ (شَدَّةٌ *shaddah*): نَزَّلَ *nazzala*, بَشَّارٌ *bashshārun*, نَوَّرَ *nawwara*, سَيِّدٌ *sayyidun*, سَآّلٌ *saʾʾālun*. Since *ī* is the same as *iy* and *ū* the same as *uw* (§28), the sequences *īy* and *ūw* can be transliterated *iyy* and *uww*: صَبِيٌّ *ṣabīyun* (*ṣabiyyun*), عَدُوٌّ ʿ*adūwun* (ʿ*aduwwun*).

Note 1. The sign ـّ is derived from ش, that is, *shaddah*.

Note 2. In modern printing, ـِ *kasrah* is usually placed immediately under ـّ, while ـَ *fatḥah* lies on top: نَزِّلْ = نَزِّلْ *nazzil*.

Note 3. When part of a doubled consonant is an element of inflection, only one letter is written, and it bears the *shaddah*: إِتَّرَكَ (ʾ*i*)*t-t-araka* (§170), ثَبَتُّ *thabat-tu* (§207). One spells forms resulting from assimilation in the same way: مِمَّنْ *mimman* < *min-man*, أَلَّا ʾ*allā* < ʾ*an-lā* (§45).

§**18.** The *l* of the definite article (ʾ*a*)*l-* is assimilated to the following consonant, if the forward part of the tongue is involved in its articulation (the "sun" letters [§44]). ل is always written, and the assimilation is indicated by ـّ placed over the following letter. ل does not take *sukūn*: أَلدَّارُ ʾ*ad-dāru* < ʾ*al-dāru*, أَلرَّجُلُ ʾ*ar-rajulu* < ʾ*al-rajulu*, أَلسَّنَةُ ʾ*as-sanatu* < ʾ*al-sanatu*, أَلنَّارُ ʾ*an-nāru* < ʾ*al-nāru*, but أَلْجَارُ ʾ*al-jāru*, أَلْبَابُ ʾ*al-bābu*. Before *l*, the article behaves as it does in assimilation: أَللَّيْلَةُ ʾ*al-laylatu*, أَللِّسَانُ ʾ*al-lisānu*; also أَللّٰهُ ʾ*al-lāhu* "God" < ʾ*al-ʾilāhu* "the god" (§49d).

Note 1. Note the writing of only one ل in the following forms of relative pronouns: أَلَّذِي ʾ*alladhī*, أَلَّذِينَ ʾ*alladhīna*, أَلَّتِي ʾ*allatī*, while the other forms are spelled with two ل's: أَللَّذَانِ ʾ*al-ladhāni*, أَللَّتَانِ ʾ*al-latāni*, أَللَّوَاتِي ʾ*al-lawātī*, etc. (§281).

Note 2. In the same way as with articles, the spelling of other words may occasionally reveal assimilation, for example: شَهِدتُّ *sh̲ahidtu* > *sh̲ahittu*, غَفُورٌ رَّحِيمٌ *gh̲afūrun raḥīmun* > *gh̲afūrur-raḥīmun* (Koran 2:173, 182, 192, etc.); cf. §48.

Waṣlah

§19. Classical Arabic does not allow a double consonant at the beginning of a word and avoids the possibility by introducing an auxiliary vowel that precedes an initial double consonant. The orthography requires that an ا introduce a word that would otherwise begin with a double consonant. In non-classical Arabic, on which the orthography is based, the auxiliary vowel became an essential component of the word: إسم *ʾism*, classical (*ʾi*)*smun* 'name', إبن *ʾibn*, classical (*ʾi*)*bnun* 'son', إنصرف *ʾinṣaraf*, classical (*ʾi*)*nṣarafa* 'turn away', أخرج *ʾukh̲ruj*, classical (*ʾu*)*kh̲ruj* 'go away!'. In such cases, in classical Arabic context, the ʾ is not pronounced. The ا that is written is therefore merely a silent sign augmented by ـٓ (وَصْلَةٌ *waṣlah* or صِلَةٌ *ṣilah*): وَٱسْمُهُ *wa-'smuhu* 'and his name', فَٱنْصَرَفَ *fa-'nṣarafa* 'then he turned away', يَا ٱبْنِي *yā 'bnī* 'oh my son'; at the beginning of a phrase, however: أُخْرُجْ *ʾukh̲ruj*.

Note 1. The ـٓ sign derives from ص, that is, صِلَةٌ *ṣilah* 'connection'.

Note 2. In Arabic grammatical terminology, *alif* that takes *waṣlah* is called أَلِفُ ٱلْوَصْلِ *alif al-waṣl*.

Note 3. In foreign words, initial double consonants are likewise eliminated; nevertheless, the preceding auxiliary vowel becomes an essential component of the word and is maintained within a phrase: إِقْلِيمٌ *ʾiqlīmun* 'region' < Greek κλῖμα, أَفْلَاطُونُ *ʾaflāṭūnu* 'Plato', أُسْطُولٌ *ʾusṭūlun* 'fleet' < στόλος.

§20. Within a phrase, if a vowel precedes a word that begins with a double consonant, no auxiliary vowel is needed: هٰذَا ٱبْنُهُ *hād̲h̲ā 'bnuhū* 'This is his son', قَالَ ٱخْرُجْ *qāla 'kh̲ruj* 'He said, go away!'. If a consonant precedes, however, an auxiliary vowel *i, u, a* (§54) that produces another syllable is attached to the final consonant of the preceding word: قَدِ ٱنْصَرَفَ *qad-i 'nṣarafa* 'He has gone away', رَأَوُا ٱلْبَابَ *raʾaw-u 'l-bāba* 'They saw the door' مِنِ ٱبْنِهِ *min-i 'bnihī* 'from his son'.

Note 1. Note how the article precedes *alif al-waṣl*: أَلِاسْمُ (ʾa)*l-i-'smu* 'the name', أَلِاشْتِرَاءُ (ʾa)*l-i-'shtirāʾu* 'the act of buying'.

Note 2. If *tanwīn* (*-un, -in, -an* §§11; 12) precedes *alif al-waṣl* within a phrase, there is no way to represent the auxiliary vowel in writing. Yet, the auxiliary vowel is pronounced: رَجُلٌ ٱبْنَتُهُ جَمِيلَةٌ *rajulun-i 'bnatuhū jamīlatun* 'a man whose daughter is beautiful', مُحَمَّدٌ ٱلْقُرَشِيُّ *Muḥammadun-i 'l-Qurashiyyu*.

§21. In the following cases, ا is *alif al-waṣl*:

a) In the words إِسْمٌ (ʾi)*smun* 'name', إِبْنٌ (ʾi)*bnun* 'son', إِبْنَةٌ (ʾi)*bnatun* 'daughter', إِسْتٌ (ʾi)*stun* 'buttocks', إِمْرُؤٌ (ʾi)*mruʾun* 'man', إِمْرَأَةٌ (ʾi)*mraʾatun* 'woman', إِثْنَانِ (ʾi)*thnāni*, fem. إِثْنَتَانِ (ʾi)*thnatāni* 'two'.

b) In the article أَلْ (ʾa)*l-* (§142b).

c) In the imperative of the basic verbal stem (§220b).

d) In the perfect, imperative, and verbal noun of the derived verbal stems VII إِنْفَعَلَ (ʾi)*nfaʿala*, VIII إِفْتَعَلَ (ʾi)*ftaʿala*, IX إِفْعَلَّ (ʾi)*fʿalla*, X إِسْتَفْعَلَ (ʾi)*stafʿala*, XI إِفْعَالَّ (ʾi)*fʿālla*, XII إِفْعَوْعَلَ (ʾi)*fʿawʿala*, XIII إِفْعَوَّلَ (ʾi)*fʿawwala*, XIV إِفْعَنْلَلَ (ʾi)*fʿanlala*, XV إِفْعَنْلَى (ʾi)*fʿanlā*, and the verbal stems III إِفْعَنْلَلَ (ʾi)*fʿanlala*, IV إِفْعَلَلَّ (ʾi)*fʿalalla* of quadriliteral root verbs (§169 ff.).

§22. In a few fixed constructions, *alif al-waṣl* is not written:

a) In the construction consisting of the particles *li-* and *la-* and the article: لِلرَّجُلِ *lir-rajuli* (not لالرجل), لَلْمَجْدُ *lal-majdu* (not لالمجد). If in such cases the following noun begins in ل, the ل of the article is not written: لِلَّيْلَةِ *li-llaylati* (not لالليلة), لِلّٰهِ *li-llāhi* 'for God' (not لالله).

b) In إِبْنٌ (ʾi)*bnun* 'son' and إِبْنَةٌ (ʾi)*bnatun* 'daughter' in apposition in genealogical phrases, مَالِكُ بْنُ سَعْدِ بْنِ ثَعْلَبَةَ *Maliku bnu Saʿdi bni Thaʿlabata*. If بن, بنة are at the beginning of a line, however, they are written with ا.

c) In the word إِسْمٌ *ʾismun* in the formula بِسْمِ ٱللّٰهِ *bi-smi 'l-lāhi* 'in the name of God'.

Words Joined in Writing

§**23.** The particles and prepositions بِ *bi-*, تَ *ta-*, سَ *sa-*, فَ *fa-* , كَ *ka-*, لَ *la-*, لِ *li-*, وَ *wa-*, which consist of single letters, are joined to the words that follow: بِبَلَدٍ *bi-baladin* 'in a country', تَاللّٰهِ *ta-'l-lāhi* 'by God!', سَيَأْتِي *sa-yaʾtī* 'he will come', لِيَفْرَحْ *li-yafraḥa* 'let him be happy', وَٱسْوَدَّ *wa-'swadda* 'and became black'. With the enclitic particle *mā*, the spelling varies between unjoined and joined forms: بَعْدَ مَا *baʿda mā* or بَعْدَمَا *baʿda-mā*, طَالَ مَا *ṭāla mā* or طَالَمَا *ṭāla-mā*. The elements must be written as one word when *mā* is shortened to *ma* (§285b): فِيمَ *fī-ma* 'in what?', عَلَامَ *ʿalā-ma* 'on what?' (= مَ + عَلَى).

Abbreviations

§**24.** Abbreviations are generally idiosyncratic. Only a few formulaic expressions are abbreviated, and they are marked as such with ‾ over the abbreviation:

عم = عَلَيْهِ ٱلسَّلَامُ *ʿalayhi 's-salām(u)* 'Upon him be peace!'

صلعم = صَلَّى ٱللّٰهُ عَلَيْهِ وَسَلَّمَ *ṣallā 'l-llāhu ʿalayhi wa-sallam(a)* 'God bless him and grant him salvation' (eulogy for the Prophet Muhammad).

رضه = رَضِيَ ٱللّٰهُ عَنْهُ *raḍiya 'l-lāhu anhu* 'May God be pleased with him' (eulogy for the Companions of the Prophet).

رحه = رَحِمَهُ ٱللّٰهُ *raḥimahu 'l-lāhu* 'May God have mercy upon him' (eulogy for the dead).

ألخ = إِلَى آخِرِهِ *ʾilā ʾākhirihī* 'To its end', i.e., 'etc'.

أه = إِلَى هٰهُنَا *ʾilā hāhunā* 'To here', i.e., 'the citation goes this far'.

ثنى = حَدَّثَنِي *ḥaddathanī* 'He reported to me'.

ثنا = حَدَّثَنَا *ḥaddathanā* 'He reported to us'.

انا = أَخْبَرَنَا *ʾakhbaranā* 'He transmitted to us'.

Numerals

§**25.** The numbers, which the Arabs borrowed from India, are written as follows:

٠	١	٢	٣	٤ or ۴	٥	٦	٧	٨	٩
0	1	2	3	4	5	6	7	8	9

For example: ٣٧٩ 379, ١٣٢٠ 1320.

Note 1. Notice that the numerals are written from left to right.

The letters of the alphabet can also be used to represent numbers (see p. 4, table of the Arabic writing system): يا 11, مه 45, قط 109.

Phonology

Phonemes

§**26.**

a) Vowels:

sonant	short	*a*	*i*	*u*
	long	*ā*	*ī*	*ū*
consonantal			*y*	*w*

b) Consonants:

	Non-emphatic	Emphatic
Labial	*f b m*	
Apical	*t d th dh*	*ṭ ḍ (ẓ)*
Sibilant	*s z sh*	*ṣ ḍ*
Liquid	*r l n*	
Dorsal	*k g (j) kh gh*	*q*
Pharyngeal	*ʿ ḥ*	
Laryngeal	*ʾ h*	

Note 1. All consonants, including the semi-vowels *y, w*, can be geminated: *nazala* 'come down' : *nazzala* 'send down', *qawāmun* 'uprightness' : *qawwāmun* 'established'.

Pronunciation

§**27.** The Arab grammarians described the phonemes of classical Arabic according to place and manner of articulation. The earliest classification is that of al-Khalīl (d. 786/7). Sībawayh (d. 793) and later grammarians provided an array of elaborate systems in which they classified the phonemes variously according to manner of articulation. The following description of articulation is based on Classical Arabic as it is spoken today in the Arab world.

Note 1. The Arab grammarians' conception of phonetics was influenced by the written form. They called the vowels (*a, i, u*), which are represented by diacritical marks (§5), حَرَكَاتٌ *ḥarakātun* (sing. حَرَكَةٌ *ḥarakatun*, 'movement'). The other phonemes, represented by letters, including ا *ā*, ʾ, ي *ī, y*, و *ū, w*, were حُرُوفٌ *ḥurūfun* (sing. حَرْفٌ *ḥarfun* 'edge, letter').

Note 2. The orthography distinguishes two phonemes ض *ḍ* and ظ *ḏ̣* (*ẓ*) that have merged in modern Arabic dialects. Originally, the articulation of ض was probably lateral. The present-day pronunciation of ض — ظ is *ḏ̣* in Bedouin speech, and *ḍ* in urban speech. This variation is secondarily used to distinguish ض from ظ, as ض is associated with the sound *ḍ*, and ظ, with *ḏ̣* or *ẓ* (§31.1). Therefore, it is customary to transliterate ض *ḍ*, and ظ, *ẓ*. In this chapter on phonology, ظ is rendered by *ḏ̣*; elsewhere in the grammar, it is romanized as *ẓ*.

Vowels

§28. a) The short vowels *a, i, u* are sonant. They never occur at the beginning of a syllable (§51). *y* and *w* are consonantal vowels. They can appear at the beginning and the end of a syllable. Sonant and consonantal vowels may combine homogeneously or heterogeneously: homogeneous contact *iy* = *ī*, *uw* = *ū*, heterogeneous contact *ay, aw*. The long vowel *ā* is ambiguous in that it can be regarded as a double sonant or as a sonant-consonantal combination: *nāma* 'sleep' with *ā* = *a-a* (morpheme type *faʿala*), *k͟hālun* 'uncle' with *ā* = *a* + consonant (morpheme type *faʿlun*).

b) The consonantal nature of *y* and *w* is evident in pronunciation only at the beginning of a syllable. At the end of a syllable, *y* and *w* are sonantized by the preceding sonant, so that homogeneous combinations are pronounced as long vowels *ā, ī, ū*, heterogeneous combinations, as diphthongs [ai], [au].

Note 1. The sound sequences *iyy* (*īy*) and *uww* (*ūw*) are written ـِيّ *iyy*, ـُوّ *uww* (§17). A distinction between transliterations *iyy* and *īy*, *uww* and *ūw* should be made for morphological reasons: عَدُوٌّ *ʿadūwun* 'enemy' (morpheme pattern *faʿūlun*), قُوَّادٌ *quwwādun* 'leaders' (pl.) (morpheme pattern *fuʿʿālun*).

Note 2. In the passive of verbal stems II, III, V, and VI, the orthography distinguishes for morphological reasons between *ūw* and *uww* in II-*w* verbs: قُووِمَ *qūwima* (*fūʿila*), قُوِّمَ *quwwima* (*fuʿʿila*).

§**29.** The vowels exhibit a number of variants conditioned by contact. Contact with emphatic consonants usually results in back (velarized) variants. Contact with non-emphatic apicals, sibilants, and liquids commonly causes palatalization. The tense articulation of the pharyngeals is likewise transferred to following vowels. Precise rules for the distribution of conditioned variants do not exist for classical Arabic.

Note 1. Arab grammarians called the palatalized articulation إِمَالَةٌ *ʾimālah* and the velarized articulation, تَفْخِيمٌ *tafkhīm*.

Note 2. The word *allāh(u)* 'God' is pronounced with distinct *tafkhīm*: [ʾaḷḷāh]. The velarized articulation does not occur if *i* precedes the *ll*: *bi-llāh(i)* [billāh].

Consonants

§**30.** Non-emphatic consonants:

Labial: *b* and *m* are bilabial. *f* is labio-dental.

Note 1. *f* replaces *p* in foreign words and personal names: *ʾaflāṭūnu* < Πλάτων (§19.3), *farādīsu* 'paradise' (plural) < Greek παράδεισος.

Apical: *t* and *d* are alveolar stops. *t* is aspirated. *th* and *dh* are interdental spirants.

Note 2. Speakers of dialects lacking *th* and *dh* occasionally substitute *s* for *th*, *z* for *dh*, and *ẓ* for *ḍ* (§31a).

Sibilants: *s* is voiceless; *z* is voiced; *sh* is voiceless.

Liquid: *r* is a voiced dental vibrant ('r' flapped at the tip of the tongue); *l* is lateral; *n* is nasal.

Note 3. Before *b*, *n* is usually assimilated partially [m]: *janbun* [jambun] 'side'.

Dorsal: *k* and *g* are palatal stops. *kh* and *gh* are velar spirants. *k* and *kh* are voiceless; *g* and *gh* are voiced.

Note 4. The original pronunciation of *g* is preserved in Lower Egypt (Cairo). In other dialects, *g* is pronounced as a pre-palatal affricate [j], as a voiced sibilant [zh] (voiced correspondent of *sh*), or as a palatal semivowel [y]. The description of *g* by Arab grammarians indicates that they had in mind a [j] pronunciation. Therefore, it is common to pronounce classical Arabic *g* as [j] and transliterate it also as *j*.

Pharyngeals: ʿ and *ḥ* are produced by tightening the glottis while raising the larynx against the pharynx. ʿ is a voiced, *ḥ* an unvoiced, spirant.

Note 5. Since there is not any oral constriction in the articulation of *h*, ʿ, *ḥ*, these sounds have an affinity to *a*. One perceives an *a* after ʿ and *ḥ*, which is only an attendant feature of their articulation; frequently, however, *a* after ʿ, *ḥ*, *h* acquires the status of a phoneme: *shaʿarun* occurs alongside *shaʿrun* 'hair' (§38).

Laryngeal: ʾ (*hamzah*) is a glottal stop. In Arabic it is a consonantal phoneme and appears not only before vowels but also after vowels at syllable end: *yaʾmuru* 'he ordered', *raʾsun* 'head'. *h* is a laryngeal spirant, which, like ʾ, can occur at syllable end: *fahmun* 'understanding'.

§**31.** a) The emphatic consonants, in contrast to their non-emphatic counterparts, have an additional feature of articulation: velarization. Velarization is the raising of the back portion of the tongue against the velum to further constrict the space. The raising of the back of the tongue involves the larynx and the base of the tongue, and the result is a slightly constricted articulation. Velarization in the production of *ṭ*, *ḍ*, *ṣ* shifts the apical constriction back from the alveolar ridge toward the base of the tongue. According to rules of pronunciation for Koran reciters, *ḏ̣* is an emphatic interdental spirant (§27.2).

Note 1. Speakers of dialects that have no interdental spirant substitute *ẓ* (the emphatic counterpart of *z*) for *ḏ̣* (§30.2). It is common, therefore, to transliterate the letter ظ in classical Arabic with *ẓ*.

Note 2. In contrast to *t*, emphatic *ṭ* is not aspirated.

b) *q* is a voiceless postvelar, or uvular, stop, the emphatic counterpart of *k* and *g*. Commonly described as velarization, the palato-dorsal articulation of *k, g* moves back, as the back of the tongue is raised towards the uvula.

Note 3. In Bedouin dialects, *q* is pronounced as a voiced [g]. This pronunciation was recognized by the Arab grammarians.

Stress

§**32.** Nothing is known about stress in classical Arabic at the time of its codification by the Arab grammarians. Egyptian Koran readers determine the placement of word stress according to the following rules:

a) The final syllable never carries the word stress.

b) The main word stress never falls back beyond the antepenultimate syllable.

c) The penultimate syllable is stressed, if it is closed (§51): *qátala* : *qatálta*, *raqábatun* : *raqabā́tun*, *raqabatā́ni*.

d) In the construct state (§146), the final syllable counts as part of the following word: *ṭalábatun* : *ṭálaba|tu 'l-ʿílmi*.

e) One-syllable proclitic particles are not stressed: *fa-má<u>sh</u>ā, ʾal-ʾábu, bi-ʾábi, ʾal-lá<u>dh</u>i* (§281).

In some regions, different stress patterns are used, in which the pre-antepenultimate syllable may receive stress: *mámlakatun* vs. *mamlákatun*, *qátalahū* vs. *qatálahū*.

Combinatory and Historical Phonology

Vowels

§**33.** When the sequence *iw* and *uy* occurs, the similarity of *i* and *y*, *u* and *w* usually produces a levelling of the heterogeneous vowels.

a) *iw* regularly becomes *iy* (*ī*), when *w* ends a syllable: *ʾīqāʿun* < **ʾiwqāʿun* (root *w-q-ʿ*), *mīzānun* < **miwzānun* (root *w-z-n*), *mītatun* < **miwtatun* (root *m-w-t*). *īw* also becomes *īy*: *ʿalīyun* < **ʿalīwun* (root *ʿ-l-w*).

Note 1. *iw* becomes *iy* in verbal nouns and plural morphemes of the pattern *fiʿālun*, even though *w* would be at the beginning of a syllable: *qiyāmun* 'standing' (root *q-w-m*), *t͟hiyābun* 'garment', plural of *t͟hawbun*. In other cases, *w* is maintained: *qiwāmun* 'foundation' (§248.4). In morphemes of the pattern *fiʿalatun iw* > *iy* is optional: *t͟hiwaratun, t͟hiyaratun*, plural of *t͟hawrun* 'bull'.

b) *uy* becomes *iy* (*ī*), or, infrequently, *uw* (*ū*): *bīḍun* < **buyḍun* (root *b-y-ḍ*), stem *talaqqī-* < **talaqquy-* (§34), *ʾaydin*, stem *ʾaydī-* < **ʾayduy-* plural of *yadun* 'hand' (root *y-d-y*). *ūy* also becomes *īy*: *marmīyun* < **marmūyun* (root *r-m-y*), *huwīyun* < **huwūyun* (root *h-w-y*) (§34), *ʾug͟h-nīyatun* < **ʾug͟hnūyatun*. In verb stem IV of I-*y* roots, morphologically distinctive *u* is preserved. Thus, *uy* must become *uw* (*ū*): *yūqinu, mūqinu* < **yuyqinu, *muyqinun*.

Note 2. *uy* is maintained, if *y* is geminated (*yy*): *ṣuyyira*; cf. §68 c. In cases like *liyyun, luyyun*, i.e., pattern *fuʿlun* of the root *l-w-y*, either possibility exists.

Note 3. Notice *ūy* > *īy*, when the personal pronoun suffix *-ya* (§269 c) is added. In morpheme pattern *fūʿila* of II-*y* roots, morphological *ū* is preserved: *zūyila* 'was separated'.

Note 4. Infrequently in pre-classical texts, *uy* > *iy* in morpheme patterns *fuʿūlun* and *fuʿaylun* of II-*y* roots is observed: *ʿiyūnun* for *ʿuyūnun* and *s͟hiyaymun* for *s͟huyaymun*, *ḥiyayyun* for *ḥuyayyun*.

c) *yw* and *wy* as a rule assimilate to *yy*: *ʾayyāmun* < **ʾaywāmun* (root *y-w-m*), *g͟hayyun* < **g͟haywun* (root *g͟h-w-y*), *ʾubayyun* < **ʾubaywun*, diminutive of *ʾabun* 'father' (root *ʾ-b-w*). After *u*, *ww* replaces *yy*: *quwwat-un* 'power' (root *q-w-y*).

Note 5. Sometimes, *yw* is maintained for morphological reasons: *ʾaywamu* = pattern *ʾafʿalu* of root *y-w-m*, *judaywilun*, diminutive of *jadwalun*.

§**34.** a) Although -*ā*, -*ī*, or -*ū* may occur in stem final position in verbs of III-weak roots, in nouns only -*ā* and -*ī* may occur in that position (§69 a). Accordingly, forms of the patterns *tafaʿʿul*, *tafāʿul*, *ʾafʿul* with stem final *ī* are treated as forms of III-*y* with *uy* > *iy* (§33 b): *tarāmī*- = *tafāʿul* pattern of the root *r-m-y*. In the same way, nominal *fuʿūlun* (§88) is formed with *y* as the third radical: *ʿuṣīyun* = *fuʿūlun* of the root *ʿ-ṣ-w/y*. In verbal *fuʿūlun*, as well as *faʿūlun* and *mafʿūlun*, however, there is variation between III-*w* and III-*y* (§§256 b; 257.1).

b) Sonant suffixes are contracted into stem-final -*ā*, -*ī*, -*ū*. Suffixed sonants *a*, *i*, *u* merge into *ā*: *yalqā* = **yalqā-a* (*yafʿala*) or **yalqā-u* (*yafʿalu*), *ʾaʿlā* = **ʾaʿlā-u*, -*i*, -*a* (*ʾafʿalu*, *ʾafʿali*, *ʾafʿala*). Only *i*, *u* are contracted into stem-final -*ī*, -*ū*; suffixed *a*, however, is preserved after -*ī*, -*ū*: *talaqqī* = **talaqqī-u*, -*i* (*tafaʿʿulu*, *tafaʿʿuli*), *talaqqiya* (*tafaʿʿula*); *yadʿū* = **yadʿū-u* (*yafʿulu*), *yadʿuwa* (*yafʿula*); cf. §252.

Note 1. After *uww* (*ūw*) and *iyy* (*īy*), contraction does not occur: *yamānī* = **yamānī-u*, -*i* (§116.1), but *yamaniyyu*, *yamaniyyi*.

§**35.** a) The following contractions and vowel combinations occur when suffixes consisting of long vowels are attached to stems ending in vowels:

ī-ī	>	*ī*:	**tarmī-īna* > *tarmīna*, **qāḍī-īna* > *qāḍīna*
ī-ū	>	*ū*:	**yarmī-ūna* > *yarmūna*, **qāḍī-ūna* > *qāḍūna*
ū-ī	>	*ī*:	**tadʿū-īna* > *tadʿīna*
ū-ū	>	*ū*:	**yadʿū-ūna* > *yadʿūna*
ā-ī	>	*ay*:	**talqā-īna* > *talqayna*, **ʾaʿlā-īna* > *ʾaʿlayna*
ā-ū	>	*aw*:	**ramā-ū* > *ramaw*, **ʾaʿlā-ūna* > *ʾaʿlawna*
ā-ā	>	*ayā*:	**ramā-ā* > *ramayā*, **fatā-āni* > *fatayāni*
	>	*awā*:	**daʿā–ā* > *daʿawā*, **ʿaṣā-āni* > *ʿaṣawāni*

The distribution of *ayā*/*awā* is determined by the root consonant: *ramayā* (root *r-m-y*) and *daʿawā* (root *d-ʿ-w* §250).

Note 1. In nouns, sometimes both *ayā* and *awā* are possible: *qanawātun*, *qanayātun*, plurals of *qanātun* (stem *qanā*-) ‘cane’.

b) If *ā* is suffixed to a noun ending in *-ā* (§§10; 64 b), *ā-ā* always becomes *ayā*: **dhikrā-ātun* > *dhikrayātun*, **ḥublā-āni* > *ḥublayāni*. If the noun ends in *-āʾu*, *-āʾun* (§64 c), *ā-ā* always becomes *āwā*: **ṣaḥrā-āni* > *ṣaḥrāwāni* (*ṣaḥrāʾu*) 'desert', **khaḍrā-ātun* > *khaḍrāwātun* (*khaḍrāʾu*) 'herbs', **ḥirbā-āni* > *ḥirbāwāni* (*ḥirbāʾun*) 'chameleon'.

Note 2. In nouns of III-weak roots with stem-final *-āʾu* (§69 b), ʾ is retained before the ending: *kisāʾ-āni* (*kisāʾun*) 'garment'. An exception is *samāwātun*, plural of *samāʾun* 'heaven'.

Note 3. In the formation of the *nisbah* adjective (§117), *ā-iyy* regularly becomes *awiyy*, but also in many cases *āwiyy*.

c) ʾ is inserted to prevent contraction of the sequence *ā-i* in stem morphemes: *qāʾilun* = *fāʿilun* (stem *qāl-*) (§247 a), *faḍāʾilu* = *faʿāʾilu* (*faḍīlatun*) (§98). ʾ also prevents contraction in *-āʾu*, *-āʾun*, inflected variants of *-ā* (§64c).

§36. a) Consonantal vowels *w* and *y* as a rule do not fall between sonants. This is why, for example, there is no morpheme pattern *fuʿul* formed from III-weak roots and, for the most part, II-*w*. On this, cf. §60.

Note 1. II-*y* roots do have a *fuʿulun* pattern: *buyuḍun*, plural of *bayūḍun* '(egg-)laying'. Exceptionally, there is a *fuʿulun* pattern of root II-*w*: *suwukun*, plural of *siwākun* 'tooth cleaner'. Usually, the pattern *fuʿlun* (a contraction of *uwu* > *ū*) occurs instead: *sūkun*.

Note 2. *y* or *w* between sonants in II-weak roots is sometimes avoided by forms with *yy*: *bayyūtun* 'stale' (otherwise *faʿūlun*, root *b-y-t*), *sayyidun* 'master' (otherwise *faʿilun*, *fāʿilun*, root *s-w-d*).

b) *w* and *y*, if they precede long vowels, can, however, fall between sonants: *qawāmun*, *qiwāmun* (§33.1), *ṭawīlun*, *khawūnun*, *ḥuwūlun*. In forms based on II-*w* roots, *wu*, *wū* may be replaced by *ʾu*, *ʾū*: *nawūmun* or *naʾūmun* (root *n-w-m*), *khuwūlatun* or *khwʾūlatun* (root *kh-w-l*), *ʾanwuqun* or *ʾanʾuqun* (root *n-w-q*).

Note 3. There are occasional variants of I-*w* roots which appear with ʾ : *ʾirthun* 'inheritance' from *wartha* 'inherit'.

Note 4. There are some II-weak roots that consistently have fixed consonantal *w* and *y*: *ʿiwajun, ʿawajun, ʾaʿwaju* (§245.3).

§37. a) In the *fuʿūlun* pattern of III-*y* roots, like **huwūyun* > *huwīyun* (§§33 b; 34 a), the *u* of the first syllable can be assimilated to the following *īy*: *ʾutīyun, ʾitīyun* 'coming', *ʿuṣīyun, ʿiṣīyun* 'sticks', *qusīyun, qisīyun* 'bows' (§88).

b) In the words (*ʾi*)*mruʾun* 'man' and (*ʾi*)*bnumun* = (*ʾi*)*bnun* 'son', the stem vowel assimilates to the inflectional ending: (*ʾi*)*mruʾun*, (*ʾi*)*mriʾin*, (*ʾi*)*mraʾan*, and (*ʾi*)*mraʾatun* 'woman'; (*ʾi*)*bnumun*, (*ʾi*)*bnimin*, (*ʾi*)*bnaman*.

Note 1. Alternation of the stem vowel in harmony with inflectional ending was originally regular in several two-radical words (§70 b): *sanatun* 'year', plural *sunūna, sinīna*; *kuratun* 'ball', plural *kurūna, kirīna*. In classical Arabic, the alternation was discontinued: *sinūna, sinīna*; *kurūna, kurīna*.

Vowel Epenthesis

§38. Frequently after *r, l* and ʿ, *gh, ḥ, h*, non-morphologically conditioned sonants are generated. These extra vowels are usually *a*, less often *i*: **ṭalbun* > *ṭalabun* 'desire', *ṭardun* or *ṭaradun* 'hunting', *halkatun, halakatun* 'ruin', *raghbatun, raghabatun* 'wish', **sarqun* > *saraqun, sariqun* 'theft', *nahrun, naharun* 'river', *shaʿrun, shaʿarun* 'hair', *ḍaʿfun, ḍaʿafun* 'weakness'.

Consonants

§39. Classical Arabic has preserved almost unchanged the proto-Semitic inventory of consonantal phonemes. Only the sibilants have undergone simplification. Arabic *sh* is the successor of proto-Semitic **ś*. In Arabic, *s* represents the coalescence of proto-Semitic **s* and **sh*.

Root consonants (radicals) exhibit stability in all morphological variations. No assimilation occurs between root consonants in contact. Any assimilation that takes place is caused by consonants that are elements of inflectional morphology (§44 ff.).

Dissimilation of ʾ (_hamzah_)

§40. ʾ is dropped at the end of a syllable, if the syllable also begins with ʾ : ʾaʾ > ʾā, ʾuʾ > ʾuw, ʾiʾ > ʾiy: *ʾaʾthara > ʾāthara, *ʾuʾminu > ʾūminu, *ʾiʾmānun > ʾīmānun, *ʾaʾfāqun > ʾāfāqun.

Note 1. In cases like *(ʾi)ʾtamara > ʾītamara (§21 d), ʾiʾ necessarily dissimilates only at the beginning of a phrase. Within a phrase, this form is pronounced ʾtamara (spelled فَأْتَمَرَ fa-ʾtamara). See §237.1.

§41. a) If two syllables beginning with ʾ follow one another, the second is usually dissimilated: ʾaʾimmatun > ʾayimmatun (root ʾ-m-m), *jāʾiʾun > *jāʾiyun > jāʾin 'coming'. In *riʾāʾun > riyāʾun 'hypocrisy' and *dhaʾāʾibu > dhawāʾibu 'forelocks', the second ʾ has to be preserved.

Note 1. As a rule, dissimilation does not occur in verbs I-ʾ after the prefix ʾu-: ʾuʾammilu 'I hope', ʾuʾānisu 'I am familiar with'. There are, however, forms with w root variants: ʾuwāmiru, ʾuʾāmiru 'I seek advice', ʾuwāsī, ʾuʾāsī 'I share'.

Note 2. In buraʾāʾu > burāʾu (§90.3), the syllable is dropped following dissimilation of ʾ. Cf. §49 d.

b) If the first of two consecutive syllables beginning with ʾ ends in a consonant, the second ʾ may be dropped as the vowel of the first syllable is lengthened: ʾabʾārun or ʾābārun, plural of biʾrun 'well', ʾarʾāmun or ʾārāmun, plural of riʾmun 'white gazelle', ʾabʾurun or ʾāburun, plural of biʾrun. The same process takes place where secondary ʾu < wu (§36 b): ʾanʾuqun < ʾanwuqun or ʾānuqun, plural of nāqatun 'she-camel'.

Note 3. The plural of raʾyun is ʾārāʾun (< *ʾarʾāʾun).

Note 4. The merger of roots I-ʾ and II-ʾ in the plural morpheme pattern *ʾafʿālun* occasionally produces new formations: *ʾadabun* 'custom', a back-formation from *ʾādābun*, plural of *daʾbun* 'habit'.

c) If the particle *ʾa* (§335 a) precedes a word beginning with ʾ, both ʾ's are retained: *ʾa-ʾadkhulu* 'shall I come in?' The initial glottal stop and vowel of the article (*ʾa*)*l-* (§142 b) are not elided after *ʾa*: *ʾa-ʾal-ʿabdu* 'the slave?'. Other words beginning with double consonants (§21) use the contextual form after *ʾa*: *ʾa-shtakā* 'did he complain?'.

Dropping of ʾ (*hamzah*)

§**42.** Some I-ʾ verbs lose ʾ in the imperative: *kul* 'eat!' (root *ʾ-k-l*), likewise *khudh* 'take!', *mur* 'order!' (§238). As a change that originates in **ʾarʾā* > *ʾarā*, the imperfect forms of *raʾā* 'he saw' and verb stem IV of this root lose the root ʾ in all inflectional categories: *ʾarā, tarā, yarā*, etc. and *ʾarā, ʾarayta, ʾurī, turī, yurā*, etc. (§239 b).

§**43.** In the formation of nouns from III-ʾ roots, there often occur forms based on variants of III-weak roots (§67 a). In non-classical texts, III-weak roots very often replace III-ʾ roots, for example: (*ʾi*)*ttakā* (imperfect *yattakī*) instead of (*ʾi*)*ttakaʾa* (imperfect *yattakiʾu*) 'lean on' (root *w-k-ʾ*).

Note 1. *nabīyun* 'prophet', which etymologically belongs to the root *n-b-ʾ*, is borrowed from Aramaic *nḇīy*(*ā*). Forms like *nabīʾun*, plural *nubaʾāʾu* are hyper-classicisms.

Assimilation

§**44.** The *l* of the article (*ʾa*)*l-* (§142 b) is assimilated completely to consonants articulated with the forward part of the tongue: *t, d, th, dh, r, n, l, s, z, sh, ṣ, ḍ, ṭ, ḏ* (*ẓ*): *ʾal-taqwā* > *ʾat-taqwā* 'piety', *ʾal-ṣaydu* > *ʾaṣ-ṣaydu* 'game', *ʾal-ḏabyu* > *ʾaḏ-ḏabyu* 'antelope'. Cf. above, Writing System, §18.

Note 1. The Arab grammarians called these consonants أَلْحُرُوفُ آلشَّمْسِيَّةُ *al-ḥurūf ash-shamsiyyah* 'sun letters' after أَلشَّمْسُ (*ʾa*)*sh-shamsu* 'sun'. The rest of the letters, which are not assimilated to the *l*, are called أَلْحُرُوفُ آلْقَمَرِيَّةُ *al-ḥurūf al-qamariyyah* 'moon letters' after أَلْقَمَرُ (*ʾa*)*l-qamar* 'moon'.

§**45.** The *n* of the particles *ʾin, ʾan, min, ʿan* and of the verbal stems *(ʾi)nfaʿala* and *(ʾi)fʿanlala* is assimilated to following *m*. *n* of *ʾin, ʾan* also is assimilated to following *l*:

nm > *mm: ʾin-mā* > *ʾimmā, min-mā* > *mimmā, min-man* > *mimman, ʿan-mā* > *ʿammā, ʿan-man* > *ʿamman, (ʾi)nmaḥaqa* > *(ʾi)mmaḥaqa* 'be annihilated', *(ʾi)khranmasa* > *(ʾi)khrammasa* 'grow dumb'.

nl > *ll: ʾin-lā* > *ʾillā, ʾan-lā* > *ʾallā.*

§**46.** Infixed *-t-* of verbal stem VIII causes assimilation after *d, th, dh, z, ṣ, ḍ, ṭ, ḏ̣* as follows:

dt > *dd*: — **d-t-aʿā* > *(ʾi)ddaʿā* 'claim'
tht > *thth* or *tt*: — **th-t-aʾara* > *(ʾi)ththaʾara* or rarely *(ʾi)ttaʾara* 'get revenge'
dht > *dhdh* or *dd*: — **dh-t-akara* > *(ʾi)dhdhakara* or *(ʾi)ddakara* 'remember'
zt > *zd*: — **z-t-aḥama* > *(ʾi)zdaḥama* 'crowd'
ṣt > *ṣṭ*: — **ṣ-t-aḥaba* > *(ʾi)ṣṭaḥaba* 'accompany'
ḍt > *ḍṭ* or *ḍḍ/ṭṭ*: — **ḍ-t-arra* > *(ʾi)ḍṭarra* 'force'; **ḍ-t-alaʿa* > *(ʾi)ḍḍalaʿa* or *(ʾi)ṭṭalaʿa* 'be proficient'
ṭt > *ṭṭ*: — **ṭ-t-alaʿa* > *(ʾi)ṭṭalaʿa* 'become aware'
ḏ̣t > *ḏ̣ḏ̣* or *ṭṭ*: — **ḏ̣-t-alama* > *(ʾi)ḏ̣ḏ̣alama* or infrequently *(ʾi)ṭṭalama* 'suffer injustice'

Note 1. Orthographical convention prescribes that the assimilated forms be written: ادّعى, اثّار, اتّأر, اذّكر, ادّكر, ازدحم, اصطحب, اضطرّ, اضطلع, اطّلع, اطّلع, اظّلم, اطّلم. Cf. also اتّبع *(ʾi)ttabaʿa* < **t-t-abaʿa* 'follow'.

§**47.** The prefix of the pre-classical V and VI verbal stems was *t-* instead of *ta-*. This prefix was assimilated to following *th, dh, d, z, s, sh, ṣ, ṭ*: **t-zayyana* > *(ʾi)zzayyana* 'adorn oneself', **t-ṭayyara* > *(ʾi)ṭṭayyara* 'see an evil omen', **ya-t-ṣaddaqu* > *yaṣṣaddaqu* 'he gives alms', **ya-t-daththaru* > *yaddaththaru* 'he covers himself'.

Note 1. Forms with *t-* prefix instead of *ta-* are recognizable as such only by their spelling, which reveals the assimilation: ازّيّن, اطّيّر, يصّدّق, يدّثّر.

§**48.** Perfect suffixes beginning in *t* (*-ta, -ti, -tu, -tum, -tunna, -tumā*) can assimilate to stem-final *d, th, dh, ḍ, ṭ, ḏ*: *labith-tu* > *labittu* 'I lingered', *ʾarad-ta* > *ʾaratta* 'you desired', *basaṭ-tum* > *basaṭṭum* 'you spread out'. The unassimilated forms are always written: اردت, لبثت, بسطتم (§18.2).

Syllable Ellipsis

§**49.** If two identical or similar consonants follow one another separated only by a sonant, the sound sequence *CVCV* or *CVC$\bar{V}$* tends to be simplified, as long as no morphological ambiguity results.

a) In the prefix-conjugation, *ta-ta-* tends to be reduced to *ta-* in stems V, VI, and in stem II of quadriliteral verbs: *tataʿallamu* or *taʿallamu* 'you/she learn/s', *tatanāwamu* or *tanāwamu* 'you/she go/es to sleep'.

b) *taṭā-* may be reduced to *ṭā-* in stem X of II-weak verbs: (*ʾi*)*staṭāʿa* or (*ʾi*)*sṭāʿa* 'to be able', (*ʾi*)*staṭāla* or (*ʾi*)*sṭāla* 'to become long'.

c) *-na-* preceding the personal pronoun suffixes *-nī, -nā* (§268) may be elided: *ʾinna-nī* or *innī*, *ʾinna-nā* or *ʾinnā*, *ʾanna-nī/-nā* or *ʾannā, ʾannī*, *taḍribūna-nī* or *taḍribūnī*, *taḍribīna-nā* or *taḍribīnā*. In the same way, *-ni* in the dual is elided: *taḍribāni-nī* or *taḍribānī*.

Note 1. The shortening of *-namā* to *-nā* is evident in the pair *bayna-mā* or *baynā* 'while'.

d) After the definite article (*ʾa*)*l-* in the words *ʾilāhun* 'god', *ʾulāʾi* 'these', and *ʾunāsun* 'people', *ʾ* is dropped and the following vowel is also elided: *ʾal-ʾilāhu* 'the god' > *ʾallāhu* 'God', **ʾal-ʾilātu* > *ʾallātu* 'Allāt' (proper name of a goddess), *ʾal-ʾulāʾi* > *ʾallāʾi* 'those who', *ʾal-ʾunāsu* > *ʾan-nāsu* 'people', from which the indefinite *nāsun* 'people' developed as an independent word.

e) The prepositions *ʿalā* 'on' and *min* 'from' can be shortened to *ʿa-* and *mi-* when they precede the unassimilated form of the article (*ʾa*)*l-*: *min-a 'l-baladi* or *mil-baladi* 'from the country', *ʿalā 'l-ʾarḍi* or *ʿal-ʾarḍi* 'on the earth'. The shortened forms occur only in poetry or in non-classical texts.

Note 2. The short form (ʾ*i*)*staḥā* (*yastaḥī*) alongside (ʾ*i*)*staḥyā* (*yastaḥyī*) 'be ashamed' (root *ḥ-yy, ḥ-y-y*) developed through dissimilation, as the *y* is dropped in forms like (ʾ*i*)*staḥyaytu* > (ʾ*i*)*staḥaytu*, *yastaḥyī* > *yastaḥī*.

§**50.** Geminated root consonants, like those that appear in II-geminate ($C_2 = C_3$) roots and in verbal stems IX, XI, are usually preserved as geminates, even when the morpheme pattern requires another arrangement of the root consonants. In morphemes that call for a *CVCV* arrangement, the sonant that is expected to fall between both identical consonants is absent if a vowel appears before *CVCV*: *radda* 'return' = *faʿala* pattern of root *r-dd*, *massa* 'touch' = *faʿila* of root *m-ss*, *ḍāllun* 'erring' = *fāʿilun* of root *ḍ-ll*. If, however, a consonant precedes, *CVCV* is re-arranged as *VCCV*, that is, the sonant that is expected precedes the geminate: ʾ*aqallu* 'fewer' = ʾ*afʿalu* of root *q-ll*, *muḥibbun* 'loving' > *mufʿilun* of root *ḥ-bb*, *yaruddu* 'he returns' > *yafʿulu* of root *r-dd*. Only in morpheme patterns *faʿalun, fiʿalun, fuʿalun*, and *fuʿulun* is the geminate group split up for the sake of morphological precision: *sababun* 'cause', *sikakun* 'coins', *durarun* 'pearls', ʿ*ununun* 'reins'.

Note 1. Long vowels always break up geminates: (ʾ*i*)*ḥmirārun*, verbal-noun of (ʾ*i*)*ḥmarrra* 'redden', *takhfīfun* 'lightening' = *tafʿīlun* of root *kh-ff*, *murūrun* 'passing' = *fuʿūlun* of root *m-rr*.

Note 2. In morphemes that require the sequence (*V*)*CVC*, geminates as a rule cannot be preserved: *radadtu* 'I returned' = *faʿaltu* of root *r-dd*, (ʾ*i*)*ḥmarartu* 'I reddened' (ʾ*i*)*ḥmarra* (Cf., however, §52.2). If (*V*)*CVC* appears at the end of a word, the geminate can be preserved with an auxiliary vowel: *yardud* or *yaruddi*, *yarudda, yaruddu* 'may he return' (§53).

Syllable Structure

$51. The old Arabic syllable consists of three elements: an explosive, a vocalic nucleus, and an implosive element. In the explosive element, there is always a consonantal phoneme, or in certain cases, a long, or doubled, consonant. Every syllable contains a nucleus that is always represented by a sonant (*a,i,u*). The implosive element is realized by a consonant or is not articulated. Consonantal clusters cannot appear in any syllable element. A syllable cannot begin with a sonant. Accordingly, there are only two types of syllables:

a) open syllable: *CV*

b) closed syllable: *CVC* and *CV̄*

Note 1. After closed vocalic syllables, doubled consonants can be realized as long consonants in explosive syllable elements: *ḍā|llun*, *(ʾi)ḥ|mā|rra*, *dā|bba|tun*, *du|way|bba|tun*. In poetry, where long consonants interfere with the rhythm, doubled consonants are reduced: *ḍā|llun* > *ḍā|lun*.

Note 2. After sonants, doubled consonants behave like geminates. The first part is classified as the implosive, and the second part as the explosive element of the syllable: *naz|za|la*, *qaw|wā|mun*.

Shortening of Syllables

§**52.** If a syllable-closing consonant comes in contact with a closed vocalic syllable, the syllable as a rule is shortened through elision of the consonantal vowel element: *CāC* > *CaC*, *CīC* > *CiC*, *CūC* > *CuC*, *CayC* > *CaC*: **ʾaqām-tu* > *ʾaqamtu*, **sīr-na* > *sirna*, **qūl* > *qul*, **lays-tu* > *lastu*. Shortening also occurs when the indefinite ending *-n* (§141) is affixed to stems ending in *-ī*, *-ā*: **talaqqī-n* > *talaqqin*, **qāḍī-n* > *qāḍin*, **fatā-n* > *fatan*, **mulqā-n* > *mulqan*.

Note 1. A similar kind of shortening takes place in **ʾayn* > *ʾin* 'not' (§322).

Note 2. *CVCC* > *CVC* also occasionally affects non-vocalic consonants: **mundhu* > *mundh* > *mudh* 'since' (§300), **qaṭṭ* > *qaṭ* in *fa-qaṭ* 'only'. Such shortening does occur rarely in the classical language in the perfect of II-geminate verbs: **ḍall-tu* > *ḍaltu or ḍiltu*, **ʾaḥass-tu* > *ʾaḥastu*.

Auxiliary Vowels

§**53.** If *CVCC* cannot be shortened, the syllable structure after *CC* conditions a sonant as an auxiliary vowel. This vowel can, however, occur only at the end of a word: *mass* > *massi, massa* 'touch!', *firr* > *firri, firra* 'flee!', *yarudd* > *yaruddi/a/u* 'may he return'. The auxiliary vowel is usually *i*, infrequently *a*. It can also be *u* if the preceding syllable contains *u*.

Note 1. If there is a doubled consonant at the end of a word, either an auxiliary vowel appears or the geminate is broken up: **yarudd* > *yaruddi, yarudda*, or *yardud* (§50.2).

Note 2. Under certain circumstances, an auxiliary vowel can also appear after a closed vocalic syllable, if shortening needs to be avoided: **faʿāl* > *faʿāli* (§225.1), *-*ūn*, *-*īn*, *-*ān*, *-*ayn* > -*ūna*, -*īna*, -*āni*, -*ayni* (plural and dual endings), **hayhāt* > *hayhāti, hayhāta, hayhātu* 'not!', 'how wrong!'.

Note 3. Lengthened auxiliary vowels also appear at the end of interjections: *ʾ*uff* 'ugh, phooey' > ʾ*uffi*, ʾ*uffa*, ʾ*uffu* or ʾ*uffī*, ʾ*uffā*, written أُفًّا or أُفًّا, أُفٍّ (incorrectly with *tanwīn*; cf. also §7.4).

§54. a) Within a phrase, an auxiliary vowel must appear before a word beginning in *CC*, when the preceding word ends in *C*; cf. §§19 ff. The auxiliary is usually *i*. After *hum, tum, kum* and the plural ending -*aw*, it is *u*. After -*ī*, -*nī* (1st person singular suffix), it is *a*. It is also *a* after the preposition *min*, but only when the article follows (§21 b): *qad-i 'nṣarafa* 'he has departed', ʾ*iftaḥ-i 'l-bāba* 'open the door!', ʾ*antum-u 'r-rijālu* 'you are the men', *daʿaw-u 'n-nisāʾa* 'they called the women', *ḍaraba-niy-a 'l-waladu* 'the boy hit me', *min-a 'l-bayti* 'from the house', but *min-i 'mraʾatihī* 'from his wife'.

Note 1. After ʾ*aw* 'or', the auxiliary vowel is *i*: ʾ*imruʾun* ʾ*aw-i* ʾ*mraʾatun* 'man or woman'.

Note 2. Long vowels are shortened before *CC*, since extra-long syllables are not permitted: *laqū 'l-ʿadūwa* > *laqu 'l-ʿadūwa* 'they met the enemy', ʾ*abū 'l-ʿAbbāsi* > ʾ*abu 'l-ʿAbbāsi* 'the father of al-ʿAbbās. The orthography does not indicate the shortening. The forms are written morphemically (أَبُو ٱلْعَبَّاسِ، لَقُوا ٱلْعَدُوَّ).

Note 3. An auxiliary vowel appears before the article (ʾ*a*)*l*-, even when another auxiliary vowel comes after the article: *min-a 'l-i-ḥtijāji* 'from the argumentation'.

b) If words beginning in *CC* occur at the beginning of a phrase, ʾ must precede the auxiliary vowel. The quality of auxiliary vowel is determined by the vowel of the following syllable. It is *i* before *i* and *a*, and *u* before *u* in the following syllable: (*ʾi*)*staʿmala* 'he used', (*ʾi*)*ḍrib* 'hit!', (*ʾi*)*ftaḥ* 'open!', (*ʾu*)*stuʿmila* 'it was used', (*ʾu*)*ktub* 'write!'. The words listed in §21a always have *i*. The article is always pronounced *ʾal-* at the beginning of a phrase.

Note 1. The auxiliary vowel at the beginning of a word is transliterated vowel plus ʾ between ( ): (*ʾa*)*l-*.

Pausal Forms

§55. Before a pause in speech, it is normal to decrease the sound of the final word. Pausal forms develop as the voice and articulation subside, and the final sound segment or two fade into silence. Sonants are completely silent in pause. Long vowels sound short, and sometimes the reduced expiratory effort produces an *h*-like sound: *-ā* → (i.e., sounds in pause like) *-ah*, *-ī* → *-ih*. The noun endings *-un, in, -an* (§§11 f.) lose final *-n* or are completely deleted. Geminates are reduced: *firr* (§53) → *fir*.

§56. In poetry, rhyming words have the following pausal forms:

a) Words with final rhyming consonants are written with *sukūn* (§6). As such, there may occur words whose contextual forms end in a consonant anyway: لَمْ يَعْلَمْ *lam yaʿlam* 'he did not know'. Similarly, doubled consonants at the end of words are simplified: *firr* (§53) → فِرْ *fir*. There can also be pausal forms with rhyming consonants whose contextual forms end in sonants (*a,i,u*) or the morphemes *-un, -in, -un*: *yaʿlamu* 'he knows' → يَعْلَمْ *yaʿlam*, *muṭʿamun* 'fed' → مُطْعَمْ *muṭʿam*. Sometimes words whose stems end in *-ī* also have pausal forms ending in consonants: *yurāʿī* 'he observes' → يُرَاعْ *yurāʿ*. Pausal forms of the feminine ending *-ah* (§57 e) can occur rhyming with *-ah*. The third-person singular suffixes *-hu, -hi* (*-hū, hī*) are read *-h* in pause.

Note 1. Pausal forms in which the accusative ending *-an* is completely dropped occur rarely as rhyming forms.

Note 2. أَلْعَاصْ (ʾa)l-ʿĀṣ (a proper name) is a pausal form whose stem-final -ī has been dropped. Its contextual form is (ʾa)l-ʿāṣī 'disobedient'.

b) In words with final rhyming vowels, all vowels that rhyme are considered long. The length of ā is normally indicated in writing by ا, regardless of the underlying contextual form. ḍammah (§5) indicates ū, and و or وا (§7.2) is written only for morphemic ū. When the rhyme is ī, either *kasrah* (§5) or ى can be written. Under most circumstances, when ى is used, it is only when it is morphologically justified.

c) In words with final rhyming vowels, the following pausal forms are possible: 1. Words whose contextual forms end in long vowels show no pausal variation. 2. Sonants in words whose contextual forms end in sonants are counted as long vowels and thus are not dropped. 3. Noun endings *-un, -in, -an* drop final *-n* and are likewise considered long vowels. *-n* is also dropped from both ā and ī noun stems (§154 ff.), and the rhyming forms end in -ā and ī, respectively. 4. Words whose contextual forms end in consonants can take an auxiliary vowel *i* to fit ī rhyme. Thus, for words in which final vowels rhyme, the following pausal forms are possible:

ā-rhyme: 1. لَنْ يَعْلَمَا *lan yaʿlamā*, contextual لَنْ يَعْلَمَا
2. لَنْ يَعْلَمَا *lan yaʿlamā*, contextual لَنْ يَعْلَمَ
3. مُطْعَمَا *muṭʿamā*, contextual مُطْعَمًا
عَصَا *ʿaṣā*, contextual عَصًا

ī-rhyme: 1. لَنْ تَعْلَمِي *lan taʿlamī*, contextual لَنْ تَعْلَمِي
2. مِنَ آلدَّمِ *min-a 'd-damī*, contextual مِنَ آلدَّمِ
3. مِنْ دَمِ *min damī*, contextual مِنْ دَمٍ
عَمِ or عَمِى *ʿamī*, contextual عَمٍ
4. لَمْ يَعْلَمِ *lam yaʿlamī*, contextual لَمْ يَعْلَمْ

ū-rhyme: 1. لَنْ يَعْلَمُوا *lan yaʿlamū*, contextual لَنْ يَعْلَمُوا
2. يَعْلَمُ *yaʿlamū*, contextual يَعْلَمُ
3. مُطْعَمُ *muṭʿamū*, contextual مُطْعَمٌ

§57. There is also a system of pausal forms observed in the reading of classical Arabic prose texts. The following reductions in word-final position are occasioned by pause:

a) Sonants are dropped: *kataba* → in pause *katab*, *qāma* → *qām*, *yarmi* → *yarm* (or *yarmih*), (*ʾa*)*l-kitābu* → (*ʾa*)*l-kitab*.

b) Noun endings *-un, -in* are dropped: *kitābun, kitābin* → *kitāb*; *maqālātun, maqālātin* → *maqālāt* (feminine plural).

c) *-ī* replaces *-in* in *ī*-stems (§155): *qāḍin* → *qāḍī*, *tarāmin* → *tarāmī*.

d) *-ā* replaces final *-an*: *kitāban* (accusative) → *kitābā*, *ʿaṣan* → *ʿaṣā*, *hudan* → *hudā*, *yanfaʿan* (energetic II) → *yanfaʿā*.

e) *-ah* or *āh* replaces the feminine singular endings *-atu*(*n*), *-ati*(*n*), *-ata*(*n*) and *-ātu*(*n*), *-āti*(*n*), *-āta*(*n*) (cf. §13): *madīnatun*, *madīnatin*, *madīnatan* → *madīnah*; *ṣalātun*, *ṣalātin*, *ṣalātan* → *ṣalāh*.

In prose, orthography is unaffected by the pausal reading. Every word in pause is vocalized as in context, to the extent that vowel signs and other diacritics are used.

Note 1. When words not in context are cited in transliteration, it is usual to write the pausal form: *Muḥammad*, *madīna*(*h*), *kitāb*, *katab*, *sukūn* (§6), *shadda*(*h*) (§17), *tāʾ marbūṭa*(*h*) (§13), etc. This manner of citation is used frequently in titles of books, for example: *Kitāb al-faraj baʿd ash-shidda*(*h*) rather than *Kitābu l-faraji baʿda 'sh-shiddati*.

Note 2. In transliteration of genitive constructions in "pausal transcription", the first member is also introduced without case ending, for example with personal names: *ʿabd allāh* (*ʿAbdallāh*), *imraʾ al-qays* (*Imraʾalqays*); but *Abū Bakr*, *Abū l-Qāsim* because of the long vowel (§150). The feminine ending appears as the first member of genitive constructions in the form *-at*: *Hibat Allāh* (proper name), *sīrat rasūl Allāh* (title of a book).

Morphology

Root and Morpheme

§**58.** In addition to prefixed, infixed, and suffixed morphemes, Arabic, like the other Semitic languages, has stem pattern morphemes that determine the distribution of vowels in a word-stem. Roots, as a rule, consist only of consonants, called radicals. Vowels are usually morphologically determined. Most roots consist of three radicals, while a smaller number have four radicals. Roots with more than four radicals occur only infrequently in purely Semitic words. In pronouns, a few particles, and primary nouns (§71 f.), vowels are not morphologically determined, but are components of the root.

Separable pattern and inflectional morphemes combine with stem pattern morphemes to make up morphological units, or words. A morphologically determined word-form, or "morpheme-category", is represented paradigmatically, according to the model developed by Arab grammarians, by the root فعل *f-ʿ-l* ('do'): ف is the first, ع the second, and ل the third, root consonant, or radical. Four-radical roots are represented by فعلل *f-ʿ-*l_3*-*l_4. Thus, a word like فضيلة *faḍīlatun* 'virtue' belongs to the morpheme-category *faʿīlatun*. It consists of the stem pattern morpheme *faʿīl*, which determines the vowel distribution for the root *f-ḍ-l*, and the feminine ending *-at-* with the nominative ending *-u* and sign of indefiniteness *-n*. يضمحلّ *yaḍmaḥillu* 'he fades away' is of the morpheme-category *yafʿal*$_3$*il*$_4l_4$*u* of the root *ḍ-m-ḥ-l*. The morpheme-category here consists of the imperfect prefix *ya-*, the imperfect base *-fʿal*$_3$*il*$_4l_4$, and the ending *-u*.

§**59.** Among three-radical roots are those that have consonantal vowels (*w*, *y*) or ʾ. They are called "weak" roots, because *y* and *w*, and occasionally ʾ, are replaced by vowels or completely disappear. All other roots with stable radicals are called "strong" roots. Thus, there are the following different types of roots:

a) Strong roots with three or four different radicals

b) II-geminate roots (*mediae geminatae*): The second and third radicals are identical and form a geminate group. (§§50; 54)

c) I-ʾ roots (*primae hamzatae*): The phonological rules in §§40–43 apply to these. Other roots with ʾ as the second or third radical are, with a few exceptions, treated as "strong".

d) I-*w* and -*y* roots (*primae infirmae*): Some I-*w* root morphemes are formed as two-radical morphemes without the first radical (§240). The phonological rules in §33 apply to the rest of these roots.

e) II-*w* and -*y* roots (*mediae infirmae*): In most morphemes, long vowels replace the middle radical.

f) III-*w* and -*y* roots (*tertiae infirmae*): In most morphemes, long vowels replace the third radical. III-*w* and III-*y* are distinguished only in the basic stem of the verb and in some derived nouns.

Note 1. Within Semitic roots, consonants that are alike or share points of articulation are largely incompatible. Roots with identical first and second radicals do not occur. Roots with like first and third radicals rarely occur and, when they do, usually derive from reduplicated roots: *q-l-q* < *q-l-q-l*, *s-l-s* < *s-l-s-l*.

Note 2. There are II-weak roots in which *w* or *y* are treated as "strong" radicals (cf. §245.3).

Note 3. The last radical in four-radical roots can be "weak": IV-weak roots (cf. §251.3).

§**60.** Stems of "weak" roots containing long vowels are classified in the system of three-radical stem pattern morphemes according to the following rules:

a) Stems of the pattern *CāC, CīC, CūC* of II-weak roots correspond to one-syllable stem morphemes *faʿl, fiʿl, fuʿl* or *fʿal, fʿil, fʿul*, e.g., in the imperfect (§216) and morpheme patterns with *ma-* prefix (§78 a). *CāC* also figures in two-syllable morphemes with short vowels, *faʿal, faʿil, faʿul*. In all other morphemes, *w* and *y* are treated as consonants.

Note 1. With *fiʿl, fuʿl* of II-weak roots, the phonological rule in §33 is observed.

Note 2. With *faʿl*, *aw* or *ay* usually replaces long vowel *ā* when *w* and *y* belong to the root.

b) Stems of III-weak roots occur with final -*ā*, -*ī*, -*ū*. -*ū* occurs only in the basic stem of verbs (§250). Noun stems have only -*ā*- and *ī*- in final position: -*ā* represents a morpheme with *a* in the final syllable of the stem (*fʿal, faʿal, fiʿal*, etc.), and -*ī* represents a morpheme with *i* or *u* in the final syllable of the stem (*fʿil, fʿul, faʿil*, etc.).

Note 3. Stem final -*ā* sometimes represents the third radical in *faʿl, fiʿl, fuʿl*. Thus, these morphemes appear to be *faʿal, fiʿal, fuʿal* (§257 a).

Nominal Forms

§61. Preliminary remarks: Nominal forms are 1. substantives, 2. adjectives, and 3. quantitative expressions that cannot be classified as substantives or adjectives, such as elative forms and numerals, among others. Most morpheme categories can be substantival and adjectival. Only a few are reserved primarily for adjectives. Nominal inflectional endings (§§140 ff.) attach to the stem, whose form is determined by stem pattern morphemes. Additionally, suffixed and prefixed pattern morphemes may be appended to the stem.

Stem Pattern Morphemes

§62. Three-radical nominal stem pattern morphemes:

a) One-syllable morphemes:

faʿl, fiʿl, fuʿl

b) Two-syllable morphemes with short vowels:

faʿal, faʿil, faʿul, fiʿal, fuʿal, fuʿul

c) Two-syllable morphemes with long vowels:

faʿāl, fiʿāl, fuʿāl, faʿīl, faʿūl, fuʿūl, fuʿayl

d) Morphemes with long vowels in the first syllable:

fāʿal, fāʿil, fāʿūl, fayʿal, fawʿal, fayʿāl, fayʿūl

e) Morphemes with geminated second radical:

faʿʿil, fuʿʿal, fiʿʿil, fiʿʿal, faʿʿāl, fiʿʿāl, fuʿʿāl, fiʿʿīl, faʿʿūl, fuʿʿūl, fuʿʿayl, fiʿʿawl

f) Morphemes with geminated third radical:

fiʿall, fiʿill, fuʿull, faʿāll

g) Morphemes with reduplication:

fiʿlil, fuʿlal, fuʿlul, fiʿlāl, fiʿlīl, fuʿlāl, fuʿlūl, faʿlūl, faʿalʿal, fuʿulʿul

h) Morphemes with infixed *n*:

faʿanlā

Note 1. The substantive forms *fuʿl-un* and *fuʿul-un* are variants of the same morpheme (cf. §88). *fiʿil-un* is an occasional variant of *fiʿl-un*.

Note 2. The substantive form *faʿil-un* frequently alternates with *fiʿl-un* (§77).

Note 3. *fuʿayl-un* is a diminutive morpheme (§81).

Note 4. *fāʿil-un* is the active participle of the basic verbal stem (§223) and is used to form the ordinal numbers (§133).

Note 5. *fāʿal* and *fāʿūl* are Aramaic in origin. *fāʿūl*, however, is also formed secondarily from Arabic roots.

Note 6. The morphemes listed above in e–g are termed "expanded" morphemes.

Note 7. *faʿanlā* is a verbal adjective of the XV verbal stem (§173).

§**63.** Four-radical nominal stem pattern morphemes:

faʿlal	*fiʿlil*	*fuʿlul*	*fiʿlal*	*fuʿlal*
faʿlāl	*fiʿlīl*	*fuʿlūl*	*fiʿlāl*	*fuʿlāl*
	fiʿlill	*fuʿlull*	*fiʿlall*	
faʿl_3*al*$_4$*ī*l_4				
fiʿal$_3$$l_4$	*fuʿal*$_3$$l_4$	*fuʿal*$_3$$l_4$*ī*$l_4$		

fiʿʿal₃l₄	*fuʿʿal₃l₄*			
fuʿalil	*fuʿālil*	*fuʿaylil*	*faʿālil*	*faʿālīl*
faʿallal	*faʿanlal*	*faʿaylal*		

Note 1. Most four-radical stem morphemes have forms that correspond to the expanded three-radical morphemes (§62 e–g). In addition to these, the following correspondences between four-radical and three-radical morphemes exist: *fuʿlal* = *fuʿʿal; faʿlāl* = *faʿāl, faʿʿāl; fiʿlāl* = *fiʿāl, fiʿʿāl; fuʿālil* = *fuʿāl; fuʿaylil* = *fuʿayl*.

Note 2. *fuʿlal* has a later variant *fuʿlul*: جندب *jundabun, jundubun* 'locust'; also three-radical *fuʿlal*: سودد *sūdadun, sūdudun*, also with classicizing ʾ سؤدد *suʾdadun* 'leadership' (root *s-w-d*).

Note 3. *faʿālil* and *faʿālīl* are plural morphemes (§93 ff.).

Note 4. *faʿanlal*, corresponding to *faʿanlā* (§62.7), is a verbal adjective of the four-radical verbal stem III (§176).

Note 5. Among four-radical roots, there are very many that are derived from three-radical roots with lexicalized pattern morphemes. For example, pattern categories like *faʿwal, fiʿwal, fiʿyal*, and forms with prefixed *ha-*, *ʿa-* or suffixed *-n, -an, -am, -im, -um*, and others belong to this class.

Suffixed Pattern Morphemes

§64. The feminine endings *-at, -ā* can be added to stem pattern morphemes. These endings are so named because in substantives they often mark the naturally feminine (§110.1), and in adjectives, the grammatically feminine (§113). The suffix *-ā* has an inflected variant *-āʾu*.

a) *-at-un* (ة §13) designates the "specific", as opposed to the generic, i.e., it is used to form the naturally feminine, nominal forms that express the doing of an action once (*nomina vicis*), terms for things and individual units (*nomen unitatis*) of collectives (§84 a) and adjectives (§73), abstract and verbal substantives (§§73; 75), and abstract collectives (§89).

Note 1. A vestige of an old feminine ending *-t* is preserved in بنت *bin-t-un* 'daughter', أخت *ʾukh-t-un* 'sister' (§72), كلتا *kil-t-ā* 'both' (§109), ثنتان *thin-t-āni* 'two' (§129).

b) *-ā* (ى §10.3) is used for secondary feminine forms of adjectives (§§119; 122; 127), abstract and verbal substantives (§75 b), and, rarely, occurs to indicate things.

Note 2. Tradition varies occasionally between the use of *-ā* and *-an* to designate terms for things (III-weak nouns §69 a): معزى, *miʿzā, miʿzan* 'goats' (§12).

Note 3. Occasionally, *-ā* combines with *-(a)t-* to form *-āt-un*: سعلى *siʿlā* or سعلاة *siʿlātun* 'female demon'.

c) *-āʾu* (with diptotic inflection §152) forms the secondary adjectival feminine *faʿlāʾu* (§119) and appears in terms for things, verbal substantives (§75 b), and plural morphemes (§§90; 100).

Note 4. *-ā, -āʾu, -ātun* sometimes occur as variants: سلحفى *sulaḥfā*, سلحفاء *sulaḥfāʾu*, سلحفاة *sulaḥfātun* 'turtle'.

Note 5. The morpheme category *fiʿlāʾun* is masculine and inflects as a triptote (§§147 ff.): حرباء *ḥirbāʾun* 'chameleon'.

Note 6. In Aramaic loanwords, *-ā, -āʾu* occasionally represents the original *-ā* of the emphatic state: الثّلاثاء *(ʾa)<u>th</u>-<u>th</u>alā<u>th</u>āʾu* 'Tuesday'.

§**65.** Additional suffixed pattern morphemes are *-ān, -iy(y)*, and *-ūt*.

a) *-ān* forms adjectives (§119), verbal substantives: *faʿalānun* (§229), *fiʿlānun, fuʿlānun* (§74), and plural morphemes (§92). Rarely, *-ān* is also a suffix on other stem morphemes.

Note 1. The original individualizing function of *-ān* is noticeably present in إنسان *ʾinsānun* 'person', which belongs to إنس *ʾinsun* 'humankind'. It also figures in the origin of many personal names, such as شيبان *<u>sh</u>aybānu* ('white-haired') from شيب *<u>sh</u>aybun* 'white hair'.

b) *-iy(y)*, called the *nisbah*, or relative ending, expresses the concept of "belonging". It forms adjectives (§§116 ff.) and, mostly in combination with the feminine endings: *-iy-atun, iyy-atun, -iy-āʾu*, forms abstract substantives (§76).

Note 2. *-iyy* without the feminine ending occurs only rarely as a substantive: سخريّ *sukhriyyun* and سخريّة *sukhriyyatun* 'ridicule'. Apparently, *-iy* figures in the origin of patterns like غرقئ *ghirqiʾun* 'interior membrane of an egg, egg white' with classicizing *hamzah*.

c) *-ūt* is found in loanwords from Aramaic: ملكوت *malakūtun* 'kingdom' and infrequently in adjectives: تربوت *tarabūtun* 'navigable'. In Arabic, these words are masculine.

Prefixed Pattern Morphemes

§**66.** a) *ta- /ti- /tu-* form verbal substantives (§231) and infrequently verbal adjectives: تنبل *tinbalun*, تنبال *tinbālun* 'small of stature, dwarf', تلعاب *tilʿābun*, تلعّاب *tiliʿʿābun* 'joker'.

b) *ma- /mi- /mu-*: *ma-* forms nouns of place (*nomina loci*) (§78), verbal substantives (§230), and passive participles of the basic stem *mafʿūlun* (§223). *mi-* forms nouns that indicate instrument (*nomina instrumenti*) (§79) and adjectives (§121). *mu-* forms participles (§224) and verbal substantives (§230), and is an occasional variant of *ma-* or *mi-* (§80).

c) *ʾa- /ʾi- /ʾu-* form the elative *ʾafʿalu* (§124) and its derivative adjectives (§119). These prefixes also figure in morpheme categories like *ʾifʿīlun, ʾufʿūlun, ʾifʿillun, ʾufʿullun, ʾufāʿilun*, which are derived from elatives or represent phonetic variants of morpheme categories *fiʿillun, fuʿullun*.

d) *ya-* occurs in morpheme categories *yafʿalun, yafʿulun, yafʿīlun, yafʿūlun*, which figure almost exclusively in animal, plant, and personal names.

Note 1. Morpheme categories formed with prefixes are mostly deverbal, less often denominal, e.g.: *mafʿūlun* < **ma-faʿūl-un*, *mifʿālun* < **ma-fiʿāl-un*. All prefix patterns have in common the loss of the vowel in the open syllable (§51) following the prefix.

"Weak" Root Stem Patterns

§**67.** a) III-ʾ roots are often treated like III-weak roots. Variants with *w* and *y*, instead of ʾ, occur especially after *u, i, ū, ī*: خابية *khābiyatun* or خابئة *khābiʾatun* 'jug', مروّة *murūwatun* or مروءة *murūʾatun* 'manliness', هدوّ

hudūwun or هدوء *hudūʾun* 'rest'. In order to avoid the sequence ʾ – ʾ (§41), plural morpheme *faʿāʾilu* (§98) is not formed from III-ʾ roots; rather, *faʿālā* (§99) with *y* as the third radical appears: خطيئة *khaṭīʾatun* 'sin', plural خطايا *khaṭāyā*.

b) With II-geminate roots, phonological rules for the treatment of geminates (§50) in nominal patterns apply only for morpheme categories with prefixes. All other morphemes are formed according to the standard three-radical pattern: سرير *sarīrun* 'bed', plural أسرّة *ʾasirratun* = *ʾafʿilatun* (§100), but سرر *sururun*; أسكّ *ʾasakku* 'deaf' = *ʾafʿalu* (§119). Cf. §236.

Note 1. In poetry there are also morpheme categories formed on the standard pattern: أحرر *ʾaḥraru* instead of أحرّ *ʾaḥarru* 'very hot' (elative §§124ff.).

§68. a) In morphemes *faʿl, fiʿl, fuʿl* and in *ma-fʿal, ma-fʿil*, II-weak roots have stems with long vowels: سوق *sūqun* 'market' = *fuʿlun*, ميتة *mītatun* (< **miwtatun*) 'manner of death' = *fiʿlatun*, خال *khālun* 'maternal uncle' = *faʿlun*. The stem vowel *ā* also appears in morphemes *faʿal, faʿil, faʿul*: طاعة *ṭāʿatun* 'obedience' = *faʿalatun*, طاع *ṭāʿun* 'obedient' = *faʿilun*.

Note 1. Patterns with consonantal *w* or *y* can occur in all the above-mentioned morphemes: عوج *ʿawajun* 'crookedness', معيبة *maʿyabatun* 'object of rebuke'. This pattern holds especially for *faʿl*, which, as a verbal substantive, is always formed with *w* or *y* as root letter; cf. §248.

Note 2. Adjectives of the category *CāC* = *faʿilun* sometimes also have a III-weak *fāʿilun* variant: شاك *shākun* or شاك *shākin* (§256 a) 'thorny'.

b) All other morphemes are formed with consonantal *w* or *y*: هيام *huyāmun* 'passion', طويل *ṭawīlun* 'long', خوون *khawūnun* 'disloyal', مقياس *miqyāsun* 'measure'.

Note 3. In *fiʿālun*, *iw* becomes *iy*, when the verbal substantive of the basic stem or the plural morpheme (§88) is involved (§33 a). The sequence *wu* (*wū*) can be replaced by *ʾu* (*ʾū*) (§36 b): خؤون *khaʾūnun*.

Note 4. There is no *faʿīl* form of II-*y* roots.

c) Several morphemes with geminated second radical *yy* or *ww* originate in a non-classical variant of the active participle *fāʿilun* with *y* instead of ʾ (§247): قوّم *quwwamun* or قيّم *quyyamun*, قوّام *quwwāmun* or قيّام *quyyāmun* (§90), plural of قائم *qāʾimun* (non-classical قايم *qāyim*) 'standing'; قيّوم *qayyūmun* 'permanent' (§36.2). The adjective category *CayyiC*, formed only from II-weak roots, always has *yy*: ميّت *mayyitun* 'dead' (root *m-w-t*), بيّن *bayyinun* 'clear' (root *b-y-n*).

Note 5. *CayyiC* is on rare occasion shortened to *CaYC*: ميت *maytun* 'dead'.

Note 6. The verbal substantive *faʿlūlatun* (§248.1), formed only from II-weak roots, also always has *y*.

§**69.** a) In III-weak roots, the third radical of one-syllable morphemes is regularly consonantal. In morphemes with *a* before the final radical, the stem ends in *-ā*. In morphemes with *i*, *u* before the final radical, the stem ends in *-ī* (*-uy* > *ī* §33 b): عمي *ʿumyun*, عميان *ʿumyānun* 'blind' (§119), عمى *ʿaman* 'blindness' (stem *ʿamā* = *faʿalun*), عم *ʿamin* 'blind' (stem *ʿamī* = *faʿilun*). On the inflection of *ā* and *ī* stems, see §§154 ff.

Note 1. In morphemes *faʿl, fiʿl, fuʿl*, the last radical can also be represented by stem final *-ā*: ونى *wanan* = ونْي *wanyun*, verbal substantive of ونى *wanā* (يني *yanī*) 'weaken'. Cf. §257 a.

b) In morphemes with *-ā* in the final syllable of the stem, ʾ appears between the final sound of the stem and the inflectional ending: مقراء *miqrāʾun* 'hospitable' (§121). Cf. §257 b. Before the feminine ending *-atun*, *w* or *y* of the root appears: سماوة *samāwatun* 'tent, celestial canopy', as opposed to سماء *samāʾun* 'heaven'.

Note 2. If the form derives directly from the masculine, ʾ is preserved before the feminine ending: بكّاء *bakkāʾun*, feminine بكّاءة *bakkāʾatun* 'crying'.

c) In morphemes with *ī*, *ū*, *ay* in the final syllable of the stem, *w* and *y* are treated as consonants. Thus, the phonological rules in §§33 and 34 are observed: خفيّ *khafīyun* 'hidden', أبيّ *ʾubayyun* diminutive of 'father' (root *ʾ-b-w*). Cf. on this §§256 b and 257.1.

Note 3. Sometimes, in III-weak roots compensatory forms with the feminine ending *-atun* occur instead of morphemes with long vowels in the final syllable of the stem: رماة *rumātun* 'throwing' (§90) = *fuʿalatun* instead of *fuʿ(ʿ)ālun*, تربية *tarbiyatun* 'education' (§257.2) = *tafʿilatun* instead of *tafʿīlun*.

§70. a) Two-radical substantives of the pattern *CaC-atun, CiC-atun, CuC-atun* are classified as either I-*w* roots or III-weak roots. To I-*w* roots belong, for example, جهة *jihatun* 'direction' (root *w-j-h*), لدة *lidatun* 'contemporary' (root *w-l-d*). See §240 c. *CuC-atun* does not exist for I-*w* roots. To III-weak roots belong, e.g.: أمة *ʾamatun* 'female slave' (root *ʾ-m-w*), لثة *li<u>th</u>atun* 'gums' (root *l-<u>th</u>-y*), لغة *lu<u>gh</u>atun* 'language' (root *l-<u>gh</u>-w*). Stem pattern derivations are based on the three-radical root: أميّة *ʾumayyatun* = *fuʿayl-atun*, diminutive of *ʾamatun*.

b) Several two-radical substantives also have root variants with III-*h*: سنة *sanatun* 'year', diminutive سنيّة *sunayyatun* (root *s-n-w*), سنهاء *sanhāʾu* 'year of misfortune' (root *s-n-h*), شفة *<u>sh</u>afatun* 'lip', *nisbah* adjective شفويّ *<u>sh</u>afawiyyun* (root *<u>sh</u>-f-w*), شفهيّ *<u>sh</u>afahiyyun* 'labial' (root *<u>sh</u>-f-h*).

Note 2. Substantives in the two-radical category without the feminine ending are rare. As with many two-radical substantives with the feminine ending, they are treated like primary substantives which have assimilated to the three-radical pattern (§72).

Substantive

Primary Substantives

§71. Primary substantives, that is, those substantives that are not derived from verbal roots or other nominal forms, are not associated with any one morpheme category. They are one- and two-radical, as well as three- and more-radical, words. Substantives like رأس *raʾsun* 'head', قمر *qamarun* 'moon', جبين *jabīnun* 'forehead' are formally indistinguishable from derivatives of morpheme categories *faʿlun, faʿalun, faʿīlun*. Yet, they are not regarded as derivatives of the corresponding roots.

Note 1. Loanwords, especially those that entered Arabic in pre- and early Islamic times, have been adapted for the most part to Arabic morpheme categories, so that in form they cannot readily be distinguished from purely Arabic words: قصر *qaṣrun* 'castle, palace' < Aramaic *qaṣṭrā* < Latin *castra*.

§72. Primary substantives with one or two radicals are classed secondarily with "weak" three-radical roots (§70). In this way, denominative patterns based on the three-radical morpheme category are possible.

a) فو *fū* 'mouth' (only in the construct state §150), root *f-w-h*, e.g., plural أفواه *ʾafwāhun* (§100). In the definite and indefinite states, فم *famun* is used. — شاء *shāʾun* 'sheep' (collective; noun of individuality, or *nomen unitatis* شاة *shātun*), root *sh-w-h*: plural شياه *shiyāhun* (§33 a). — ماء *māʾun* 'water', root *m-w-h*: plural مياه *miyāhun* (§33 a).

b) أب *ʾabun* 'father', أخ *ʾakhun* 'brother', حم *ḥamun* 'father-in-law', construct state أبو *ʾabū*, أخو *ʾakhū*, حمو *ḥamū* (§150), roots *ʾ-b-w*, *ʾ-kh-w*, *ḥ-m-w*: plural آباء *ʾābāʾun*, إخوة *ʾikhwatun* (§89b), أحماء *ʾaḥmāʾun* (§100).

Note 1. The feminine of *ʾakhun* is أخت *ʾukhtun* (§64.1) 'sister', plural أخوات *ʾakhawātun*. The feminine of *ḥamun* is حماة *ḥamātun* 'mother-in-law'.

Note 2. Three-radical أمّ *ʾummun* 'mother' has an extended root in the plural: أمّهات *ʾummahātun*, in addition to أمّات *ʾummātun*.

c) إسم *(ʾi)smun* 'name', إبن *(ʾi)bnun* 'son', إست *(ʾi)stun* 'buttocks' (§21), roots *s-m-y*, *b-n-w*, *s-t-h*: plural أسماء *ʾasmāʾun*, أبناء *ʾabnāʾun*, أستاه *ʾastāhun* (§100).

Note 3. Older stem forms are preserved in سم *simun* 'name', بنت *bintun* (§64.1) in addition to إبنة *(ʾi)bnatun* 'daughter', plural بنات *banātun*.

Note 4. حر *ḥirun*, حرة *ḥiratun* 'female genitals' is *sui generis*; root *ḥ-r-ḥ* appears in the plural أحراح *ʾaḥrāḥun*. Cf. §151.1.

d) دم *damun* 'blood', يد *yadun* 'hand', هن *hanun*, هنة *hanatun* 'thing, something', شفة *shafatun* 'lip', roots *d-m-w, y-d-y, h-n-h* or *h-n-w, sh-f-h* or *sh-f-w*: plural دماء *dimāʾun*, يديّ *yudīyun* (§88), شفاه *shifāhun* or شفوات *shafawātun*, diminutive هنيهة *hunayhatun*, هنيّة *hunayyatun*.

Note 5. غد *ghadun* 'next day' is a back-formation from غدا *ghadan* (root *gh-d-w*), which as an accusative (§315 b), means 'tomorrow'.

e) إمرؤ *ʾimruʾun* 'man' (§151), إمرأة *ʾimraʾatun* 'woman', with the article ألمرء (ʾ*a*)*l-marʾu*, ألمرأة (ʾ*a*)*l-marʾatu*. These words have no plurals. The suppletive forms رجال *rijālun* 'men' (§88), نساء *nisāʾun*, نسوة *niswatun*, نسوان *niswānun* 'women' (with no singular) are used instead.

Feminine Substantive Ending -*atun*

§**73.** The feminine ending -*atun* (§64 a) affixed to adjectives transforms them into substantives that designate individuals and things, as well as abstracts (see also §§84; 232)

a) -*atun* that has transformed an adjective into a substantive indicates 'one who practices an occupation in an exemplary manner': راو *rāwin* 'narrator' : راوية *rāwiyatun* 'narrator (of poems)', علّام *ʿallāmun* 'knowing thoroughly' : علّامة *ʿallāmatun* 'distinguished scholar'.

Note 1. In its function of signifiying the 'specific', -*atun* is found in intensive adjectives of the morpheme categories *fuʿalun, fuʿʿālun* (§121).

Note 2. These forms ending in -*atun*, as they designate the individual, are treated as masculines.

b) In other cases, -*atun* forms words that designate things: دبّاب *dabbābun* 'creeping' : دبّابة *dabbābatun* 'besieging machine', راب *rābin* 'growing large' : رابية *rābiyatun* 'hill', حسن *ḥasanun* 'good' : حسنة *ḥasanatun* 'good deed', مشكل *mushkilun* 'obscure' : مشكلة *mushkilatun* 'difficulty, problem'.

c) Adjectives that have been transformed into substantives with -*atun* are often abstract in meaning: رذيل *radhīlun* 'low, base' : رذيلة *radhīlatun* 'vice, depravity', لائم *lāʾimun* 'accuser' : لائمة *lāʾimatun* 'censure'. Very frequently, *-atun* transforms *nisbah*-adjectives into abstract substantives (§§116 f.): نصراني *naṣrāniyyun* 'Christian' : نصرانيّة *naṣrāniyyatun* 'Christianity'; cf. §76.

Note 3. On the formation of abstract substantives ending in *-atun*, see also §75 a; for abstract collectives ending in *-atun*, see §89.

Abstract and Verbal Substantives

§**74.** The following morpheme categories function as abstract and verbal substantives: *faʿlun, fiʿlun, fuʿlun, faʿalun, fiʿalun, faʿālun, fiʿālun, fuʿālun, faʿīlun, faʿūlun, fuʿūlun.* In addition, morpheme categories with *-ān* suffix *fiʿlānun, fuʿlānun, faʿalānun* serve the same function. Cf. §§225 ff.

Note 1. *faʿalun, faʿilun* occur as phonetic variants of *faʿlun* (§38).

Note 2. *fuʿulun* is a variant of *fuʿlun.*

Note 3. Morpheme categories *fuʿ(u)lun, fiʿālun, fuʿālun, faʿīlun, fuʿūlun* also function as collective plurals (§88).

§**75.** a) The feminine ending *-atun* (§73 c), in its function of forming abstracts, is also added to the morphemes listed in §74: *fiʿlatun, fuʿlatun, faʿālatun, fiʿālatun, fuʿālatun, faʿīlatun, fuʿūlatun*, and occasionally *faʿalatun, fiʿalatun.* These morpheme categories are usually abstracts of words that denote qualities, among other things. As such, they also function as verbal substantives of verbs that refer to qualities (§§228 f.).

Note 1. *faʿlatun* is as a rule a *nomen vicis* (§232). Sometimes, however, especially with verbs whose action occurs once, *faʿlatun* may also function as a general verbal substantive: رغبة *ra<u>gh</u>batun* 'wish' from رغب *ra<u>gh</u>iba* (يرغب *yar<u>gh</u>abu*) 'wish, desire'. The corresponding form *faʿlalatun*, as verbal substantive from four-radical verbs, is always formed with *-atun.*

Note 2. *faʿalatun* is, like *faʿilatun, faʿulatun*, a verbal substantive variant of *faʿlatun.* Cf. §§38 and 257 a.

Note 3. See §77 concerning *fiʿlatun, fuʿlatun, fiʿālatun, fuʿālatun.*

b) The feminine ending *-ā* (§64 b) is used with the following morpheme categories to form abstracts and verbal substantives: *faʿlā, fiʿlā,* *fuʿlā, faʿalā*: دعوى *daʿwā* 'claim', ذكرى *dhikrā* 'memory', بشرى *bushrā* 'good tidings', جفلى *jafalā* 'everyone without distinction'. The suffix *-āʾu* occurs with *fuʿālāʾu, fāʿūlāʾu*: غلواء *ghulawāʾu* 'excess' ضاروراء *ḍārūrāʾu* 'necessity'.

Note 4. *-āʾu* is sometimes a variant of *-ā*: رهباء *rahbāʾu* = رهبى *rahbā, ruhbā* 'dread'.

Note 5. *-ā* forms verbal substantives from expanded morpheme categories, e.g.: *fiʿʿīl-ā, fiʿill-ā, fuʿull-ā*: زلّيلى *zillīlā* 'slip, lapse', غلّبى *ghilibbā, ghulubbā* 'conquering'.

Note 6. *fuʿalāʾu* usually functions as a plural morpheme (§90).

§**76.** Originally derived from the feminine of the *nisbah* adjective (§73 c), *-iyyatun* has become a suffix in its own right for abstract substantives: عجرفيّة *ʿajrafiyyatun* = عجرفة *ʿajrafatun* 'presumption, arrogance', عنجهيّة *ʿunjuhiyyatun* 'arrogance, pride'. Cf. §65.2. Frequently both *fuʿūliyyatun* and *fuʿūlatun* occur: فروسيّة *furūsiyyatun* = فروسة *furūsatun* 'horsemanship, knighthood'. The short form *-iy-atun* occurs with *faʿāl*: كراهية *karāhiyatun* 'antipathy', علانية *ʿalāniyatun* 'openness'.

Note 1. With the feminine ending *-āʾu* in the same function is: كبرياء *kibriyāʾu* 'arrogance, pride'.

Semantic Groups

§**77.** Many morpheme categories can be classified in groups with associated meanings. These semantic groups are identified in part by form and in part by meaning. The most important are:

fiʿlun: Objects occurring in pairs like عدل *ʿidlun* 'either of the two balanced halves of a load carried by a beast of burden', قسم *qismun* 'part', شبه *shibhun* 'counterpart, something like'. Cf. §229.

faʿilun, fiʿlun: Parts of the body like كبد *kabidun, kibdun*, رحم *raḥimun, riḥmun* 'womb', فخذ *fakhidhun, fikhdhun, fakhdhun* 'thigh'.

fiʿlatun: Nouns of kind or manner (*nomina speciei*) like مشية *mishyatun* 'gait', قبلة *qiblatun* ('the direction one turns in prayer') 'qiblah'.

fuʿlatun: Abstracts of color and form like حضرة *ḥuḍratun* 'greenness', حمرة *ḥumratun* 'redness', شنعة *shunʿatun* 'ugliness'. Cf. §119.

fiʿalun: Measure and size like ثقل *thiqalun* 'heaviness', كبر *kibarun* 'bigness' صغر *ṣigharun* 'smallness', عظم *ʿiẓamun* 'might'.

fiʿālun: Implements like حزام *ḥizāmun* 'belt', حجاب *ḥijābun* 'veil', عنان *ʿinānun* 'bridle', وعاء *wiʿāʾun* 'vessel'.

fuʿālun: Maladies like سعال *suʿālun* 'cough', صداع *ṣudāʿun* 'headache', عطاس *ʿuṭāsun* 'sneeze'.

fuʿālatun: Rubbish, leavings like براية *burāyatun* 'wood shavings', كناسة *kunāsatun* 'sweepings', occasionally *fuʿālun* as a collective (§84): براء *burāʾun* 'wood shavings'.

fāʿilāʾu: Places of refuge like قاصعاء *qāṣiʿāʾu* 'burrow of a jerboa', عانقاء *ʿāniqāʾu* 'rabbit warren'.

faʿʿālun: Occupational terms like نجّار *najjārun* 'carpenter', ملّاح *mallāḥun* 'sailor'. Occupations in the abstract have the morpheme category *fiʿālatun*: نجارة *nijāratun* 'carpentry', ملاحة *milāḥatun* 'navigation'.

fuʿʿalun (***fiʿʿalun***), ***fuʿʿālun***: Names of animals and plants like حمّر *ḥummarun* 'finch', حمّص *ḥimmaṣun* 'chick pea', تفّاح *tuffāḥun* 'apple', رمّان *rummānun* 'pomegranate'.

fuʿālun, fuʿālā: Birds like غراب *ghurābun* 'raven', عقاب *ʿuqābun* 'eagle', حبارى *ḥubārā* 'bustard'.

ʾufʿūlatun: Literary genres like أرجوزة *ʾurjūzatun* '*Rajaz* poem', أحدوثة *ʾuḥdūthatun* 'story', أغنيّة *ʾughnīyatun* 'song' (§33 b).

Nouns of Place (*Nomina Loci*) and Nouns of Time (*Nomina Temporis*)

§78. a) Morphemes with *ma-* prefix *mafʿalun, mafʿilun* are deverbal substantives of place and time. As a rule, when the verb is an *i*-imperfect, the pattern is *mafʿilun*; when it is a *u-* or *a*-imperfect, the pattern is *mafʿalun* (§216): منزل *manzilun* 'place where one alights' from نزل *nazala* (ينزل *yanzilu*) 'go down, alight', موعد *mawʿidun* 'place or time of an appointment' from وعد *waʿada* (يعد *yaʿidu*) 'give a pledge', مشرب *ma<u>sh</u>rabun* 'drinking place' from شرب *<u>sh</u>ariba* (يشرب *ya<u>sh</u>rabu*) 'drink'. Sometimes, however, *mafʿilun* occurs when the verb has an *u*-imperfect: مسجد *masjidun* 'mosque' from سجد *sajada* (يسجد *yasjudu*) 'bow in prayer'.

Note 1. II-*w* and *y* roots have *ā* and *ī* as stem vowels. *ī* occurs only in II-*y* roots: مكان *makānun* 'place' from كان *kāna* (يكون *yakūnu*) 'to be', مصير *maṣīrun* 'place at which one arrives' from صار *ṣāra* (يصير *yaṣīru*) 'become'.

b) Morpheme categories *mafʿilatun, mafʿalatun, mafʿulatun* are formed with the feminine ending *-atun*: مظنّة *maẓinnatun* 'place where one presumes to find something/one' from ظنّ *ẓanna* 'think' (يظنّ *yaẓunnu*), مقبرة *maqbaratun, maqburatun* 'grave' from قبر *qabara* (يقبر *yaqburu*) 'bury'. Morpheme category *mafʿalatun* forms denominal terms for places: مأسدة *maʾsadatun* 'place frequented by lions' from أسد *ʾasadun* 'lion'. Sometimes the feminine ending is used to establish a specialized meaning: منزل *manzilun* 'place of alighting, stopping place': منزلة *manzilatun* 'position, rank'.

Note 2. Morpheme categories *mafʿalun, mafʿilun, mafʿilatun, mafʿa/ulatun* also function as verbal substantives (§§230, 248.3, 257.3).

Note 3. In the derived verbal stems, the passive participle assumes the role of *ma*-formations: مصلّى *muṣallan* 'place of prayer' from صلّى *ṣallā* 'pray' (II), منصرف *munṣarafun* 'departure, or place, time of departure' from إنصرف (*ʾi*)*nṣarafa* 'depart' (VII), ملتقى *multaqan* 'meeting place, place or time of meeting' from إلتقى (*ʾi*)*ltaqā* 'meet' (VIII).

Note 4. Sometimes, denominal *mafʿalatun* has the meaning of a noun indicating cause (*nomina causae*) or abstract collective: مندمة *mandamatun* 'reason for repenting' from ندم *nadima* 'repent', مشيخة *ma<u>sh</u>ya<u>kh</u>atun* 'office or dignity of a sheik, sheikdom' (§89).

c) Infrequently, substantives indicating place and time are formed from I-*w* roots according to the *mifʿālun* morpheme category (§79): ميعاد *mīʿādun* 'appointment' from وعد *waʿada* 'make a promise', ميلاد *mīlādun* 'time of birth, birthday' from ولد *walada* 'give birth'.

Nouns of Instrument (*Nomina Instrumenti*)

§**79.** Morpheme categories with *mi-* prefix *mifʿalun, mifʿalatun, mifʿālun* are used for terms that indicate instrument: مخلب *mikhlabun* 'claw', مكنسة *miknasatun* 'broom', مفتاح *miftāḥun* 'key' from فتح *fataḥa* 'open', ميزان *mīzānun* 'scales' from وزن *wazana* 'weigh', مكواة *mikwātun* 'hot iron' from كوى *kawā* 'burn'.

Note 1. These morpheme categories of II-weak roots always have consonantal *iw* or *y*: معول *miʿwalun* 'pick', مقياس *miqyāsun* 'measure'.

Note 2. Concerning *mifʿālun* as a substantive of place and time, see §78c. Concerning adjectival *mifʿālun*, see §121.

§**80.** The prefix *mu-* occurs as a variant of *ma-* and *mi-* in forms that are legacies of the pre-classical language: منخل *munkhulun, munkhalun* 'sieve', منصل *munṣulun, munṣalun* 'sabre', مدقّ *muduqqun*, later *midaqqun*, 'pestle', مكحلة *mukḥulatun*, later *mikḥalatun*, 'kohl jar'. In some cases, various vocalizations have come down: منخر *munkhurun, munkharun, mankharun, mankhirun, minkhirun, minkharun* 'nostril', مغزل *mighzalun, maghzalun, mughzalun* 'spindle', مصحف *muṣḥafun, maṣḥafun, miṣḥafun* 'book, codex'.

Note 1. *mufʿalun* verbal substantives can be interpreted to be passive participles of verbal stem IV (§230) or *mu-* variants of *mafʿalun*.

Diminutives

§**81.** a) The morpheme *fuʿayl* is used for diminutives of one- and two-syllable morphemes with short vowels: كلب *kalbun* 'dog' : كليب *kulaybun*, جبل *jabalun* 'mountain' : جبيل *jubaylun*. In III-weak roots, the third radical is always *y*: فتى *fatan* 'youth' : فتيّ *futayyun*, أب *ʾabun* father' (root *ʾ-b-w* §72 b) : أبيّ *ʾubayyun*. Besides indicating smallness, the diminutive often expresses contempt, endearment, or occasionally, even enhancement.

Note 1. In II-*y* roots, the sequence *yay* may be dissimilated to *way*: بيت *baytun* 'house' : بييت *buyaytun*, بويت *buwaytun*.

Note 2. Note بنيّ *bunayya* 'my little son!' instead of **bunayy-iya*.

Note 3. *fuʿaylun* is the diminutive pattern for personal names even for morphemes other than those mentioned above (§81 a): حميد *Ḥumaydun* for أحمد *ʾAḥmadu*. Often *fuʿaylun* has become the only form of a personal name, independent of the diminutive: قريش *Qurayshun*, حنين *Ḥunaynun*.

b) Derivational suffixes are added to *fuʿayl* without modification: أمة *ʾamatun* 'maid' (root *ʾ-m-w* §70 a) : أميّة *ʾumayyatun*, حمراء *ḥamrāʾu* 'red' : حميراء *ḥumayrāʾu*, سلمى *Salmā* : سليمى *Sulaymā* (proper name). The naturally and grammatically feminine (§§110 ff.) take the feminine ending *-atun* in the diminutive: أمّ *ʾummun* 'mother' : أميمة *ʾumaymatun*, عين *ʿaynun* 'eye' : عيينة *ʿuynaynatun*.

Note 4. Diminutives only rarely become independent lexical entities: بحيرة *buḥayratun* 'lake'. كميت *kumaytun* 'bay horse' is a Persian loanword.

§82. a) Diminutives of four-radical morphemes are expanded from *fuʿayl* to *fuʿaylil*. *fuʿaylīl* is the corresponding diminutive of a basic form with a long vowel in the final syllable: أكدر *ʾakdaru* 'turbid' : أكيدر *ʾukaydiru*, صندوق *ṣundūqun* 'trunk' : صنيديق *ṣunaydīqun*, كذّاب *kadhdhābun* 'liar' : كذيذيب *kudhaydhībun*.

Note 1. With substantives ending in *-ān-un*, *-ān* usually figures as part of the stem; سرحان *sirḥānun* 'wolf' : سريحين *surayḥīnun*.

Note 2. Names of plants of the morpheme category *fuʿʿālun* (§77) frequently have a later form *fuʿʿaylun*: خبّاز *khubbāzun*, خبّيز *khubbayzun* 'mallow'.

Note 3. Note that *yw* > *yy* (§33 c) in: أسود *ʾaswadu* 'black' : أسيود *ʾusaywidu* or أسيّد *ʾusayyidu* (proper name).

Note 4. The plural of a small number (§100) can have a diminutive form: *ʾufayʿilun* from *ʾafʿulun* and *ʾafʿilatun*, but *ʾufayʿālun* from *ʾafʿālun*: أخيبار *ʾukhaybārun* 'several trivial accounts' from أخبار *ʾakhbārun* 'news', singular خبر *khabarun*, أثيّاب *ʾuthayyābun* (< **ʾuthaywābun* §33 c) 'several small pieces of clothing' from أثواب *ʾathwābun* 'articles of clothing', singular ثوب *thawbun*.

b) As with plural patterns (§93 b), two-syllable morphemes with long vowels *fāʿil, fāʿal, fāʿūl* and *faʿāl, fiʿāl, fuʿāl, faʿīl, faʿūl*, etc., are regarded as four-consonant morphemes: *fāʿilun* : *fuwayʿilun*; *fa/i/uʿālun, faʿū/īlun*: *fuʿayyilun*, e.g.: شاعر *shāʿirun* 'poet' : شويعر *shuwayʿirun*, غلام *ghulāmun* 'boy' : غليّم *ghulayyimun*, عروس *ʿarūsun* 'bride' : عريّس *ʿurayyisun* (contrary to §81 b, without the feminine ending!).

Note 5. The morphological correspondence *ā* : *uway* comes from nominal forms of II-weak roots, like باب *bābun* 'door' : بويب *buwaybun*.

Note 6. Morphemes *fa/i/uʿāl, faʿū/īl*, etc., of III-weak roots form diminutives after the *fuʿayl* pattern: سماء *samāʾun* 'heaven' : سميّة *sumayyatun*, عدوّ *ʿadūwun* 'enemy' : عديّ *ʿudayyun*, صبيّ *ṣabīyun* 'boy' : صبيّ *ṣubayyun*.

Note 7. Words consisting of more than four consonants have abbreviated diminutives: عنكبوت *ʿankabūtun* 'spider' : عنيكب *ʿunaykibun*.

Number of Substantives

§83. Arabic has three numbers: singular, dual, and plural. Additionally, there is a collective that is considered either singular and treated masculine, or plural and feminine. The collective plural has, moreover, an individual plural and a plural of a small number (*pluralis paucitatis*).

The basic form of the substantive appears in the singular and the collective. The dual and the so-called external plural, or inflected plural (§§101 ff.), are derived with suffixed inflectional morphemes from the singular. The collective plural and the plural of a small number have several stem pattern morphemes that are secondarily associated with singular morphemes. As such, these are called "internal" or "broken" plurals.

Note 1. Unless there is a semantic reason to prevent it, the dual and the different plurals can be formed from any singular: فرخ *farkhun* 'young bird' (singular) : dual فرخان *farkhāni* 'two young birds', individual plural فرخان *firkhānun*, collective plural فراخ *firākhun*, فروخ *furūkhun*, *pluralis paucitatis* أفراخ *ʾafrākhun*, أفرخ *ʾafrukhun*. A singular collective can replace a collective plural: شجرة *shajaratun* 'one tree' (singular = *nomen unitatis* §84 a) : singular collective شجر *shajarun* 'trees, tree (as a genus)'

(= collective plural), individual plural شجرات *shajarātun* 'trees (as individuals), *pluralis paucitatis* أشجار *'ashjārun* '(several) trees'. As a result of numerous analogical formations that have occurred in the system of plurals, in usage classical Arabic has given up the distinction among plurals largely in favor of a general plural category: collective plurals can replace individual plurals; the plural of a small number can function as a general plural. Nevertheless, the distinctive plurals can always become productive features again.

Note 2. The term "broken" plural comes from Arabic الجمع المكسّر *al-jam' al-mukassar*. It refers to all plural morpheme categories that are not formed with inflectional endings (§§101 ff.). These are called الجمع الصّحيح *al-jam' aṣ-ṣaḥīḥ* or الجمع السّالم *al-jam' as-sālim* "sound plural". All "broken" plurals are treated grammatically as feminines.

Singular Collectives

§84. a) Generic collectives as a rule have corresponding forms with the feminine ending *-atun* to indicate individual members in a class or of a species (*nomen unitatis*): دمع *dam'un* 'tears' : دمعة *dam'atun* 'a tear', حمام *ḥamāmun* 'pigeon(s)' : حمامة *ḥamāmatun* 'a (particular) pigeon'. For substances, the individual noun indicates a piece of that substance: حديد *ḥadīdun* 'iron' : حديدة *ḥadīdatun* 'a piece of iron'.

Note 1. A collective for which a *nomen unitatis* is formed is masculine. Only rarely, if the relationship of the *nomen unitatis* to the collective is construed as a singular to collective plural, is the collective treated as feminine (§91).

b) Once in a while, generic collectives that have no *nomen unitatis* occur. The collective is then understood to be the individual noun as well: طير *ṭayrun* 'bird, birds' (collective and singular), plural طيور *ṭuyūrun* 'birds, flocks of birds', ذباب *dhubābun* 'fly, flies'.

Note 2. In post-classical Arabic, these collectives sometimes have individual nouns: ذبابة *dhubābatun* 'a fly' (but not so for طير).

§**85.** Collectives referring to a multitude or masses have no corresponding form indicating the individual. In this category belong such words as: عسكر *ʿaskarun* 'army (camp)' إبل *ʾibilun*, *ʾiblun* 'herd of camel, camels', غنم *ghanamun* '(herd of) small livestock', جمهور *jumhūrun* 'multitude of people'. Depending upon whether the quantity is regarded as indicating a plurality or a unit, such words are treated, respectively, as feminine or, less frequently, masculine.

> **Note 1.** In post-classical Arabic, عسكريّ *ʿaskariyyun* 'soldier' is the individual noun of عسكر *ʿaskarun* (§86 b).

§**86.** Collectives referring to persons are masculine. For the most part, however, they are treated grammatically according to their meaning as masculine plurals. Counted among them are many words of the morpheme category *faʿlun* (§228), with variants of the pattern *faʿalun*: قوم *qawmun* ('standing together' =) 'people, tribe', شرب *sharbun* ('drinking party' =) 'binge, drinking crowd', صحب *ṣaḥbun* ('company' =) 'companions', حرس *ḥarasun* ('guarding' =) 'guard, guards', خدم *khadamun* 'servants', and others like معشر *maʿsharun* 'clan, kinfolk'.

> **Note 1.** When *faʿlun* is used as a personal collective, its use as a verbal substantive of the basic stem is normally avoided. Cf., for example, شرب *shurbun* 'drinking', قيام *qiyāmun* 'standing'.

> **Note 2.** *fāʿilun* (active participle) frequently functions as a suppletive individual noun to the personal collective: شارب *shāribun* 'drinker', صاحب *ṣāḥibun* 'companion', حارس *ḥārisun* 'guard'.

> **Note 3.** A personal collective can have *ʾafʿālun* (§100) as a *pluralis paucitatis* form: نصر *naṣrun* 'helpers', plural أنصار *ʾanṣārun* '(several) helpers' (Name of the Medinan followers of Muḥammad).

b) Collective names of tribes and people are treated as feminines: يهود *yahūdun* 'Jews', هند *hindun* 'Indians' and 'India', قريش *Qurayshun* (the principal Meccan tribe). The related *nisbah* adjective (§§116 f.) functions at the same time as an individual noun: يهوديّ *yahūdiyyun* 'Jew', هنديّ *hindiyyun* 'Indian', قرشيّ *qurashiyyun* Qurayshite'.

Note 4. Occasionally there are special forms for individual nouns: إنس *ʾinsun* 'human race' : إنسان *ʾinsānun* (§65.1) 'human being', along with إنسيّ *ʾinsiyyun* 'human, human being', جنّ *jinnun* 'jinn, demons' : جانّ *jānnun* 'demon', and جنّيّ *jinniyyun* 'demonic, demon'.

"Broken" Plurals

§**87.** Plural inflectional endings (§101) are used for only a portion of nouns to form plurals. The majority of substantives, as well as adjectives (§§122 f.), have a number of stem pattern morphemes in the plural, which cannot be derived from the singular morpheme. Only four-consonant morphemes have a consistent plural formation that is based on a singular morpheme that typically has the morphemic vowel sequence *a-ā-i* (§§93 ff.). The most likely or usual plural forms must be determined individually from the lexicon.

§**88.** Morpheme categories *fuʿulun, fiʿālun, fuʿūlun* are used very frequently (*faʿīlun* rarely) (§74) as plural morphemes. *fuʿulun* occurs mostly as plural of singular morphemes that have long vowels in the second stem syllable. *fiʿālun, fuʿūlun* often occur as plurals of singular morphemes that have one or two syllables with short vowels.

Note 1. See §122 concerning *fuʿulun, fiʿālun, fuʿūlun* as plurals of adjectives.

fuʿulun, often shortend to *fuʿlun*: كتاب *kitābun* 'book' : كتب *kutubun, kutbun*, سرير *sarīrun* 'bed' : سرر *sururun*, سقف *saqfun* 'roof, ceiling' : سقف *suqufun*, ناقة *nāqatun* 'camel' : نوق *nūqun* (§36 a).

Note 2. *fuʿlun* is avoided in II-geminate roots. In II-*y* roots, *uy* in *fuʿlun* becomes *ī* (§33 b): ناب *nābun* 'old camel' : نيب *nībun*.

fiʿālun: رجل *rajulun* 'man' : رجال *rijālun* (§72 e), كلب *kalbun* 'dog' : كلاب *kilābun*. Cf. §33 a.

fuʿūlun: عين *ʿaynun* 'eye' : عيون *ʿuyūnun*, ملك *malikun* 'king' : ملوك *mulūkun*, عصا *ʿaṣan* 'stick' : عصيّ *ʿuṣīyun*, *ʿiṣīyun* (§§34 a; 37). Notice قوس *qawsun* 'bow' : قسيّ *qusīyun, qisīyun* (*q-s-y*).

faʿīlun: (infrequently as a plural morpheme): عبد *ʿabdun* 'slave' : عبيد *ʿabīdun*, حمار *ḥimārun* 'ass' : حمير *ḥamīrun*.

§**89.** a) Abstract substantives formed with the feminine ending *-atun* from substantivized adjectives (§73 c) that refer to persons often function as plural collectives: حمّال *ḥammālun* 'porter' : حمّالة *ḥammālatun* 'carrier, porters', صوفيّ *ṣūfiyyun* 'mystic, sufi' : صوفيّة *ṣūfiyyatun* 'Sufism, Sufis', مسلم *muslimun* 'Muslim' : مسلمة *muslimatun* 'Muslims in general, Muslims'.

Note 1. The individual plural is formed with the inflectional ending *-ūna* (§102): حمّالون *ḥammālūna*, صوفيّون *ṣūfiyyūna*, مسلمون *muslimūna*.

b) *-atun* in combination with the morphemes *fiʿl, fiʿal, faʿal, fiʿāl* and *fuʿūl* forms abstract collectives that function as plurals:

fiʿlatun: غلام *ghulāmun* 'lad' : غلمة *ghilmatun*, فتى *fatan* 'youth' : فتية *fityatun*, أخ *ʾakhun* 'brother' (§72 b) : إخوة *ʾikhwatun*.

fiʿalatun, predominantly with names of animals: قرد *qirdun* 'ape' : قردة *qiradatun*, دبّ *dubbun* 'bear' : دببة *dibabatun*.

faʿalatun, *fāʿilun, faʿīlun* as terms referring to persons: طالب *ṭālibun* 'student' : طلبة *ṭalabatun*, ضعيف *ḍaʿīfun* 'weakling' : ضعفة *ḍaʿafatun*.

Note 2. With II-weak roots, *faʿalatun* is formed with stem vowel *ā* as well as with consonantal *w* or *y*: سيّد *sayyidun* 'master' : سادة *sādatun*, خائن *khāʾinun* 'traitor' : خونة *khawanatun*.

fiʿālatun: حجر *ḥajarun* 'stone' : حجارة *ḥijāratun*, جمل *jamalun* 'camel' : جمالة *jimālatun* (see also §106 b).

Note 3. *faʿālatun* occurs as a variant: صاحب *ṣāḥibun* 'companion' : صحابة *ṣaḥābatun* 'companions', specifically the 'Companions of the Prophet'.

fuʿūlatun with terms of relationship, etc.: عمّ *ʿammun* 'paternal uncle' : عمومة *ʿumūmatun*, فحل *faḥlun* 'male animal, stallion' : فحولة *fuḥūlatun*.

Note 4. *mafʿalatun, mafʿulatun* (§230) also occur on occasion as abstract collectives: مشيخة *mashyakhatun* 'office or dignity of a sheik, sheikdom, community of sheiks' from شيخ *shaykhun* 'elder, master, religious scholar'.

§**90.** Plural morpheme categories derived from the expanded morpheme catagory *fuʿal/fuʿāl* occur almost exclusively as broken plurals of *fāʿilun, faʿīlun* which refer to persons. In addition, they are used on occasion as plurals of the active participle *fāʿilun*.

Note 1. Morpheme categories *fiʿillā, fiʿillāʾu, fiʿillatun, fiʿillānun*, which are derived from the expanded *fiʿill*, and *mafʿūlāʾu*, which is formed from the passive participle, are cited by the Arab grammarians as plural morphemes without, however, being attested.

fuʿālun (rare): راعٍ *rāʿin* 'shepherd' : رعاء *ruʿāʾun*, إنسان *ʾinsānun* 'human' : أناس *ʾunāsun* (§49 d), توأم *tawʾamun* 'twin' : تؤام *tuʾāmun*.

fuʿalatun (§69.3), *fāʿilun* of III-weak roots: رامٍ *rāmin* 'throwing, archer' : رماة *rumātun*, قاضٍ *qāḍin* 'judge' : قضاة *quḍātun*.

fuʿalāʾu: شاعر *sh̲āʿirun* 'poet' : شعراء *sh̲uʿarāʾu*, وزير *wazīrun* 'minister, vizier' : وزراء *wuzarāʾu*, خليفة *kh̲alīfatun* (§73 a) 'successor, caliph' : خلفاء *kh̲ulafāʾu*. See §§152 f. on the inflection.

Note 2. See §122 on *fuʿālā*, plural of *faʿlā*.

Note 3. The plural of بريء *barīʾun* 'innocent' : *buraʾāʾu* is shortened to براء *burāʾu* or *burāʾun* to avoid the sequence ʾ–ʾ.

fuʿʿalun: ساجد *sājidun* 'bowing in prayer' : سجّد *sujjadun*, باهل *bāhilun* 'free' : بهّل *buhhalun*.

fuʿʿālun: كاتب *kātibun* 'scribe' : كتّاب *kuttābun*, كافر *kāfirun* 'unbeliever' : كفّار *kuffārun*.

Note 4. The second radical in *fuʿʿalun, fuʿʿālun* of II-*w* roots as a plural of *fāʿilun* can be *w* or *y* (§68 c): نائم *nāʾimun* 'sleeping' : plural نوّم *nuwwamun*, نوّام *nuwwāmun* or نيّم *nuyyamun*, نيّام *nuyyāmun*.

§**91.** In analogy with the generic collective that takes the *nomen unitatis* ending *-atun* (§84 a), the collective plural of singular *faʿlatun, faʿalatun, fiʿlatun, fuʿlatun* is formed conversely by the dropping of *-atun*: *faʿalun* plural of *faʿlatun* and *faʿalatun, fiʿalun* plural of *fiʿlatun*, *fuʿalun* plural of *fuʿlatun*.

fa'alun: حلقة *ḥalqatun, ḥalaqatun* 'ring' : حلق *ḥalaqun*, بكرة *bakratun* 'reel' : بكر *bakarun*, شامة *shāmatun* 'mole' : شام *shāmun*, علاة *'alātun* 'anvil' : علا *'alan*.

fi'alun: حكمة *ḥikmatun* 'wisdom' : حكم *ḥikamun*, لمّة *limmatun* 'lock of hair' : لمم *limamun*, قيمة *qīmatun* 'value' : قيم *qiyamun*.

fu'alun: ركبة *rukbatun* 'knee' : ركب *rukabun*, فوطة *fūṭatun* 'apron' : فوط *fuwaṭun*, كلية *kulyatun* 'kidney' : كلى *kulan*.

Note 1. In the plural of *fa'latun* of II-weak roots, the vowel of the first syllable is determined by the radical *w* or *y*: نوبة *nawbatun* 'change' : نوب *nuwabun*, خيمة *khaymatun* 'tent' : خيم *khiyamun*.

Note 2. The vocalization of the plural of قرية *qaryatun* 'village' : قرى *quran* is exceptional.

Note 3. *fu'alu*, with diptotic inflection (§152), occurs as plural of *fu'lā* (§127): أخرى *'ukhrā* 'another' : أخر *'ukharu* (§127 b).

Note 4. Individual plurals ending in *-ātun* retain in these words the plural morpheme pattern: *fa'alātun, fi'alātun, fu'alātun*. See §105 a.

§**92.** Plural morphemes formed with the suffix *-ān*, *fi'lānun* and *fu'lānun*, function primarily as individual plurals for animate beings. Through numerous analogical formations, however, the use of this plural formation has become widespread.

fi'lānun: غزال *ghazālun* 'gazelle' : غزلان *ghizlānun*, فتى *fatan* 'youth' : فتيان *fityānun*, جار *jārun* 'neighbor' : جيران *jīrānun*; *fi'lānun* is above all the plural of II-weak root substantives: تاج *tājun* 'crown' : تيجان *tījānun*, كوع *kū'un* 'wrist bones' : كيعان *kī'ānun*, حائط *ḥā'iṭun* 'wall' : حيطان *ḥīṭānun*.

Note 1. The collective plural of *fi'lānun* is *fi'latun* (§89 b): غزلة *ghizlatun*, فتية *fityatun*. إخوة *'ikhwatun* is the usual plural of أخ *'akhun*, with the meaning '(natural) brothers'. إخوان *'ikhwānun* is used in the sense of 'brethren' or 'members of an order'.

fuʿlānun: فارس *fārisun* 'rider, knight' : فرسان *fursānun*, صبيّ *ṣabīyun* 'boy' : صبيان *ṣubyānun* or *ṣibyānun*. *fuʿlānun* is frequently associated with *fuʿulun* (*fuʿlun*): غدير *ghadīrun* 'pond' : غدر *ghudurun* (§88), غدران *ghudrānun*.

Note 2. *fuʿlānun* is also an extended form of adjectival plural *fuʿlun* (§119).

Plural of Four-Consonant Morpheme Categories

§**93.** a) All four-consonant morpheme categories have as "broken" plurals a lengthened stem that is morphologically marked by the vowel sequence *a-ā-i/ī*. A basic rule applies, namely, that singular stems with short vowels in the final syllables have *i* in the plural, while those with long vowels in the final syllables have *ī* in the plural. Morpheme categories formed with *a-ā-i/ī*, except for *faʿālilatun* (§96), are diptotically inflected (§152).

b) With regard to their plural formation, four-consonant morpheme categories are: 1. four-radical and three-radical (four-consonant) morphemes (§62 e–g); 2. morpheme categories formed with prefixes (§66); 3. morpheme categories formed with long vowels or *aw, ay* in initial syllables (§62 d); 4. morpheme categories with long vowels in the second syllable of the stem (§62 c); 5. three-radical morpheme categories formed with suffixes *-ā, -āʾu, -ān* and endings *-ātun, iyatun, -uwatun* that are treated like IV-weak roots.

Note 1. The basic categories *faʿālilu, faʿālīlu* have variants with prefixed morpheme categories *ʾa-/ta-/ma-fāʿilu* and *ʾa-/ta-/ma-/ya-fāʿīlu* and with morpheme categories with doubled second radical *faʿāʿilu, faʿāʿīlu*.

Note 2. Stem final *ī* in *faʿālilu* of III- and IV-weak roots is treated triptotically (*-in*) in the nominative and genitive, but diptotically (*-iya*) in the accusative (§156).

Note 3. The plural of ليلة *laylatun* 'night' is formed from four-radical root *l-y-l-y*: ليال *layālin* (stem *layālī*).

§**94.** ***faʿālilu*** (*ʾa-/ta-/ma-fāʿilu*, etc.): درهم *dirhamun* 'drachma' : دراهم *dirāhimu*, كوكب *kawkabun* 'star' : كواكب *kawākibu*, تجربة *tajribatun* 'trial' : تجارب *tajāribu*, إصبع *ʾiṣbaʿun* 'finger' : أصابع *ʾaṣābiʿu*; (II-geminate roots) محلّ *maḥallun* 'station' : محالّ *maḥāllu*; (III- and IV-weak roots) أفعى *ʾafʿan* 'viper' : أفاع *ʾafāʿin*, مرثية *mar<u>th</u>iyatun* 'elegy': مراث *marā<u>th</u>in*, سعلاة *siʿlātun* 'female demon' : سعال *saʿālin*, ترقوة *tarquwatun* 'collarbone' : تراق *tarāqin*.

Note 1. In II-weak roots, *w* or *y*, insofar as it is a root element, regularly appears as a consonant: ملام *malāmun*, ملامة *malāmatun*, 'rebuke' : ملاوم *malāwimu*, معاب *maʿābun* 'fault' : معايب *maʿāyibu*. Sometimes, however, its usual plural is formed on the pattern *faʿāʾilu* (§98): مصيبة *muṣībatun* 'misfortune' : مصائب *maṣāʾibu*, منارة *manāratun* 'minaret' : منائر *manāʾiru*.

Note 2. Root I-*w* words of the pattern *mifʿalun* form plurals with the *w* of the root or with *y*: ميسم *mīsamun* 'branding iron' : مواسم *mawāsimu*, مياسم *mayāsimu*.

Note 3. Some words of the pattern *mafāʿilu*, like محاسن *maḥāsinu* 'good qualities', مساوئ *masāwiʾu* (often مساو *masāwin*) 'bad qualities' are encountered only in the plural.

§**95.** ***faʿālīlu*** (*ʾa-/ta-/ma-/ya-fāʿīlu*, etc.): شيطان *<u>sh</u>ayṭānun* 'devil' : شياطين *<u>sh</u>ayāṭīnu*, تصريف *taṣrīfun* 'change' : تصاريف *taṣārīfu* 'vicissitudes', ميزان *mīzānun* (< **miwzānun*) 'scales' : موازين *mawāzīnu*, ينبوع *yanbūʿun* 'spring, well' : ينابيع *yanābīʿu*; (III- and IV-weak roots) أغنيّة *ʾu<u>gh</u>nīyatun* 'song' (§33 b): أغانيّ *ʾa<u>gh</u>ānīyu*, كرسيّ *kursīyun* 'throne' : كراسيّ *karāsīyu*.

Note 1. The *faʿālīlu* pattern of III- and IV-weak roots can be abbreviated to *faʿālilu* (§93.2): أغان *ʾa<u>gh</u>ānin*, كراس *karāsin*.

Note 2. *Nisbah* formations are infrequently treated like IV-weak roots: بختيّ *bu<u>kh</u>tiyyun* 'Bactrian (two-humped) camel' : بخاتيّ *ba<u>kh</u>ātīyu*, بخات *ba<u>kh</u>ātin*.

Note 3. *mafʿūlun* (passive participle, §223) has the plural *mafāʿīlu* only as a substantive: مرسوم *marsūmun* 'decree' : مراسيم *marāsīmu*.

Note 4. Words with *ī* in the first syllable frequently form their plurals by repeating the second radical: ديوان *dīwānun* 'divan' : دواوين *dawāwīnu*, دينار *dīnārun* 'dinar' : دنانير *danānīru*, similarly ديباج *dībājun* 'brocade', قيراط *qīrāṭun* 'inch, unit of measure'; regular, however, نيشان *nīs͟hānun* 'sign' : نياشين *nayās͟hīnu*.

Note 5. Contrary to the basic rule in §93, sometimes *faʿālīlu* occurs in place of *faʿālilu*: سلّم *sullamun* 'leader' : سلالم *salālimu*, سلاليم *salālīmu*; مطفل *muṭfilun* 'mother animal' : مطافل *maṭāfilu*, مطافيل *maṭāfīlu*. In poetry, the use of *faʿālīlu* or *faʿālilu* is largely determined by metre.

Note 6. Words with more than four consonants are abbreviated in the plural *faʿāli/īlu*: منجنيق *manjanīqun* 'catapult' : مجانيق *majānīqu*, عنكبوت *ʿankabūtun* 'spider' : عناكب *ʿanākibu*.

§**96.** ***faʿālilatun*** functions as a collective plural of forms that refer to people (§89 a): جبّار *jabbārun* 'despot' : جبابرة *jabābiratun*, تلميذ *tilmīd͟hun* 'student' : تلامذة *talāmid͟hatun*, فيلسوف *faylasūfun* 'philosopher' : فلاسفة *falāsifatun*, ملحد *mulḥidun* 'heretic' : ملاحدة *malāḥidatun*.

Note 1. This morpheme category can also occur in *nisbah* forms: بغداديّ *bag͟hdādiyyun* 'Baghdadi' : بغاددة *bag͟hādidatun*, مهلّبيّ *muhallabiyyun* 'follower of Muhallab' : مهالبة *mahālibatun*; similarly in genitive construct names: عبد الله *ʿAbdu 'llāh* : عبادلة *ʿAbādilah*, إمرؤ القيس *'Imruʾu 'l-Qays* : مراقسة *Marāqisah*.

Note 2. The plural ملائكة *malāʾikatun* 'angel' of ملك *malakun* comes from an older form ملأك *malʾakun*.

§**97.** *fawāʿilu/fawāʿīlu* is a plural morpheme of words that have *ā*, infrequently *ū*, in the first syllable of the stem. The regular plural of substantive *fāʿilatun* is *fawāʿilu*.

fawāʿilu: ناحية *nāḥiyatun* 'direction' : نواح *nawāḥin*, قائمة *qāʾimatun* 'leg' : قوائم *qawāʾimu*, فارس *fārisun* 'horseman': فوارس *fawārisu*, قالب *qālabun* 'mold' : قوالب *qawālibu*, (II-geminate root) خاصّة *k͟hāṣṣatun* 'peculiarity' : خواصّ *k͟hawāṣṣu*, تونية *tūniyatun* 'tunic': توان *tawānin*.

Note 1. *fawāʿilatun* is also formed on the pattern *faʿālilatun*: تونسيّ *tūnisiyyun* 'Tunisian' : توانسة *tawānisatun*.

fawāʿīlu: تاريخ *tārīkhun* (< *taʾrīkhun*) 'history' : تواريخ *tawārīkhu*, طاعون *ṭāʿūnun* 'plague' : طواعين *ṭawāʿīnu*, طومار *ṭūmārun* 'scroll' : طوامير *ṭawāmīru*.

Note 2. Singular forms with long vowels in the first or second syllable originate secondarily in post-classical plurals like عواميد *ʿawāmīdu* 'columns', خواتيم *khawātīmu* 'seals': عامود *ʿāmūdun* instead of عمود *ʿamūdun*, خاتام *khātāmun* instead of خاتم *khātamun*.

§**98.** ***faʿāʾilu*** occurs in morpheme categories that have long vowels in the second syllable of the stem, especially those formed with the feminine ending *-atun*: سحابة *saḥābatun* 'cloud': سحائب *saḥāʾibu*, ذؤابة *dhuʾābatun* 'lock' (of hair): ذوائب *dhawāʾibu* (< **dhaʾāʾibu* §41 a), عجيبة *ʿajībatun* 'miracle' : عجائب *ʿajāʾibu*, دليل *dalīlun* 'indication': دلائل *dalāʾilu*, عروس *ʿarūsun* 'bride': عرائس *ʿarāʾisu*.

Note 1. حرائر *ḥarāʾiru* (without a singular) occurs suppletively as a feminine plural of singular حرّ *ḥurrun* 'noble, free'.

§**99.** a) The plural of *faʿlā, fiʿlā, fuʿlā* and substantive *faʿlāʾu* can be regular *faʿālin* (stem *faʿālī*), on the pattern *faʿālilu*, or *faʿālā*, which retains the *-ā* suffix: فتوى *fatwā* 'legal opinion' : فتاو *fatāwin*, فتاوى *fatāwā*, ذفرى *dhifrā* 'camel's sweat gland behind the ear' : ذفار *dhafārin*, ذفارى *dhafārā*, عذراء *ʿadhrāʾu* 'virgin' : عذار *ʿadhārin*, عذارى *ʿadhārā*.

Note 1. By analogy with the formation described in §95.1, *faʿālīlu* forms also occur, but infrequently: عذاريّ *ʿadhārīyu*, ذفاريّ *dhafārīyu*.

Note 2. Occasionally, *nisbah* formations also have the *faʿālā* plural pattern (cf. §95.2): بختيّ *bukhtiyyun* 'Bactrian camel' : بخاتى *bakhātā*, مهريّ *mahriyyun* 'Mahra camel' : مهار *mahārin*, مهارى *mahārā*, مهاريّ *mahārīyu*; نصرانيّ *naṣrāniyyun* 'Christian' : نصار *naṣārin*, نصارى *naṣārā*, نصاريّ *naṣārīyu*.

Note 3. The adjective pattern *faʿlā* (singular feminine or plural, §§119; 122) mostly has the plural *faʿālā*, variant *fuʿālā*. In several cases, the primary singular morpheme has become obsolete: يتامى *yatāmā* 'orphans', plural of يتيم *yatīmun*.

b) ***faʿālā*** occurs with III-weak roots in place of *faʿāʾilu* (§98) and infrequently instead of *fāʿilatun*: هديّة *hadīyatun* 'gift' : هدايا *hadāyā*, هراوة *hirāwatun* 'club' : هراوى *harāwā*, زاوية *zāwiyatun* 'corner, angle' : زوايا *zawāyā*.

Note 4. Note خطيئة *khaṭīʾatun* 'sin' : خطايا *khaṭāyā* (§67 a).

Plural of "Paucity", or a Small Number

§100. The plural of a small number (3–10) *pluralis paucitatis* is indicated by prefixed *ʾa-*: *ʾafʿulun* for *fuʿulun*, *ʿafʿālun* for *fiʿālun*, *ʾafʿilatun* for *faʿalatun* or *fiʿalatun*, *ʾafʿilāʾu* for *fuʿalāʾu*.

ʾafʿulun: نهر *nahrun* 'river' : أنهر *ʾanhurun*, عين *ʿaynun* 'eye' : أعين *ʾaʿyunun*, (III-weak root §34 a) دلو *dalwun* 'bucket' : أدل *ʾadlin*, أمة *ʾamatun* 'maid' (§70a): آم *ʾāmin* (§40).

Note 1. With a II-*w* root, أدور *ʾadwurun*, plural of دار *dārun* 'dwelling', has the variants أدؤر *ʾadʾurun*, آدر *ʾādurun* (§41 b). ناقة *nāqatun* 'female camel' has additionally an alternative plural أينق *ʾaynuqun*.

ʾafʿālun: قدم *qadamun* 'foot' : أقدام *ʾaqdāmun*, باب *bābun* 'gate' : أبواب *ʾabwābun*, يوم *yawmun* 'day' : أيّام *ʾayyāmun* (§33 c), أب *ʾabun* 'father' : آباء *ʾābāʾun* (§§40 and 72 b), بئر *biʾrun* 'well' : أبآر *ʾabʾārun*, آبار *ʾābārun* (§41 b).

Note 2. The *ʾafʿāl* pattern of شيء *shayʾun* 'thing' is treated as a diptote under influence of the ending *-āʾu* (§64 c): أشياء *ʾashyāʾu*.

ʾafʿilatun: جناح *janāḥun* 'wing' : أجنحة *ʾajniḥatun*, دواء *dawāʾun* 'remedy' : أدوية *ʾadwiyatun*, إله *ʾilāhun* (§8) 'deity' : آلهة *ʾālihatun* (§40), (II-geminate root) إمام *ʾimāmun* 'model' : أيمّة *ʾayimmatun* (§41 a).

ʾafʿilāʾu: قريب *qarībun* 'relative' : أقرباء *ʾaqribāʾu*, غنيّ *ghanīyun* 'wealthy' : أغنياء *ʾaghniyāʾu*.

Note 3. A small number is also expressed by the plural diminutive: سنيّات *sunayyātun* 'several years', from سنة *sanatun* 'year' (§70 b), نسيّة *nusayy-atun* 'several women', from نسوة *niswatun* 'women' (§72 e).

"Sound" (Inflected) Plural

§101. The inflected plural endings, masculine *-ūna/-īna*, feminine *-ātun/-ātin*, are used only to a limited extent for substantives. Adjectives (participles) used as substantives frequently take inflected plurals. As such, *-ūna* may be used for masculines referring to people, and *-ātun* for feminines referring to people and things: سارق *sāriqun* 'stealing, thief', سارقة *sāriqatun* 'thief' (fem.) : سارقون *sāriqūna* 'thieves', سارقات *sāriqātun* 'thieves' (fem.); مسروق *masrūqun* 'stolen, loot' : مسروقات *masrūqātun*; طالبيّ *ṭālibiyyun* 'descended from Abū Ṭālib, Talibite' : طالبيّون *ṭālibiyyūna*. Generally, corresponding "broken" plurals also occur for such "sound" plurals: سرقة *saraqatun*, سرّاق *surrāqun* 'thieves', سوارق *sawāriqu* (fem.).

§102. The pattern *faʿʿālun*, *nisbah*-forms (§216), and diminutives form inflected plurals exclusively and, as a rule, have no corresponding "broken" plurals: شويعر *shuwayʿirun* 'lesser poet' : شويعرون *shuwayʿirūna*, شويء *shuwayʾun* 'trifle' : شويآت *shuwayʾātun*. Exceptions are rare; cf. §§95.2; 96.1; 99.2. In addition, verbal substantives and participles of the derived verbal stems, as well as the passive participle *mafʿūlun*, usually have only inflected plurals: تغيّر *taghayyurun* 'change' : تغيّرات *taghayyurātun*, مسير *musīrun* 'mentor' : مسيرون *musīrūna*. *tafāʿīlu* and *mafāʿi/īlu* (§95) can occur on occasion as plurals for morpheme categories *tafʿīlun* and *mufʿi/alun*, *mafʿūlun*. Occasionally, *ʾafāʿīlu* occurs as plural of *ʾifʿālun*: إملاء *ʾimlāʾun* 'dictation': أمالٍ *ʾamālin* (§95.1).

Note 1. Personal names can take the inflected plural: العمرون *(ʾa)l-ʿumarūna* 'the Umars', الطّلحتات *(ʾa)ṭ-ṭalaḥatātu* 'the Ṭalḥas' (masc.), العبلات *(ʾa)l-ʿabalātu* (§105) 'women named Abla'; the names of months may have *-ātun*: المحرّمات *(ʾa)l-muḥarramātu*, rarely المحاريم *(ʾa)l-maḥārīmu*, 'the months of Muḥarram'. The plural of four-consonant names is usually *faʿāli/īlu*: اليرابيع *(ʾa)l-yarābīʿu* 'the people of Banū Yarbūʿ'.

§103. a) The following primary substantives form plurals with *-ūna*: أرض *ʾarḍun* 'earth' : أرضون *ʾarḍūna*, *ʾaraḍūna* (also أرضات *ʾaraḍātun*; cf. §105), أهل *ʾahlun* 'people, inhabitants' : أهلون *ʾahlūna*, إبن (*ʾi*)*bnun* 'son' (§72 c): بنون *banūna*. In pre-classical Arabic, *-ūna* is sometimes used for the individual plural of living beings: عبد *ʿabdun* 'slave' : عبدون *ʿabdūna*.

Note 1. See §131 concerning the use of *-ūna* with numerals.

Note 2. علّيّون *ʿilliyyūna* 'highest spheres' is treated as a plural, even though its origin is Hebrew *ʿelyōn*.

b) Substantives of the pattern *Ca/i/uC-atun* (§70 a) mainly have *-ūna* and *-ātun* plural forms: كرة *kuratun* 'ball' : كرون *kurūna* (§37.1), كرات *kurātun*; رئة *riʾatun* 'lung' : رئون *riʾūna*, رئات *riʾātun*; سنة *sanatun* 'year' : سنون *sinūna* (§37.1), سنوات *sanawātun*; هن *hanun* 'something' (§72 d) : هنات *hanātun*, هنوات *hanawātun* 'things, whatnot', هنون *hanūna* 'this one and that one'.

Note 3. The following words do not have *-ūna* plurals: حمة *ḥumatun* 'sting' : حمات *ḥumātun*, لثة *lithatun* 'gum' : لثات *lithātun*, لثى *lithan*.

§104. a) *-ātun* forms individual plurals of feminine living beings: أمّ *ʾummun* 'mother' : أمّات *ʾummātun*, أمّهات *ʾummahātun*; بنت *bintun*, ابنة (*ʾi*)*bnatun* 'daughter' : بنات *banātun*, أخت *ʾukhtun* 'sister' : أخوات *ʾakhawātun*, عمّة *ʿammatun* (paternal) 'aunt' : عمّات *ʿammātun*.

b) Unless usage favors a "broken" plural (§102), all abstracts, verbal substantives, and nouns referring to inanimate objects may form plurals with *-ātun*: جهة *jihatun* 'direction' : جهات *jihātun*, لباس *libāsun* 'clothing' : لباسات *libāsātun*.

Note 1. In foreign words of recent origin, *-ātun* occurs also as a plural of forms referring to masculine individuals; باشا *bāshā* 'Pasha' : باشوات *bāshawātun*.

§105. a) In singulars which have the feminine ending *-atun*, *-ātun* replaces the singular ending, and in the process morpheme categories *faʿlatun, fiʿlatun, fuʿlatun* undergo variation in the stem to *faʿal-*, *fiʿal-* (*fiʿil-*), *fuʿal-*

(*fuʿul-*): ضربة *ḍarbatun* 'blow' : ضربات *ḍarabātun*, كسرة *kisratun* 'fragment' : كسرات *kisarātun*, *kisirātun*, ظلمة *ẓulmatun* 'darkness' : ظلمات *ẓulamātun*, *ẓulumātun*. The stem variation may be suppressed in *fi/uʿlatun* : *kisrātun*, *ẓulmātun*.

Note 1. There is no such change in the stem in II-geminate and II-weak roots: شدّة *shaddatun* 'assault' : شدّات *shaddātun*, هيئة *hayʾatun* 'form' : هيئات *hayʾātun*.

Note 2. The feminine plural of adjectival *faʿlun* is *faʿlātun* (§115).

b) -*ātun* is suffixed to -*ā*, -*āʾu* and, as a result, the phonological rules in §35 b take effect: ذكرى *dhikrā* 'memory' : ذكريات *dhikrayātun*, حبلى *ḥublā* 'pregnant' : حبليات *ḥublayātun*, خضراء *khaḍrāʾu* 'herb' : خضراوات *khaḍrāwātun*.

Note 3. Exceptionally, stem final -*āʾ* behaves in the same way in سماء *samāʾun* 'heaven' : سموات *samāwātun* (§8).

Note 4. *w* or *y* appears before -*ātun* in III-weak roots with stem-final -*ā*: صلاة *ṣalātun* 'prayer' : صلوات *ṣalawātun*, قناة *qanātun* 'tube' : قنوات *qanawātun*, قنيات *qanayātun*; ملتقى *multaqan* 'meeting' : ملتقيات *multaqayātun* (§35 a).

Combined Plural Morphemes

§106. a) Since the plural of a small number (§100) is interpreted as a collective, its plural is formed accordingly as *ʾafāʿi/īlu*: رهط *rahṭun* 'one's people' : أرهط *ʾarhuṭun* 'several of such groups of people' = 'tribe' : أراهط *ʾarāhiṭu* 'tribes', قول *qawlun* 'saying, doctrine' : أقوال *ʾaqwālun* 'doctrines, sayings' : أقاويل *ʾaqāwīlu* 'groups of (common) doctrines, sayings', يد *yadun* 'hand' : أيد *ʾaydin* 'several hands, assistance' : أياد *ʾayādin* 'acts of assistance'.

Note 1. The *faʿālilu* plural pattern for plurals ending in -*ūna* figures in: أرض *ʾarḍun* 'earth' : أرضون *ʾaraḍūna* : أراض *ʾarāḍin* 'grounds', أهل *ʾahlun* 'people, inhabitants' : أهلون *ʾahlūna* : أهال *ʾahālin* 'population'.

Note 2. بلد *baladun* 'place' : بلاد *bilādun* 'places' = 'country' : بلدان *buldānun* 'countries' is unique.

b) Occasionally *-ātun* forms individual plurals of "broken" plurals: صاحبة *ṣāḥibatun* 'companion' (fem.) : صواحب *ṣawāḥibu* : صواحبات *ṣawāḥibātun*; جمل *jamalun* 'camel' : جمال *jimālun* : جمالات *jimālātun*; بيت *baytun* 'tent, house, family' : بيوت *buyūtun* : بيوتات *buyūtātun* 'noble families'.

Dual

§107. The dual indicates two individuals or examples of the same. It is formed by adding to the singular the endings *-āni/-ayni* (§147) where the case suffixes would be: عام *ʿāmun* 'year' : عامان *ʿāmāni* 'two years', سنة *sanatun* 'year': سنتان *sanatāni* 'two years'.

Note 1. When the dual endings are added to *-ā, -āʾ*, the phonological rules in §35 a and b are in effect: فتى *fatan* 'youth' : فتيان *fatayāni*, عصى *ʿaṣan* 'stick' : عصوان *ʿaṣawāni*, شكوى *shakwā* 'complaint' : شكويان *shakwayāni*, حرباء *ḥirbāʾun* 'chameleon' : حرباوان *ḥirbāwāni*.

§108. a) Two paired persons or things can be expressed by the dual of one of them: الأبوان *(ʾa)l-abawāni* 'the parents', dual of أب *ʾabun* 'father', الحسنان *(ʾa)l-Ḥasanāni* 'Hasan and Husayn', القمران *(ʾa)l-qamarāni* 'sun and moon', dual of *qamarun* 'moon'.

Note 1. Adjectives and elatives have substantive duals with enigmatic meanings: الأبيضان *(ʾa)l-ʾabyaḍāni* 'the two whites', i.e., 'water and milk', الأبردان *(ʾa)l-ʾabradāni* 'the two colds', i.e., evening and morning'.

Note 2. When pairs are distinguished by different attributes, the attributes are in the singular: كساءان أبيض وأخضر *kisāʾāni ʾabyaḍu wa-ʾakhḍaru* 'two pieces of clothing, one white and one green', i.e., 'a white and a green garment'.

b) The dual of collectives or of collective plurals indicates duality of the example or quantity: غنم *ghanamun* 'small livestock' : غنمان *ghanamāni* 'two small livestock herds', رماح *rimāḥun* (sing. رمح *rumḥun*) 'lances' : رماحان *rimāḥāni* 'two groups of lances'.

Note 3. A *nomen unitatis* (§84 a) may form an individual dual: حمامتان *ḥamāmatāni* 'two doves'.

§**109.** a) The dual particle كلا *kilā*, fem. كلتا *kiltā* (§64.1) is followed by a genitive or personal pronoun suffix: كلا هذين *kilā hādhayni* 'both of these', كلتا الجنّتين *kiltā 'l-jannatayni* 'both gardens', or كلانا *kilānā* 'both of us', كلاكما *kilākumā* 'both of you'.

Note 1. Instead of a genitive dual, two genitives in the singular may occur: كلا السّيف والرّمح *kilā 's-sayfi wa-'r-rumḥi* 'both, the sword and the lance'.

b) *kilā, kiltā* are indeclinable in combination with substantives in the genitive: في كلا البلدين *fī kilā 'l-baladayni* 'in both places'. With personal suffixes, the oblique forms are: *kilay, kiltay*: بكلينا *bi-kilaynā* 'with us both', في الواديين كليهما *fī 'l-wādiyayni kilayhimā* 'in both wadis'.

Note 2. Expressions with *kilā, kiltā* are treated grammatically as singulars: كلا العبدين رآها *kilā 'l-ʿabdayni raʾāhā* 'both slaves saw her'. Dual constructions *ad sensum* occasionally occur.

Gender of Substantives

§**110.** Substantives are classified into two grammatical genders: masculine and feminine. Masculine substantives are those that are not distinguished by the feminine ending or are not treated as feminine because of meaning. Feminines by morphological form are those substantives with the feminine ending *-atun, -ā, -āʾu* (§64): مدّة *muddatun* 'period of time', ذكرى *dhikrā* 'memory', فسيفساء *fusayfisāʾu* 'mosaic'.

Note 1. As a feminine ending *-atun* forms feminines that refer to persons: خال *khālun* 'maternal uncle' : خالة *khālatun* 'maternal aunt', فتى *fatan* 'youth' : فتاة *fatātun* 'young woman'.

Note 2. Masculines ending in *-atun* that refer to persons (§73 a) are treated grammatically as masculines. Usually, حيّة *ḥayyatun* 'snake' is masculine, but also occasionally feminine.

§**111.** Because of their meanings, the following substantives are grammatically feminine:

a) Words that indicate feminine beings: أمّ *ʾummun* 'mother', عجوز *ʿajūzun* 'old woman'. Cf. for this §113.1, adjectives.

Note 1. The names of animals are treated as feminines, if the female is intended: ثعلب *th̲aʿlabun* 'fox', as feminine 'vixen'. Conversely, فرس *farasun* 'mare', when it means 'horse', is masculine.

b) The names of countries, cities, etc., if they are diptotes (§153): مصر *miṣru* 'Egypt', جهنّم *jahannamu* 'Hell'.

c) Collectives and "broken plurals" (§84 ff.).

Note 2. Generic collectives are as a rule masculine (§84.1). All collectives and collective plurals may be treated, contrary to the basic rule, as *ad sensum* plurals, if they are intended as individual plurals of living beings, especially people.

d) A series of words, such as نفس *nafsun* 'soul' (§273), أرض *ʾarḍun* 'earth', ريح *rīḥun* 'wind', نار *nārun* 'fire', شمس *s̲h̲amsun* 'sun', بئر *biʾrun* 'well', دار *dārun* 'dwelling', حرب *ḥarbun* 'war', as well as the names of body parts that appear in pairs, such as يد *yadun* 'hand', رجل *rijlun* 'foot', عين *ʿaynun* 'eye', أذن *ʾud̲h̲nun* 'ear', and still others details about which can be found in the lexicons.

§**112.** a) In analogy to the words enumerated in §111, many semantically related words are optionally treated as feminines, e. g.: روح *rūḥun* 'spirit', جحيم *jaḥīmun* 'hellfire', صلح *ṣulḥun* 'peace', the names of winds like صبا *ṣaban* 'east wind', the names of body parts like سنّ *sinnun* 'tooth', the names of substances like ذهب *d̲h̲ahabun* 'gold', ملح *milḥun* 'salt' or مركب *markabun* 'ship', by association with سفينة *safīnatun* 'ship', etc. For gender, usage fluctuates in such cases from period to period, occasionally from author to author, so that no consistent rule can be laid down.

b) With reference to general concepts like كلمة *kalimatun* 'word', حرف *ḥarfun* 'letter, particle', when cited in a text, words, particles, morphemes, etc., are usually feminine, less frequently masculine: ما الحجازيّة *mā 'l-ḥijāziyyatu* 'the ḥijāzī "*mā*"', الالف المقصورة (*ʾa*)*l-alifu 'l-maqṣūratu* (see §10.3).

Adjective

§113. a) As attribute and predicate, the adjective agrees in gender with the substantive it modifies. The masculine is unmarked. The feminine is indicated by *-atun* (cf. §110.1) on primary adjectives that agree in gender: يوم بارد *yawmun bāridun* 'a cold day', ليلة باردة *laylatun bāridatun* 'a cold night'. Primary adjectives can form plurals with the *-ūna* (masc.), *-ātun* (fem.) endings.

Note 1. Adjectives that specifically refer to feminine qualities, as a rule, do not take the feminine ending: امرأة طالق *(ʾi)mraʾatun ṭāliqun* 'divorced women'; nevertheless, there are rare exceptions: مرضعة *murḍiʿatun*, rarely مرضع *murḍiʿun* 'nursing, wet nurse'.

b) Adjectives that agree secondarily have suppletive feminine and plural morpheme patterns (§119). Adjectives that do not agree have no distinguishing feminine or plural morpheme (§121).

Note 2. Adjectives can become substantives: خادم *khādimun* 'serving' and 'servant, maid-servant', باطل *bāṭilun* 'null' and 'nothingness, prattle'. Cf. also §73.

§114. a) The ending of the inflected plural *-ūna* may refer only to masculine individuals, and *-ātun* to feminine individuals and to the names of things: مسلمون صالحون *muslimūna ṣāliḥūna* 'pious Muslims', مسلمات صالحات *muslimātun ṣāliḥātun* 'pious Muslim women', عادات صالحات *ʿādātun ṣāliḥātun* 'pious practices'. In analogy to "broken" plurals, the names of things are usually treated in the plural as feminine singulars: عادات صالحة *ʿādātun ṣāliḥatun*.

b) The plural adjective forms may function independently of the grammatical gender of the modified substantive. Thus, these adjectival forms may modify "broken" plurals and collectives *ad sensum*, even if grammatically the substantives are singulars (masc. or fem.): رجال صالحون *rijālun ṣāliḥūna* 'pious men', نساء صالحات *nisāʾun ṣāliḥātun* 'pious women', دموع ذارفات *dumūʿun dhārifātun* and دموع ذارفة *dumūʿun dhārifatun* 'flowing tears', نخل باسقات *nakhlun bāsiqātun* and نخل باسق *nakhlun bāsiqun* or باسقة *bāsiqatun* 'towering datepalms' (§84 a), قوم صالحون *qawmun ṣāliḥūna* 'pious people, pious nation' (§86 a).

Note 1. With substantives that refer to people, grammatical agreement occurs infrequently : قوم صالح *qawmun ṣāliḥun*, نساء صالحة *nisāʾun ṣāliḥatun.*

Note 2. The "broken" plural is frequently preferred in adjectives (§122 f.) over the inflected plural.

c) Strict agreement is the rule in the dual: رجلان صالحان *rajulāni ṣāliḥāni* 'two pious men', ليلتان باردتان *laylatāni bāridatāni* 'two cold nights'.

§**115.** Primary adjectives that agree include: 1. Participles (§§223 f.); 2. *nisbah* adjectives (§§116 f.); 3. verbal adjectives in the morpheme categories *faʿalun, faʿilun* (*faʿulun*), *faʿlun* (§105.2), *fuʿlun* like: حسن *ḥasanun* 'good, handsome', صعب *ṣaʿbun* 'difficult', مرّ *murrun* 'bitter'; 4. intensive adjectives in the morpheme categories *faʿʿālun, fiʿʿīlun* like بكّاء *bakkāʾun* 'weepy', صدّيق *ṣiddīqun* 'upright'; 5. adjectives in the morpheme category *fuʿlānun* like عريان *ʿuryānun* 'naked'; cf. also §119.1.

Note 1. *faʿilun* of II-weak roots is always formed with *yy* (§68 c).

Note 2. A verbal substantive in the role of adjective does not agree: عدل *ʿadlun* 'probity': شاهد عدل *shāhidun ʿadlun* 'an honest witness', حلم *ḥulumun* 'dream': ذكرة حلم *dhikratun ḥulumun* 'a dreamlike memory'.

§**116.** The so-called *nisbah*-ending *-iyyun* forms denominal adjectives that indicate belonging or relationship (نسبة *nisbatun*): عقل *ʿaqlun* 'reason' : عقليّ *ʿaqliyyun* 'rational', مصر *miṣru* 'Egypt' : مصريّ *miṣriyyun* 'Egyptian', أسد *ʾasadun* (name of a tribe) : أسديّ *ʾasadiyyun* 'belonging to Asad, a member of the Asad tribe'. The feminine *-iyyatun* frequently forms abstract substantives (§§73 c; 76).

Note 1. The short form *-iy-un* > *-in* (*-ī* §155) occurs in تهامٍ *tahāmin* from تهامة *tihāmatun* 'Tihamah' (West Arabian coastal plain), يمانٍ *yamānin* from أليمن (ʾ*a*)*l-Yamanu* 'Yemen', شآمٍ *sha*ʾ*āmin* from ألشّأم (ʾ*a*)*sh-Sha*ʾ*mu* 'Syria'. The regular *nisbah*'s يمنيّ *yamaniyyun* and شأميّ *sha*ʾ*miyyun* also occur.

Note 2. *-iyy-īna* (oblique plural §147) is occasionally abbreviated to *-īna*: أعجمين ʾ*a*ʿ*jamīna* from أعجميّ ʾ*a*ʿ*jamiyyun* 'non-Arab'.

Note 3. See §§95.2 and 99.2 concerning the plural *fa*ʿ*ālīyu* (*fa*ʿ*ālī, fa*ʿ*ālā*) of the *nisbah*-ending.

Note 4. See §§86.4; 119.4 concerning *-iyyun* in the formation of terms indicating individuals.

Note 5. *Nisbah*-adjectives can also be formed from adjectives: أعوجيّ ʾ*a*ʿ*wajiyyun* (pedigree of horses) from أعوج ʾ*a*ʿ*waju* 'crooked'.

Note 6. *Nisbah*-adjectives formed from plurals that signify objects serve as names of occupations: كتبيّ *kutubiyyun* 'book dealer' from كتب *kutubun* 'books' (sing. كتاب *kitābun*), ساعاتيّ *sā*ʿ*ātiyyun* 'clock maker' from ساعات *sā*ʿ*ātun* 'clocks' (sing. ساعة *sā*ʿ*atun* 'hour, clock').

§**117.** When the *nisbah*-ending is affixed, the feminine ending *-atun* is dropped: بصريّ *baṣriyyun* 'coming from Basrah' from البصرة (ʾ*a*)*l-Baṣratu*, عامّيّ ʿ*āmmiyyun* 'popular' from عامّة ʿ*āmmatun* 'common people'. On the other hand, it is added to *-ā*, *-ā*ʾ*u*: دنيا *dunyā* 'this world' : دنيويّ *dunyawiyyun* 'earthly', صحراء *ṣaḥrā*ʾ*u* 'desert' : صحراويّ *ṣaḥrāwiyyun* 'desert-like' (§35.3). In the same way, *w* comes between stem final *-ā* of III-weak noun forms and the *nisbah*-ending: معنى *ma*ʿ*nan* 'meaning, idea' : معنويّ *ma*ʿ*nawiyyun* 'pertaining to meaning, conceptual'. Two-radical substantives (III-weak roots; §72 a) are treated analogically: لغة *lughatun* 'language' : لغويّ *lughawiyyun* ', lexic(ographic)al, linguistic, philological'.

Note 1. A post-classical *nisbah*-ending in *-āwiyyun* is added to place names with the feminine ending *-atun*: مكّة *Makkatun* 'Mecca' : مكّاويّ *makkāwiyyun*, instead of classical مكّيّ *makkiyyun*. On occasion, *-āniyyun* occurs instead: صنعاء *Ṣan*ʿ*ā*ʾ*u* 'Sanʿaʾ' : صنعانيّ *ṣan*ʿ*āniyyun*.

Note 2. In several cases, *-ān-iyyun* replaces *-iyyun*: فوقانيّ *fawqāniyyun* 'upper' from فوق *fawqu* 'up' (§317), روحانيّ *rūḥāniyyun* 'spiritual' from روح *rūḥun* 'spirit'.

§**118.** When the *nisbah*-ending is affixed to the morphemes *faʿil, faʿīl*, they change to *faʿal*, while *fuʿayl* changes to *fuʿal*: نمر *namirun* (name of a tribe) : نمريّ *namariyyun*, نبيّ *nabīyun* 'prophet' : نبويّ *nabawiyyun*, قريش *quraysh̲un* (name of a tribe) : قرشيّ *quras̲h̲iyyun*. There is no such change with II-geminate roots: حقيقة *ḥaqīqatun* 'reality' : حقيقيّ *ḥaqīqiyyun* 'real'.

Note 1. يثربيّ *yat̲h̲rabiyyun*, in addition to يثربيّ *yat̲h̲ribiyyun*, are formed analogously from يثرب *Yat̲h̲ribu* (the former name of Medina). Note also طائيّ *ṭāʾiyyun* from طيّئ *ṭayyiʾun* (name of a tribe).

Note 2. Frequently there is no change in the stem in post-classical Arabic: مدينيّ *madīniyyun* for classical مدنيّ *madaniyyun* from المدينة (ʾ*a*)*l-Madīnatu* 'Medina'. Nevertheless, such formations are attested early: ردينيّ *rudayniyyun* 'well-straightened spear, spear of Rudaynah'.

Note 3. *Nisbah* forms of compound names and names that belong to no particular morpheme category are shortened: حضرميّ *ḥaḍramiyyun* from حضرموت *ḥaḍramawtu* 'Hadramaut' (province in South Arabia), طالبيّ *ṭā-libiyyun* 'from the family of Abū Ṭālib'.

§**119.** Adjectives that agree secondarily are: *faʿlānu*, fem. *faʿlā*, pl. *faʿālā*, *fuʿālā* like كسلان *kaslānu* 'lazy', fem. كسلى *kaslā*, plural كسالى *kasā-lā*, *kusālā*, as well as adjectival ʾ*afʿalu* that indicates colors and physical defects: ʾ*afʿalu*, fem. *faʿlāʾu*, pl. *fuʿlun* (*fuʿlānun*) like أعرج ʾ*aʿraju*, fem. عرجاء ʿ*arjāʾu*, pl. عرج ʿ*urjun* 'lame'; أبيض ʾ*abyaḍu*, fem. بيضاء *bayḍāʾu*, pl. بيض *bīḍun* (§33 b) 'white'; آدم ʾ*ādamu* (§40), fem. أدماء ʾ*admāʾu*, pl. أدم ʾ*udmun*, أدمان ʾ*udmānun* 'light-colored'.

Note 1. *faʿlānu* and ʾ*afʿalu*, *faʿlāʾu* are diptotically inflected (§152). Occasionally, *faʿlānun* occurs as a triptote, from which a feminine with *-atun* is formed: ندمان *nadmānu* or ندمان *nadmānun*, fem. ندمانة *nadmānatun* 'repentant'.

Note 2. Contrary to the rules of agreement (§§113 f.), *faʿlāʾu* may occur only for feminine singulars, but not for plurals and collectives. *fuʿlun* must always be used instead: حمام ورق *ḥamāmun wurqun* 'ash-color doves', بيوت صفر *buyūtun ṣufrun* 'yellow houses'.

Note 3. كميت *kumaytun* 'bay' (horse) and جون *jawnun* 'colorful, dark' take *fuʿlun* as plural: كمت *kumtun*, جون *jūnun*.

Note 4. كدري *kudriyyun* 'Qaṭā-bird of the *kudr*-type' and جوني *jūniyyun* 'Qaṭā-bird of the *jūn*-type' occur as individual nouns of كدر *kudrun* 'drab' (sing. أكدر *ʾakdaru*) and جون *jūnun* 'colorful' (Note 3), as they are used as the names of birds.

§**120.** Adjectives in the morpheme categories *faʿīlun* and *faʿūlun* agree grammatically to a limited extent. As a basic rule, *faʿīlun* with a passive sense and *faʿūlun* with an active sense do not agree: عين كحيل *ʿaynun kaḥīlun* 'eye darkened with kohl' (§111 d), رؤيا كذوب *ruʾyā kadhūbun* 'false vision'. Usage, however, is frequently at odds with the basic rule, and *faʿūlun* is the form that usually does not agree.

Note 1. كثير *kathīrun* 'many' and قليل *qalīlun* 'few' sometimes do not agree in the plural: رجال (نساء) كثير *rijālun (nisāʾun) kathīrun* 'many men (women)'.

Note 2. An inflected plural can be formed on *faʿīlun* when it does agree: قليلون *qalīlūna* 'few'. *faʿūlun* has only a "broken" plural, usually *fuʿulun*.

§**121.** Adjectives in the expanded morpheme categories *fuʿalun, fuʿālun, fuʿʿālun, faʿālun, fiʿālun* and *mifʿalun, mifʿālun, mifʿīlun* do not agree. They do not vary as they modify masculines, feminines, and plurals: بنت ملاح *bintun mulāḥun* (*mullāḥun*) 'an exceptionally beautiful girl', فتاة مكسال *fatātun miksālun* 'a lady who does not need to work', نوق هجان *nūqun hijānun* 'well-bred camels (fem.)'.

Note 1. *mifʿālun, mifʿīlun* can have *mafāʿilu* (§95) as plural. "Broken" plurals also occur for other morpheme categories: هجان *hijānun*: plural هجائن *hajāʾinu*.

"Broken" Plurals of Adjectives

§**122.** The following morpheme categories are used as plural masculines and feminines of adjectives:

faʿlā: حمق *ḥamiqun* 'stupid' : حمقى *ḥamqā*, هالك *hālikun* 'perishing' : هلكى *halkā*, قتيل *qatīlun* 'killed' : قتلى *qatlā*.

faʿālā, fuʿālā (for *faʿlā*, §99): سمج *samjun, samijun*, سميج *samījun* 'ugly' : سماجى *samājā, sumājā*; cf. also §119.

fuʿulun (*fuʿlun* §88): كذوب *kadhūbun* 'lying': كذب *kudhubun*, بادن *bādinun*, بدين *badīnun* 'corpulent': بدن *budunun, budnun.*

fiʿālun (§88): خفيف *khafīfun* 'light' (of weight) : خفاف *khifāfun*, جيّد *jayyidun* 'good' : جياد *jiyādun.*

ʾafʿālun (§100): حرّ *ḥurrun* 'free, noble' : أحرار *ʾaḥrārun*, صفر *ṣifrun, ṣafrun, ṣafirun* 'empty' : أصفار *ʾaṣfārun.*

fuʿūlun (§88): قاعد *qāʿidun* 'sitting' : قعود *quʿūdun.*

fuʿʿalun, fuʿʿālun see §90.

§**123.** a) The morpheme categories *fuʿalāʾu* (of III-weak roots, *fuʿalatun* §90) and *ʾafʿilāʾu* (§100) function as masculine plurals: جبان *jabānun* 'cowardly, coward' : جبناء *jubanāʾu*, فقير *faqīrun* 'poor, poor person' : فقراء *fuqarāʾu*, كاس *kāsin* 'clothed' : كساة *kusātun*, غنيّ *ghanīyun* 'wealthy, wealthy person' : أغنياء *ʾaghniyāʾu.*

b) *fawāʿilu* (§97) is used as a feminine plural, but also as a common plural: نساء كوافر *nisāʾun kawāfiru* 'unbelieving women'. Occasionally, *faʿāʾilu* occurs as a feminine plural of adjectives (§§98; 121.1).

Quantity

Elative *ʾafʿalu*

§**124.** The morpheme category *ʾafʿalu* designates an attribute or thing as preeminent: أكرم *ʾakramu* 'especially noble, very noble, more noble, most noble'. It functions as an elative of all nominal derivatives, whatever the root might be: ألحن *ʾalḥanu* 'more melodious' from لحن *laḥnun* 'melody', أعقد *ʾaʿqadu* 'more knotted' from معقّد *muʿaqqadun* 'knotted', أقلّ *ʾaqallu* 'fewer' from قليل *qalīlun* 'few', أقصى *ʾaqṣā* 'very far' from قصيّ *qaṣīyun* 'far'. Often, several derivations are possible: أكرم *ʾakramu*. 1. 'more noble' from كريم *karīmun* 'noble'; 2. 'bestowing more honor' from مكرم *mukrimun* 'bestowing honor'.

Note 1. In II-weak roots, *w* or *y* is always consonantal: أطوع *ʾaṭwaʿu* 'more obedient' from طائع *ṭāʾiʿun* or مطيع *muṭīʿun* 'obedient' (root *ṭ-w-ʿ*), أخوف *ʾakhwafu*. 1. 'more fearful' from خائف *khāʾifun* 'fearful'; 2. 'more dreaded' from مخوف *makhūfun* 'dreaded' (root *kh-w-f*), أطيب *ʾaṭyabu* 'better' from طيّب *ṭayyibun* 'good' (root *ṭ-y-b*).

Note 2. خير *khayrun* 'good' and شرّ *sharrun* 'evil, bad' also function as elatives without any change in form: 'better, best' and 'worse, worst'. Only in post-classical Arabic do أخير *ʾakhyaru*, أشرّ *ʾasharru* occasionally occur as elatives.

Note 3. Adjectival *ʾafʿalu* (§119) is not used in classical Arabic as an elative. Paraphrases, like أشدّ بياضا *ʾashaddu bayāḍan* 'even whiter' (Note 4), are used instead. The comparative use (§125) occurs not infrequently in post-classical Arabic: أبيض من *ʾabyaḍu min* 'whiter, brighter than . . . '.

Note 4. In combination with the indefinite accusative (§384), elatives are used in a general sense to paraphrase an otherwise ambiguous elative: أسرع عدوا *ʾasraʿu ʿadwan* 'swifter in running' rather than أعدى *ʾaʿdā*, to distinguish it from أعدى *ʾaʿdā* 'more hostile' from عدوّ *ʿadūwun* 'enemy'.

§125. a) The elative is inflected as a diptote (§152). As a rule, it may not take the article (exception §127) and does not, therefore, agree grammatically with the substantive that it modifies. Besides indicating a quality of preeminence, the elative also functions as a comparative. When followed by the genitive (§126), it expresses the superlative.

b) To express the comparative, the elative is paired with من *min* (§299 d) ('than'): أطول من نخلة *ʾaṭwalu min nakhlatin* 'taller than a date-palm', النّاقة أسمن من ناقتنا *(ʾa)n-nāqatu ʾasmanu min nāqatinā* 'that camel (fem.) is fatter than ours'. The comparative usage can also be determined by context: أعطيناهم درهما أو أكثر *ʾaʿṭaynāhum dirhaman ʾaw ʾakt͟hara* 'we gave them one dirham or more', أيّ المالين أقرّ لعينك *ʾayyu ʾl-mālayni ʾaqarru li-ʿaynika* 'which of these two possessions gives you more pleasure?'.

Note 1. In a comparative sentence, the subject of the contrasted phrase follows and is dependent on من *min*, if it is a nominal phrase: أنا لك أشرف منك لي *ʾanā laka ʾas͟hrafu minka lī* 'I am more respectful of you than you are of me'. A verbal phrase begins with subordinating ما *mā* (§416): كنت أخوف عليك ممّا كنت على نفسي *kuntu ʾak͟hwafa ʿalayka mimmā* (§45) *kuntu ʿalā nafsī* 'I was more fearful for you than I was for myself'.

c) The elative without the article and with or without *min* can appear in all positions in which an indefinite noun can occur, i.e., especially as predicate or in apposition to an indefinite governing form (*regens*): أللّه أكبر *ʾal-lāhu ʾakbaru* 'God is (incomparably) great', لستم بأكذب *lastum bi-ʾakd͟haba* 'you are no more deceitful (than anyone else)', ما لقيت ناسا أقبح منهم *mā laqītu nāsan ʾaqbaḥa minhum* 'Never have I met worse people than them'. The elative also occurs as an object: فإنّه يعلم السّرّ وأخفى *fa-ʾinnahū yaʿlamu ʾs-sirra wa-ʾak͟hfā* (Koran 20:7) 'for He knows all that is secret (in man) and what is more deeply hidden'.

§**126.** The elative has the superlative meaning when followed by the genitive:

a) When the genitive is indefinite (§387), the superlative has an absolute sense: أفضل رجل *ʾafḍalu rajulin* 'the most excellent man (there is)', أعلى جبال *ʾaʿlā jibālin* 'the highest (known) mountains'. Often, a restrictive complement follows: كنت أحدث رجل فيهم *kuntu ʾaḥdat͟ha rajulin fīhim* 'I was the youngest man among them'.

Note 1. Note expressions with the elative such as: كان أشدّ شيء عليه *kāna ʾas͟hadda s͟hayʾin ʿalayhi* 'he was extremely violent against him', يكتب أقلّ ما يكون *yaktubu ʾaqalla mā yakūnu* 'he writes as little as possible', أقبح ما يكون الصّدق في السّعاية *ʾaqbaḥu mā yakūnu ʾṣ-ṣidqu fī ʾs-siʿāyati* 'sincerity is worst in slander' (في السّعاية *fī ʾs-siʿāyati* is the predicate!).

'The more . . . the more' is expressed by using this phrase two times: أخوف ما تكون العامّة آمن ما تكون الوزراء *ʾakhwafu mā takūnu ʾl-ʿāmmatu ʾāmanu mā takūnu ʾl-wuzarāʾu* 'the more fearful are the people, the more sure are the viziers' (cf. also §463).

b) In the same way, the elative has a superlative meaning with the (always definite) partitive genitive (§387 b). It is always substantivized: أعلى الجبال *ʾaʿlā ʾl-jibāli* 'the highest of the mountains', بأعلى صوته *bi-ʾaʿlā ṣawtihī* 'with his loudest voice'.

Note 2. خير *khayrun* and شرّ *sharrun* (§124.2) are treated like elatives that do not agree grammatically: في خير دار *fī khayri dārin* 'in the best home', أنتم خير العرب *ʾantum khayru ʾl-ʿarabi* 'you are the best of the Arabs'.

§**127.** a) With the article, the definite elative (ʾ*a*)*l*-ʾ*afʿalu* is used for the masculine singular. As its feminine counterpart, the suppletive form *fuʿlā* is used. ʾ*afʿalūna* or ʾ*afāʿilu* (§94) is used for the masculine plural. *fuʿlayātun* or *fuʿalu* is used for the feminine plural. In this form, the elative is used as a substantive or adjective modifying a definite substantive: الأصغر (ʾ*a*)*l*-ʾ*aṣgharu* 'the younger, the youngest', الصّغرى (ʾ*a*)*ṣ-ṣughrā* 'the younger, the youngest (fem.)', الأكابر (ʾ*a*)*l-akābiru* 'the oldest ones', بصوته الأعلى *bi-ṣawtihī ʾl-ʾaʿlā* 'with his loudest voice', الدّرجات العليا (ʾ*a*)*d-darajātu ʾl-ʿulyā* 'the upper (highest) steps'.

Note 1. In post-classical Arabic, *fuʿlā* also appears with indefinite substantives: درجة عليا *darajatun ʿulyā* 'a higher (highest) step'.

b) The suppletive forms *fuʿlā* and *fuʿalu* also occur with أوّل *ʾawwalu* 'first' and آخر *ʾākharu* (< *ʾ*aʾkharu*) 'other': fem. sing. أولى *ʾūlā*, أخرى *ʾukhrā*, masc. pl. أوّلون *ʾawwalūna*, آخرون *ʾākharūna* and أوائل *ʾawāʾilu*, fem. pl. أول *ʾuwalu*, أخر *ʾukharu* and أخريات *ʾukhrayātun*. أوّل *ʾawwalu*, as an elative that does not agree grammatically, also appears in constructions with the genitive: أوّل كتاب *ʾawwalu kitābin* 'the first book', أوّل الأمر *ʾawwalu ʾl-ʾamri* 'the beginning of the matter', أوّل امرأة *ʾawwalu ʾmraʾatin* or المرأة الأولى *al-marʾatu ʾl-ʾūlā* 'the first woman'.

Note 2. The construction of آخر *ʾākhirun* follows that of أوّل *ʾawwalu*. It can occur in combination with a following indefinite genitive: آخر يوم *ʾākhiru yawmin* 'the last (possible) day', as opposed to اليوم الآخر *(ʾa)l-yawmu ʾl-ʾākhiru* 'the last day (of a series of days)', آخر مرّة *ʾākhira marratin* 'for the last time' (§315 b), آخر اللّيل *ʾākhiru ʾl-layli* 'the end of the night'.

Formulas of Astonishment *mā ʾafʿala*

§128. In combination with *mā* 'what', *ʾafʿala* forms the so-called formula of astonishment. The subject follows in the accusative or as a pronominal suffix: ما أكرم الأمير *mā ʾakrama ʾl-ʾamīra* 'how noble is the prince!', ما أبغضك إليّ *mā ʾabghaḍaka ʾilayya* 'how loathsome are you to me!', ما أعلمني لذلك *mā ʾaʿlamanī li-dhālika* 'how well do I know that!'. Indeclinable كان *kāna* coming before *ʾafʿala* indicates the preterite (§190): ما كان أصبره *mā kāna ʾaṣbarahū* 'how patient was he!'.

Note 1. Infrequently, and only in poetry, the formula occurs without the following accusative: ما أكرم *mā ʾakrama* 'how noble!'.

Note 2. The formula *ʾafʿil bi-* has the same meaning: أهون به *ʾahwin bihī* 'how disdainful is he!'. Often it appears with the accusative of specificity (§384) or with *min* (§299 c): أكرم بها فتاة *ʾakrim bihā fatātan* or من فتاة *min fatātin* 'what a noble woman is she!'.

Numerals

§129. a) The cardinal numbers from 1 to 10 are:

	For masculine	For feminine
1	واحد *wāḥidun*	واحدة *wāḥidatun*
2	اثنان *(ʾi)thnāni*	اثنتان *(ʾi)thnatāni*, ثنتان *thintāni* (§64.1)
3	ثلاثة *thalāthatun*	ثلاث *thalāthun*
4	أربعة *ʾarbaʿatun*	أربع *ʾarbaʿun*
5	خمسة *khamsatun*	خمس *khamsun*
6	ستّة *sittatun*	ستّ *sittun*
7	سبعة *sabʿatun*	سبع *sabʿun*
8	ثمانية *thamāniyatun*	ثمان *thamānin* (§155)
9	تسعة *tisʿatun*	تسع *tisʿun*
10	عشرة *ʿasharatun*	عشر *ʿashrun*

Note 1. *wāḥidun* is an adjective: قرية واحدة *qaryatun wāḥidatun* 'a single village' (§141 b). When used as a substantive, 'one' is أحد *ʾaḥadun*, fem. إحدى *ʾiḥdā*: أحدهم *ʾaḥaduhum* 'one of them'. Cf. also §131.1.

Note 2. (*ʾi*)*thnāni* has the dual inflection (§147). It can appear with the dual for emphasis: قريتان اثنتان *qaryatāni 'thnatāni* 'two villages'.

b) The numbers 3–10 have forms with *-atun* in combination with masculine counted substantives, the basic form with feminines. This also holds true when the counted is unnamed: هؤلاء الثّلاثة *hāʾulāʾi 'th-thalāthatu* 'these three (men)', مضت أربع *maḍat ʾarbaʿun* 'four (nights) passed'. The substantive follows the numeral in the genitive plural: سبع سارقات *sabʿu sāriqātin* 'seven thieves (fem.)'. With "broken" plurals, the gender of the singular governs: خمسة رجال *khamsatu rijālin* 'five men', خمس نساء *khamsu nisāʾin* 'five women'. A personal pronoun suffix may appear instead of a substantive: ثلاثتهم *thalāthatuhum* 'the three of them'. The numbers can follow as attributives: رجال ثمانية *rijālun thamāniyatun* 'eight men', النّساء الثّماني (*ʾa*)*n-nisāʾu 'th-thamānī* 'the eight women'. On the agreement in such contructions, see §§354; 399.

Note 3. Collectives can occur in the genitive singular: عشرة رهط *ʿasharatu rahṭin* 'ten persons'.

Note 4. To make numerical expressions definite, the article is placed either before the substantive, before the number, or even before both: تسعة الكتب *tisʿatu 'l-kutubi*, or التّسعة كتب (*ʾa*)*t-tisʿatu kutubin*, or التّسعة الكتب (*ʾa*)*t-tisʿatu 'l-kutubi* 'the nine books'.

Note 5. Forms of the numerals ending in *-atun* are used to express abstract numbers and, like proper names, are inflected diptotically (§152): ستّة أكثر من خمسة *sittatu ʾaktharu min khamsata* 'six is more than five'.

Note 6. Similarly, بضع *biḍʿun* 'several' occurs with the genitive: بضع رجال (نساء) *biḍʿu rijālin* (*nisāʾin*) 'several men (women)'. See also §130.2.

§**130.** a) The cardinal numbers from 11 to 19 are:

	For masculine	For feminine
11	أحد عشر *ʾaḥada ʿa<u>sh</u>ara*	إحدى عشرة *ʾiḥdā ʿa<u>sh</u>rata*
12	اثنا عشر *(ʾi)<u>th</u>nā ʿa<u>sh</u>ara*	اثنتا عشرة *(ʾi)<u>th</u>natā ʿa<u>sh</u>rata*
13	ثلاثة عشر *<u>th</u>alā<u>th</u>ata ʿa<u>sh</u>ara*	ثلاث عشرة *<u>th</u>alā<u>th</u>a ʿa<u>sh</u>rata*
14	أربعة عشر *ʾarbaʿata ʿa<u>sh</u>ara*	أربع عشرة *ʾarbaʿa ʿa<u>sh</u>rata*
15	خمسة عشر *<u>kh</u>amsata ʿa<u>sh</u>ara*	خمس عشرة *<u>kh</u>amsa ʿa<u>sh</u>rata*
16	ستّة عشر *sittata ʿa<u>sh</u>ara*	ستّ عشرة *sitta ʿa<u>sh</u>rata*
17	سبعة عشر *sabʿata ʿa<u>sh</u>ara*	سبع عشرة *sabʿa ʿa<u>sh</u>rata*
18	ثمانية عشر *<u>th</u>amāniyata ʿa<u>sh</u>ara*	ثماني عشرة *<u>th</u>amāniya ʿa<u>sh</u>rata*
19	تسعة عشر *tisʿata ʿa<u>sh</u>ara*	تسع عشرة *tisʿa ʿa<u>sh</u>rata*

Note 1. The oblique of "12" is اثني عشر *(ʾi)<u>th</u>nay ʿa<u>sh</u>ara*, اثنتي عشرة *(ʾi)<u>th</u>natay ʿa<u>sh</u>rata*. The rest of the numbers, 11 and 13–19, do not vary with case.

Note 2. بضع *biḍʿun* (§129.6) is treated analogously: بضعة عشر *biḍʿata ʿa<u>sh</u>ara*, بضع عشرة *biḍʿa ʿa<u>sh</u>rata* 'ten plus several'.

b) The counted follows the number in the indefinite accusative singular: ستّة عشر رجلا *sittata ʿa<u>sh</u>ara rajulan* 'sixteen men'. The article always precedes the number in this construction: السّبع عشرة ليلة *(ʾa)s-sabʿa ʿa<u>sh</u>rata laylatan* 'the seventeen nights'.

§**131.** The plural ending *-ūna/-īna* (§101) indicates the tens: عشرون *ʿi<u>sh</u>rūna* 20, ثلاثون *<u>th</u>alā<u>th</u>ūna* 30, أربعون *ʾarbaʿūna* 40, خمسون *<u>kh</u>amsūna* 50, ستّون *sittūna* 60, سبعون *sabʿūna* 70, ثمانون *<u>th</u>amānūna* 80, تسعون *tisʿūna* 90. The units come before the tens, and the counted follows in the indefinite accusative singular: واحد و عشرون رجلا *wāḥidun wa ʿi<u>sh</u>rūna rajulan* 'twenty-one men', ثمان وعشرون ليلة *<u>th</u>amānin wa-ʿi<u>sh</u>rūna laylatan* 'twenty-eight nights'. The article precedes the units and tens: بعد التّسعة والتّسعين يوما *baʿda 't-tisʿati wa-'t-tisʿīna yawman* 'after ninety-nine days'.

Note 1. In combination with larger numbers, "one" is always expressed by واحد *wāḥidun*. See §399 concerning agreement in numerical expressions.

§**132.** a) Hundreds: مائة, مئة *mi'atun* 100 (§15.4), مائتان *mi'atāni* 200, ثلاث مائة *thalāthu mi'atin* 300, أربع مائة *'arba'u mi'atin* 400, etc. (also written ثلاثمائة, أربعمائة, etc.). Thousands: ألف *'alfun* 1,000, ألفان *'alfāni* 2,000, ثلاثة آلاف *thalāthatu 'ālāfin* 3,000 (§100), أربعة آلاف *'arba'atu 'ālāfin* 4,000, أحد عشر ألفا *'aḥada 'ashara 'alfan* 11,000.

b) The counted follows the hundreds and the thousands in the genitive singular: ستّة آلاف درهم *sittatu 'ālāfi dirhamin* '6,000 dirhams'. In compound numerals, the hundreds and the thousands usually, but not always, precede the lower numerals. The case and number of the counted is determined by the immediately preceding numeral: واحد ومائة رجل *wāḥidun wa-mi'atu rajulin* '101 men', ألف وثماني مائة وأربع سنين *alfun wa-thamānī mi'atin wa-'arba'u sinīna* '1,804 years'.

Note 1. The plural forms مئات *mi'ātun*, مئون *mi'ūna* (§103 b) 'hundreds', ألوف *'ulūfun* 'thousands' occur with the genitive plural: مئو سنين *mi'ū sinīna* 'hundreds of years'.

Note 2. To make these numerical expressions definite, as with the ones (§129.4), the article is placed either before the substantive, before the number, or before both: مائة النّاقة *mi'atu 'n-nāqati*, or المائة ناقة *('a)l-mi'atu nāqatin*, or المائة النّاقة *('a)l-mi'atu 'n-nāqati* 'the hundred camels'.

§**133.** a) The ordinal numbers from 2–10 are in the adjectival morpheme category *fā'ilun*, fem. *fā'ilatun*: أوّل *'awwalu*, fem. أولى *'ūlā* 'first' (§127 b), ثان *thānin*, fem. ثانية *thāniyatun* 'second', ثالث *thālithun* 'third', رابع *rābi'un* 'fourth', خامس *khāmisun* 'fifth', سادس *sādisun* 'sixth', سابع *sābi'un* 'seventh', ثامن *thāminun* 'eighth', تاسع *tāsi'un* 'ninth', عاشر *'āshirun* 'tenth'.

b) The ordinal numbers 11–19 correspond to the cardinals inasmuch as they are indeclinable: حادي عشر *ḥādiya 'ashara*, fem. حادية عشرة *ḥādiyata 'ashrata* 'eleventh', ثاني عشر *thāniya 'ashara*, fem. ثانية عشرة *thāniyata 'ashrata* 'twelfth', ثالث عشر *thālitha 'ashara*, fem. ثالثة عشرة *thālithata 'ashrata* 'thirteenth', etc.: اللّيلة التّاسعة عشرة *('a)l-laylatu 't-tāsi'ata 'ashrata* 'the nineteenth night'.

c) From 20 up, the ones are in the morpheme category *fāʿilun, -atun*, while the tens, hundreds, thousands have the form of the cardinal: حاد وعشرون *ḥādin wa-ʿi<u>sh</u>rūna* 'twenty-first', الثّاني والخمسون (ʾa)*<u>th</u>-<u>th</u>ānī wa-'l-<u>kh</u>amsūna* 'the fifty-second', اللّيلة الحادية والسّبعون والثّمانيمائة (ʾa)*l-laylatu 'l-ḥādiyatu wa-'s-sabʿūna wa-'<u>th</u>-<u>th</u>amānī-miʾatin* 'the eight-hundred and seventy-first night'.

Note 1. As is typical of all large numbers, cardinal numbers replace the ordinal when referring to dates. In such constructions, the cardinal is in the genitive after the counted substantive: في سنة ألف ومائتين وثلاث وستّين *fī sanati ʾalfin wa-miʾatayni wa-<u>th</u>alā<u>th</u>in wa-sittīna* 'in the year 1263'.

Note 2. The adverbial accusative of ordinal numbers (§315): أوّلا *ʾawwalan*, ثانيا *<u>th</u>āniyan*, ثالثا *<u>th</u>āli<u>th</u>an*, etc., has the meaning 'firstly, first', 'secondly', 'thirdly', etc.

§134. Fractions have the morpheme category *fuʿlun* (*fuʿulun*), pl. *ʾafʿālun*: ثلث *<u>th</u>ul<u>th</u>un* 'a third', ربع *rubʿun* 'a quarter', سدس *sudsun* 'a sixth', ثمن *<u>th</u>umnun* 'an eighth', etc.; ثلثان *<u>th</u>ul<u>th</u>āni* 'two-thirds', ثلاثة أرباع *<u>th</u>alā<u>th</u>atu ʾarbāʿin* 'three-quarters'.

§135. The distributive numbers have the morpheme category *fuʿālu* or *mafʿalu* with diptotic inflection (§152): ثناء *<u>th</u>unāʾu*, مثنى *ma<u>th</u>nā* 'two at a time', ثلاث *<u>th</u>ulā<u>th</u>u*, مثلث *ma<u>th</u>la<u>th</u>u* 'three at a time', etc. 'Alone' is expressed by وحد *waḥda-*, always with a personal pronominal suffix, and it generally follows in apposition in the accusative: أبوك وحده *ʾabū-ka waḥdahū* 'your father alone', بقينا وحدنا *baqīnā waḥdanā* 'we remained alone'.

Note 1. Distributive adjectives are frequently expressed by repeating the number: جاءوا اثنين اثنين أو ثلاثة ثلاثة *jāʾū '<u>th</u>nayni '<u>th</u>nayni ʾaw <u>th</u>alā<u>th</u>atan <u>th</u>alā<u>th</u>atan* 'they came two or three at a time'.

Note 2. Adjectival *fuʿāliyyun* (§116) is formed from *fuʿālu*: ثلاثيّ *<u>th</u>ulā<u>th</u>iyyun* 'three-part', رباعيّ *rubāʿiyyun* 'four-part, quadriliteral'.

Totality

§**136.** كلّ *kullun* 'each, every, all': كلّ قد ذهب *kullun qad dhahaba* 'everyone has left'; usually with the genitive: كلّ إنسان *kullu ›insānin* 'every human', كلّ الإنسان *kullu 'l-›insāni* 'the entire human being', كلّ النّاس *kullu 'n-nāsi* 'all mankind'. In emphatic apposition: القوم كلّ القوم (›a)*l-qawmu kullu al-qawmi* 'the one and only people'. As a permutative in apposition (§395) *kullu* often follows with a personal pronoun suffix: اليوم كلّه (›a)*l-yawmu kulluhū* 'the whole day'. See §353 for gender agreement.

Note 1. Post-classical *kullun* is occasionally a substantive: كلّ *kullun* 'a whole', الكلّ (›a)*l-kullu* 'the whole' (§144.2).

Note 2. In combination with numbers, *kullun* has a distributive sense: في كلّ سبعة أيّام مرّة *fī kulli sab‹ati ›ayyāmin marratan* 'once every seven days'. In pre-classical Arabic, it sometimes has the meaning 'every, all, possible': على كلّ فرس *‹alā kulli farasin* 'on all kinds of horses'.

§**137.** جميع *jamī‹un* 'totality' usually occurs in constructions with the definite genitive: جميع النّاس *jamī‹u 'n-nāsi* 'all mankind', جميع أمره *jamī‹u ›amrihī* 'his entire affair'. The conditional accusative جميعا *jamī‹an* 'altogether, completely' can follow in apposition: أهل نجد جميعا *›ahlu najdin jamī‹an* 'the people of the Najd, altogether', أمرنا جميعا *›amrunā jamī‹an* 'our affair, all of us'.

Note 1. Similarly, عامّة *‹āmmatun* and كافّة *kāffatun* 'encompassing, totality' are used like *jamī‹un*: عامّة (كافّة) النّاس *‹āmmatu (kāffatu) 'n-nāsi* 'the totality of mankind', النّاس عامّة (كافّة) (›a)*n-nāsu ‹āmmatan (kāffatan)* 'mankind in its entirety'.

§**138.** أجمع *›ajma‹u*, fem. جمعاء *jam‹ā›u*, pl. أجمعون *›ajma‹ūna* 'entire, whole, all' occurs in apposition to substantives but never takes the article: يوم أجمع *yawmun ›ajma‹u* 'a whole day', الملائكة كلّهم أجمعون (›a)*l-malā›ikatu kulluhum ›ajma‹ūna* (Koran 15:30, 38:73) 'all the angels altogether'. In apposition to a personal pronominal suffix: هداكم أجمعين *hadā-kum ›ajma‹īna* 'he rightly guided you all'.

Note 1. The synonyms of *›ajma‹u*, أكتع *›akta‹u*, أبتع *›abta‹u*, أبصع *›abṣa‹u* are treated similarly. Occasionally, they appear with *›ajma‹u* for emphasis.

Note 2. In combination with the preposition *bi-* (§294.8) and with a personal pronominal suffix, *ʾajmaʿu* may follow in apposition: النّاس بأجمعهم *(ʾa)n-nāsu bi-ʾajmaʿihim* 'mankind in its entirety'. Expressions like بجمعهم *bi-jamʿihim*, بأسرهم *bi-ʾasrihim*, and others (§394.8) also occur in this type of construction.

§139. بعض *baʿḍun* ('part') with the definite genitive indicates a part or any number of something: بعض الكافرين *baʿḍu 'l-kāfirīna* 'one of the unbelievers' or 'some unbelievers', بعض ماله *baʿḍu mālihī* 'some (part) of his wealth' (§146 b), بعض العذاب *baʿḍu 'l-ʿa<u>dh</u>ābi* 'some' or 'a certain kind of suffering'. Often *baʿḍun* is used to show reciprocity. In this paired construction, the first member has the personal pronominal suffix, while the second is always indefinite: راقب بعضنا بعضا *rāqaba baʿḍunā baʿḍan* 'some of us watched the others', or 'we watched each other', رفعنا بعضهم فوق بعض *rafaʿnā baʿḍahum fawqa baʿḍin* (Koran 43:32) 'we raised some of them above the others'.

Note 1. Note expressions like: بعض اللّوم *baʿḍa 'l-lawmi* 'only some blame!', i.e., 'do not blame so much!'.

Nominal Inflection

§140. All nouns have three case-forms that express syntactic relationships: nominative (§§352; 362 f.), genitive (§385 ff.), accusative (§372 ff.). In the dual and plural, the genitive and accusative are formally indistinguishable (oblique case). There are three different states: the indefinite (or indetermined), the definite (or determined), and the construct. In the singular, the definite and construct states, with a few exceptions (§150), are identical. In the dual and plural, they are morphologically distinguished.

§141. Indefinite state: a) The indefinite state indicates something unspecified introduced into the context. It is marked by *-n* (*tanwīn* §11 f.) in triptotic inflection and is unmarked in diptotic inflection.: رجل *rajulun* 'a man', فوارس *fawārisu* '(any, some) horsemen'.

Note 1. Personal names that are inflected as triptotes lose the sign of indefiniteness (*-n*) in genealogical citations before بن *(ʾi)bnu* (§22 b) 'son of ...': مالك بن سعد بن محمّد *māliku bnu saʿdi bni muḥammadin* (but not *Mālikun, Saʿdin*).

Note 2. Expressions of time that specify the future are usually indefinite: غدا *ghadan* 'tomorrow', بعد غد *ba'da ghadin* 'the day after tomorrow', قابلا *qābilan* 'next year'.

Note 3. In poetry, the indefinite state occurs not infrequently where one would expect the definite: أعزّي عنك قلبا مستهاما *'u'azzī 'anka qalban mustahāman* 'I console over you a (i. e., my) love-sick heart', كلّما ذرّ شارق *kulla-mā dharra shāriqun* 'whenever a (i.e., the) rising sun flares up'.

Note 4. Explicit indefiniteness is often indicated by ما *mā* (§285 c) following a noun: أمر ما *'amrun mā* 'a certain affair', إلى يوم *'ilā yawmin* or إلى يوم ما *'ilā yawmin mā* 'until some day'.

b) The indefinite state also indicates numerical singularity: كلّهم لأمّ *kulluhum li-'ummin* 'all of them come from one and the same mother', يقدر على ذلك رجل *yaqdiru 'alā dhālika rajulun* 'one man is capable of this', يوما *yawman* 'one day long'. In this case, واحد *wāḥidun* (§129) can be added for clarity: لأمّ واحدة *li-'ummin wāḥidatin.*

c) The indefinite state often simply indicates the genus, namely, in the predicate (§363 a), with accusatives (§384), with genitives (§387 a), and in combination with من *min* (§299 a): كم درهما *kam dirhaman* 'how many dirhams', حبّذا أنت من رجل *ḥabbadhā 'anta min rajulin* 'what a likeable man you are!' (§263).

§**142.** Definite state: a) The definite state in the singular triptotic inflection does not have *-n*. The definite state occurs when a nominal form is marked definite by the article, ألْ *'al-*, by the vocative after يا *yā* (§157 a), and by general negation after لا *lā* (§318 c).

b) The article is (*'a*)*l-* (§§21; 22 a; 54): ألكتاب (*'a*)*l-kitābu* 'the book', هذا الكتاب *hādhā 'l-kitābu* 'this book' (§§274 ff.), بالكتاب *bi-'l-kitābi* 'with the book'. See §§18; 44 concerning the assimilation of the *l* to the following consonant.

§**143.** The definiteness indicated by the article is occasioned by the context, by the situation at hand, or by generally understood conditions.

a) When context expresses definiteness, the article often appears in place of the personal pronoun suffix, which otherwise would express definiteness: أتيت بيت الوزير فخرج الخادم إليّ *ʾataytu bayta ʾl-wazīri fa-<u>kh</u>araja ʾl-<u>kh</u>ādimu ʾilayya* 'I came to the vizier's house, and out came the (i.e., his) servant toward me'. Frequently, if no defining agent is specified, definiteness has a distributive meaning: جاء الرّجل بعد الرّجل *jāʾa ʾr-rajulu baʿda ʾr-rajuli* 'they came one after the other', إنّ الرّجل يأكل في المجلس الواحد ما لا تأكل المرأة *ʾinna ʾr-rajula yaʾkulu fī ʾl-majlisi ʾl-wāḥidi mā lā taʾkulu ʾl-marʾa-tu* 'the man eats at a single sitting an amount the woman cannot', الرّجل من المسلمين (ʾ*a*)*r-rajulu min-a ʾl-muslimīna* 'every single one of the Muslims'.

b) Definiteness expressed by the situation occurs in cases like: من الرّجل *man-i ʾr-rajulu* 'who is the man?', i.e., 'you there, who are you?' (in direct discourse), اليوم (ʾ*a*)*l-yawmu* 'the present day', إلى السّاعة *ʾilā ʾs-sāʿati* 'until now'.

c) Nouns that refer to the generic, abstract, substance, etc., are definite if they are thought of as unique in kind: مثله كمثل الكلب *ma<u>th</u>aluhū ka-ma<u>th</u>ali ʾl-kalbi* 'with him it is like it is with the dog', من الكبر *min-a ʾl-kibari* 'out of arrogance'.

Note 1. Uniqueness defines words like الشمس (ʾ*a*)*<u>sh</u>-<u>sh</u>amsu* 'the sun', الخليفة (ʾ*a*)*l-<u>kh</u>alīfatu* 'the Caliph' and all proper names, even if they appear formally in the indefinite state: محمّد *Muḥammadun* (Muhammad), رجب *Rajabun* 'the month of Rajab'.

§**144.** The article transforms nouns that refer to individuals into generic nouns by defining them in a generic sense: خلق الانسان ضعيفا *<u>kh</u>uliqa ʾl-insānu ḍaʿīfan* (Koran 4:28) 'man was created weak', العلماء (ʾ*a*)*l-ʿulamāʾu* 'scholars'.

Note 1. When expressing quantity, this general kind of definiteness indicates individual parts: الكثير منهم (ʾ*a*)*l-ka<u>th</u>īru minhum* 'the majority of them', العدد القليل منه (ʾ*a*)*l-ʿadadu ʾl-qalīlu minhu* 'a small number of it'. لم نزد على المائة *lam nazid ʿalā ʾl-miʾati* 'we did not exceed (the number) 100'.

Note 2. Non-substantive nominal forms (§§113–139) are made substantives by the the definite article or the lack of it: جاهل *jāhilun*, الجاهل (ʾ*a*)*l-jāhilu* 'an ignorant person, the ignorant'.

Note 3. Concerning the definiteness of predicate nouns, see §363 b.

§**145.** Construct state: a) Words in the singular construct state are identical to those in the definite state. In the plural, *-na*, and in the dual, *-ni*, are dropped. A word in the construct state is followed immediately by a dependent substantive in the genitive or by a personal pronoun suffix: مال تاجر *mālu tājirin* 'the wealth of a merchant', ماله *māluhū* 'his wealth', جنّتا سبأ *jannatā Sabaʾin* 'both gardens of Sheba', جنّتاهم *jannatāhum* 'both of their gardens'.

b) Anything else qualifying the word in the construct state must come after the genitive or pronominal suffix: سيف الفارس البتّار *sayfu 'l-fārisi 'l-battāru* 'the sharp sword of the horseman', ربّك الأكرم *rabbuka 'l-ʾakramu* 'your incomparably noble lord'.

Note 1. Once in a while, interjections and the like come between the word in the construct state and the genitive: حرّ والله الظّهيرة *ḥarru wa-'l-lāhi 'ẓ-ẓahīrati* 'the heat — by God! — of mid-day'. See also §285 c.

c) If there are two substantives in the construct state but one dependent genitive, the genitive must be represented by a personal pronoun suffix on the second member of the construct: سيوف الأعداء وأرماحهم *suyūfu 'l-ʾaʿdāʾi wa-ʾarmāḥuhum* 'the swords and spears of the enemies', قصير القامة نحيفها *qaṣīru 'l-qāmati naḥīfuhā* 'short and thin in stature' (§388).

Note 2. Contrary to this rule, genitives may with increasing frequency depend on two substantives in post-classical Arabic: طرق وأراضي تلك البلدان *ṭuruqu wa-ʾarāḍī tilka 'l-buldāni* 'the roads and lands of those countries'.

§**146.** a) By itself, the construct state is neither definite nor indefinite. A definite genitive or a personal pronoun suffix makes the construction definite. If the genitive is indefinite, the construction is indefinite: كلب دار نابح *kalbu dārin nābiḥun* 'a barking dog of a dwelling', كلب الدّار النّابح *kalbu 'd-dāri 'n-nābiḥu* 'the barking dog of the dwelling'.

Note 1. The indefinite state is combined with a dependent genitive by *li-* (§295 b). If the sense is partitive, it is combined with the dependent genitive by *min* (§299.1): كلب لدارهم *kalbun li-dārihim* 'a dog belonging to their dwelling', كلب من كلابهم *kalbun min kilābihim* 'one of their dogs' = أحد كلابهم *ʾaḥadu kilābihim* (§129.1) or بعض كلابهم *baʿḍu kilābihim* 'one of their dogs' (§139).

b) The construct state of words like أحد *ʾaḥadun* (§129.1), بعض *baʿḍun* (§139) or of words indicating comparison like مثل *mithlun* 'one like ..., something like ...' (§297 c), غير *ghayru-* 'other than' (§325), نظير *naẓīrun*, شبه *shibhun* 'similar to', and the like are considered indefinite, even when combined with a definite genitive or a personal pronoun suffix: فتى مثلي *fatan mithlī* 'a youth like me', رجال غيركم *rijālun ghayrukum* 'men other than you'.

c) The construct state of adjectives and participles is not made definite by the definite specifying genitive (§388) or the genitive expressing an object (§386 b): رجل كريم النّسب *rajulun karīmu 'n-nasabi* 'a man of noble lineage', ضارب أخيه *ḍāribu ʾakhīhi* = ضارب أخاه *ḍāribun ʾakhā-hu* 'one who strikes his brother'. The adjective can be made definite by the article: الرّجل الكريم النّسب *(ʾa)r-rajulu 'l-karīmu 'n-nasabi*. In such constructions, making the participle definite is avoided, but it occasionally occurs: التّابعي *(ʾa)t-tābiʿī* 'he who follows me', الضّاربو أولادهم *(ʾa)ḍ-ḍāribū ʾawlādihim* 'those who strike their children'.

Note 2. The perfective participle (§201) is considered a substantive in the construct state and is made definite by the genitive: قاتل أخي *qātilu ʾakhī* 'the one who killed my brother, my brother's murderer'.

Note 3. Cases like *karīmu 'n-nasabi*, *(ʾa)l-karīmu 'n-nasabi* are called "the improper annexation" الاضافة غير الحقيقيّة *al-iḍāfah ghayr al-ḥaqīqiy-yah* by the Arab grammarians, because the genitive can be joined with a substantive in the definite state.

Triptotic Inflection

§**147.** Indefinite state: سارق *sāriqun* 'thief', سارقة *sāriqatun* (fem.).

Sg.	nom. masc.	سارق	*sāriq-un*	fem.	سارقة	*sāriq-at-un*
	gen.	سارق	*sāriq-in*		سارقة	*sāriq-at-in*
	acc.	سارقا	*sāriq-an*		سارقة	*sāriq-at-an*
Du.	nom.	سارقان	*sāriq-āni*		سارقتان	*sārirq-at-āni*
	obl.	سارقين	*sāriq-ayni*		سارقتين	*sāriq-at-ayni*
Pl.	nom.	سارقون	*sāriq-ūna*		سارقات	*sāriq-āt-un*
	obl.	سارقين	*sāriq-īna*		سارقات	*sāriq-āt-in*

Note 1. On the orthography of the endings, see §§11 and 13.

Note 2. On the formation of the plural, see §§101 ff.; for the dual, see §§107ff.

§**148.** Definite state

Sg.	nom.	السارق	*(ʾa)s-sāriq-u*	fem.	السارقة	*(ʾa)s-sāriq-at-u*
	gen.	السارق	*(ʾa)s-sāriq-i*		السارقة	*(ʾa)s-sāriq-at-i*
	acc.	السارق	*(ʾa)s-sāriq-a*		السارقة	*(ʾa)s-sāriq-at-a*
Du.	nom.	السارقان	*(ʾa)s-sāriq-āni*		السارقتان	*(ʾa)s-sāriq-at-āni*
	obl.	السارقين	*(ʾa)s-sāriq-ayni*		السارقتين	*(ʾa)s-sāriq-at-ayni*
Pl.	nom.	السارقون	*(ʾa)s-sāriq-ūna*		السارقات	*(ʾa)s-sāriq-āt-u*
	obl.	السارقين	*(ʾa)s-sāriq-īna*		السارقات	*(ʾa)s-sāriq-āt-i*

§**149.** Construct state

Sg.	nom.	سارق	*sāriq-u*	fem.	سارقة	*sāriq-at-u*
	gen.	سارق	*sāriq-i*		سارقة	*sāriq-at-i*
	acc.	سارق	*sāriq-a*		سارقة	*sāriq-at-a*
Du.	nom.	سارقا	*sāriq-ā*		سارقتا	*sāriq-at-ā*
	obl.	سارقي	*sāriq-ay*		سارقتي	*sāriq-at-ay*
Pl.	nom.	سارقو	*sāriq-ū*		سارقات	*sāriq-āt-u*
	obl.	سارقي	*sāriq-ī*		سارقات	*sāriq-āt-i*

Note 1. On the attachment of personal pronominal suffixes to the construct state, see §269.

§150. أب *ʾabun* 'father' (definite الأب *(ʾa)l-ʾabu*), أخ *ʾakhun* 'brother' (definite الأخ *(ʾa)l-ʾakhu*), حم *ḥamun* (definite الحم *(ʾa)l-ḥamu*), 'father-in-law' (§72 b) have alternative forms in the construct state (as also the words that exist only in the construct state, فو *fū* 'mouth' (§72 a) and ذو *dhū* (§283)):

Nom.	أبو *ʾabū*	أخو *ʾakhū*	حمو *ḥamū*	فو *fū*	ذو *dhū*
Gen.	أبي *ʾabī*	أخي *ʾakhī*	حمي *ḥamī*	في *fī*	ذي *dhī*
Acc.	أبا *ʾabā*	أخا *ʾakhā*	حما *ḥamā*	فا *fā*	ذا *dhā*

Note 1. On the attachment of the personal pronoun suffixes, see §269.3.

Note 2. Dual: أبوان *ʾabawāni* (§108 a), أخوان *ʾakhawāni.*

§151. In إمرؤ *(ʾi)mrwʾun* 'man' (§72 e) and the infrequently occurring إبنم *(ʾi)bnumun* 'son' (§37 b), the vowel of the stem assimilates to the vowel of inflectional ending:

Nom.	إمرؤ	*(ʾi)mrwʾun*	إبنم	*(ʾi)bnumun*
Gen.	إمرئ	*(ʾi)mriʾin*	إبنم	*(ʾi)bnimin*
Acc.	إمرءا	*(ʾi)mraʾan*	إبنما	*(ʾi)bnaman*

(ʾi)mrwʾun in the definite state with the article is المرء *(ʾa)l-marʾu*, in the construct state امرؤ *(ʾi)mrwʾu*.

Note 1. Occasionally, uninflected forms of words and expressions that are semantically identified with non-standard language enter classical Arabic poetic texts, e.g., حر *ḥir* for *ḥirun* 'vulva', هن *han* for *hanun* with the same meaning as *ḥir* (§72).

Diptotic Inflection

§152. Diptotically inflected nominal forms do not have the sign of indefiniteness -*n* in the indefinite state, and the genitive has -*a* instead of -*i*. When such words form duals and inflected plurals, they do not differ from triptotes.

Sg.	nom.	أسود	*ʾaswadu* 'black'	الأسود	*(ʾa)l-ʾaswadu*
	gen.	أسود	*ʾaswada*	الأسود	*(ʾa)l-ʾaswadi*
	acc.	أسود	*ʾaswada*	الأسود	*(ʾa)l-ʾaswada*

Diptotes in the definite and construct states are inflected like triptotic nominal forms.

§**153.** The following groups of nominal forms have the diptotic inflection in the indefinite state:

a) Nominal forms in morpheme category *ʾafʿalu* (§§119; 124; 138), *fuʿalu* (§127), *faʿlānu* (§119), *fuʿālu*, and *mafʿalu* (§135).

b) Morpheme categories with the feminine ending *-āʾ* (§64 c) like *faʿlāʾu* (§§75 b; 119; 138), *fiʿliyāʾu*, *fuʿalāʾu*, *fāʿūlāʾu* (§§75 b; 90), and *ʾafʿilāʾu* (§100).

Note 1. The indeclinable feminine ending *-ā* (§64 b) is also diptotic. It does not take the sign of indefiniteness *-n*. See §100.2 on the diptotic plural *ʾa<u>sh</u>yāʾu* of *<u>sh</u>ayʾun* 'thing'.

c) Plural morpheme categories *faʿālilu, faʿālīlu*, etc. (§93 ff.).

d) If they consist of more than three consonants, all proper names that have the feminine ending *-at-* or are of foreign origin, like دمشق *Dima<u>sh</u>qu*, 'Damascus', زينب *Zaynabu* (fem. personal name), مكّة *Makkatu* 'Mecca', طلحة *Ṭalḥatu* (masc. personal name), أهواز *ʾAhwāzu* (place name).

e) All proper names that are feminine in meaning, like مصر *Miṣru* 'Egypt', حلب *Ḥalabu* 'Aleppo', هند *Hindu* (fem. personal name).

f) Masculine personal names, if they do not belong to morpheme categories *faʿlun, fiʿlun, fuʿlun, faʿalun, faʿilun* or are not participles (§§223 f.). Compare عمر *ʿUmaru* 'Omar', عثمان *ʿUthmānu* 'Uthman', يوسف *Yūsufu* 'Joseph' to عمرو *ʿAmrun* (§11.1), نوح *Nūḥun* 'Noah', محمّد *Muḥammadun* 'Muhammad'.

Note 2. Proper names with diminutive forms *fuʿaylun* and *fuʿayyilun* (§§81 f.) are inflected as triptotes: زهير *Zuhayrun*, كثيّر *Ku<u>th</u>ayyirun*. The diminutive is diptotic, however, if it has the feminine ending *-at-*: فطيمة *Fuṭaymatu*.

Note 3. All diptotic nominal forms can be treated as triptotes in poetry. The opposite also occurs sometimes in poetry (though much more rarely).

Inflection of III- and IV-Weak Nominal Forms

§154. a) Nominal forms ending in stem-final *-ā* are indeclinable in the singular (§34 b). When the sign of indefiniteness *-n* is affixed, *-ā-n* is abbreviated > *-an* (§52); *-ā-atun* is shortened to *-ātun*. When the dual and plural endings are affixed, the phonological rules in §35 a are observed.

Sg.	masc.	ملقى	*mulqan* 'thrown' (§256 c)	fem.	ملقاة	*mulqātun* (gen. *-in*, acc. *-an*)
Du.	nom.	ملقيان	*mulqayāni*		ملقاتان	*mulqātāni*
	obl.	ملقيين	*mulqayayni*		ملقاتين	*mulqātayni*
Pl.	nom.	ملقون	*mulqawna*		ملقيات	*mulqayātun*
	obl.	ملقين	*mulqayna*		ملقيات	*mulqayātin*

b) The definite and construct states are formed according to the rules mentioned above (§§142 ff.): Definite الملقى (ʾa)*l-mulqā*, plural nominative الملقون (ʾa)*l-mulqawna*, feminine الملقاة (ʾa)*l-mulqātu*, etc.; construct state ملقى *mulqā*, plural nominative ملقو *mulqaw*, oblique ملقي *mulqay*, dual nominative ملقيا *mulqayā*, oblique ملقيي *mulqayay*, feminine ملقاة *mulqātu*, etc.

Note 1. See §10 on the orthography.

Note 2. As they do in the definite and construct states, diptotes in the indefinite state have indeclinable stem-final *-ā* in the singular: أعلى *ʾaʿlā* 'highest' = *ʾafʿalu/a* of root *ʿ-l-w*, الأعلى (ʾ*a*)*l-ʾaʿlā* 'the highest' = (ʾ*a*)*l-ʾafʿalu/i/a*.

Note 3. The feminine ending *-ā* (§64 b) is treated like diptotic stem-final *-ā*: حبلى *ḥublā* 'pregnant', plural حبليات *ḥublayātun*, dual حبليان *ḥublayāni* (§35 b).

§155. a) Nominal forms with stem-final *-ī* have the ending *ī* (= **-iyu*, **-iyi* §34 b) in the nominative and genitive. In the accusative, it is *-iya*. When the sign of indefiniteness *-n* is affixed, *ī-n* is shortened to *-in* (§52). When the dual and plural endings are affixed, the rules in §35 a are followed. There are no peculiarities with the feminine ending in *-iy-atun*.

Sg.	nom.	داعٍ	*dāʿin* 'calling' (§256 a)	الدّاعي	(ʾ*a*)*d-dāʿī*
	gen.	داعٍ	*dāʿin*	الدّاعي	(ʾ*a*)*d-dāʿī*
	acc.	داعيا	*dāʿiyan*	الدّاعيَ	(ʾ*a*)*d-dāʿiya*
Du.	nom.	داعيان	*dāʿiyāni*	الدّاعيان	(ʾ*a*)*d-dāʿiyāni*
	obl.	داعيين	*dāʿiyayni*	الدّاعيين	(ʾ*a*)*d-dāʿiyayni*
Pl.	nom.	داعون	*dāʿūna*	الدّاعون	(ʾ*a*)*d-dāʿūna*
	obl.	داعين	*dāʿīna*	الدّاعين	(ʾ*a*)*d-dāʿīna*

b) The construct state resembles the forms in §149: داعي *dāʿī*, accusative داعيَ *dāʿiya*, dual داعيا *dāʿiyā*, داعيي *dāʿiyay*, plural داعو *dāʿū*, داعي *dāʿī*.

Note 1. The short form of the *nisbah*-ending *-iy* is treated like stem-final *-ī*: يمانٍ *yamānin* 'Yemenite', accusative يمانيا *yamāniyan*, etc. (§116.1).

§156. Diptotic nominal forms with stem-final *ī* are distinctive in that they take the sign of indefiniteness *-n* in the nominative and genitive of the indefinite state: أفاعٍ ʾ*afāʿin* 'vipers', plural of أفعى ʾ*afʿan* (§94).

Sg.	nom.	أفاعٍ	ʾ*afāʿin*	الأفاعي	(ʾ*a*)*l-*ʾ*afāʿī*
	gen.	أفاعٍ	ʾ*afāʿin*	الأفاعي	(ʾ*a*)*l-*ʾ*afāʿī*
	acc.	أفاعيَ	ʾ*afāʿiya*	الأفاعيَ	(ʾ*a*)*l-*ʾ*afāʿiya*

Vocative

§157. a) In vocative expressions, such as appeals or exhortations, the substantive is in the definite state, as a rule introduced by the particle يا *yā* or (يا) أيّها (*yā*) ʾ*ayyuhā*. The definite state follows *yā* without the article, ʾ*ayyuhā* with the article (ʾ*a*)*l-*: يا غلامُ *yā ghulāmu* 'O lad!', يا فتى *yā fatā* 'O young man!', يا أيّها الأميرُ *yā* ʾ*ayyuhā* ʾ*l-*ʾ*amīru* 'O prince!'.

Note 1. In pre-classical Arabic, أيّتها ʾ*ayyatuhā* occurs occasionally along with ʾ*ayyuhā* with feminine substantives.

b) The construct state must be in the accusative in vocative expressions: يا ابن عمّي *yā* ʾ*bna ʿammī* 'O son of my uncle!', يا عبد الله *yā ʿAbda* ʾ*l-lāhi* 'O Abd Allah!'.

Note 2. The vocative particle *yā* may be lacking: زيدُ *Zaydu* 'O Zayd!', أبا عامرٍ ʾ*abā ʿĀmirin* 'O Abū Āmir!', ربّنا *rabbanā* 'our lord!'.

Note 3. The personal pronominal suffix *-ī* 'my' is sometimes shortened and thus not written: يا ربّ *yā rabbi* 'o my Lord (God)!'. There are alternative forms of أب *ʾabun* 'father', أمّ *ʾummun* 'mother': يا أبت *yā ʾabati* 'O my father!', يا أمّت *yā ʾummati* 'O my mother!'.

Note 4. Poetry has vocative constructions with the accusative in the indefinite state following the particles أ *ʾa*, يا *yā*, أيا *ʾayā*. The indefinite accusative must be followed by an additional element: أراكبا كميّا *ʾa-rākiban kamīyan* 'O you heroic horseman!', يا موقدا نارا *yā mūqidan nāran* 'O you who would kindle a fire!'

§158. The vocative can be marked by the ending *-ā*, *-āh* (pausal form). *-āh* usually occurs after the particle وا *wā*: يا عمّا (عمّاه) *yā ʿammā* (*ʿammāh*) 'O (my) uncle!', يا عجبا *yā ʿajabā*, وا عجباه *wā ʿajabāh* 'O (what a) miracle!', يا حسرتا *yā ḥasratā* 'O pity!', وا صباحاه *wā ṣabāḥāh* 'O (how bad is) the morning!'.

Note 1. *-ā* is often interpreted as an indefinite accusative *-an* (§157.4): يا عجبا *yā ʿajaban* 'O miracle!', يا رجلا *yā rajulan* 'hey, any man!'. Cf. §53.3.

Note 2. In expressions referring to family relatives, *-ā* is often abbreviated to *-a*: يا ابن عمّ (عمّاه) *yā 'bna ʿamma* (*ʿammāh*) 'O (my) cousin!'. These vocatives of أب, أمّ (§157.3) are أبت *ʾabata*, أبتاه *ʾabatāh* and أمّ *ʾumma*, أمّت *ʾummata*, أمّتاه *ʾummatāh*.

§159. After the vocative particles *ʾa* and *yā*, personal names and words frequently employed in exhortations are often shortened. Abbreviation (ترخيم *tarkhīm*) affects the inflectional endings and the preceding consonants: يا صاح *yā ṣāḥi* (= صاحب *ṣāḥibu*) 'O companion!', يا عاذل *yā ʿādhila* (= عاذلة *ʿādhilatu*) 'O blamer (fem.)!', يا فاطم *yā fāṭima* (= فاطمة *Fāṭimatu*) 'O Fatima!', يا عثم *yā ʿuthma* (= عثمان *ʿUthmānu*) 'O Uthman!'.

Verb

§160. Preliminary remarks: The Arab grammarians considered the third person singular masculine to be the simplest form of the verb, in that it embodies orthographically the stem unencumbered by any morpheme: فعل 'he did' from the root فعل *f-ʿ-l*. Therefore, it is customary for grammars and dictionaries to present the 3rd pers. sg. masc. as the basic form of the verb. Every verb has a perfect and an imperfect primary form. These are usually distinguished from each other by the stem vowel. Since in the basic stem (§163) there is no predictable distribution of vowel classes in the perf. and imperf. base, dictionaries give the stem vowel of the imperf. base: *qatala* (*u*) 'kill', i.e., perf. base *qatal-a*, imperf. base *ya-qtul-u*.

Formation of the Stem

§161. Most verbs by far are three-radical (§§58 f.). A smaller number consists of four-radical verbs. The basic stem and the derived verbal stems are classified in 15 three-radical morpheme categories and 4 four-radical categories, excluding a few alternative formations (§178). In grammars and dictionaries, verbal stems are usually identified by roman numerals (I–XV), beginning with the basic stem as stem I.

§162. The derived verbal stems are formed in the following ways:

a) Doubling of the middle or final consonantal radical: three-radical verbs: *faʿʿala* (II), (*ʾi*)*fʿalla* (IX); four-radical (*ʾi*)*fʿal*$_3$*all*$_4$*a* (IV).

b) Vowel lengthening *a* > *ā*: in three-radical verbs: *fāʿala* (III), (*ʾi*)*fʿālla* (XI) from (*ʾi*)*fʿalla*.

c) *aw*(*w*) infixed into the stem: three-radical verbs: (*ʾi*)*fʿawʿala* (XII), (*ʾi*)*fʿawwala* (XIII).

Note 1. Morpheme categories *fawʿala* and *fayʿala* are classified as in the basic stem *faʿl*$_3$*al*$_4$*a* (I) of the four-radical verb.

d) Causative prefix *ʾa*-: in three-radical verbs: *ʾafʿala* (IV).

Note 2. On vestiges of the *ha*- causative prefix, see §178 b.

e) Causative prefix *sa*-: only in combination with the *t*-infix in three-radical verbs (*ʾi*)*stafʿala* (X).

Note 3. Evidence of the *sa*-prefix is also found in the basic stem of three- and four-radical verbs: *sabaqa* 'leave behind' from *baqiya* 'remain', *salqā* 'throw down on the back' from *laqiya* 'meet'.

f) Reflexive prefix *ta-*: three-radical verbs: *tafa‘‘ala* (V) from *fa‘‘ala*, *tafā‘ala* (VI) from *fā‘ala*; four-radical verbs: *tafa‘l₃al₄a* (II) from *fa‘l₃al₄a*.

g) Reflexive infix *-t-*: three-radical verbs: (*ʾi*)*fta‘ala* (VIII), (*ʾi*)*staf‘ala* (X) from **sa-f‘ala* (§162 e).

Note 4. Pre-classical Arabic had a *t*-prefix: (*ʾi*)*tfa‘‘ala* (= V), (*ʾi*)*tfā‘ala* (= VI). See §47.

h) Reflexive-passive prefix *n-*: three-radical verbs: (*ʾi*)*nfa‘ala* (VII).

i) Infix *-n-*: three-radical verbs: (*ʾi*)*f‘anlala* (XIV), (*ʾi*)*f‘anlā* (XV); four-radical verbs: (*ʾi*)*f‘anl₃al₄a* (III).

Note 5. Other derivations, like morpheme categories originating in (*ʾi*)*f‘ālla* (XI), namely, (*ʾi*)*f‘aʾalla*, (*ʾi*)*f‘ahalla*, (*ʾi*)*f‘a‘alla*, and similar forms, or denominal formations, *fa‘lala*, and others, correspond formally to verbal stems I through IV of four-radical verbs. They are therefore classed there (§§174ff.).

Verbal Stems of Three-Radical Verbs

§163. I. (Basic stem): The basic stem occurs in three vowel classes of the perfect base: 1. *fa‘ala* (imperfect *yaf‘a/i/alu*), 2. *fa‘ila* (imperfect *yaf‘alu*), 3. *fa‘ula* (imperfect *yaf‘ulu*). *fa‘ala* includes transitive and intransitive action verbs like قتل *qatala* (يقتل *yaqtulu*) ‘kill’, ضرب *ḍaraba* (يضرب *yaḍribu*) ‘beat’, ذهب *dhahaba* (يذهب *yadhhabu*) ‘go away’. *fa‘ila* includes mostly non-action verbs and verbs expressing attributes such as علق *‘aliqa* (يعلق *ya‘laqu*) ‘hang’, بله *baliha* (يبله *yablahu*) ‘be simple-minded’. *fa‘ula* includes exclusively verbs expressing qualities or attributes like حسن *ḥasuna* (يحسن *yaḥsunu*) ‘be handsome, good’, عمق *‘amuqa* (يعمق *ya‘muqu*) ‘be deep’.

Note 1. In poetry, *fa‘la* occurs occasionally in place of *fa‘ila*.

Note 2. In the following description, only the most important of the typical semantic groups of the derived verbs are included.

§**164.** II. *faʿʿala* (imperf. *yufaʿʿilu* forms intensives like قطّع *qaṭṭaʿa* 'cut to pieces' from قطع *qaṭaʿa* 'cut off'; transitives like ثبّت *thabbata* 'make firm' from ثبت *thabata* 'be firm', علّم *ʿallama* 'teach' from علم *ʿalima* 'know'; sometimes declaratives like كذّب *kadhdhaba* 'call a liar' from كذب *kadhaba* 'lie'. Transitive denominal verbs are frequently in this morpheme category: سلّم *sallama* 'to offer greetings (سلام *salāmun*)'.

§**165.** III. *fāʿala* (imperf. *yufāʿilu*) has the sense of 'intend, try to do something' or 'intend, try, to do something to someone': قاتل *qātala* 'fight' ('intend, try, to kill'), لاين *lāyana* 'treat with kindness' from لان *lāna* (imperf. يلين *yalīnu*) 'be soft, gentle'. These kinds of meanings of verbal stem III occur with the accusative. In combination with بين *bayna* 'between', verbal stem III is frequently a transitive of stem VI. See §308.1.

§**166.** IV. *ʾafʿala* (imperf. *yufʿilu*) forms causatives like أذهب *ʾadhhaba* 'cause to go away' from ذهب *dhahaba* 'go away', أحسن *ʾaḥsana* 'do right, good' from حسن *ḥasuna* 'be good'; sometimes declarative: أنكر *ʾankara* 'consider objectionable, censure'. There are other characteristic meanings, e.g., أخطأ *ʾakhṭaʾa* 'make an error', أصبح *ʾaṣbaḥa* 'begin a new day' (§190.1), أعرق *ʾaʿraqa* 'march to Iraq', أطلب *ʾaṭlaba* 'acquiesce to a demand'.

Note 1. The causative is usually not used if an action is carried out by an agent: قتله *qatalahū* 'he killed him' or 'he had him killed'.

Note 2. On the formulaic expressions *mā ʾafʿala* and *ʾafʿil bi-*, see §128.

§**167.** V. *tafaʿʿala* (imperf. *yatafaʿʿalu*) is the reflexive of stem II: تعلّم *taʿallama* 'teach one self, learn', تثبّت *tathabbata* 'ascertain'; occasionally with the meaning of pretending: تنبّأ *tanabbaʾa* 'pretend, claim to be a prophet', تكلّف *takallafa* 'force oneself, pretend to do something'.

Note 1. Concerning (*ʾi*)*tfaʿʿala* (*yatfaʿʿalu* > *yaffaʿʿalu*), see §47.

§**168.** VI. *tafāʿala* (imperf. *yatafāʿalu*) is the reflexive of stem III and often has a reciprocal meaning: تعالج *taʿālaja* 'undergo treatment' from عالج *ʿālaja* 'treat someone', تنازع *tanāzaʿa* 'contend with one another' from نازع *nāzaʿa* 'fight'; occasionally, like stem V, it has the meaning of pretending: تناوم *tanāwama* 'to feign sleep'.

Note 1. Concerning (ʾ*i*)*tfāʿala* (*yatfāʿalu* > *yaffāʿalu*) see §47.

§169. VII. (ʾ*i*)*nfaʿala* (imperf. *yanfaʿilu*) is reflexive-passive of the basic stem: انهزم (ʾ*i*)*nhazama* 'be put to flight' from هزم *hazama* 'put to flight'.

Note 1. The prefixed *n*- can be assimilated to a following *m* (§45). Of I-*n* roots, only *n*-*m*-*s* has a stem VII: انّمس (ʾ*i*)*nnamasa* 'conceal oneself'. As a rule, stem VIII occurs instead for these roots.

§170. VIII. (ʾ*i*)*ftaʿala* (imperf. *yaftaʿilu*) is reflexive-intransitive of the basic stem: ارتفع (ʾ*i*)*rtafaʿa* 'rise' from رفع *rafaʿa* 'lift'; frequently with the meaning 'do something for oneself': اتّخذ (ʾ*i*)*ttakhadha* (§238) 'take for oneself' from أخذ ʾ*akhadha* 'take', and the meaning 'do something with someone else': اختصم (ʾ*i*)*khtaṣama* 'fight with each other' from خاصم *khāṣama* 'fight'.

Note 1. Concerning the assimilation of the -*t*- infix to the first radical, see §46.

§171. IX. (ʾ*i*)*fʿalla* (imperf. *yafʿallu*) and XI. (ʾ*i*)*fʿālla* (imperf. *yafʿāllu*), with lengthening of the stem vowel, belong almost without exception to adjectives of the morpheme category ʾ*afʿalu* (§119): اصفرّ (ʾ*i*)*ṣfarra* and اصفارّ (ʾ*i*)*ṣfārra* 'turn yellow, become pale' from أصفر ʾ*aṣfaru* 'yellow', ازورّ (ʾ*i*)*zwarra* and ازوارّ (ʾ*i*)*zwārra* become crooked, turn aside' from أزور ʾ*azwaru* 'oblique, crooked'.

§172. X. (ʾ*i*)*stafʿala* (imperf. *yastafʿilu*) is reflexive of extinct **safʿala* (§162 e): استوحش (ʾ*i*)*stawḥasha* 'feel lonely' from **sawḥasha* = أوحش ʾ*awḥasha* 'make lonely', استغفر (ʾ*i*)*staghfara* 'apologize', i.e., 'ask for forgiveness'; frequently reflexive of the causative-declarative: استكبر (ʾ*i*)*stakbara* 'consider oneself great, important, be haughty' from أكبر ʾ*akbara* 'deem great, important'.

§173. Verbal stems XII–XV are rare: XII. (ʾ*i*)*fʿawʿala* (imperf. *yafʿawʿilu*): احدودب (ʾ*i*)*ḥdawdaba* 'be hunchback' from أحدب ʾ*aḥdabu* 'hunchback', احلولى (ʾ*i*)*ḥlawlā* 'be sweet' from حلو *ḥulwun* 'sweet'. XIII. (ʾ*i*)*fʿawwala* (imperf. *yafʿawwilu*): اعلوّد (ʾ*i*)ʿ*lawwada* 'be strong' from علد ʿ*alida* 'be strong'. XIV. (ʾ*i*)*fʿanlala* (imperf. *yafʿanlilu*): احلنكك (ʾ*i*)*ḥlankaka* 'be pitch-black' from حلك *ḥalika* 'be pitch-black'. XV. (ʾ*i*)*fʿanlā* (imperf. *yafʿanlī*): اعلندى (ʾ*i*)ʿ*landā* 'be strong' from علد ʿ*alida* 'be strong'.

Verbal Stems of Four-Radical Verbs

§**174.** I. *faʿl₃al₄a* (imperf. *yufaʿl₃il₄u*) includes roots of diverse origin: four-radical roots like جمهر *jamhara* 'gather', reduplicated roots like لألأ *laʾlaʾa* 'glisten', denominals like منطق *manṭaqa* 'gird' from منطقة *minṭaqatun* 'belt', جلبب *jalbaba* 'clothe in a جلباب *jilbābun*', formulaic expressions like بسمل *basmala* 'to utter the formula بسم الله *bi-smi 'l-lāhi*' (§22 c), and others.

§**175.** II. *tafaʿl₃al₄a* (imperf. *yatafaʿl₃al₄u*) is reflexive-intransitive of the basic stem (I.): تجمهر *tajamhara* 'congregate', تمنطق *tamanṭaqa* 'gird oneself'.

§**176.** III. (*ʾi*)*fʿanl₃al₄a* (imperf. *yafʿanl₃il₄u*) is exceptionally rare: اخرنطم (*ʾi*)*k͟hranṭama* 'turn up one's nose' from خرطوم *k͟hurṭūmun* 'elephant trunk'.

Note 1. Infixed -*n*- can be assimilated to the following *m*; see §45.

§**177.** IV. (*ʾi*)*fʿal₃all₄a* (imperf. *yafʿal₃ill₄u*: اشمخرّ (*ʾi*)*s͟hmak͟harra* 'be lofty, arrogant' from شمخر *s͟hamk͟hara* 'be lofty, proud'; cf. §162.5.

§**178.** a) Instead of (*ʾi*)*fʿalla* (IX), (*ʾi*)*fʿalā* (imperf. *yafʿalī*) is formed from III-weak roots: احووى (*ʾi*)*ḥwawā* 'be dark-colored' from أحوى *ʾaḥwā* 'dark-colored', ارعوى (*ʾi*)*rʿawā* 'pay attention'.

b) The causative prefix *ha*- (§162 d) is still preserved in هراق *harāqa* 'spill' and in several other rarely used words. On the inflection, see §249.

Note 1. Variant verbal stems of these morpheme categories occur with exceeding rarity and mostly only in one attestation.

System of Verb Forms

§**179.** The verb has a suffix conjugation and a prefix conjugation. The suffix conjugation is used to form the perfect. The prefix conjugation is used to form the imperfect, subjunctive, jussive, and energetic. Both conjugations have active and passive forms. The passive is distinguished from the active by stem vowels and prefix vowels. The imperative, which is formed from the imperfect base, occurs in the active only. Active and passive participles and verbal substantives (infinitive) are inflected nominal forms of the verb.

§**180.** The perfect and imperfect and, under special circumstances, the jussive and active participle serve as finite verb forms. The verbal system is based on the opposing aspects inherent in the perfect and the imperfect:

The perfect indicates completed action (perfective aspect).
The imperfect indicates incomplete action in process (imperfective aspect).
When the perfect and imperfect refer to time:
the perfect is used to express the past,
the imperfect is used to express the present,
and the imperfect combined with *sawfa, sa-* is used to express the future.

Note 1. To distinguish more precisely different aspects and tenses, the particles *qad* and *sawfa* (*sa-*) and verb forms combined with *kāna* (*yakūnu*) 'to be', *jaʿala* 'make, do', among others (§190) are used.

Use of the Perfect

§**181.** The perfect indicates completed action. It is used to:

a) refer to events that have already taken place (preterite): دعاني يوما فدخلت إليه *daʿānī yawman fa-da͟khaltu ʾilayhī* 'One day he called me, and I went in before him', خلق الله السّموات والأرض *k͟halaqa 'l-lāhu 's-samāwāti wa-'l-ʾarḍa* (Koran 29:44; 30:8) 'God created heaven and earth'.

b) establish facts: اختلفت العلماء (*ʾi*)*k͟htalafat-i 'l-ʿulamāʾu* 'Scholars are of differing opinions', علم أنّه *ʿalima ʾannahū* 'He knows that . . .', ألّذين كفروا (*ʾa*)*llad͟hīna kafarū* (Koran 2:6, 26, 89, etc.) 'those who are unbelievers'. This use of the perfect is limited primarily to pre-classical Arabic, nevertheless it is preserved in maxims and formulas in the classical period: أنجز حرّ ما وعد *ʾanjaza ḥurrun mā waʿada* 'A free man fulfills what he promises'.

Note 1. If the action is conceived of as a continuing process, the imperfect may be used: أعلم أنّه *ʾaʿlamu ʾannahū* 'I know that . . .'.

Note 2. The perfect كان *kāna* 'he was' (cf. §190 ff.) is also used in the Koran and infrequently in other pre-classical texts to establish facts: كان الله غفورا رحيما *kāna 'l-lāhu g͟hafūran raḥīman* (Koran 4:96, 100, 152; 25:70, etc.) 'God is merciful'.

c) verify an action that is completed at the same time as the establishment of a fact (coincidental occurrence): بعثت إليك بهذا *baʿathtu ʾilayka bi-hādhā* 'I herewith (hereby) send this to you', حلفت *ḥalaftu* 'I hereby swear ...'.

Note 3. The perfect which establishes facts or verifies completed action is negated with *mā* (§321). The jussive in combination with the negative particle *lam* is used as a negative preterite (§194). Concerning the negative particle *lā* in combination with the perfect, see §§182 b; 318 b; 335 b.

Note 4. Note that many verbs can be interpreted as expressing both durative and punctual-ingressive actions: قام *qāma* 'He stood upright' or 'He stood up', ركب *rakiba* 'He rode' or 'He mounted'.

§182. a) The perfect is used to express "wished for" or "conceived of" actions: رحمه الله *raḥimahū 'l-lāhu* 'May God have mercy on him!', 'May God be merciful to him!', بوركت *būrikta* 'May you be blessed!'.

Note 1. In post-classical Arabic the imperfect is frequently used to express wish: يرحمك الله *yarḥamuka 'l-lāhu* 'God will bless you', 'May God bless you'.

b) The perfect that expresses wish is negated by لا *lā* (§318): لا قاتلك الله *lā qātalaka 'l-lāhu* 'May God not condemn you (fight against you)!'. This use also occurs in oaths: حلفت والله لا فعلت هذا *ḥalaftu wa-'l-lāhi lā faʿaltu hādhā* 'I hereby swear, by God! May I never have done this!', i.e. 'I would never do this'.

§183. In a subordinate clause, the action or event that is indicated by the perfect is dependent on the situation in the main clause: جلس حيث جلس أبوه *jalasa ḥaythu jalasa ʾabūhu* 'He sat where his father had sat', لمّا اجتمع النّاس إليّ قلت لهم *lammā 'jtamaʿa 'n-nāsu ʾilayya qultu lahum* 'After the people had assembled around me, I said to them ...'.

Note 1. Concerning the use of the perfect without reference to time in generally valid conditional clauses and clauses with conditional implication, see §446 a.

Note 2. In pre-classical Arabic, the perfect was sometimes used to represent a hypothetical occurrence: أسرّك أن أخرج *ʾa-sarraka ʾan ʾakhruja* 'Would you really rejoice over my departure?', وددت أنّه رآني *wadidtu ʾannahū raʾānī* 'I wished that he had seen me'. In classical prose usage, the imperfect (§185 d) or *kāna* with the imperfect (192.3) has replaced the perfect here.

Use of the Imperfect

§184. The imperfect indicates a continuing or possibly continuing process independent of the time in which the event takes place. It can be a single continuing process, a repeatedly occurring event, or an act that occurs over and over (habitual action). If the context does not refer to the past, the imperfect indicates the present or future.

Note 1. The imperfect is as a rule negated with لا *lā* (§318).

Note 2. Note that only verbs of durative aspect can be interpreted as expressing a single continuing process: يتحرّك *yataḥarraku* 'He is just moving, he is in movement'. The imperfect of verbs of punctual aspect refers to either immediately impending action or a continuously occurring process: يجد *yajidu* 'He is about to find' or 'He finds again and again', يأتي *yaʾtī* 'He is about to come' or 'He comes again and again (every day, etc.)'.

§185. For present-time actions, the imperfect is used:

a) to portray an act occurring in the present: أراك تبكي *ʾarāka tabkī* 'I see you crying (literally, that you are crying)', ماذا تفعل *māḏā tafʿalu* 'What are you doing?'.

b) to relate a repeatedly occurring act: أعفو عن الجاهل وأعطي السّائل *ʾaʿfū ʿan-i 'l-jāhili wa-ʾuʿṭī 's-sāʾila* 'I always forgive fools and give to those who ask'.

c) to describe a universally occurring act (not limited to any time): التّمساح يعيش في الماء (*ʾa*)*t-timsāḥu yaʿīshu fī 'l-māʾi* 'Crocodiles live in the water'.

d) to introduce an act that is about to occur or might occur: ننظر *nanẓuru* 'We are watching (waiting for what will happen)', أولائك يرجون رحمة الله *ʾulāʾika yarjūna raḥmata ʾl-lāhi* (Koran 2:218) 'These should hope for the mercy of God', تسيرون إلى الجبال *tasīrūna ʾilā ʾl-jibāli* 'Now they will go into the mountains!'.

§186. If the context refers to the past, that which occurred in the past may be described with the imperfect: إذا أصبح عمرو قال من عدا على إلهنا ثم يغدو يلتمسه حتّى إذا وجده غسله *ʾidhā ʾaṣbaḥa ʿAmrun qāla man ʿadā ʿalā ʾilāhinā thumma yaghdū yaltamisahū ḥattā ʾidhā wajadahū ghasalahū* 'When morning came, Amr said, who blasphemed against our God? Then he set out (imperf.) very early to look for him. When he finally found him, he purged him'. Not infrequently, it describes a process that is repeated or continues: لم تقتلون أنبياء الله من قبل *lima taqtulūna ʾanbiyāʾa ʾl-lāhi min qablu* (Koran 2:91) 'Why did you keep killing the prophets of God before?', بكى ويبكي ما شاء الله *bakā wa-yabkī mā shāʾa ʾl-lāhu* 'He cried and kept crying, as long as God willed it'. In this case, the imperfect is usually combined with كان *kāna* (§192).

Note 1. Dreams and eyewitness reports are frequently rendered in the imperfect: قال الملك إنّي أرى سبع بقرات *qāla ʾl-maliku ʾinnī ʾarā sabʿa baqarātin* (Koran 12:43) 'The king said, I saw (in a dream) seven cows'.

§187. a) The reported action can also be rendered in the future: لا يموت في النار ولا يحيا *lā yamūtu fī ʾn-nāri wa-lā yaḥyā* 'He will not die in hell-fire and will not live'.

b) سوف *sawfa* or سـ *sa-* may be used to indicate the future tense: إنّه سوف يزورك *ʾinnahū sawfa yazūruka* 'He will (certainly) visit you', سوف أستغفر لكم ربّي *sawfa ʾastaghfiru lakum rabbī* 'I shall ask my Lord to forgive you' (Koran 12:98), لقد علمنا أن سيكون ذلك *la-qad ʿalimnā ʾan sa-yakūnu dhālika* 'We already knew that this will be (so)'.

Note 1. *sawfa, sa-* are not combined with negative particles. لن *lan* with the subjunctive (§196) is used instead.

§188. As it depends on a perfect in the main clause, the imperfect is used to:

a) describe an action occurring at the same time: مرّ بي وأنا أقعد *marra bī wa-ʾanā ʾaqʿudu* 'He went by me while I was sitting' (§§407 ff.), بينا أنا أمشي إذ أقبل رجل *baynā ʾanā ʾamshī ʾidh ʾaqbala rajulun* 'While I was going there, a man (suddenly) approached' (§444).

b) describe an action that occurs in the immediate future with respect to a perfect in the main clause: أتى العين يشرب *ʾatā ʾl-ʿayna yashrabu* 'He came to the spring to drink', بعثني في جلب أبيعه *baʿathanī fī jalabin ʾabīʿuhū* 'He sent me with cattle that I was supposed to sell'.

The Verbal Particle *qad*

§189. قد *qad* occurs immediately before the perfect and imperfect.

a) In combination with *qad*, the perfect indicates an action completed already or previous to a certain time. The perfect cannot be used in its narrative function (§181 a) when *qad* appears: قد مات *qad māta* 'He had (at a certain time already) died', قد جعت *qad juʿtu* 'I have become (am already) hungry'.

b) In combination with *qad*, the imperfect indicates an action that possibly or probably would occur: 'sometimes, perhaps, might occur ...', 'it could be that it will occur': قد أكتب *qad ʾaktubu* 'It could be that I shall write', 'sometimes I write', قد ينامون وقد يأكلون *qad yanāmūna wa-qad yaʾkulūna* 'They might sleep, they might eat'.

Note 1. Only the negative particle لا *lā* or short interjections like والله *wa-ʾl-lāhi* 'by God' can come between *qad* and the verb.

Note 2. In pre-classical Arabic, *qad* before the imperfect is sometimes used to indicate the past: قد أرى غوايتهم *qad ʾarā ghawāyatahum* 'Then I noticed their error', قد أدخل الخباء *qad ʾadkhulu ʾl-khibāʾa* 'Then I went (sometimes, would always go) into their tent'.

Use of Compound Verb Forms

§190. The perfect of كان *kāna* 'he was' is used in combination with the perfect and imperfect to indicate the past. The imperfect يكون *yakūnu* 'he will be' is used with the perfect to indicate the future. A nominal subject comes between *kāna* / *yakūnu* and the following verb: *kāna 'r-rajulu faʿala* (*yafʿalu*) and *yakūnu 'r-rajulu faʿala*.

Note 1. There are also other verbs that are used to define the tenses with more precision. These verbs specify modes of action (*Aktionsarten*) appropriate to their meanings. The most important verbs of this type are: أصبح *ʾaṣbaḥa*, أمسى *ʾamsā* meaning 'to become', ظلّ *ẓalla*, بات *bāta* meaning 'keep (doing)', جعل *jaʿala*, أخذ *ʾakhadha* meaning 'begin' (§192.1), and عاد *ʿāda* meaning 'do again'. See §432.

Note 2. كان *kāna* is also used to indicate the past in relation to a nominal clause that describes a condition (§360): أخوه غائب *ʾakhūhu ghāʾibun* 'His brother is missing': كان أخوه غائبا *kāna ʾakhūhu ghāʾiban* 'His brother was missing' (§382 a).

§191. a) كان *kāna* with the perfect refers to actions that have occurred in the past (pluperfect): هذه أتانك الّتي كنت خرجت عليها *hādhihī ʾatānuki 'llatī kunti kharajti ʿalayhā* 'This is your (fem.) she-ass on which you had gone out'.

b) قد *qad* comes either before *kāna* or before the following perfect: قد كان رأى منك مثل ما رأينا *qad kāna raʾā minka mithla mā raʾaynā* = كان قد رأى *kāna qad raʾā* ... 'he had already noticed the same (qualities) in you that we noticed'.

Note 1. Concerning *kāna* referring to the past in conditional clauses, see §446 b.

§192. When used with the imperfect, كان *kāna* describes an action that is occurring, is continuing, or occurs repeatedly in the past: كان الملك يمرّ به *kāna 'l-maliku yamurru bihī* 'The king was passing by him then', يوما خرجت كما كانت تصنع *yawman kharajat kamā kānat taṣnaʿu* 'One day she went out, just as she used to do', كان يكون في البيت *kāna yakūnu fī 'l-bayti* 'He always (usually, continually) was in the house'.

Note 1. جعل *jaʿala* or أخذ *ʾa<u>kh</u>a<u>dh</u>a* is used to express an action begun in the past: فجعل يستبطئ الأمر *fa-jaʿala yastabṭiʾu ʾl-ʾamra* 'From now on, he found (began to find) that the matter was proceeding too slowly'. See also §432.

Note 2. The negative equivalent of *kāna* is *lam yakun* (§194.1).

Note 3. Sometimes *kāna* is used with the imperfect to express an action that could have occurred in the past or should have: كان يكون سوء أدب *kā-na yakūnu sūʾa ʾadabin* 'It would have been a misbehavior', فكيف كان يقول *fa-kayfa kāna yaqūlu* 'How should he have said it?'.

Note 4. If it occurs in combination with more than one imperfect form joined by *wa-* 'and', *kāna* is used only once.

§193. يكون *yakūnu* in combination with the perfect indicates that the action is conceived of as having been completed in the future (future perfect): فلنأخذه فنكون قد أخذنا عوضا *fal-naʾ<u>kh</u>u<u>dh</u>hu fa-nakūnu qad ʾa<u>kh</u>a<u>dh</u>nā ʿiwaḍan* 'Let us take him, for then we should have taken a substitute'.

Note 1. Concerning the subjunctive يكون *yakūna* in this construction, see §197; see §222.2 on the imperative كن *kun*.

Use of the Jussive

§194. The jussive is used as a perfect: a) in combination with لم *lam* 'not' and لما *lammā* 'not yet': لم يأت *lam yaʾti* 'He did not come', لما يأت *lammā yaʾti* 'He has not yet come'.

Note 1. لم يكن *lam yakun* is the negative equivalent of *kāna* in verbal constructions: أولم أكن حذّرتك *ʾa-wa-lam ʾakun ḥa<u>dh</u><u>dh</u>artuka* 'Had I not warned you?', لم يكن يسمع *lam yakun yasmaʿu* 'As usual, he heard nothing then'.

b) In conditional clauses (§446 a) and in the apodosis after imperatives (§412).

§195. The jussive implies an order: a) It is combined with the particle *li-* in the positive: ليأت *li-yaʾti* 'Let him come!'.

Note 1. After *wa-* and *fa-* (§§328 f), *li* is abbreviated to *l-*: فلنأخذ *fal-naʾkhudh* 'So let us take!'.

b) In combination with the negative لا *lā*, the jussive implies a negative order (prohibition): لا تقتل *lā taqtul* 'You shall not kill, do not kill!', لا يحزنكم الله *lā yuḥzinkum-u 'l-lāhu* 'May God not cause you grief!'.

Use of the Subjunctive

§**196.** a) The subjunctive indicates an action as intended or expected; it occurs only in a subordinate clause: اغفر لي يا ربّ فأدخل الجنّة *(ʾi)ghfir lī yā rabbi fa-ʾadkhula 'l-jannata* 'Forgive me, my Lord, so that I might enter Paradise!', ما منعك ألّا تسجد إذ أمرتك *mā manaʿaka ʾallā tasjuda ʾidh ʾamartuka* (Koran 7:12) 'What prevented you from prostrating yourself when I had given you the command?'. The subjunctive is negated with لا *lā*.

b) The subjunctive comes after the particles: أن *ʾan* 'that' and ألّا *ʾallā* (< *'an-lā* §45) 'that not, lest' (§414), كي *kay* and ل *li-* 'that, in order that' (§438), ف *fa-* 'so that' (§410), أو *ʾaw* 'unless' (§411), and حتّى *ḥattā* 'until (that)' (§439 b); see also §345.

Note 1. The subjunctive follows *ʾan* and *ḥattā* only if an intention or possible result is expressed. Otherwise, the perfect or imperfect is used: أعلم أن نام (ينام) *ʾaʿlamu ʾan nāma (yanāmu)* 'I know that he slept (sleeps)', مرض حتّى لا يرجونه *mariḍa ḥattā lā yarjūnahū* 'He is so sick that they have no hope for him'. In post-classical Arabic, however, the subjunctive is used most of the time indiscriminately after *ʾan* and *ḥattā*.

Note 2. In pre-classical Arabic, the subjunctive is attested on occasion even after إذا *ʾidhan* 'then', ثمّ *thumma* 'then', and و *wa-* 'and then'.

c) لن *lan* with the subjunctive (< **lā ʾan*) is used to negate future actions (§187): لن يزوركم أبدا *lan yazūrakum ʾabadan* 'He will never visit you'.

Note 3. The subjunctive is not used after the future particles *sawfa, sa-*.

§**197.** An action that might have occurred is expressed after a subjunctive particle with يكون *yakūna* and a following perfect: عسى أن يكون سمع منّي *ʿasā ʾan yakūna samiʿa minnī* 'Perhaps he has heard about me' (§342.2),

خاف أن يكون قد أخطأ *khāfa ʾan yakūna qad ʾakhṭaʾa* 'He feared that he could have committed an error', لا تطلب الفساد في الدّنيا فتكون قد نسيت نصيبك من الآخرة *lā taṭlub-i ʾl-fasāda fī ʾd-dunyā fa-takūna qad nasīta naṣībaka min-a ʾl-ʾākhirati* 'Do not seek evil in this world, lest you would have forgotten your share in the hereafter' (§410).

Use of the Energetic

§198. The energetic is used to introduce an action that is certain to occur (e.g., in an oath). In the positive, it occurs with the prefixed particle *la-* (§334): لتبايعنّ أو لأحرّقنّكم *la-tubāyiʿunna ʾaw la-ʾuḥarriqannakum* 'You will absolutely pay homage, or I shall certainly burn you up', حلف ليقتلنّ *ḥalafa la-yaqtulanna* 'He swore he will certainly kill'. The energetic is negated with لا *lā*.

Note 1. The second person frequently has the sense of an order: لا تقولنّ *lā taqūlanna* 'Do not indeed say anything!'.

Note 2. In pre-classical Arabic, the energetic also occurs in conditional sentences (§§450.1; 451) and in interrogative sentences (without *la-*).

Use of the Passive

§199. a) The passive is the form of the verb in which the agent is not named. The agent either is unknown or is intentionally not identified: قتل أخوك *qutila ʾakhūka* 'Your brother was killed', أمرت *ʾumirta* 'you were ordered, instructed'; cf. §405 b.

Note 1. Divine or supernatural powers (God, fate, etc.) are often left unmentioned: توفّي *tuwuffiya* 'He was taken (by God)', i.e., 'he died'.

Note 2. The cause, origin, and instrument of passive action are occasionally rendered by *li-*, *min*, and *bi* (§§294 ff.): تراع له *turāʿu lahū* 'He was terrified of him', أسكر من الخمر *ʾuskira min-a ʾl-khamri* 'He was made drunk by the wine', أرضعنا بها *ʾurḍiʿnā bihā* 'we were suckled by her'.

b) Intransitive reflexive verbs do not have a subject in the passive. As a rule, they then have have a prepositional complement: يسار إليها *yusāru ʾilayhā* 'It was traveled to, one travels to it', أختلف في ذلك (ʾ*u*)*khtulifa fī dhālika* 'There was disagreement over that'.

Note 3. Transitive verbs too can be used in the passive without subject, if they have a complement: غشي عليه *ghushiya ʿalayhi* 'It was covered over him', i.e., 'He became unconscious'.

§**200.** In passive constructions with transitive verbs, the direct object (§373) becomes the subject. All additional complements, whether accusatives or prepositions, remain unchanged.

a) Verbs with accusatives: أوتيت الكتاب *ʾūtīta 'l-kitāba* 'You were brought the book', يسمّى عليّا *yusammā ʿAlīyan* 'He is called Ali', تبّروا تتبيرا *tubbirū tatbīran* 'They were completely mangled' (§376)

b) Verbs with prepositions: أتي بكتاب *ʾutiya bi-kitābin* 'He was brought a book', يلقّب بالجاحظ *yulaqqab bi-'l-Jāḥiẓi* 'He is called by the *laqab* "goggle-eyed"'.

Note 1. The passive participle is treated the same way: المسمّى عليّا *(ʾa)l-musammā ʿAlīyan* 'the one named Ali', المعروف بالجاحظ *(ʾa)l-maʿrūfu bi-'l-Jāḥiẓi* 'The one known as al-Jāḥiẓ'. See also §204.

Use of the Participle

§**201.** Participles are adjectives that represent the meaning of the verb as an attribute. Active and passive participles can have both perfect and imperfect (§180) meanings: ضارب *ḍāribun* 'one who has hit' and 'one who hits, will hit, can hit', مشروب *mashrūbun* 'drunk' and 'something that is drunk, can be drunk; drinkable'. The imperfect meaning is associated more often with the active participle, perfect meaning more often with the passive participle.

Note 1. Other verbal adjectives, especially those of the morpheme categories *faʿīlun, faʿūlun* (§120), *faʿʿālun* (§115), may also assume participle-like functions. Participles are ususally not formed from verbs that refer to qualities (§163); rather, verbal adjectives in morpheme categories *faʿalun, faʿilun, faʿulun* (§115) are used.

§**202.** The active participle as a nominal predicate (§361) functions very much like an imperfect. It is used:

a) as a perfect participle, to represent an action that has begun and still continues: غدوت إليه فإذا هو قائم يصلّي *ghadawtu ʾilayhi fa-ʾidhā huwa qāʾimun yuṣallī* 'I went in the early morning to him, just as he was engaged in prayer' ('having stood up'), بينا نحن متوقّفون إذ نودي *baynā naḥnu mutawaqqifūna ʾidh nūdiya* 'As we stood there ('having stopped'), he was called'.

b) as an imperfect participle, to represent an action that has not yet been realized but is expected to be taken: هو كاتب *huwa kātibun* 'He is in a position to, just about to write' or simply 'He is a writer', أنا راجع إليهم فداعيهم إلى الإسلام *ʾanā rājiʿun ʾilayhim fa-dāʿīhim ʾilā 'l-ʾislāmi* 'I was about (have already decided) to return to them and call them to Islam'. Frequently, it occurs after the negative particles ما *mā* and ليس *laysa* (§§321; 323): لست بفاعل (فاعلا) *lastu bi-fāʿilin (fāʿilan)* or ما أنا بفاعل *mā ʾanā bi-fāʿilin* 'I will not (cannot) do it'.

Note 1. Infrequently, there is no subject: أفهادم ما قد بنيت *ʾa-fa-hādimun mā qad banaytu* 'Will you destroy what I have built?'.

c) as a circumstantial accusative (§§380 ff.), the participle functions much like the imperfect (§188): رآه باكيا (يبكي) *raʾāhu bākiyan (yabkī)* 'He saw him crying (cry)', خرج هاربا (يهرب) *kharaja hāriban (yahrubu)* 'He went out to flee'. The perfect participle can be used in place of *qad* with the perfect (§189 a): لا آتيك مجرما (وقد أجرمت) *lā ʾātīka mujriman (wa-qad ʾajramtu)* 'I shall not come to you as one who has committed a crime'.

§**203.** The active participle can behave like a verb in constructions with an accusative object and like a noun in constructions with a genitive object (§386b).

a) The perfect participle as a rule is found in constructions with the genitive and thus functions as a substantive: اللّه خالق الأرض *al-lāhu khāliqu 'l-ʾarḍi* 'God is the creator of the earth'. Cf. §146.2.

b) The imperfect participle occurs in constructions with the accusative or the genitive: ضارب أخيه *ḍāribu ʾakhīhi* = ضارب أخاه *ḍāribun ʾakhāhu* 'striking his brother', كلّ نفس ذائقة الموت *kullu nafsin dhāʾiqatu 'l-mawti* (Koran 3:185; 21:35; 29:57) 'Every soul will taste death'. The accusative may also follow when the participle functions as a substantive: طالب الثّأر *ṭālibun-i 'th-tha'ra*, الطّالب الثّأر (ʾa)*ṭ-ṭālibu 'th-tha'ra* 'one who seeks blood revenge', 'the one who seeks blood revenge'. See §146 concerning the definiteness of the construct state.

Note 1. Personal pronominal suffixes on participles are usually interpreted as genitives: ضاربه *ḍāribuhū* 'hitting him', ضاربي *ḍāribī* 'hitting me', rarely ضاربني *ḍāribunī* 'hitting me' (§268).

Note 2. The accusative can be replaced by *li-* (§295 a): الطّالب للعلم (ʾ*a*)*ṭ-ṭālibu lil-*ʿ*ilmi* 'the one who seeks knowledge'. This construction is obligatory when the object precedes the participle: للضّيف مكرم *liḍ-ḍayfi mukrimun* 'honoring the guest'.

Note 3. Verbal adjectives (§201.1) and elatives occur in constructions similar to those of the corresponding participles: هو أطلب للعلم منكم *huwa* ʾ*aṭlabu lil-*ʿ*ilmi minkum* 'He seeks knowledge more eagerly than you'.

Note 4. Concerning the active participle in the role of indeterminate subject, see §358 b.

§**204.** The prepositional complement (§199 b) associated with a participle of a passive without subject takes a personal pronominal suffix that refers to the thing or person mentioned: مغشيّ عليه *maghshīyun* ʿ*alayhi* 'covered over him', 'unconscious', parallel to غشي عليه *ghushiya* ʿ*alayhi* 'It was covered over him', موثوق به *mawthūqun bihī* 'someone on whom one relies', i.e., 'reliable', parallel to وثق به *wuthiqa bihī* 'It is relied on him, he is relied on'. Although the passive participle without subject does not agree grammatically, the personal suffix does agree with the substantive to which it is subordinate: أنت موثوق بك ʾ*anta mawthūqun bika* 'You are reliable', صحيفة مختوم على أسفلها *ṣaḥīfatun makhtūmun* ʿ*alā* ʾ*asfalihā* 'a leaf the verso of which bears a seal', رجال مغضوب عليهم *rijālun maghḍūbun* ʿ*alayhim* 'men at whom they are annoyed, annoying men'.

Note 1. The prepositional complement is lacking in passive participles of the derived verbal stems, if they are used as *nomen loci* or as verbal substantives (§78.3): مستنقع *mustanqa*ʿ*un* 'where water collects, bog'.

Use of Verbal Substantives

§**205.** Verbal substantives embody the meaning of the verb without any of its functional properties: قتل *qatlun* 'killing, having killed, being killed'. They are used to rephrase a verb as a noun: إنّ خروجه كان غضبا *ʾinna khurūjahū kāna ghaḍaban* 'His exit was undertaken in anger'; to change a verb into a nominal subordinate: يستطيع بلوغ حاجته *yastaṭīʿu bulūgha ḥājatihī* 'He is able to attain what he needs'; as an inner object (§§376 f.): ضربه ضربا *ḍarabahū ḍarban* 'He struck him a blow, i.e., hit him hard'.

§**206.** A verbal substantive can be combined, like a noun, with a genitive or, like a verb, with an accusative or preposition:

a) The genitive takes the place of the subject or object (or passive subject) of the verb: قتل أخيه *qatlu ʾakhīhi* 'the fact that his brother has killed' and 'the fact that someone has killed his brother, or the fact that his brother has been killed'.

Note 1. A verbal substantive of a verb that takes a prepositional complement also appears with the same complement: الاطّلاع على الكتب *(ʾa)l-iṭṭilāʿu ʿalā al-kutubi* 'studying books'.

b) The accusative occurs for the object when the genitive position is occupied by a subject genitive, when the verbal substantive is made definite by the article, or when the substantive is indefinite: قتلك أخاه *qatluka ʾakhāhu* 'your having killed his brother', ضعيف النّكاية أعداءه *ḍaʿīfu 'n-nikāyati ʾaʿdāʾahū* 'weak in injuring his enemies', ضرب بالسّيوف رؤوسهم *ḍarbun bi-'s-suyūfi ruʾūsahum* 'cutting off their heads with the swords'.

Note 2. See §271.1 on the adding of personal pronominal suffixes to the verbal substantive.

Note 3. The accusative can be replaced by the preposition *li-* (§295 a): منافستي له *munāfasatī lahu* 'my rivalry with him', بأخذ لدينار *bi-ʾakhdhin li-dīnārin* 'by taking a dinar'.

c) The subject can be in the nominative: الضّرب أبوك ولده (ʾa)ḍ-ḍarbu ʾabūka waladahū 'the act of your father having struck his child'. More often, the agent of the action is introduced with *min* (§299 c): الحبّ منّي إليك (ʾa)l-ḥubbu minnī ʾilayka 'the love of me (I have) for you'.

Inflection of the Verb

Suffix Conjugation (Perfect)

§**207.** The following morphemes suffixed to the perfect base (§§163 ff.) constitute the personal inflectional forms:

Sg.	3rd m.	*-a*	f.	*-at*	2nd m.	*-ta*	f.	*-ti*	1st	*-tu*
Du.		*-ā*		*-atā*		*-tumā*		*-tumā*		—
Pl.		*-ū*		*-na*		*-tum*		*-tunna*		*-nā*

Cf. the tables of paradigms, pp. 237–258.

Note 1. On the orthography of the 3rd pl. masc. قتلوا *qatalū*, see §7.2.

Note 2. If a suffix beginning with *t* or *n* attaches to stem-final *-t* or *-n*, only one ت or ن is written: ثبتّ *th̲abat-tu* 'I stood firm', آمنّا *ʾāman-nā* 'We believed' (§17.3).

Note 3. On the assimilation of suffixes beginning with *t* to stem-final consonants, see §48.

Note 4. In poetry, تمو *-tumū* (§7.5) occurs besides *-tum*.

§**208.** As a rule, the perfect bases end in single consonants: *qatal-a*, 'He killed' *qatal-tu* 'I killed'. In verb-stems IX and XI, as well as stem IV of four-radical verbs, the final double consonant must be broken up before a suffix that begins with a consonant (§50.2): إحمرّ (ʾi)ḥmarr-a 'He turned red', 3rd fem. احمرّت (ʾi)ḥmarr-at, 3rd pl. احمرّوا (ʾi)ḥmarrū, etc., but 1st sg. احمررت (ʾi)ḥmarartu, 1st pl. احمررنا (ʾi)ḥmararnā, etc. Also, اصفارّ (ʾi)ṣfārra 'He turned yellow', but 3rd pl. fem. اصفاررن (ʾi)ṣfārarna, etc. اطمأنّ (ʾi)ṭmaʾanna 'He became quiet', but 2nd pl. masc. اطمأننتم (ʾi)ṭmaʾnantum, etc.

Note 1. Stem XV is inflected like III-weak verbs (§§250 ff.): إعلندى (ʾi)ʿlandā 'He was strong', 3rd sg. fem. إعلندت (ʾi)ʿlandat, 1st sg. إعلنديت (ʾi)ʿlandaytu, etc.

§**209.** The inflection of negative ليس *laysa* 'he is not' (§323) follows that of the suffix conjugation: sg. 3rd masc. ليس *laysa*, fem. ليست *laysat*, 2nd masc. لست *lasta*, fem. لست *lasti*, 1st لست *lastu*, dual 3rd masc. ليسا *laysā*, fem. ليستا *laysatā*, 2nd لستما *lastumā*, pl. 3rd masc. ليسوا *laysū*, fem. لسن *lasna*, 2nd masc. لستم *lastum*, fem. لستنّ *lastunna*, 1st لسنا *lasnā*. Cf. §52.

§**210.** Passive: Rather than the perfect stem-vowels *a* - *a*, and, in the basic stem, also *a* - *i*, the passive has the vowel sequence *u* - *i*.

a) Passive perfect: فعل *fuʿila* from *faʿala* (I), فعّل *fuʿʿila* from *faʿʿala* (II), فوعل *fūʿila* from *fāʿala* (III), أفعل *ʾufʿila* from *ʾafʿala* (IV), فعلل *fuʿl_3il_4a* from *faʿl_3al_4a* (four-radical I).

b) In verb stems formed with *ta-*, the vowel of the prefix is assimilated to the *u* of the stem: تفعّل *tufuʿʿila* from *tafaʿʿala* (V), تفوعل *tufūʿila* from *tafāʿala* (VI), تفعلل *tufuʿl_3il_4a* from *tafaʿl_3al_4a* (four-radical II).

c) Auxiliary vowels in stems beginning with double consonants are likewise assimilated (§54 b): انفعل (ʾu)*nfuʿila* from (ʾi)*nfaʿala* (VII), افتعل (ʾu)*ftuʿila* from (ʾi)*ftaʿala* (VIII), استفعل (ʾu)*stufʿila* from (ʾi)*stafʿala* (X), افعنلل (ʾu)*fʿunl$_3$il_4a* from (ʾi)*fʿanl$_3$al_4a* (four-radical III), افعللّ (ʾu)*fʿul$_3$ill_4a* from (ʾi)*fʿa$l_3$all_4a* (four-radical IV).

Note 1. In poetry, فعل *fuʿla*, fem. فعلت *fuʿlat* occur occasionally for *fuʿila*, fem. *fuʿilat*. Cf. §163.1.

Prefix Conjugation

§**211.** The imperfect base is inflected with prefixed morphemes to indicate person and suffixes to indicate plural and dual. The prefixes appear in two series:

a) *a*-series:

	3rd m.	f.	2nd m.	f.	1st
Sg.	*ya-*	*ta-*	*ta-*	*ta-* . . . *ī*	*ʾa-*
Du.	*ya-* . . . *-ā*	*ta-* . . . *-ā*	*ta-* . . . *-ā*	*ta-* . . . *-ā*	—
Pl.	*ya-* . . . *-ū*	*ya-* . . . *-na*	*ta-* . . . *-ū*	*ta-* . . . *-na*	*na-*

The *a*-series occurs in the active of the basic stem, stems V–XV, and stems II–IV of four-radical stems.

Note 1. If *ta-* appears before *ta-* when it is part of the stem in forms V, VI, or II (four-radical), the sequence *ta-ta-* of the prefix can be simplified to *ta-* (§49 a): تعلّم *taʿallamu* for تتعلّم *tataʿallamu* 'you learn, she learns'.

b) *u*-series:

	3rd m.	f.	2nd m.	f.	1st
Sg.	*yu-*	*tu-*	*tu-*	*tu-* . . . *-ī*	*ʾu-*
Du.	*yu-* . . . *-ā*	*tu-* . . . *-ā*	*tu-* . . . *-ā*	*tu-* . . . *-ā*	—
Pl.	*yu-* . . . *-ū*	*yu-* . . . *-na*	*tu-* . . . *-ū*	*tu-* . . . *-na*	*nu-*

The *u*-series occurs in the active of stems II, III, and IV, as well as in the basic stem of four-radical verbs. In addition, it occurs in the passive of all the verb stems. See the paradigms, pp. 237–258 ff.

Note 2. As a dialect variant, an *i*-series is attested in the *a*-class of the imperfect basis (§216): *ʿalima* 'know' : non-classical imperfect *tiʿlamu* (Cf. §§241.3; 244.3).

§**212.** A distinctive feature of the imperfect in all forms that do not have supplementary suffixes is the *u-* morpheme: يقتل *ya-qtul-u* 'He kills', تقتل *ta-qtul-u* 'She kills', 'you (masc.) kill', أقتل *ʾa-qtul-u* 'I kill', نقتل *na-qtul-u* 'We kill'. The supplementary suffixes *-ī, -ā, -ū* are extended in the imperfect by the addition of *-na/ni* to *-īna, -āni, -ūna*: تقتلين *ta-qtul-īna* 'You (fem. sg.) kill', يقتلان *ya-qtul-āni* 'Both of them kill', تقتلان *ta-qtul-āni* 'Both of them (fem.) kill', both of you kill', يقتلون *ya-qtul-ūna* 'They (masc.) kill, تقتلون *ta-qtul-ūna* 'You (masc. pl.) kill'. The plural feminine forms are: يقتلن *ya-qtul-na* 'They (fem.) kill', تقتلن *ta-qtul-na* 'You (fem.) kill'.

§**213.** The subjunctive is distinguished by the *-a* morpheme. The supplementary suffixes are not extended: يقتل *ya-qtul-a*, تقتل *ta-qtul-a*, تقتلي *ta-qtul-ī*, أقتل *ʾa-qtul-a*, يقتلا *ya-qtul-ā*, تقتلا *ta-qtul-ā*, يقتلوا *ya-qtul-ū*, يقتلن *ya-qtul-na*, تقتلوا *ta-qtul-ū*, نقتل *na-qtul-a*.

§**214.** The jussive is distinguished by the absence of endings. The supplementary suffixes are not extended: يقتل *ya-qtul*, تقتل *ta-qtul*, تقتلي *ta-qtul-ī*, أقتل *ʾa-qtul*, يقتلا *ya-qtul-ā*, تقتلا *ta-qtul-ā*, يقتلوا *ya-qtul-ū*, يقتلن *ya-qtul-na*, تقتلوا *ta-qtul-ū*, تقتلن *ta-qtul-na*, نقتل *na-qtul*.

§**215.** The energetic is distinguished by the *-anna* morpheme (energetic I) or by the *-an* morpheme (energetic II): يقتلنّ *ya-qtul-an(na)*, تقتلنّ *ta-qtul-an(na)*, أقتلنّ *ʾa-qtul-an(na)*, نقتلنّ *na-qtul-an(na)*. The supplementary suffixes *-ī, -ū,* are shortened before *-n(na)*: تقتلنّ *ta-qtul-in(na)*, يقتلنّ *ya-qtul-un(na)*, تقتلنّ *ta-qtul-un(na)*. In the dual, **-ā-ann(a)* becomes *-ānni* without the shortening of *ā*; and in the fem. pl., **-na-ann(a)* becomes *-nānni*: يقتلانّ *ya-qtul-ānni*, تقتلانّ *ta-qtul-ānni*, يقتلنانّ *ya-qtul-nānni*, تقتلنانّ *ta-qtul-nānni*.

> **Note 1.** On the spelling of يقتلن or يقتلا *yaqtulan*, see §11.3. The pausal form is يقتلا *yaqtulā*.

Imperfect Base

§**216.** The imperfect base in the active of the basic stem has three vowel classes: *-fʿal, -fʿil, -fʿul*. Among the vowel classes of the perfect base (§163) and the imperfect base, six combinations are possible:

1st	Perf. *faʿala* : Imperf.	*yafʿulu*	4.	Perf. *faʿila* : Imperf.	*yafʿalu*
2nd	*faʿala* :	*yafʿilu*	5.	*faʿula* :	*yafʿulu*
3rd	*faʿala* :	*yafʿalu*	6.	*faʿila* :	*yafʿilu*

Most verbs of the pattern *faʿala* belong to classes 1 and 2 (see §163). The *a* of the imperfect base of those in class 3 is conditioned by a laryngeal or pharyngeal: قرأ *qaraʾa* (يقرأ *yaqraʾu*) 'read, recite', ذهب *dhahaba* (يذهب *yadhhabu*) 'go away'. The perfect base *faʿila* regularly has the imperfect *yafʿalu* (class 4): شرب *shariba* (يشرب *yashrabu*) 'drink'. Likewise the imperfect *yafʿulu* (class 5) consistently belongs to perfect *faʿula*. Class 6 is represented solely by حسب *ḥasiba* (يحسب *yaḥsibu, yaḥsabu*) 'consider'.

Note 1. The imperfect base can belong to more than one vowel class without any variation in meaning: دبغ *dabagha* (يدبغ *yadbughu, yadbighu, yadbaghu*) 'tan' (hide), نسج *nasaja* (ينسج *yansuju, yansiju*) 'weave'. Sometimes variation in the vowel class makes a distinction in meaning: فصل *faṣala* (يفصل *yafṣilu*) 'separate', فصل *faṣala* (يفصل *yafṣulu*) 'depart'.

Note 2. Frequently with attributive verbs, the imperfect base *u*-class can be conjoined with both *faʿula* and *faʿala*: شحب *shaḥaba* or *shaḥuba* (يشحب *yashḥubu*) 'look sickly'.

Note 3. Not all verbs with a laryngeal or pharyngal as second or third radical belong in the imperfect to the *a*-class: رجع *rajaʿa* (يرجع *yarjiʿu*) 'return', طلع *ṭalaʿa* (يطلع *yaṭluʿu*) 'rise'.

§**217.** a) Verb stems formed with *ta-*, namely, V, VI, and four-radical II, have the same stem form with the vowel sequence *a* - *a* in both perfect and imperfect: Perf. *tafaʿʿala* : Imperf. *ya-tafaʿʿal-u*. See §§167 f.; 175.

b) All other derived stems have the vowel sequence *a* - *i* in the imperfect base: *yu-faʿʿil-u* (II), *ya-nfaʿil-u* (VII), *ya-fʿanlil-u* (four-radical III), etc. Stem IV drops *ʾa-* from the stem after the inflectional prefix: *ʾarsala* 'send': **yu-ʾarsilu* > *yursilu*. Cf. §164 ff.

§**218.** The final double consonant in stems IX, XI, and four-radical IV must be broken up before the supplementary suffix *-na*, beginning with a consonant, and in forms of the jussive without an ending (§208). The imperfect base is then: IX *-fʿalil*, XI *-fʿālil*, four-radical IV *-fʿal$_3$l$_4$il$_4$*: يحمرّ *yaḥmarru* 'he becomes red' : يحمررن *yaḥmarirna*, يصفارّ *yaṣfārru* 'he turns yellow' : يصفاررن *yaṣfārirna*, يطمئنّ *yaṭmaʾinnu* 'he becomes quiet' : يطمأننّ *yaṭmaʾnin-na*. In the jussive forms without an ending, the consonant cluster can be preserved with an auxiliary vowel (§53): يحمرر *yaḥmarir* or يحمرّ *yaḥmarr-i*, etc.

Note 1. Stem XV imperfect *yafʿanlī* follows the category of III-weak verbs with stem final *ī* (§§250 ff.).

Passive

§**219.** Instead of *i/u*, *a* occurs uniformly in the imperfect base of all passive verb forms. All passive forms are inflected with the *u*-series of prefixes (§211 b): يفعل *yafʿa/i/ulu* : passive *yufʿalu* (I), يفعّل *yufaʿʿilu* : passive *yufaʿʿalu* (II), يتفعّل *yatafaʿʿalu* : passive *yutafaʿʿalu* (V), يستفعل *yastafʿilu* : passive *yustafʿalu* (X), etc.

Note 1. As a result of the dropping of prefixed *ʾa-* in stem IV, the passive of the basic stem and stem IV merge: يطعم *yuṭʿamu* 'He was eaten', from طعم *ṭaʿama* (I) 'eat', or 'He was fed', from أطعم *ʾaṭʿama* 'feed' (IV).

Imperative

§**220.** a) The imperfect base without prefix functions as the imperative of the masculine singular. The feminine is marked by *-ī*, the dual by *-ā*, the plural by *-ū*, the feminine plural by *-na* : قاتل *qātala* (يقاتل *yu-qātil-u*) 'fight': *qātil* 'Fight!', fem. قاتلي *qātilī*, masc. pl. قاتلوا *qātilū*, fem. قاتلن *qātilna*; تفكّر *tafakkara* (يتفكّر *ya-tafakkar-u*) 'think' : *tafakkar* 'Think!', fem. تفكّري *tafakkarī*, masc. pl. تفكّروا *tafakkarū*, fem. تفكّرن *tafakkarna*. The prefix *-ʾa* of stem IV is retained in the imperative: أرسل *ʾarsala* 'send' (يرسل *yursilu*) : أرسل *ʾarsil* 'Send!', fem. أرسلي *ʾarsilī*, masc. pl. أرسلوا *ʾarsilū*, fem. أرسلن *ʾarsilna*.

b) An auxiliary vowel (§54 b) is inserted before stems beginning with double-consonant clusters. Within a phrase, the auxiliary is dropped (§§19 ff.). The auxiliary is *u* in *u*-series of the basic stem and *i* in all other stems; أكتب (*ʾu*)*ktub* 'Write!' from كتب *kataba* (يكتب *yaktubu*), إفتح (*ʾi*)*ftaḥ* 'Open!' from فتح *fataḥa* (يفتح *yaftaḥu*), إنزل (*ʾi*)*nzil* 'Come down!' from نزل *nazala* (ينزل *yanzilu*), إعترف (*ʾi*)*ʿtarif* 'Confess!' from اعترف (*ʾi*)*ʿtarafa*, استأذن (*ʾi*)*staʾdhin* 'Ask for permission!' from استأذن (*ʾi*)*staʾdhana*.

Note 1. In stems IX, XI, and four-radical IV, stem-final double-consonant clusters in the imperative behave as they do in jussives (§218).

§**221.** a) The imperative can additionally take the energetic ending *-an* (§215): إفتحن (*ʾi*)*ftaḥan* 'Open up!', fem. إفتحن (*ʾi*)*ftaḥin*, masc. pl. إفتحن (*ʾi*)*ftaḥun*.

b) The imperative cannot be negated. The jussive negated with *lā* (§195 b) functions as a negative imperative (prohibition): لا تفتح *lā taftaḥ* 'Do not open!'.

Note 1. Sometimes the particle يا *yā* occurs before the imperative: يآنفر *yā 'nfir* 'Up and into battle!'

§**222.** In combination with *bi-nā* 'with us', the imperative calls for an action: قم بنا *qum binā* 'Stand up with us!', i.e., 'Let's stand up!', أخرجوا بنا (ʾ*u*)*khrujū binā* 'Go out with us!', i.e., 'Let's get out of here!'

Note 1. The jussive appears in the apodosis of an imperative phrase (§412).

Note 2. Occasionally the imperative is expressed with the imperative of كان *kāna* 'be' (§§190 ff.) in combination with the imperfect: فكن أنت تكلّمهم *fa-kun ʾanta tukallimuhum* 'So you speak to them!'.

Note 3. In pre-classical Arabic, the imperative is linked to a preceding emphatic clause with *fa-* (§329): بل الله فاعبد *bal-i 'l-lāha fa-'ʿbud* (Koran 39:66) 'Rather worship God!', وفي مالنا فاحتكم *wa-fī mālinā fa-'ḥtakim* 'And with our property, proceed as you will!'.

Participles

§**223.** The active participle of the three-radical basic stem belongs to the morpheme category *fāʿilun*, fem. *fāʿilatun*. The corresponding passive participle has the morpheme category *mafʿūlun*, fem. *mafʿūlatun*: قاتل *qātilun*, fem. قاتلة *qātilatun* 'killing, having killed', مقتول *maqtūlun*, fem. مقتولة *maqtūlatun* 'killed, one who can (should) be killed'. Participles as a rule form inflected plurals (§§101 f.).

Note 1. See §97 on the plural *fawāʿilu* of *fāʿil(at)un*, and §95.3 on the plural *mafāʿīlun* of *mafʿūlun*.

§**224.** The participles of the derived and four-radical stems are formed from the imperfect base by the addition of the prefix *mu-*. They are inflected as triptotes (§§147 ff.). All stems in the active have the vowel sequence *a* - *i*, in the passive *a* - *a*: II. مفعّل active *mufaʿʿilun*, passive *mufaʿʿalun*; III. مفاعل active *mufāʿilun*, passive *mufāʿalun*; IV. مفعل active *mufʿilun*, passive *mufʿalun*; V. متفعّل active *mutafaʿʿilun* (!), passive *mutafaʿʿalun*; VI. متفاعل active *mutafāʿilun*, passive *mutafāʿalun*; VII. منفعل active *munfaʿilun*, passive *munfaʿalun*; VIII. مفتعل active *muftaʿilun*, passive *muftaʿalun*; X. مستفعل active *mustafʿilun*, passive *mustafʿalun*; four-radical I. مفعلل active *mufaʿ*l_3*i*l_4*un*, passive *mufaʿ*l_3*a*l_4*un*; II. متفعلل active *mutafaʿ*l_3*i*l_4*un*, passive *mutafaʿ*l_3*a*l_4*un*; III. مفعنلل active *mufʿan*l_3*i*l_4*un*, passive *mufʿan*l_3*a*l_4*un*; IV. مفعلّ active *mufʿa*l_3*i*$l_4$$l_4$*un*, passive *mufʿa*$l_3$*a*$l_4$$l_4$*un*.

Note 1. Stems IX and XI form only active participles مفعلّ *mufʿallun*, مفعالّ *mufʿāllun*.

Verbal Substantives

§**225.** The verbal substantive is formed from the perfect base. Where the perfect base exhibits the vowel sequence *a* - *a*, the verbal substantive has *i* - *ā*. The triptotic inflectional endings (§§147 ff.) attach to the stem. I. *faʿala* : *fiʿālun*, e.g., حسب *ḥasaba* 'reckon' : حساب *ḥisābun*, شفى *shafā* 'cure' : شفاء *shifāʾun* (§257 b). This form of the verbal substantive occurs infrequently in the basic stem. Most often the morpheme category *faʿlun* and other categories (§§228 f.) are used.

Note 1. In addition to *fiʿālun*, *faʿālun* occurs: هلك *halaka* 'perish' : هلاك *halākun*, فسد *fasada* 'spoil' : فساد *fasādun*. Without an ending, **faʿāl* > *faʿāli* (§53.2) in pre-classical Arabic is used as a command form: نزال *nazāli* 'Come down!', سماع *samāʿi* 'Listen!' and as a proper name: كساب *Kasābi* 'Fetch!' (a dog's name).

II. *faʿʿala* : *fiʿʿālun*, very rare, e.g., كذّب *kadhdhaba* 'call a liar' : كذّاب *kidhdhābun*. Instead of this form, *tafʿīlun* (§231) is regularly used in form II for the verbal substantive.

III. *fāʿala* : *fiʿālun* (instead of **fīʿālun*): قاتل *qātala* 'fight' : قتال *qitālun*.

Note 2. Because of the semantic ambiguity of the morpheme category *fiʿālun*, the feminine passive participle frequently occurs as a verbal substantive: جادل *jādala* 'quarrel' : مجادلة *mujādalatun* (cf. §230.1).

IV. *ʾafʿala* : *ʾifʿālun*: أكمل *ʾakmala* 'complete': إكمال *ʾikmālun*.

VII. (*ʾi*)*nfaʿala*: انفعال (*ʾi*)*nfiʿālun*.

VIII. (ʾi)*ftaʿala*: افتعال (ʾi)*ftiʿālun*.

IX. (ʾi)*fʿalla*: افعلال (ʾi)*fʿilālun*.

X. (ʾi)*stafʿala*: استفعال (ʾi)*stifʿālun*.

XI. (ʾi)*fʿālla*: افعيلال (ʾi)*fʿīlālun*.

XII. (ʾi)*fʿawʿala*: افعيعال (ʾi)*fʿīʿālun*.

XIII. (ʾi)*fʿawwala*: افعوّال (ʾi)*fʿiwwālun*.

XIV. (ʾi)*fʿanlala*: افعنلال (ʾi)*fʿinlālun*.

XV. (ʾi)*fʿanlā*: افعنلاء (ʾi)*fʿinlāʾun*.

§**226.** Four-radical verbal substantives have the same formation pattern: *faʿ*l_3*a*l_4*a* : *fiʿ*l_3*ā*l_4*un*: زلزل *zalzala* 'shake' : زلزال *zilzālun*. More often the morpheme category *faʿ*l_3*a*l_4*atun* (§75.1) occurs instead.

Note 1. Four-radical *faʿ*l_3*ā*l_4*un*: زلزال *zalzālun* corresponds to the morpheme category *faʿālun* (§225.1).

III. (ʾi)*fʿan*l_3*a*l_4*a*: افعنلال (ʾi)*fʿin*l_3*ā*l_4*un*.

IV. (ʾi)*fʿa*l_3*a*$l_4$$l_4$*a*: افعلال (ʾi)*fʿi*$l_3$$l_4$*ā*$l_4$*un*.

Note 2. *fuʿa*$l_3$$l_4$*ī*$l_4$*atun* occurs also in form IV of four-radical stems: اطمأنّ (ʾi)*ṭmaʾanna* 'become calm' : طمأنينة *ṭumaʾnīnatun* = اطمئنان (ʾi)*ṭmiʾnānun*.

§**227.** Verbal stems formed with *ta*-prefix change the last *a* of the perfect base to *u* in verbal substantives:

V. *tafaʿʿala*: تفعّل *tafaʿʿulun*.

VI. *tafāʿala*: تفاعل *tafāʿulun*.

II. four-radical *tafaʿ*l_3*a*l_4*a*: تفعلل *tafaʿ*l_3*u*l_4*un*.

Note 1. A verbal substantive of stem V *tifiʿʿālun*, which is formed on the *fiʿālun* model, is occasionally attested: تملّق *tamallaqa* 'flatter' : تملّاق *timillāqun*.

§**228.** In the basic stem, abstract substantives of various morpheme categories occur as verbal substantives. The following classes occur commonly:

faʿala : *faʿlun*, e.g.: لمس *lamasa* 'touch' : لمس *lamsun*.

faʿila : *faʿalun*, e.g.: كدر *kadira* 'be turbid' : كدر *kadarun*.

faʿula : *faʿālatun*, e.g.: رذل *ra<u>dh</u>ula* 'be lowly, common' : رذالة *ra<u>dh</u>ālatun*.

faʿ$l_3$al$_4$a : *faʿ$l_3$al$_4$atun*, e.g.: قلقل *qalqala* 'disturb' : قلقلة *qalqalatun*.

Note 1. In roots with *r, l, h, ḥ, <u>gh</u>,* ʿ as the second radical, *faʿlun* frequently becomes *faʿalun*, more rarely *faʿilun*, with the addition of a secondary vowel (§38): طلب *ṭalaba* 'seek' : طلب *ṭalabun* (rather than **ṭalbun*).

§**229.** In addition to the verbal substantives cited thus far, numerous other morpheme categories occur in the basic stem. As verbal substantives they are typically associated with specific semantic groups. The most important types are:

fuʿūlun, motion: دخل *da<u>kh</u>ala* 'enter' : دخول *du<u>kh</u>ūlun*, جلس *jalasa* 'sit up' : جلوس *julūsun*.

faʿīlun, sound and motion: صفر *ṣafara* 'whistle' : صفير *ṣafīrun*, رحل *raḥala* 'depart' : رحيل *raḥīlun*.

fuʿālun, sound: سأل *saʾala* 'ask' : سؤال *suʾālun*, نبح *nabaḥa* 'bark' : نباح *nubāḥun*.

fuʿūlatun, attribution: صعب *ṣaʿuba* 'be difficult' : صعوبة *ṣuʿūbatun*, سهل *sahula* 'be easy' : سهولة *suhūlatun*.

faʿalānun, repetition: خفق *<u>kh</u>afaqa* 'flutter' : خفقان *<u>kh</u>afaqānun*, سجم *sajama* 'shed (tears)' : سجمان *sajamānun*.

fiʿlun, remembering: حفظ *ḥafiẓa* 'preserve, retain in memory' : حفظ *ḥifẓun*, علم *ʿalima* 'know' : علم *ʿilmun*.

Other morpheme categories that occur as verbal substantives are: فعل *fuʿlun*, فعلان *fiʿlānun*, *fuʿlānun*, فعول *faʿūlun*, فعالة *fiʿālatun*.

§**230.** Morpheme categories formed with *ma-* prefix (§78) frequently function as verbal substantives: *maf'alun, maf'ilun, maf'alatun, maf'ilatun, maf'ulatun*, e.g., حمل *ḥamala* 'carry' : محمل *maḥmalun*, قرب *qaruba* 'be near' : مقربة *maqrabatun, maqrubatun*, عرف *'arafa* 'recognize' : معرفة *ma'rifatun*, قدر *qadara* 'possess power' : مقدرة *maqdaratun, maqdiratun, maqduratun*. In the derived verbal stems, the passive participle (§224) also assumes the function of the verbal substantive: أقدم *'aqdama* 'go forward' : مقدم *muqdamun*, انصرف (*'i*)*nṣarafa* 'turn away' منصرف *munṣarafun*.

Note 1. As a rule, in verbal stem III, the feminine singular passive participle is used as a verbal substantive rather than the masculine singular passive participle: خاطب *khāṭaba* 'address' : مخاطبة *mukhāṭabatun*. In pre-classical Arabic, the passive participle of the basic stem is sometimes used also as a verbal substantive: ردّ *radda* 'send back' (§233) : مردود *mardūdun*.

§**231.** Verbal substantives formed with prefixed *ta-/ti-/tu-* are intensive in meaning:

taf'ālun from the basic stem: طلب *ṭalaba* 'seek' : تطلاب *taṭlābun* '(intensive) search'.

taf'īlun, regularly the verbal substantive of form II: علّم *'allama* 'teach': تعليم *ta'līmun*.

Note 1. In III-weak verbs, *taf'ilatun* (§257.2) replaces *taf'īlun*. On occasion, *taf'ilatun* also occurs with other types of roots: جرّب *jarraba* 'test' : تجربة *tajribatun*. cf. also §237.3.

Note 2. Other morpheme categories formed with *ta-/ti-/tu-* occur only rarely: تفعال *tif'ālun*, تفعالة *tif'ālatun*, تفعول *taf'ūlun*, تفعلة *taf'ulatun, tuf'ulatun*. See also §240.3.

Nouns Expressing a Single Action (*Nomen Vicis*)

§**232.** *faʿlun*, etc., with the feminine ending *-at* (cf. §84) indicates an action taken once: ضرب *ḍarbun* 'striking' : ضربة *ḍarbatun* 'one strike, blow', جلوس *julūsun* 'sitting' : جلسة *jalsatun* 'a sitting (court)'. This kind of formation is quite rare in other morpheme categories: تكبيرة *takbīratun* 'one cry of *Allāhu akbar*' from تكبير *takbīrun* (verbal substantive form II).

Note 1. The *nomen vicis* is also used in the dual and plural: ضربتان *ḍarbatāni* 'two blows', ضربات *ḍarabātun* 'several blows' (§105 a).

II-Geminate Verbs (*Verba mediae geminatae*)

§**233.** a) The two like radicals of verbs with identical second and third radicals form a geminate group, unless syllabification requirements break it up (§50.2). The morphologically conditioned vowel between the second and third radicals is omitted if a morpheme vowel precedes: ردّ *radda* 'return' = *faʿala*, ردّوا *raddū* = *faʿalū*, رادّ *rāddun* = *fāʿilun*. The vowel precedes the geminate group if no morpheme vowel precedes: يردّ *yaruddu* = *yafʿulu*, أحبّ *ʾaḥabba* (يحبّ *yuḥibbu*) 'love' = *ʾafʿala* (*yufʿilu*), stem IV.

Note 1. In stems III and VI and in the participle *fāʿilun*, forms based on three-radical root patterns occasionally occur: تشادد *tashādada* and تشادّ *tashādda* 'argue with one another', فارر *fārirun* and فارّ *fārrun* 'fleeing'.

Note 2. In certain cases, stem I *faʿila* and *faʿula* attributive verbs can be formed as three-radical roots: قطط *qaṭiṭa* 'be curly-haired', لبب *labuba* and لبّ *labba* 'be sensible'.

Note 3. Observe in the imperfect of stems VII, VIII, and X the inconsistent behavior of the stem vowel: انردّ (ʾ*i*)*nradda* (ينردّ *yanraddu*) = (ʾ*i*)*nfaʿala* (*yanfaʿilu*), ارتدّ (ʾ*i*)*rtadda* (يرتدّ *yartaddu*) = (ʾ*i*)*ftaʿala* (*yaftaʿilu*), استردّ (ʾ*i*)*staradda* (يستردّ *yastariddu*) = (ʾ*i*)*stafʿala* (*yastafʿilu*).

b) In stems II and V, II-geminate roots are treated as three-radical roots: ردّد *raddada* (يردّد *yuraddidu*) 'repel', تردّد *taraddada* (يتردّد *yataraddadu*) 'be repelled'.

Note 4. In pre-classical Arabic, analogical formations from III-weak verbs (§§250 ff.) occur on occasion: تظنّيت *taẓannaytu* 'I thought' instead of تظنّنت *taẓannantu*, verbal substantive تظنٍّ *taẓannin* instead of تظنّن *taẓannunun*.

§234. Syllable structure breaks up the geminate group if it is not followed by a vowel. Accordingly, morphologically conditioned forms occur before consonantal endings: ردّ *radda* 'return' : رددت *radadtu*, شمّ *shamma* 'smell': شممت *shamimtu* or *shamamtu*, أحبّ *ʾaḥabba* 'love' : أحببت *ʾaḥbabtu* (IV), اغتمّ (ʾi)*ghtamma* 'be distressed' : يغتممن *yaghtamimna* (VIII).

Note 1. In pre-classical Arabic, the geminate group before a consonant suffix in the perfect could be simplified: ظلّ *ẓalla* 'remain' : ظلت *ẓaltu* or *ẓiltu* along with ظللت *ẓaliltu*; أحسّ *ʾaḥassa* 'feel' : أحست *ʾaḥastu* as well as أحسست *ʾaḥsastu* (IV).

Note 2. On rare occasion, analogical formations from the III-weak verb occur: قصّ *qaṣṣa* : قصّيت *qaṣṣaytu* rather than قصصت *qaṣaṣtu*, أحسّ *ʾaḥassa* : أحسيت *ʾaḥsaytu* instead of أحسست *ʾaḥsastu*.

§235. In forms of the prefix conjugation and the imperative that do not have endings, the geminate group is preserved when an auxiliary vowel (§53) is inserted. Otherwise, morphologically conditioned forms occur. Either possibility may occur: Jussive يردّ *yarudd-i* (-*a*/*u*) or يردد *yardud*, يحبّ *yuḥibb-i* (-*a*) or يحبب *yuḥbib*, imperative ردّ *rudd-i* (-*a*/*u*) or اردد (ʾ*u*)*rdud*, أحبّ *ʾaḥibb-i* (-*a*) or أحبب *ʾaḥbib*.

§236. Nominal morpheme categories are likewise treated according to the rules cited in §50. Observe the verbal substantive تسرّة *tasirratun* from سرّ *sarra* = *tafʿilatun* 'be happy', مذمّة *madhammatun* from ذمّ *dhamma* 'blame' = *mafʿalatun*. Should a long vowel appear between the second and third radicals, II-geminate roots are treated as three-radical roots: قرار *qarārun* from قرّ *qarra* 'dwell', تأنان *taʾnānun* from أنّ *ʾanna* 'groan'. The same is true for verbal substantives of the derived verb stems: ترديد *tardīdun* (II), رداد *ridādun* (III), إرداد *ʾirdādun* (IV), انرداد (ʾ*i*)*nridādun* (VII), etc.

Note 1. Frequently, *faʿlun* with the preservation of the geminate group occurs alongside *faʿalun* (§50): بحّ *baḥḥun* and بحح *baḥaḥun* from بحّ *baḥḥa* 'be hoarse'.

Verbs with Weak Radicals

Verbs with *hamzah*

§**237.** Verbs from roots with ʾ (*hamzah*) as the first, second, or third radical for the most part exhibit no variation from the inflectional forms of the three-radical verb. In verbs with I-ʾ the rule of dissimilation of the sequence ʾ—ʾ (§40) is in effect for the 1st. sg. imperfect of stems I and IV and for perfect and verbal substantive of stem IV: أذن *ʾa<u>dh</u>ina* 'allow' : imperfect 1st. sg. آذن *ʾā<u>dh</u>anu*, but يأذن *yaʾ<u>dh</u>anu*; stem IV: آمن *ʾāmana* < *ʾaʾmana* 'believe', imperfect 1st. sg. أومن *ʾūminu*, but يؤمن *yuʾminu*, verbal substantive إيمان *ʾīmānun* < *ʾiʾmānun*.

Note 1. Forms beginning with *alif al-waṣl* (§§19 ff.) undergo dissimilation only in initial position forms. See §40.1. Note the spelling of imperative forms after و *wa-* and ف *fa-*: أوجر *ʾūjur* (< (*ʾu*)*ʾjur*) 'reward!': وأجر *wa-ʾjur*, إيتلف *ʾītalif* (< (*ʾi*)*ʾtalif*) 'unite!': وآئتلف or وأتلف *wa-ʾtalif*.

Note 2. See §§247.1; 41 concerning dissimilation of ʾ—ʾ in II-weak verbs with ʾ as the first or third radical.

Note 3. In non-classical Arabic, III-ʾ verbs usually merge with III-weak verbs. Non-classical forms sometimes enter classical texts, e.g., نبّى *nabbā* (ينبّي *yunabbī*) in place of نبّأ *nabbaʾa* (ينبّئ *yunabbiʾu*) 'inform'. In such cases, the verbal substantive *tafʿilatun* (§257.2) is written in a classicizing manner with ʾ: *tanbiʾatun* = *tanbiyatun*.

§**238.** I-ʾ verbs exhibit the following alternative formations: The imperatives of أخذ *ʾa<u>kh</u>a<u>dh</u>a* 'take', أكل *ʾakala* 'eat', أمر *ʾamara* 'order' are: خذ *<u>kh</u>u<u>dh</u>*, كل *kul*, مر *mur*. أخذ *ʾa<u>kh</u>a<u>dh</u>a* forms verbal stem VIII like I-*w* verbs (§242 b): اتّخذ (*ʾi*)*tta<u>kh</u>a<u>dh</u>a* 'assume'. In addition to إيتزر *ʾītazara* ((*ʾi*)*ʾtazara* §40.1) 'wrap oneself in an *izār*', اتّزر (*ʾi*)*ttazara* also occurs.

Note 1. A three-radical imperative form of أمر *ʾamara* also occurs after و *wa-*: وأمر *wa-ʾmur*, in addition to ومر *wa-mur* 'and order!'.

§**239.** *Hamzah* in the very frequently occurring verbs سأل *sa'ala* 'ask' and رأى *ra'ā* 'see, look' is elided:

a) *sa'ala*: Imperative سل *sal*, fem. سلي *salī* and regular اسأل (*'i*)*s'al*, jussive يسل *yasal* and يسأل *yas'al*.

b) *ra'ā* (§42) in the prefix conjugation: أرى *'arā*, يرى *yarā*, jussive ير *yara*, imperative ره *rah* (§240 b), fem. ري *ray*, pl. روا *raw*, fem. رين *rayna*; also, in all forms of verbal stem IV: perfect أرى *'arā* 'show', passive أري *'uriya*, imperfect يري *yurī*, jussive ير *yuri*, imperative أر *'ari*; imperfect passive (stems I and IV) يرى *yurā*. The inflection follows otherwise that of III-weak verbs (§§250 ff.). See the paradigms, p. 245.

Note 1. In poetry, forms like يرأى *yar'ā* are occasionally encountered. Conversely, ' can more often be found elided. Note cases like سال *sāla* 'he asked' < *sa'ala*.

Note 2. Of **'al'aka* 'send', only the imperative ألك *'alik* < **'al'ik* exists.

Note 3. All other verbs with ' exhibit stable ' in classical Arabic, e.g., وأى *wa'ā* (يأي *ya'ī*, 1st. sing. أءي *'a'ī*) 'promise' (§240 b).

I-Weak Verbs (*Verba primae infirmae*)

§**240.** a) In the basic stem, most I-*w* verbs form the imperfect base (active) without *w*: وجد *wajada* 'find' : يجد *ya-jid-u*, وضع *waḍa'a* 'put down' : يضع *ya-ḍa'-u*, وطئ *waṭi'a* 'step' : يطأ *ya-ṭa'-u*, وثق *wathiqa* 'rely' : يثق *ya-thiq-u*. Otherwise, the inflection corresponds to that of three-radical verbs. See paradigms, p. 244.

Note 1. The imperfect passive is formed from the *w* stem: يوجد *yūjadu* (= *yuwjadu*) 'he is found'.

Note 2. ودع *wada'a* (يدع *yada'u*) 'let' usually occurs only in the prefix conjugation: Jussive يدع *yada'*, imperative دع *da'*. Thus, يذر *yadharu*, which is found exclusively in the prefix conjugation, jussive يذر *yadhar*, imperative ذر *dhar*, is classed as if it belonged to a root **w-dh-r*. The imperative عم *'im*, which occurs in the formula عم صباحا *'im ṣabāḥan* 'Good morning!', is actually an abbreviation of أنعم صباحا *'an'im ṣabāḥan* (root *n-'-m*).

b) Some verbs are both I-*w* and III-*y*: وقى *waqā* 'guard' : imperfect يقي *yaqī*, jussive يق *yaqi*; ولي *waliya* 'be near', imperfect يلي *yalī*, jussive يل *yali*. To avoid the short forms *qi, li*, the imperative of such verbs always appears in the pausal form (§55): قه *qih*, له *lih*; but feminine قي *qī*, لي *lī*, etc. Otherwise, they are inflected like III-*y* verbs (§§250 ff.).

c) The imperfect base without *w* is used to form verbal substantives: ثقة *thiqatun* from وثق *wathiqa* (يثق *yathiqu*) 'rely', سعة *sa'atun* from وسع *wasi'a* (يسع *yasa'u*) 'be wide', شية *shiyatun* from وشى *washā* (يشي *yashī*) 'embellish'.

Note 3. In some verbal substantives, *tu-* appears in place of *w*: تراث *turāthun* 'inheritance' from ورث *waritha* (يرث *yarithu*) 'inherit', تخمة *tukhamatun* 'indigestion' from وخم *wakhima* (يخم *yakhimu*) 'suffer from indigestion'.

§**241.** A few verbs in the category *fa'ila* and all in the category *fa'ula* preserve *w* in the imperfect: وجل *wajila* 'be afraid' : يوجل *yawjalu*, وضؤ *waḍu'a* 'be pure' : يوضؤ *yawḍu'u*. According to §33 a, the imperative becomes إيجل *'ījal* < *('i)wjal.

Note 1. Some I-*w* verbs have both types of imperfect: وحم *waḥima* 'have a craving' : يحم *yaḥimu* or يوحم *yawḥamu*.

Note 2. All I-*w*/II-geminate verbs have stable *w*: ودّ *wadda* 'like' : imperfect يودّ *yawaddu*, jussive يودّ *yawadd-i* or يودد *yawdad*, imperative ودّ *wadd-i* or إيدد *'īdad* < *('i)wdad.

Note 3. **tiw* became *tī* with the *i*-series of the personal prefixes (§211.2): تيجل *tījalu* 'You are afraid'. When such forms make their way into literature, their vocalization is frequently classicized: تيجل *tayjalu*. Isolated occurrences of the pre-classical imperfect type ياجل *yājalu* are attested.

§**242.** a) The derived verbal stems are formed like three-radical verbs. When the sequence *iw* occurs, it must become *iy* = *ī*: أوقع *'awqa'a* (يوقع *yūqi'u* = *yuwqi'u*) 'let fall': Verbal substantive إيقاع *'īqā'un* (IV), استودع *('i)stawda'a* (يستودع *yastawdi'u*) 'deposit': Verbal substantive استيداع *('i)stīdā'un* (X), **('i)wraqqa* > إيرقّ *'īraqqa* (يورقّ *yawraqqu*) 'turn ashen' (IX).

b) In verbal stem VIII, *tt* replaces **wt-*: اتّسع (ʾ*i*)*ttasaʿa* 'expand' (يتّسع *yattasiʿu*) (root *w-s-ʿ*), اتّفق (ʾ*i*)*ttafaqa* (يتّفق *yattafiqu*) 'agree' (root *w-f-q*).

Note 1. See §238 concerning اتّخذ (ʾ*i*)*tta<u>kh</u>a<u>dh</u>a* (root ʾ*-<u>kh</u>-<u>dh</u>*) and اتّزر (ʾ*i*)*ttazara* (root ʾ*-z-r*).

Note 2. In the basic stem, back-formations with I-*t* from verbal stem VIII can occur: تقى *taqā* (يتقي *yatqī*) 'be pious' from اتّقى (ʾ*i*)*ttaqā* 'fear (God)' (root *w-q-y*).

§**243.** I-*y* verbs are inflected like three-radical verbs: يقظ *yaqiẓa* 'be awake' : imperfect ييقظ *yayqaẓu*. The sequence *uy* must become *uw* = *ū* (§33 b): أيقظ ʾ*ayqaẓa* 'wake up' : imperfect يوقظ *yūqiẓu*, passive يوقظ *yūqaẓu*, verbal substantive إيقاظ ʾ*īqāẓun* (IV). Stem VIII of the root *y-s-r* is formed as if it were a I-*w* root: اتّسر (ʾ*i*)*ttasara* (يتّسر *yattasiru*) 'draw lots'.

II-Weak Verbs (*Verba mediae infirmae*)

§**244.** Verbs with II-*w* and -*y* have a long vowel in place of the second radical. In the basic stem there are three classes of vowels:

II – *w*	1. قام *qāma* 'stand',	1st sg. قمت *qumtu* :	imperf. يقوم *yaqūmu*
	2. نام *nāma* 'sleep',	1st sg. نمت *nimtu* :	imperf. ينام *yanāmu*
II – *y*	حار *ḥāra* 'confused',	1st sg. حرت *ḥirtu* :	imperf. يحار *yaḥāru*
	3. صار *ṣāra* 'become',	1st sg. صرت *ṣirtu* :	imperf. يصير *yaṣīru*

The perfect base exhibits the vowel alternation *ā* : *u/i*, which occurs only in the basic stem. Stems with long vowels (*ā*) occur before vocalic inflectional suffixes: قام *qāma*, قامت *qāmat*, قاما *qāmā*, قامتا *qāmatā*, قاموا *qāmū*. Stems with short vowels (*qum-*, *nim-*, *ḥir-*, *ṣir-*) occur before consonantal suffixes: قمت *qumta*, نمتم *nimtum*, حرنا *ḥirnā*, صرن *ṣirna*, etc. In the prefix conjugation, the long vowel stem also occurs before vocalic endings: يقومون *yaqūmūna*, يصير *yaṣīra*, etc. The stem vowel is shortened (§52) before the consonantal ending *-na* (fem. pl.) and in forms without endings (jussive, imperative): يقمن *yaqumna*, ينمن *yanamna*, يحرن *yaḥarna*, يصرن

yaṣirna, قم *qum*, نم *nam*, حر *ḥar*, صر *ṣir*, but feminine قومي *qūmī*, نامي *nāmī*, etc. See the paradigms, pp. 246 ff.

Note 1. In addition to jussive يكن *yakun* from كان *kāna* (يكون *yakūnu*) 'be', there is a short form يك *yaku*, which, however, cannot be used before the article (ʾ*a*)*l*- (§142).

Note 2. مات *māta* (يموت *yamūtu*) 'die' has a short-vowel perfect base *mit*- and *mut*-: متّ *mitta* or متّ *mutta*.

Note 3. اخال *ikhālu* (only in the 1st sing.) from خال *khāla* (يخال *yakhālu*) 'fancy, believe' originates from a dialect variant *i*-series of personal prefixes (§211.2).

§**245.** a) In the derived verbal stems with long vowels, there is no difference between II-*w* and II-*y*. There is no vowel alternation in the perfect base:

IV:	perf.	أقام	ʾ*aqāma*	1st sing.	أقمت	ʾ*aqamtu*
	imperf.	يقيم	*yuqīmu*	imperat.	أقم	ʾ*aqim*
X:	perf.	استقام	(ʾ*i*)*staqāma*	1st sing.	استقمت	(ʾ*i*)*staqamtu*
	imperf.	يستقيم	*yastaqīmu*	imperat.	استقم	(ʾ*i*)*staqim*
VII:	perf.	انقام	(ʾ*i*)*nqāma*	1st sing.	انقمت	(ʾ*i*)*nqamtu*
	imperf.	ينقام	*yanqāmu*	imperat.	انقم	(ʾ*i*)*nqam*
VIII:	perf.	اقتام	(ʾ*i*)*qtāma*	1st sing.	اقتمت	(ʾ*i*)*qtamtu*
	imperf.	يقتام	*yaqtāmu*	imperat.	اقتم	(ʾ*i*)*qtam*

Note 1. The distribution of vowels in the imperfect base conforms to that of the corresponding stems of II-geminate verbs (§233.3).

Note 2. See §49 b concerning اسطاع (ʾ*i*)*sṭāʿa* (يسطيع *yasṭīʿu*) 'be in a position to' in addition to استطاع (ʾ*i*)*staṭāʿa* and اسطال (ʾ*i*)*sṭāla* (يسطيل *yasṭīlu*) 'become long' in addition to استطال (ʾ*i*)*staṭāla*.

b) In verbal stems II, III, V, VI, and IX, *w* and *y* behave like consonants: قوّم *qawwama* (يقوّم *yuqawwimu*) 'set right', صيّر *ṣayyara* (يصيّر *yuṣayyiru*) 'induce' (II); قاوم *qāwama* (يقاوم *yuqāwimu*) 'resist', لاين *lāyana* (يلاين *yulāyinu*) 'treat with kindness' (III), etc.; اسودّ (ʾ*i*)*swadda* (يسودّ *yaswaddu*) 'become black', ابيضّ (ʾ*i*)*byaḍḍa* (يبيضّ *yabyaḍḍu*) 'become white' (IX). The inflection corresponds to that of three-radical "strong" verbs.

Note 3. Formations with consonantal *w* or *y* also exist in other verbal stems. They are regularly denominal in origin: عوج *ʿawija* (يعوج *yaʿwaju*) 'be crooked' (I), أحوج *ʾaḥwaja* (يحوج *yuḥwiju*) 'require' (IV), استصوب (*ʾi*)*staṣwaba* (يستصوب *yastaṣwibu*) 'approve of' (X). Cf. §68.1.

§**246.** By analogy with *fuʿila* : *yufʿalu*, the passive of long vowel stems has *ī/i* in the perfect base and *ā/a* in the imperfect base: قيم *qīma* (يقام *yuqāmu*), نيم *nīma* (ينام *yunāmu*), صير *ṣīra* (يصار *yuṣāru*), jussive يقم *yuqam*, etc. The prefixed morphemes in the perfect are taken from the *u* of *fuʿila*: أقيم *ʾuqīma* (يقام *yuqāmu*) IV, انقيد (*ʾu*)*nqīda* ينقاد *yunqādu* VII, استقيم (*ʾu*)*stuqīma* (يستقام *yustaqāmu*) X.

Note 1. Verbal stems II, III, V, VI form the passive as three-radical morpheme categories (§§210; 219): قوّم *quwwima*, قووم *qūwima* (§28.2), تقوّم *tuquwwima*, تقووم *tuqūwima*.

Note 2. Instead of (*ʾu*)*nqīda*, (*ʾu*)*qtīda* with auxiliary vowel *u* in verbal stems VII and VIII, the auxiliary vowel can be *i*: (*ʾi*)*nqīda*, (*ʾi*)*qtīda*.

Note 3. In poetry, non-classical perfect forms with *ū/u* instead of *ī/i* occasionally occur: قول *qūla*, 'was said', اختور (*ʾu*)*k͟htūra* 'was chosen' (VIII of root *k͟h-y-r*).

§**247.** a) The active participle (§223) has the morpheme sequence *ā-i*, with *ʾ* in between, in place of the stem vowel: قائم *qāʾimun*, نائم *nāʾimun*, حائر *ḥāʾirun*, صائر *ṣāʾirun*. In the passive participle, which has *ma-* (§223) prefixed to the stem, the stem vowel varies — it is *ū* in II-*w* verbs and *ī* in II-*y* verbs: مقود *maqūdun* from قاد *qāda* (يقود *yaqūdu*) 'lead', مخوف *mak͟hūfun* from خاف *k͟hāfa* (يخاف *yak͟hāfu*) 'fear', مبيع *mabīʿun* from باع *bāʿa* (يبيع *yabīʿu*) 'sell'.

Note 1. In I- and III-ʾ verbs, the ʾ—ʾ sequence in the active participle is dissimilated (§41): آيب *ʾāyibun* from آب *ʾāba* (يؤوب *yaʾūbu*) 'return', جاء *jāʾin* (< **jāʾiyun* < **jāʾiʾun*) from جاء *jāʾa* (يجيء *yajīʾu*) 'come'.

Note 2. In II-*y* verbs, the passive participle *mafʿūlun* appears occasionally with consonantal *y*: مبيوع *mabyūʿun* 'sold'.

b) In the derived stems, participles are formed according to §224 from the imperfect base: مقوّم *muqawwimun, muqawwamun* (II), مقيم *muqīmun,* مقام *muqāmun* (IV), منقام *munqāmun* (VII, active and passive!), etc.

§**248.** a) Radical *w* and *y* appear in verbal substantives *faʿlun, faʿlatun*: قود *qawdun,* نوم *nawmun,* خوف *khawfun,* حيرة *ḥayratun,* صير *ṣayrun.*

Note 1. *faylūlatun* is a morpheme category that occurs only in II-weak roots as a verbal substantive of the basic stem: ديمومة *daymūmatun* from دام *dāma* (يدوم *yadūmu*) 'last', بينونة *baynūnatun* from بان *bāna* (يبين *yabīnu*) 'part, separate'.

b) Verbal substantive *fiʿālun* of II-*w* roots also has *y* as the second radical (§33 a): قيام *qiyāmun,* نيام *niyāmun.* By analogy, verbal substantives of stems VII and VIII follow the same pattern: انقيام *(ʾi)nqiyāmun,* اقتيام *(ʾi)qtiyāmun.* In verb stems IV and X, the morpheme pattern *i-ā* is distributed over prefix and stem, to which, in addition, the feminine ending *-atun* is attached: إقامة *ʾiqāmatun,* استقامة *(ʾi)stiqāmatun.*

Note 2. Rarely occurring are verbal substantives of stems IV and X lacking *-atun*: إقام *ʾiqāmun,* استقام *(ʾi)stiqāmun.*

Note 3. Verbal substantives formed with prefixed *ma-* (§230) have the stem vowel *ā*, or frequently with II-*y* roots, *ī*: ملام *malāmun,* ملامة *malāmatun* from لام *lāma* (يلوم *yalūmu*) 'blame', معاش *maʿāshun,* معيش *maʿīshun,* معيشة *maʿīshatun* from عاش *ʿāsha* (يعيش *yaʿīshu*) 'live'.

c) Verb stems with consonantal *w* or *y* form verbal substantives according to the three-radical morpheme category: تقويم *taqwīmun,* تصيير *taṣyīrun* (II), قوام *qiwāmun* (III), تقوّم *taqawwumun* (V), اسوداد *(ʾi)swidādun,* ابيضاض *(ʾi)byiḍāḍun* (IX).

Note 4. Note the distinction: *qiyāmun* = *fiʿālun* from the basic stem and *qiwāmun* = *fiʿālun* from verb stem III.

§**249.** هراق *harāqa* 'pour, shed' (§178 b) is inflected in the following manner: Perf. 1st sing. هرقت *haraqtu,* pass. هريق *hurīqa,* هرقت *huriqtu;* imperf. يهريق *yuharīqu, yuhrīqu,* juss. يهرق *yuhriq,* pass. يهراق *yuharāqu, yuhrāqu;* active part. مهريق *muharīqun, muhrīqun,* pass. مهراق *muharāqun,* *muhrāqun*; verbal substantive هراقة *hirāqatun*, إهراقة *ʾihrāqatun*. Derived from the latter form are the secondary perfect forms: أهراق *ʾahrāqa*, pass. أهريق *ʾuhrīqa*.

III-Weak Verbs (*Verba tertiae infirmae*)

§**250.** III-*w* and -*y* verbs have a long vowel in place of the third radical. The six classes of vowel combinations of the basic stem correspond to those of the three-radical verb (§216):

1. *faʿala* — *yafʿulu*: دعا *daʿā* — يدعو *yadʿū* 'call' (§10) III-*w*
2. *faʿala* — *yafʿilu*: رمى *ramā* — يرمي *yarmī* 'throw' III-*y*
3. *faʿala* — *yafʿalu*: سعى *saʿā* — يسعى *yasʿā* 'run' III-*y*
4. *faʿila* — *yafʿalu*: لقي *laqiya* — يلقى *yalqā* 'meet' III-*y*
5. *faʿula* — *yafʿulu*: سرو *saruwa* — يسرو *yasrū* 'be noble' III-*w*
6. *faʿila* — *yafʿilu*: ولي *waliya* — يلي *yalī* 'be near' (§240 b) III-*y*

§**251.** The derived verb stems, except for stems V and VI, which belong to the third class, belong to the second class: غنّى *ghannā* (يغنّي *yughannī*) 'sing' (II), لاقى *lāqā* (يلاقي *yulāqī*) 'meet' (III), أهدى *ʾahdā* (يهدي *yuhdī*) 'give' (IV), تلقّى *talaqqā* (يتلقّى *yatalaqqā*) 'receive' (V), تلاقى *talāqā* (يتلاقى *yatalāqā*) 'get together' (VI), انجلى (*ʾi*)*njalā* (ينجلي *yanjalī*) 'reveal oneself' (VII), التقى (*ʾi*)*ltaqā* (يلتقي *yaltaqī*) 'meet' (VIII), استولى (*ʾi*)*stawlā* (يستولي *yastawlī*) 'take possession of' (X), احلولى (*ʾi*)*ḥlawlā* (يحلولي *yaḥlawlī*) 'be sweet' (XII).

Note 1. There are no verb stems IX or XI. Instead, there are occasional alternative formations (§178 a): ارعوى (*ʾi*)*rʿawā* (يرعوي *yarʿawī*) 'watch'.

Note 2. Verb stem XV (*ʾi*)*fʿanlā* (*yafʿanlī*) is inflected according the second class (§173).

Note 3. Four-radical verb stems of IV-weak verbs correspond to three-radical derived stems: سلقى *salqā* (يسلقي *yusalqī*) (§162.3) 'overturn' (I), تسلقى *tasalqā* (يتسلقى *yatasalqā*) 'fall onto the back' (II), اسلنقى (*ʾi*)*slanqā* (يسلنقي *yaslanqī*) 'fall onto the back' (III).

§**252.** The vocalic stem ending undergoes complex variation (cf. §§34; 35 a) as a result of the addition of inflectional suffixes:

a) *u* and *i* merge into the stem vowel, while *a* merges only into -*ā*, but not into -*ū* and -*ī*: subjunctive يرمي *yarmiya*, يدعو *yadʿuwa*, but يلقى *yalqā*. 3rd pers. fem. sing. *-*āt* must be shortened: رمت *ramat*, دعت *daʿat*, but لقيت *laqiyat*, سروت *saruwat*; by analogy, 3rd dual fem. رمتا *ramatā*, دعتا *daʿatā*, لقيتا *laqiyatā*, سروتا *saruwatā*.

b) Before consonantal suffixes and before -*ā* (-*āni*), the stem ending is treated consonantally: *ī* = *iy*, *ū* = *uw*, *ā* becomes *ay* or *aw*, depending on whether the root is III-*y* or III-*w*: perf. رميت *ramayta*, -*ti*, -*tu*, etc., دعونا *daʿawnā*, دعون *daʿawna*; لقيت *laqīta* (= *laqiyta*), سروت *sarūta* (= *saruwta*); imperf. fem. pl. يرمين *yarmīna* (= *yarmiy-na*), يدعون *yadʿūna* (= *yadʿuw-na*), يلقين *yalqayna*; dual رميا *ramayā*, دعوا *daʿawā*, لقيا *laqiyā*, سروا *saruwā*; يرميان *yarmiyāni*, يدعوان *yadʿuwāni*, يلقيان *yalqayāni*.

c) -*ū*, -*ī*, -*ūna*, -*īna* undergo the following contractions when vocalic suffixes are added: *ā* - *ū* > *aw*, *ā* - *ī* > *ay*: perf. رموا *ramaw*, دعوا *daʿaw*; imperf. يلقون *yalqawna*, تلقين *talqayna*. In the following contractions *ī* - *ī* > *ī*, *ū* - *ū* > *ū* and *ī* - *ū* > *ū*, *ū* - *ī* > *ī*, the suffix vowel prevails: perf. لقوا *laqū*, سروا *sarū*; imperf. يرمون *yarmūna*, يدعون *yadʿūna*, يسرون *yasrūna*; ترمين *tarmīna*, تدعين *tadʿīna*, تسرين *tasrīna*.

§253. a) The subjunctive ending -*a* is added to the imperfect base: يرمي *yarmiya*, يدعو *yadʿuwa*, but يلقى *yalqā* (§252 a). The supplementary suffixes lose -*na*, -*ni*: يرموا *yarmū*, ترمي *tarmī*, يرميا *yarmiyā*; يدعوا *yadʿū*, تدعي *tadʿī*, يدعوا *yadʿuwā*, يلقوا *yalqaw*, تلقي *talqay*, يلقيا *yalqayā*. The ending -*na* of the fem. pl. is not dropped: يرمين *yarmīna*, يدعون *yadʿūna*, يلقين *yalqayna* (like the imperf.).

b) The jussive's lack of endings is represented in III-weak verbs by a shortening of the stem vowel: يرم *yarmi*, يدع *yadʿu*, يلق *yalqa*, يسر *yasru*, يغنّ *yughanni* (II), يتلقّ *yatalaqqa* (V). Forms with supplementary suffixes are identical to those of the subjunctive.

c) The imperative has the endings of the 2nd person jussive: ارم (ʾi)rmi, fem. ارمي (ʾi)rmī, pl. ارموا (ʾi)rmū, fem. ارمين (ʾi)rmīna; ادع (ʾu)dʿu, fem. ادعي (ʾu)dʿī, pl. ادعوا (ʾu)dʿū, fem. ادعون (ʾu)dʿūna; الق (ʾi)lqa, fem. القي (ʾi)lqay, pl. القوا (ʾi)lqaw, fem. القين (ʾi)lqayna; غنّ ghanni, غنّي ghannī, etc. (II), تلقّ talaqqa, fem. تلقّي talaqqay, etc. (V).

§**254.** The energetic forms (§215) are: يرمين yarmiyan(na), 2nd fem. ترمنّ tarminna, pl. يرمنّ yarmunna, fem. يرميناّن yarmīnānni; يدعون yadʿuwan(na), 2nd fem. تدعنّ tadʿinna, pl. يدعنّ yadʿunna, fem. يدعوناّن yadʿūnānni; يلقين yalqayan(na), 2nd fem. تلقينّ talqayinna, pl. يلقونّ yalqawunna, fem. يلقيناّن yalqaynānni.

§**255.** The passive is formed according to morpheme category fuʿila : yufʿalu: رمي rumiya (يرمى yurmā), دعي duʿiya (يدعى yudʿā), لقي luqiya (يلقى yulqā); stem III لوقي lūqiya (يلاقى yulāqā), stem IV أهدي ʾuhdiya, (يهدى yuhdā), etc. The inflection follows the pattern of the fourth vowel class (§250).

> **Note 1.** In poetry, there are also forms in the category fuʿla (§210.1): رمى rumā, fem. رمت rumat; رمّى rummā, fem. رمّت rummat (II).

§**256.** The phonological rules in §252 hold for nominal stems ending in -ī, -ā. When the sign of indefiniteness -n is added, the final long vowel of the stem must be shortened. Cf. §§154 f. on the inflection.

a) rāmī, dāʿī, lāqī correspond to the active participle category fāʿil-: رام rāmin, fem. رامية rāmiyatun, داع dāʿin, fem. داعية dāʿiyatun, لاق lāqin, fem. لاقية lāqiyatun.

b) The passive participle mafʿūlun is formed with consonantal w or y: مدعوّ madʿūwun, مرميّ marmīyun (< *marmūyun §33 b).

> **Note 1.** On occasion, mafʿūlun of III-w roots is formed with y: مدعيّ madʿīyun instead of madʿūwun.

c) All derived verb stems have stem-final -ī in the active participle and -ā in the passive participle: مغنّ mughannin, fem. مغنّية mughanniyatun 'singing', مغنّى mughannan, fem. مغنّاة mughannātun 'sung' (II); مهد muhdin 'giving', مهدى muhdan 'given' (IV), etc.

§**257.** The rules followed in the formation of III-weak roots (§69) hold for verbal substantives.

a) In morpheme categories *faʿlun, fiʿlānun*, and the like, consonantal *w* or *y* appears: رمي *ramyun*, دعوة *daʿwatun*, نسيان *nisyānun* from نسي *nasiya* (ينسى *yansā*) 'forget'. For *fuʿlun* and *fiʿlun*, usually *fiʿalun, fuʿalun* occur with a vocalic stem-ending: رضى *riḍan* from رضي *raḍiya* (يرضى *yarḍā*) 'be satisfied', هدى *hudan* from هدى *hadā* (يهدي *yahdī*) 'lead on the right way'. In the same way, morpheme category *faʿalatun* occurs in place of *faʿlatun*: نجاة *najātun* from نجا *najā* (ينجو *yanjū*) 'escape' (§60.3).

Note 1. *fuʿūlun* is formed with radical *w* or *y*: صفوّ *ṣufūwun* from صفا *ṣafā* (يصفو *yaṣfū*) 'be pure', هويّ *huwīyun* (< **huwūyun* §33 b) from هوى *hawā* (يهوي *yahwī*) 'fall'.

b) Morpheme categories with *-ā* in the second syllable, *faʿālun, fiʿālun*, etc., have ʾ before the inflectional ending (§69 b): بقاء *baqāʾun* from بقي *baqiya* (يبقى *yabqā*) 'remain'. The forms of verbal substantives of the derived stems correspond: لقاء *liqāʾun* (III), إهداء *ʾihdāʾun* (IV), انجلاء (ʾ*i*)*njilāʾun* (VII), التقاء (ʾ*i*)*ltiqāʾun* (VIII), استيلاء (ʾ*i*)*stīlāʾun* (X), etc. According to §33 b, verb stems V and VI have تلقّ *talaqqin* (*talaqqī-* < **talaqquy*), ترام *tarāmin*.

Note 2. The verbal substantive of stem II is formed like *tafʿilatun* rather than *tafʿīlun*: تغنية *taghniyatun*.

Note 3. Verbal substantives formed with the prefix *ma-* occur as *mafʿalun, mafʿalatun, mafʿilatun*: منجى *manjan*, منجاة *manjātun* from *najā* 'escape', معصية *maʿṣiyatun* from عصى *ʿaṣā* (يعصي *yaʿṣī*) 'disobey'.

III-Weak—II-Weak Verbs (*Verba tertiae et mediae infirmae*)

§**258.** a) *w* in II-*w*–III-weak verbs is always treated consonantally: روى *rawā* (يروي *yarwī*) 'give to drink, water', روي *rawiya* (يروى *yarwā*) 'drink one's fill'. In verbal substantives in the category *faʿlun*, **wy* becomes *yy* (§33 c): ريّ *rayyun*.

b) II-*y*–III-weak verbs in the basic stem can be treated either as III-weak or as II-geminate verbs: حيي *ḥayiya* (يحيا *yaḥyā*) or حيّ *ḥayya* (يحيّ *yaḥayyu*) 'live', عيي *ʿayiya* (يعيا *yaʿyā*) or عيّ *ʿayya* (يعيّ *yaʿayyu*) 'be incapable'. In the derived stems, all forms are constructed like III-weak verbs: stem IV أحيا *ʾaḥyā* (يحيي *yuḥyī*), 'lend life', أعيا *ʾaʿyā* (يعيي *yuʿyī*) 'incapacitate'.

Note 1. Stem II حيّا *ḥayyā* (يحيّي *yuḥayyī*) 'greet' forms its verbal substantive like a II-geminate verb (§236): تحيّة *taḥiyyatun*.

Note 2. In addition to استحيا (*ʾi*)*staḥyā* (يستحيي *yastaḥyī*) 'be ashamed' (X), a shortened form occurs: استحا (*ʾi*)*staḥā* (يستحي *yastaḥī*).

Emphatic Qualification

§259. The words نعم *niʿma* 'What a wonderful...', بئس *biʾsa* 'What an evil...', as well as several words in the morpheme category *faʿla, fuʿla* (*faʿula*) (§262) are used for emphatic qualification. That which is qualified always follows in the nominative and is determined by the article, although the entire phrase is considered indefinite: نعم الرّجل *niʿma 'r-rajulu* 'What a wonderful man!', 'a wonderful man to be sure!', بئس النّساء *biʾsa 'n-nisāʾu* 'What evil women!', 'bad women for sure!'.

Note 1. Occasionally, feminine نعمت *niʿmat*, بئست *biʾsat* are formed and come before feminine terms: نعمت المرأة *niʿmat-i 'l-marʾatu* 'What a perfect woman', in addition to normal نعم المرأة *niʿma 'l-marʾatu*.

§260. The invariable formula *niʿma* (*biʾsa*) with following article and substantive in the nominative may occupy different places within the phrase: لبئس الرّجلان أنتما *la-biʾsa 'r-rajulāni ʾantumā* 'What evil men are you two', نعم الفتى كنت *niʿma 'l-fatā kunta* 'What a perfect lad you were', أليس ببئس الظّالم *ʾa-laysa bi-biʾsa 'ẓ-ẓālimu* 'Is he not indeed an evil doer?'.

Note 1. Note the formula فبها ونعمت *fa-bihā wa-niʿmat* '(If you do it) in that case, it's all right!' used as the apodosis of a conditional sentence.

§261. a) The nominative coming after *niʿma* (*biʾsa*) may be replaced by a clause introduced by ما *mā* (§289), in which case *niʿma* (*biʾsa*) with relative *mā* (§421) means 'something very wonderful (evil) indeed':

نعم ما أمرت به *niʿma mā ʾamarta bihi* 'You have issued a wonderful order indeed', بئس ما صنعت *biʾsa mā ṣanaʿta* 'What an evil thing you have created'. The action is qualified with subordinating *mā* (§416): بئس ما سافرتم *biʾsa mā sāfartum* 'You have traveled very badly'.

Note 1. نعمّا *niʿimmā* occurs as a variant of *niʿma-mā*.

b) Sometimes, an indefinite in the accusative (§384) occurs in place of the definite nominative: بئس للظّالمين بدلا *biʾsa liẓ-ẓālimīna badalan* 'How evil is that exchange for the evildoers!' (Koran 18:50).

§**262.** Other words that are used on occasion to qualify emphatically are, for example: جلّ *jalla*, شدّ *shadda*, عزّ *ʿazza*, هدّ *hadda* 'how mighty, great', كبر *kabura*, ساء *sāʾa* 'how evil, bad', حسن *ḥasuna*, *ḥusna*, *ḥasna* 'how beautiful, magnificent', عظم *ʿaẓuma*, *ʿuẓma*, *ʿaẓma* 'how powerful, mighty'. They are used much like *niʿma*, *biʾsa*: جلّ الخطب فقدانه *jalla 'l-khaṭbu fiqdānuhu* 'How great a mishap is his loss!', لشدّما أحببتها *la-shadda-mā ʾaḥbabtahā* 'How much do you love her!', كبرت كلمة تخرج من أفواههم *kaburat kalimatan takhruju min ʾafwāhihim* 'How nasty a word comes from their mouths!' (Koran 18:5).

Note 1. Used more as particles are: قلّ ما, قلّما *qalla-mā* 'very rarely', طال ما, طالما *ṭāla-mā* 'how often, very often': قلّما يكون بالدّبور المطر *qalla-mā yakūnu bi-'d-dabūri 'l-maṭaru* 'How infrequently does the rain come with the westerly wind', طالما قد سألتني *ṭāla-mā qad saʾaltanī* 'How often have you asked me'.

Note 2. Other particles of emphatic qualification include: شتّان *shattā-na* 'how unlike', سرعان *surʿāna*, *sirʿāna* 'how swift': شتّان الطّامع واليائس *shattāna 'ṭ-ṭāmiʿu wa-'l-yāʾisu* 'How different are those who still have hope from those who have given up hope!', سرعان ما نسيتم *surʿāna mā nasītum* 'How quickly have you forgotten!'.

§**263.** The emphatic qualification حبّ *ḥabba* (*ḥubba*) 'how loveable' is almost always combined with ذا *dhā* (§274.2), in which case *dhā* is in the position of the definite nominative and can be accompanied by an indefinite accusative or *min* (§299): حبّذا أنت *ḥabba-dhā ʾanta* 'How lovely are you!', حبّذا الفوارس *ḥabba-dhā 'l-fawārisu* 'How wonderful are the knights!',

حبّذا البصرة أرضا (من أرض) *ḥabba-dhā 'l-Baṣratu ʾarḍan* (or *min ʾarḍin*) 'What a lovely spot of earth is Basra!'.

Note 1. Frequently يا *yā* (§347) precedes *ḥabba-dhā*.

Note 2. *ḥabba, ḥubba* without *-dhā* occurs in combination with *bi-* (§294 d) as predicate: يا حبّ بالمنزل *yā ḥabba bi-'l-manzili* 'How lovely is the dwelling!', حبّ به رجلا *ḥabba bihī rajulan* 'What a lovely man is he!'.

Pronouns and Particles

Personal Pronouns

§**264.** Independent personal pronouns:

Sing.	1st pers.	أنا	*ʾanā*	dual	—		pl.	نحن	*naḥnu*
	2nd m.	أنت	*ʾanta*		أنتما	*ʾantumā*		أنتم	*ʾantum*
	2nd f.	أنت	*ʾanti*		أنتما	*ʾantumā*		أنتنّ	*ʾantunna*
	3rd m.	هو	*huwa*		هما	*humā*		هم	*hum*
	3rd f.	هي	*hiya*		هما	*humā*		هنّ	*hunna*

Note 1. أنا *ʾanā* 'I' in poetry is usually *ʾana* (§7.6).

Note 2. Pronouns ending in *-um* may in poetry end in *-umū* (§7.5).

Note 3. After *wa-* and *fa-* (§§328 f.), *huwa, hiya* may be shortened to وهو *wa-hwa*, وهي *wa-hya*, فهو *fa-hwa*, فهي *fa-hya*.

Note 4. On occasion in poetry, the non-classical forms هو *hū*, هي *hī* may occur in addition to *huwa, hiya*.

§**265.** The independent personal pronoun as a rule functions as a nominative. See §§266.1; 267 for exceptions. It can be the subject and predicate of a nominal sentence (§§360 ff.) and precede the definite nominal predicate (§363 b).

Note 1. إنّ *ʾinna* (§339) with a personal suffix may occur instead of the independent personal pronoun as the subject.

Note 2. The independent personal pronoun or the personal suffix (§455) may come after لولا *law-lā*.

§**266.** Since the verb incorporates the pronominal subject (§§207; 211), the personal pronoun is used in the verbal sentence to emphasize the subject: كان هو السّارق *kāna huwa 's-sāriqa* '*He* was the thief'. It usually also appears when the word order subject–predicate is required (§§368 ff.), e.g.: مرّ بي وأنا أنظر إليه *marra bī wa-ʾanā ʾanẓuru ʾilayhi* 'He went by me as I watched him'.

> **Note 1.** On occasion, the personal pronoun is also used to emphasize a personal suffix (§268): بيتي أنا *baytī ʾanā* '<u>my</u> house'.

§**267.** The personal pronoun is used to coordinate more than one subject with one verbal predicate: أتينا أنا والحكم *ʾataynā ʾanā wa-'l-Ḥakam* 'We, al-Ḥakam and I, came'. In the same way, different pronominal objects can be coordinated with one verb: بعثني أنا وأنت *baʿathanī ʾanā wa-ʾanta* 'He sent you and me'. Cf. §328 b.

§**268.** The dependent personal suffixes can be attached to substantives, prepositions (§292), verbs, and particles:

				dual		pl.	
Sing.	1st pers.	ي	*-ī, -ya*			نا	*-nā*
		ني	*-nī*				
	2nd m.	ك	*-ka*	كما	*-kumā*	كم	*-kum*
	2nd f.	ك	*-ki*	كما	*-kumā*	كنّ	*-kunna*
	3rd m.	ه	*-hu, -hū*	هما	*-humā*	هم	*-hum*
		ه	*-hi, -hī*	هما	*-himā*	هم	*-him*
	3rd f.	ها	*hā*	هما	*-hu/imā*	هنّ	*-hu/inna*

> **Note 1.** In the 1st person sing., *-ī, -ya* is suffixed to substantives and prepositions, and *nī* is suffixed to verbs and particles. The form *-ya* comes after *ā, ī, ū, ay, aw* (§269 c).

> **Note 2.** The suffix of the 1st sing. is *-iya, -niya* (§54 a) when it precedes the article (*ʾa*)*l-* (§142). In classical Arabic, however, *-ī, -nī* are also permitted. In poetry, *-iya, -niya* often occur in place of *-ī, -nī* to fit the metre.

> **Note 3.** The suffix of the 3rd masc. sing. is short (*-hu, -hi*) when it comes after a closed syllable, but long (*-hū, -hī*) after an open syllable. See §7.3.

> **Note 4.** Plural suffixes that end in *-um* may become *-umū, -imū* in poetry: كم *kumū*, هم *humū, himū* (§7.5). Cf. also §54 a.

Note 5. When additional suffixes (§271) are attached, *-kum, -hum* become كمو *-kumū*, همو *-humū* (*-himū*). كا *-kā*, كي *-kī* also occur in post-classical Arabic in the 2nd sing. in this situation.

§269. a) The personal suffixes are added to the construct state of nouns (§145), and in this construction function as genitives: كتابك *kitābu-ka, kitābi-ka, kitāba-ka* 'your book' (nom., gen., acc.), أبوكما *ʾabū-kumā*, أبيكما *ʾabī-kumā*, أباكما *ʾabā-kumā* 'your [du.] father' (nom., gen., acc.), داعيكم *dāʿī-kum* 'your caller', قنانا *qanā-nā* 'our spears', سارقوها *sāriqū-hā*, سارقيها *sāriqī-hā* 'her thieves' (nom., obl.), etc.

Note 1. The personal suffixes may function as accusatives when affixed to verbal substantives or participles. Cf. §271.1. See §386.2 concerning the use of personal suffixes with terms expressing time.

b) After *i, ī, ay*, the 3rd person suffixes are *-hi* (*-hī*), *-himā, -him, -hinna*: سارقه *sāriqi-hī* 'his thief' (gen.), سارقيه *sāriqay-hi* 'both his thieves' (obl.), سارقيه *sāriqī-hi* 'his thieves' (obl.), as contrasted to nominative *sāri-qu-hū, sāriqā-hu, sāriqū-hu*

Note 2. In the dialect of Ḥijāz, *-hu* (*-hū*), *-humā, -hum, -hunna* remained unchanged after *i, ī, ay*: في كتابه *fī kitābi-hū* 'in his book'.

c) The case suffixes *-u, -i, -a* disappear before the 1st sing. suffix *-ī*: كتابي *kitābī* 'my book', عمّتي *ʿammatī* 'my aunt', عمّاتي *ʿammātī* 'my aunts'. After *ā, ī, ū, ay, aw*, the suffix is *-ya*, in which case the sequence *ū - y* becomes *ī - y*, and *aw - y* becomes *ay - y* (§33): سارقيّ *sāriqī-ya* 'my thieves' (nom., obl.), عمّتاي *ʿammatā-ya* (nom.), عمّتيّ *ʿammatay-ya* (obl.) 'my two aunts'.

Note 3. See §157.3 on the shortening of *-ī* > *-i* in the vocative.

Note 4. When the 1st sing. suffix is added to the substantives listed in §150, they are: أبي *ʾabī* 'my father', أخي *ʾakhī* 'my brother', حمي *ḥamī* 'my uncle', and فيّ *fīya* 'my mouth'.

§270. In combination with verbs, the personal suffixes function as objects. The suffix of the 1st sing. is always *-nī, -niya*. Only the 2nd pl. of the perfect (§207) undergoes variation due to the addition of the personal suffix:

ضربتم *ḍarabtum* 'You struck' : ضربتموني *ḍarabtumū-nī* 'You struck me'. The suffix of the 3rd person after *i, ī, ay* becomes: *-hi* (*-hī*), *-himā, -him, -hinna*: يرميه *yarmī-hi* 'He throws him', but رماه *ramā-hu* 'He threw him'.

Note 1. The ا that is written after the plural ending (§7.2) is dropped before the suffix: كتبوا *katabū* : كتبوها *katabū-hā*.

Note 2. The *-ti* of the 2nd fem. sing. of the perfect may be *-tī* before suffixes in post-classical Arabic: ضربتيني *ḍarabtī-nī* for ضربتني *ḍarabti-nī*.

Note 3. The imperfect endings *-īna, -ūna, -āni* may be shortened before *-nī, -nā* (§50 c). As a result, the imperfect forms are the same as the jussive and subjunctive: تضربيني *taḍribīnī* and تضربينني *taḍribīna-nī* 'You (fem.) hit me', يضربونا *yaḍribūnā* and يضربوننا *yaḍribūna-nā* 'They hit us', etc.

§**271.** There may be two personal suffixes added to the verb. In this case, the 1st person precedes the 2nd and the 3rd, and the 2nd person precedes the 3rd: أعطانيه *ʾaʿṭā-nī-hi* 'He gave it to me', أعطيتكه *ʾaʿṭaytu-ka-hū* 'I gave it to you', أعطيناكموها *ʾaʿṭaynā-kumū-hā* 'We gave her to you' (§268.5).

Note 1. If two personal suffixes are attached to a verbal substantive, the first functions as the subject, the second as the object: ذكركها *dhikru-ka-hā* 'your remembering her', طلبيكم *ṭalab-ī-kum* 'my searching for you'.

Pronominal Object Particle

§**272.** Instead of the second personal suffix, إيّا *ʾiyyā* with personal suffixes is used, if directly adding the suffix is impossible or is better avoided: إيّاي *ʾiyyā-ya* 'me', إيّاك *ʾiyyā-ka, -ki* 'you', إيّاه *ʾiyyā-hu*, him, etc. أعطاها إيّاي *ʾaʿṭāhā ʾiyyāya* 'He gave me to her' as opposed to أعطانيها *ʾaʿṭānīhā* 'He gave her to me'.

Note 1. *ʾiyyā* is also used to place the pronominal object first: إيّاك نعبد وإيّاك نستعين *ʾiyyāka naʿbudu wa-ʾiyyāka nastaʿīnu* (Koran 1:5) 'You alone do we worship, and You alone we ask for help'.

Note 2. Independent إيّاك *ʾiyyāka, -ki*, إيّاكم *ʾiyyākum*, إيّاكنّ *ʾiyyākunna*, mostly with *wa-* (§328.3) or *ʾan* (§414) following, has the meaning 'beware...!, 'take care not to...!'.

Reflexive

§273. The reflexive relationship to the object is expressed by نفس *nafsun* 'soul, self' (§111 d) with the addition of corresponding personal suffixes: رأيت نفسي *ra'aytu nafsī* 'I saw myself', قال لنفسه *qāla li-nafsihī* 'He said to himself'. In the other reflexive relationships, the simple personal suffixes are usually used: كنت في بيتي *kuntu fī baytī* 'I was in my house'.

Demonstratives

§274. Demonstratives that indicate direct deixis ('this'):

Sing.	m.	هذا *hādhā*	dual	هذان *hādhāni*	pl. هؤلاء *hā'ulā'i*
	f.	هذه *hādhihī*		هتان *hātāni*	هؤلاء *hā'ulā'i*

Sing. and pl. demonstratives are not inflected. The dual has the nominal inflection: Obl. هذين *hādhayni*, fem. هتين *hātayni*.

> **Note 1.** In the singular, *hādhihī* has almost completely replaced the original form هذي *hādhī*. See §§7.4; 7.7; 8 on the orthography.

> **Note 2.** Forms without *hā-* occur very rarely in classical Arabic: sing. masc. ذا *dhā*; fem. تي *tī*, ته *tihī*, ذي *dhī*, ذه *dhihī*, تا *tā*; dual masc. ذان *dhāni*, ذين *dhayni* (obl.), fem. تان *tāni*, تين *tayni* (obl.); pl. أولا, أولى *'ulā*, أولاء *'ulā'i*.

§275. Demonstratives that indicate indirect deixis ('that'):

a) Formed with *-ka*:

Sing. m.	ذاك *dhāka*	dual	ذانك *dhānika*	pl.	أولاك *'ulāka* / أولائك *'ulā'ika*
		(obl.)	ذينك *dhaynika*		أولاك *'ulāka* / أولائك *'ulā'ika*
f.	تاك *tāka*		تانك *tānika*		أولاك *'ulāka* / أولائك *'ulā'ika*
	تيك *tīka*	(obl.)	تينك *taynika*		أولاك *'ulāka* / أولائك *'ulā'ika*

b) Formed with *-lika*:

Sing.	m.	ذلك *dhālika*	dual	ذانّك *dhānnika*	pl.	أولالك *'ulālika*
			(obl.)	ذينّك *dhaynnika*		أولالك *'ulālika*
	f.	تلك *tilka*		تانّك *tānnika*		أولالك *'ulālika*
				تينّك *taynnika*		أولالك *'ulālika*

Note 1. In the singular, forms with *-lika* are preferred. On occasion, forms with *-hā* occur: sing. masc. هذاك *hādhāka*, fem. هذيك *hādhīka*, pl. هؤلاك *hāʾulāka*, هؤلاءك *hāʾulāʾika*.

Note 2. Sometimes in pre-classical Arabic, other forms of the personal suffix of the 2nd person occur instead of *-ka*: ذاكِ *dhāki*, ذاكم *dhākum*, ذلكم *dhālikum*, ذلكنّ *dhālikunna*, تلكم *tilkum*, تلكما *tilkumā*, etc. Reference to the particular person, however, no longer holds. Cf. §278.1.

§**276.** a) Direct deixis refers in time and space to something present: يا هذا *yā hādhā* 'oh, this one here!', i.e., 'hey, you there!', أهذا أم هذا *ʾa-hādhā ʾam hādhā* 'this one here or this one here?'; referring to context دع ذا *daʿ dhā* 'leave this!'. Sometimes, هذا *hādhā* anticipates the context that follows: هذا ما اشترى فلان *hādhā mā 'shtarā fulānun* 'This (that follows) is what so-and-so bought'.

b) Indirect deixis refers in time and space to something at a distance: يوم ذلك (ذاك) *yawma dhālika* (*dhāka*) 'on the day of that (event), then'. ذلك *dhālika* is the demonstrative that most frequently refers back to context.

Note 1. In some usages, demonstratives refer to preceding contexts in a comprehensive way: هذا و ... *hādhā wa*... 'besides, moreover, on the other hand'; ذلك أنّ ... *dhālika ʾanna* ... 'that is (to say), namely, to wit...'.

§**277.** Demonstratives come before definite substantives with articles (§142): هذا الكتاب *hādhā 'l-kitābu* 'this book'. Otherwise, demonstratives come after substantives: كتبي هذه *kutubī hādhihī* 'these my books', أصحاب الحديث أولائك *ʾaṣḥābu 'l-ḥadīthi ʾulāʾika* 'those followers of Ḥadith'. Demonstratives agree with respect to gender in the same way that attributive adjectives do (§§113 f.).

Note 1. When used with proper names which have the article, demonstratives may precede: هذا الحكم *hādhā 'l-Ḥakamu* or الحكم هذا *(ʾa)l-Ḥakamu hādhā* 'this al-Ḥakam', but always محمّد هذا *Muḥammadun hādhā* 'this Muhammad', and so forth.

§**278.** When they introduce clauses, direct deixis demonstratives call attention to the presence of the predicate ('here is/are'): هؤلاء بناتي *hāʾulāʾi banātī* 'Here are my daughters!' The predicate may be expanded with a circumstantial accusative (§§380 ff.) or clause (§§431 ff.): هذا رسول الله قد دخل *hādhā rasūlu 'l-lāhi qad dakhala* 'Now the Messenger of God has come in'. This usage is restricted primarily to pre-classical Arabic.

Note 1. When ذاك *dhāka*, ذاكم *dhākum*, تلك *tilka*, etc., (§275.2) occur with this function, the direct deixis refers to the person being addressed: ذاكم صاحبكم *dhākum ṣāḥibukum* 'Here is your companion!'.

§279. a) A demonstrative referring to a person may occur in combination with the personal pronoun at the beginning of a phrase: أنا ذا *ʾanā dhā*, أنت ذا *ʾanta dhā*, هم هؤلاء *hum hāʾulāʾi*, etc.; هو ذا واقف (واقفا) في دارك *huwa dhā wāqifun (wāqifan) fī dārika* 'There he is in your house' (§383 a).

b) In classical Arabic, *hā-* usually precedes the personal pronoun:

هأنذا (هَآءَنَذَا) or ها أنا ذا *hā-ʾanā-dhā*, f. ها أنا ذي *hā-ʾanā-dhī* 'Here am I!';
ها أنت ذا *hā-ʾanta-dhā*, f. ها أنت ذي (تا) *hā-ʾanti-dhī* (*-tā*);
ها هو ذا *hā-huwa-dhā*, f. ها هي ذي (تا) *hā-hiya-dhī* (*-tā*);
هانحن أولاء *hā-naḥnu-ʾulāʾi*, etc.

Note 1. إنّ *ʾinna* (§339) may replace the personal pronoun: ها إنّ ذا *hā-ʾinna-dhā*, ها إنّ ذي (تا) *hā-ʾinna-dhī* (*-tā*): ها إنّ ذي عذرة *hā-ʾinna-dhī ʿidhratun* 'There is an excuse!'.

Note 2. On occasion, the demonstrative is lacking: ها أنتم تعلمون *hā ʾantum taʿlamūna* 'You there sure know it!'

§280. Demonstratives that introduce clauses are: إذ *ʾidh*, إذا *ʾidhā*, usually فإذا *fa-ʾidhā* 'there was (and all of a sudden there was)...'.

a) إذ *ʾidh* introduces a verbal clause (§§355 ff.): إنّي لعندهم إذ أقبل عير *ʾinnī la-ʿindahum ʾidh ʾaqbala ʿīrun* 'I was with them, and there came a caravan' (§407.2).

b) A substantive or pronoun follows إذا (ف) (*fa-*)*ʾidhā*: نظرت إليها فإذا (هي) امرأة *naẓartu ʾilayhā fa-ʾidhā (hiya) 'mraʾatun* 'I looked at her, and lo! it was a woman', دخل عليها فإذا هي قد نامت *dakhala ʿalayhā fa-ʾidhā hiya qad nāmat* 'He went in to her, and there she was already asleep'. The subject of the clause, which is something that appears suddenly, is frequently introduced by *bi-* (§294 d): فإذا بأبيه *fa-ʾidhā bi-ʾabīhi* 'There all of a sudden was his father', فإذا هو بأبيه *fa-ʾidhā huwa bi-ʾabīhi* 'All of a sudden, he was face-to-face with his father'.

Note 1. See §§443; 444 on *ʾidh, ʾidhā* introducing a main clause. See §442 on *ʾidh* introducing a subordinate clause, and §§464 f. on *ʾidhā* introducing a subordinate clause.

Definite Clauses (Relative Pronouns)

§281.	Sing.	Dual	Plural
m.	الّذي *(ʾa)lladhī*	اللّذان *(ʾa)lladhāni*	الّذين *(ʾa)lladhīna*
f.	الّتي *(ʾa)llātī*	اللّتان *(ʾa)llatāni*	اللاّتي *(ʾa)llātī* or
			اللّواتي *(ʾa)llawātī*

The singular and plural are not inflected. The dual has a nominal inflection: oblique اللّذين *(ʾa)lladhayni*, اللّتين *(ʾa)llatayni*. The *(ʾa)l-* at the beginning is the definite article (§§18.1; 142 b).

Note 1. Pre-classical Arabic had masc. and fem. plurals الأولى *(ʾa)l-ʾulā* and الّائي *(ʾa)llāʾī* (§49 d).

Note 2. ذو *dhū* with the same function, found in pre-classical poetry, is invariable. It is a feature of the dialect of the Ṭayyiʾ tribe.

§282. Relative pronouns make attributive clauses definite. Like adjectives (§§113 f.), they agree with the substantives to which they refer: الرّجل الّذي ضربته *(ʾa)r-rajulu ʾlladhī ḍarabtuhū* 'the man whom I struck', (literally) 'the man who — I struck him', بالمرأتين اللّتين لقيتهما *bi-ʾl-marʾatayni ʾllatayni laqītuhumā* 'with the two women whom I encountered', الرّجال الّذين ضربتهم *(ʾa)r-rijālu ʾlladhīna ḍarabtuhum* 'the men whom I struck'. In addition, it functions without antecedent as an independent relative pronoun ('he who, that which'). See §§421 ff.

Nominal Demonstratives

§283. Meaning 'the (possessor, master) of ..., the one with ...' and always followed by a genitive (§391), the demonstrative ذو *dhū* is inflected nominally: (§150):

		m.	f.	
Sing.	nom.	ذو dhū	ذات dhātu	
	gen.	ذي dhī	ذات dhāti	
	acc.	ذا dhā	ذات dhāta	
Du.	nom.	ذوا dhawā	ذاتا dhātā,	ذواتا dhawātā
	obl.	ذوي dhaway	ذاتي dhātay,	ذواتي dhawātay
Pl.	nom.	ذوو dhawū, أولو ʾulū	ذوات dhawātu,	أولات ʾulātu
	obl.	ذوي dhawī, أولي ʾulī	ذوات dhawāti,	أولات ʾulāti

Note 1. As a substantive, ذات *dhātun* means 'being, self'.

Note 2. In the adverbial accusative, *dhū* and *dhātu* are used to express indefinite time: ذا صباح *dhā ṣabāḥin* 'one morning', ذات يوم *dhāta yawmin* 'one day'.

Demonstrative Particles

§284. a) Demonstratives referring to location: هنا *hunā*, ههنا, هاهنا *hāhunā* 'here'; هناك *hunāka*, هنالك *hunālika*, هاهناك *hāhunāka* 'there'; ثَمَّ *thamma* 'there'.

b) Demonstratives referring to time: الآن (ʾa)l-ʾāna 'now', إذًا, إذن ʾidhan 'then, consequently' (§11.2; cf. §§196.2; 447.1). إذذاك ʾidh-dhāka, إذذلك ʾidh-dhālika 'at that time'.

Note 1. (ʾa)l-ʾāna is not inflected: حتّى الآن *ḥattā 'l-ʾāna*, إلى الآن *ʾilā 'l-ʾāna* 'until now'.

Note 2. إذ *ʾidhin* 'at that time' occurs with substantives that express time: حينئذ *ḥīna-ʾidhin* 'then, at that time' (= حينذاك *ḥīna-dhāka*; cf. §276 b), غداتئذ *ghadāta-ʾidhin* 'that morning', يومئذ *yawma-ʾidhin* '(on) that day', etc.

c) Demonstratives referring to manner: كذا *kadhā*, هكذا *hākadhā*, كذاك *kadhāka*, كذلك *kadhālika* 'thus, in this/that way'; كذا وكذا *kadhā wa-kadhā*, كيت وكيت *kayta wa-kayta* 'so and so, such and such'.

Interrogatives

§**285.** a) من *man* 'who?', ما *mā* 'what?' are used for the singular, dual, and plural: من الرّجلان *man-i 'r-rajulāni* 'Who are the two men?'. ذا *dhā*, as it introduces a clause, may directly follow: ماذا تصنع *mā-dhā taṣnaʿu* 'What are you making?'.

Note 1. *mā* may be followed by *li-* (§295): ما لك *mā laka* 'What is with you?', 'What do you have?'. It may be followed by a verb or an accusative: ما له كاذبا *mā lahū kādhiban* 'For what is he lying?', ما لك تبكين *mā laka tabkīna* 'Why are you (fem.) crying?' (§434.1).

b) من *man* and ما *mā* may function as genitives and be combined with prepositions: أخت من انت *ʾukhtu man anti* 'Whose sister are you?', في من, فيمن *fī-man* 'among whom, among which people?', ممّن *mimman* (§45) 'from whom?'. Interrogatives like *mā* may be abbreviated after prepositions to *ma* (pausal form مه *mah*): لم *lima* 'why?', بم *bima*, عمّ *ʿamma* (§45), علام *ʿalā-ma* (على م), حتّام *ḥattā-ma* (حتّى م), etc.

Note 2. Occasionally, *lima, bima* become لم *lim*, بم *bim* in poetry.

c) Indefinite ما *mā* 'some' comes after the indefinite state (§141): رجل ما *rajulun mā* (also رجل مّا *rajulum-mā*) 'a certain man', أمر ما *ʾamrun mā* (also أمر مّا *ʾamrum-mā*) 'a certain affair'. It may also appear between the construct state and a following genitive (§145): يا طول ما شوق *yā ṭūla mā shawqin* 'O so long yearning!'. Similarly, after prepositions: عمّا قليل *ʿammā qalīlin* = عن قليل *ʿan qalīlin* 'shortly, soon'; also frequently, غير ما *ghayru mā* = غير *ghayru* 'other than' (§325). Cf. §424.2.

§**286.** a) أيّ *ʾayyun* 'which?' (§419.2), almost always with the genitive following: أيّ رجل *ʾayyu rajulin* 'which man?', أيّ رجال *ʾayyu rijālin* 'which men?', أيّ النساء *ʾayyu 'l-nisāʾi* 'which of the women?', أيّنا *ʾayyunā* 'which of us?'. See §287.1 on كأيّ *ka-ʾayyin*.

Note 1. Occasionally, fem. أيّة *ʾayyatun* 'which' occurs: أيّة قرية *ʾayyatu qaryatin* 'which village?'.

Note 2. Sometimes, non-classical أيش *ʾayshin*, أيش *ʾaysh* < أيّ شيء *ʾayyu shayʾin* 'which thing, what?' occurs in classical texts.

b) Indefinite أيّ *ʾayyun* 'any, every': أكرمه أيّ إكرام *ʾakramahū ʾayya ʾikrāmin* 'He bestowed every honor on him'. As an exclamation, it is used to express great admiration: رأينا فارسا أيّ فارس *raʾaynā fārisan ʾayya fārisin* 'We saw a rider, and what a rider he was!'.

§**287.** كم *kam* 'how much, how often?'; the substantive to which it refers is in the indefinite accusative singular (§384): كم لك درهما *kam laka dirhaman* 'How many dirhams do you have?'. As an exclamation, is used with the genitive or من *min* (§299 a): كم درهم أنفقت *kam dirhamin ʾanfaqta* 'How many dirhams have you spent indeed!', كم لاقينا من عدوّ *kam lāqaynā min ʿadūwin* 'How many enemies have we encountered'.

Note 1. كأيّن كأيّ *ka-ʾayyin* has the same meaning, in poetry often > كائن *kāʾin*: كائن رأيت من ملوك *kāʾin raʾaytu min mulūkin* 'So many kings have I seen.'

§**288.** Other interrogatives: أين *ʾayna* 'where, where to?', أنّى *ʾannā* 'where, where from, why is it that?', كيف *kayfa* 'how?', متى *matā*, أيّان *ʾayyāna* 'when?'.

Note 1. *ʾayna, kayfa, ʾayyāna* are not inflected: من أين *min ʾayna* 'where from?', بلا كيف *bilā kayfa* 'without how,' i.e., 'without asking how'.

Note 2. On the interrogative particles *ʾa-, hal*, see §335. On *law-lā, law-mā* introducing an interrogative clause, see §457.1.

§**289.** Most of the interrogatives can also be used as relatives: من *man* 'who, the one who', ما *mā* 'what, the one which' أيّ *ʾayyu* with the genitive 'which of ...', أين *ʾayna* '(there) where', كيف *kayfa* 'how', متى *matā* '(then) when' (§461).

Note 1. Relative *mā* is not shortened after prepositions: لما *li-mā*, ممّا *mimmā* < *min-mā* (§45), etc. Concerning relative clauses, see §§421 ff.

Note 2. Relative *mā* has two other functions: *mā* 'the fact that' (subordinating *mā* §416), *mā* 'as long as" (§462).

§**290.** In combination with relatives, indefinite ما *mā* has a generalizing sense: مهما *mahmā* < **mā-mā* 'whatever', أيّما *ʾayyumā* 'whichever', أينما *ʾaynamā* 'wherever', متى ما, متاما *matā-mā* 'whenever', حيثما *ḥaythumā* 'wherever', among others. See §461 for syntactic constructions.

Note 1. In addition to *ʾayyu-mā*, on occasion أيّمن *ʾayyu-man* 'whoever' occurs with reference to persons.

Prepositions

§**291.** a) Primary prepositions: ب *bi-*, ل *li-*, في *fī*, ك *ka-*, مع *maʿa*, من *min*, عن *ʿan*, (§45), على *ʿalā*, إلى *ʾilā*, حتّى *ḥattā*, لدى *ladā*, لدن *ladun*; see §§294ff.

Note 1. On the orthography of constructions with *bi-*, *li-*, *ka-*, see §§23; 22. Before the article, *min* is *min-a* (§54). In poetry, مع *maʿ* sometimes appears in place of مع *maʿa*.

Note 2. In poetry, *min* and *ʿalā* may be shortened to *mi-*, *ʿa-* (§49 e): ملإبل , مالإبل *mil-ʾibili* 'from the camels', علماء *ʿal-māʾi* 'on the water'.

b) Secondary prepositions take the form of the accusative in the construct state (§145): أمام *ʾamāma* 'in front of, in the presence of', بعد *baʿda* 'after', بين *bayna* 'between' (§308), تحت *taḥta* 'under', حول *ḥawla*, حوالى *ḥawālā* 'around, about', خلف *khalfa* 'behind, after', دون *dūna* (§309), عند *ʿinda* 'with' (§307), فوق *fawqa* 'above, over, on', قبل *qabla* 'before (in time)', قبل *qibala* 'in the direction of', نحو *naḥwa* 'toward', وراء *warāʾa* 'behind', وسط *wasṭa* 'in the midst of'. More recent formations, e.g.: داخل *dākhila* 'within', ضدّ *ḍidda* 'against', etc., are also included in this group.

Note 3. Many prepositions can be combined with من *min* or إلى *ʾilā*: من بعد *min baʿdi* 'after completion of', من فوق *min fawqi* 'from above, above', إلى فوق *ʾilā fawqi* 'over', من قبل *min qibali* 'on the part of, from, by', among others; also من على *min ʿalā* 'from above, from on top of', من لدى *min ladā*, من لدن *min ladun* (§§305 f.). The preposition *min* in such constructions may indicate direction or be partitive (see §299 b and c). دون *dūna* and بدون *bi-dūni* have the same meaning.

Note 4. Diminutives (§81) are formed from several of the secondary prepositions: بعيد *buʿayda* 'soon after', قبيل *qubayla* 'shortly before', فويق *fuwayqa* 'a little above'; similarly, تحيت *tuḥayta*, دوين *duwayna* (from *dūna*).

§**292.** a) All prepositions are followed by a genitive. The same rules that apply to substantives (§268) also hold, with a few exceptions, for the addition of personal suffixes (§269) to prepositions: مع *maʿa* : معي *maʿī* 'with me', معك *maʿaka* 'with you', etc.; بعد *baʿda* : بعدي *baʿdī* 'after me', بعده *baʿdahū* 'after him', etc.; في *fī* : فيّ *fīya* 'in me', فيهم *fīhim* 'in them', etc. With *min*, *ʿan*, and *ladun*, the *n* is doubled before the addition of the suffix of the 1st sing.: منّي *minnī*, عنّي *ʿannī*, لدنّي *ladunnī*; but منك *minka*, عنك *ʿanka*, لدنك *ladunka*, etc.

Note 1. ك *ka-* 'as, like' and حتّى *ḥattā* 'until' may not take personal suffixes (§297 d).

b) ل *li-* becomes *la-* before personal suffixes: لي *lī(ya)*, لك *laka*, *laki*, له *lahū*, لها *lahā*, لكما *lakumā*, لهما *lahumā*, لنا *lanā*, لكم *lakum*, لكنّ *lakunna*, لهم *lahum*, لهنّ *lahunna*.

c) The stems of على *ʿalā*, إلى *ʾilā*, لدى *ladā*, and حوالى *ḥawālā* end in *-ay* before the personal suffixes: عليّ *ʿalayya*, عليك *ʿalayka*, *ʿalayki*, عليه *ʿalayhi*, عليها *ʿalayhā*, عليكما *ʿalaykumā*, عليهما *ʿalayhimā*, علينا *ʿalaynā*, عليكم *ʿalaykum*, عليكنّ *ʿalaykunna*, عليهم *ʿalayhim*, عليهنّ *ʿalayhinna*.

§**293.** a) Prepositions for the most part indicate position or direction. Several are used to express syntactic relationships (§§294 d; 295 a–b; 299.1). Many verbs occur in constructions with dependent prepositional predicate complements, in which the preposition is part of the lexical unit of meaning and modifies the meaning of the verb: رغب في شيء *ra<u>gh</u>iba fī <u>sh</u>ayʾin* 'He desired something' and رغب عن شيء *ra<u>gh</u>iba ʿan <u>sh</u>ayʾin* 'He desired something to be away', i.e., 'He loathed it', ظهر لنا *ẓahara lanā* 'It came into our view' and ظهر علينا *ẓahara ʿalaynā* 'He got the better of us'. The corresponding verbal substantives, verbal adjectives, and elatives (§§124 ff.) appear in constructions with the same prepositions: هو أرغب عن ذلك منك *huwa ʾar<u>gh</u>abu ʿan <u>dh</u>ālika minka* 'He detests that more than you do'.

b) Prepositional phrases may appear in various syntactic positions: 1. dependent on a verb, verbal substantive, or verbal adjective (see above); 2. as the predicate in a nominal sentence: الجارية في البيت (ʾa)l-jāriyatu fī 'l-bayti 'The maid was in her chamber'; 3. as an adverbial modifier: تنام الجارية في البيت tanāmu 'l-jāriyatu fī 'l-bayti 'The maid is asleep in her room', 4. in apposition: أخ في الدّين ʾakhun fī 'd-dīni 'brother in religion'. *ka-* 'as, like' (§297) and *min* 'from' (§299 a–b), like substantives, may occur as subject, predicate, or object.

Note 1. Prepositions may appear in the genitive position only when they depend on other prepositions (§291.3). See §308.7 for an exception.

Note 2. See §§294.5; 302.3; 303.4; 309.1 for the use of prepositional phrases as commands; cf. 351.1.

c) Prepositional phrases that depend on verbal substantives or verbal adjectives frequently come before a verbal noun, especially when the verbal noun is the predicate and the preposition has a personal suffix or appears with a demonstrative: هذا على ذلك دليل *hādhā ʿalā dhālika dalīlun* 'This is proof of that', كنت إليها مشتاقا *kuntu ʾilayhā mushtāqan* 'I was filled with longing for her'. Prepositional phrases may be placed at the beginning of a sentence for emphasis: وفيه قال الشّاعر *wa-fīhi qāla 'sh-shāʿiru* 'And about him, the poet said ...', فبالحلم سد *fa-bi-'l-ḥilmi sud* 'Reign with compassion!'

§294. ب *bi-* in the sense of 'in contact with, close by' is used in the following ways:

a) 'in contact with, by': بعثه برسالة إلى أبيها *baʿathahū bi-risālatin ʾilā ʾabīhā* 'He sent him with a message to her father', بعث برسالة *baʿatha bi-risālatin* 'He sent a message', ما بي من غضب *mā bī min ghaḍabin* 'the anger that is in me'; in oaths, and other similar constructions: أقسمت بالله *ʾaqsamtu bi-'l-lāhi* 'I swear by God', بسم الله *bi-smi 'l-lāhi* 'in the name of God' (§22 c); indicating content: أمر بقتله *ʾamara bi-qatlihī* 'He gave the order to kill him', بعد موته بيومين *baʿda mawtihī bi-yawmayni* 'after his death by two days', i.e., ' two days after his death'; – indicating time and place: بالباب *bi-'l-bābi* 'at the gate', بمصر *bi-Miṣra* 'in Egypt', باللّيل *bi-'l-layli* 'at night'.

Note 1. *bi-* indicates the object to which something happens: عمل بشيء *ʿamila bi-shayʾin* 'He occupied himself with something' as opposed to عمل شيئا *ʿamila shayʾan* 'He did something'.

Note 2. *bi-* is used as a particle to introduce an oath: بالله *bi-'l-lāhi* 'by God!'. The oath particles *wa-* and *ta-* are also used in this kind of construction: والله *wa-'l-lāhi*, تالله *ta-'l-lāhi* 'by God!', والّذي نفسي بيده *wa-'lladhī nafsī bi-yadihī* 'by Him in whose hand is my soul' (i.e., 'by God!').

Note 3. Cf. §§260.1; 452 b on فبها *fa-bihā* 'well and good'.

Note 4. بلا *bi-lā*, بغير *bi-ghayri* 'not in connection with' means 'without': بلا شكّ *bi-lā shakkin* 'without doubt', بغير ضرورة *bi-ghayri ḍarūratin* 'without necessity, unnecessarily'.

b) Intransitive verbs expressing movement take on a kind of factitive meaning with *bi-*: أتاه بكتاب *ʾatāhu bi-kitābin* 'He came to him with a book' = آتاه كتابا *ʾātāhu kitāban* 'He brought him a book', قام بغارة *qāma bi-ghāratin* 'He undertook a raid' (literally, 'stood up with ...').

Note 5. Similarly, in usages like: أنا لك بذلك *ʾanā laka bi-dhālika* 'I shall obtain that for you', عليّ به *ʿalayya bihī* 'Bring him to me!' (§302.3). See §222 on the use of the imperative with *bi-*.

c) 'By means of, with the help of': ضربه بالعصا *ḍarabahū bi-'l-ʿaṣā* 'He struck him with a stick', اشترى شاة بدرهم *(ʾi)shtarā shātan bi-dirhamin* 'He bought a sheep for a dirham'; thus, also in the meaning of 'in place of, as substitute for': باع شاة بدرهم *bāʿa shātan bi-dirhamin* 'He sold a sheep for a dirham', أعطاه بأبياته دينارا *ʾaʿṭāhu bi-ʾabyātihī dīnāran* 'I gave him a dinar for his verses', قتله بزيد *qatalahū bi-Zaydin* 'He killed him instead of Zayd', بأبي أنت وأمّي *bi-ʾabī ʾanta wa-ʾummī* 'You are instead of my father and mother', i.e., 'You take the place of my father and mother'; — with persons, often 'in the person of': شتمت به محبّبا إليّ *shatamta bihī muḥabbaban ʾilayya* 'You vilify in (him) his person one who is beloved to me'.

d) The nominal predicate or the predicate accusative (§382) in negative or interrogative sentences is frequently introduced by *bi-*: لم تكن بصغيرة *lam takun bi-ṣaghīratin* 'She was not small', هل هو بصادق *hal huwa bi-ṣādiqin* 'Is he sincere?'.

Note 6. In positive sentences, *bi-* as predicate is very infrequent (§363.1); it occurs somewhat more often with verbs with a declarative meaning: سمّاه بكريم *sammāhu bi-karīmin* 'He called him a noble man'.

Note 7. *bi-* as a predicate occurs in other usages: إذا ب *ʾidhā bi-* (§280 b), حبّ ب *ḥabba bi-* (§263.2), كأنّ ب *kaʾanna . . . bi-* (§365.1).

Note 8. Several terms indicating totality and identity occur in apposition with *bi-*: النّاس بجمعهم *(ʾa)n-nāsu bi-jamʿihim* 'the people altogether' (§138.2), هو بنفسه *huwa bi-nafsihī* 'he himself', في ذلك المكان بعينه *fī dhālika 'l-makāni bi-ʿaynihī* 'in this exact place', رجل بعينه *rajulun bi-ʿaynihī* 'a certain man'.

§**295.** ل *li-* (*la-*) 'to' is used in the following ways:

a) 'to', in space and time: انكبّ لوجهه *(ʾi)nkabba li-wajhihī* 'He fell onto his face', لأوّل مرّة *li-ʾawwali marratin* 'for the first time'; indicating the indirect object: قال له *qāla lahū* 'He said to him', قدّم له شيئا *qaddama lahū shayʾan* 'He presented him with something'; — also to paraphrase the direct object of participles and verbal substantives (§§203.2; 206.3): كان مضحكا للنّاس *kāna muḍḥikan lin-nāsi* 'He was one who made the people laugh'; with verbs, if the object must precede the verb: للّذين هم لربّهم يرهبون *li-lladhīna hum li-rabbihim yarhabūna* (Koran 7:154) 'those who fear their Lord'.

Note 1. *li-* is used in expressions of time and date: لوقته *li-waqtihī* 'at its time', i.e., 'immediately', لسنة مضت من ملكه *li-sanatin maḍat min mulkihī* 'when one year of his reign had passed', لسبع ليال خلون من شعبان *li-sabʿi layālin khalawna min shaʿbāna* 'when seven days had gone by in Shaʿbān', i.e., 'on the seventh of Shaʿbān'.

Note 2. See §294.5 on أنا لكم به *ʾanā la-kum bihī* 'I am for you with him', i.e., 'I shall get him for you'; on ما له *mā lahū* with the accusative or a verb, see §285.1.

Note 3. See §438 on *li-* with the subjunctive; §195 with the jussive.

b) 'belonging to': كتاب له *kitābun lahū* 'a book of his (written by him or owned by him)', أنشد لأبي نواس *ʾanshada li-ʾAbī Nuwāsin* 'He cited a verse of Abū Nuwās', كان للعبد حمار *kāna lil-ʿabdi ḥimārun* 'The slave had an ass', إنّا لله *ʾinnā li-llāhi* 'We belong to God'; in constructions with persons, frequently with the meaning 'be someone's right, due' ذلك لكم *dhālika lakum* 'That is your due!', ... ليس له أن *laysa lahū ʾan* ... 'It is not your right, it is not possible for you, it is not allowed for you to ...'.

Note 4. In this meaning, *li-* is used to paraphrase the genitive after the indefinite state; see §146.1.

c) 'in favor of, for': بنى لنا قصرا *banā lanā qaṣran* 'He built a castle for us'; — 'with regard to, because of': تبكي لولدها *tabkī li-waladihā* 'She cried over her child', جئتك لحاجة *jiʾtuka li-ḥājatin* 'I came to you because of a concern', لذلك *li-dhālika* 'therefore', يقال له محمّد *yuqālu lahū Muḥammadun* 'One says to him Muhammad', i.e., 'He is called Muhammad'.

Note 5. In contrast to على *ʿalā*, which expresses something to which someone has an obligation, *li-* refers to something to which one has a right: لي عليه ألف درهم *lī ʿalayhi ʾalfu dirhamin* 'He owes me 1000 dirhams'.

d) Sometimes *li-* indicates the cause or originator: تهال له العين *tuhālu lahū 'l-ʿaynu* 'One (the eye) is struck with terror by him'.

§296. في *fī* 'in, within, in the midst of' is used in the following ways:

a) location, 'in, inside' (place and direction): في البحر والبرّ *fī 'l-baḥri wa-'l-barri* 'in the sea and on land', وقع في البئر *waqaʿa fī 'l-biʾri* 'He fell into the well'; time, 'in, during': في خلافة عمر *fī khilāfati ʿUmara* 'during the caliphate of Umar', في ما مضى *fī mā maḍā* 'in that which has passed', i.e., 'in the past'; 'in the midst of, among': بعثه في جيش *baʿathahū fī-jayshin* 'He sent him in the company of, i.e., with an army', من فيكم الأكبر *man fīkum-u 'l-ʾakbaru* 'Who among you is the oldest?', سرنا في خمسة رجال *sirnā fī khamsati rijālin* 'We travelled in a party of five men'.

b) By extension, *fī* may mean 'in the realm of, with respect to, concerning, about': اختلفوا في ذلك (*ʾi*)*khtalafū fī dhālika* 'They disagreed on that', باب في الخيل *bābun fī 'l-khayli* 'a chapter on the horse', مثل الخزّ في اللّين *mithlu 'l-khazzi fī 'l-līni* 'like silk in smoothness', i.e., 'smooth as silk'.

Note 1. On occasion, *fī* may mean, like *bi-*, 'in the person of': قد كان لكم فيه أسوة *qad kāna lakum fīhi ʾuswatun* 'You had in him an example'.

Note 2. In arithmetic, *fī* indicates that number by which another is multiplied: ضرب ثلاثة في خمسة *ḍaraba thalāthata fī khamsata* 'He multiplied three by five' (See §129.5).

Note 3. *fī* indicates the object of desire in uses like: هل لك في (أن) *hal laka fī* (*ʾan*) 'Do you desire to ...?', من له في (أن) *man lahū fī* (*ʾan*) 'Who desires to ...?'

§**297.** a) ك *ka-* 'as, like' is used in qualitative comparison: رجال كأسود الغابة *rijālun ka-ʾusūdi 'l-ghābati* 'men like lions of the thicket', قد خلته كصخرة *qad khiltuhū ka-ṣakhratin* 'I imagined him as a rock', كذلك *ka-dhālika* 'so, like this, thus' (§284 c).

Note 1. The personal suffixes are not added to *ka-* ; however, they do combine with مثل *mithlu* (see below). Nevertheless, *ka-* may on rare occasion appear in constructions with independent personal pronouns: كأنا *ka-ʾanā* 'like me', كأنت *ka-ʾanta* 'like you', كهو *ka-huwa* 'like him'.

Note 2. Sporadically, كما *ka-mā* occurs in the sense of *ka-* (§285 c); cf. §418 b. Concerning كأيّ *ka-ʾayyin*, see §287.1.

b) *ka-* frequently functions as a substantive: 'one like ...', 'something like ...': كاللّيلة *ka-'l-laylati* 'something like this night, a night like this', يرينا كالدّراهم *yurīnā ka-'d-darāhimi* 'He showed us something like dirhams'. In poetry, such expressions are sometimes combined with additional prepositions: تفترّ عن كالأقحوان *taftarru ʿan ka-'l-ʾuqḥuwāni* 'When he laughed, he showed something like camomile flowers, i.e., teeth'.

Note 3. Sometimes *ka-* functions as a relative: كحين *ka-ḥīni* 'sometime when' (on حين *ḥīna*, see §346). It is also used to indicate examples: الألوان كالحمرة والصّفرة *(ʾa)l-ʾalwānu ka-ʾl-ḥumrati wa-aṣ-ṣufrati* 'colors like red, yellow . . . '.

c) مثل *mithlu*, pl. أمثال *ʾamthālu* 'something like, one like' (§§146 b; 388 b), which is inflected as a noun, has the same meaning as *ka-*: أمثالهم *ʾamthāluhum* 'people like them', قل له مثل ذلك *qul lahū mithla dhālika* 'Speak to him in that way', أتى بناقة مثل ناقتي *ʾatā bi-nāqatin mithli nāqatī* 'He came with a camel like mine'. It may also be combined with *ka-*: ليس كمثله شيء *laysa ka-mithlihī shayʾun* 'There is nothing like him'.

§**298.** مع *maʿa* 'together with, simultaneously with': خرجوا معه *kharajū maʿahū* 'They went out together with him', ذهبنا به معنا *dhahabnā bihī maʿanā* 'We took him away with us' (§294 b), إنّ الله مع الصّابرين *ʾinna ʾl-lāha maʿa ʾṣ-ṣābirīna* 'God is with those who are steadfast', مع طلوع الشّمس *maʿa ṭulūʿi ʾsh-shamsi* 'with the rising of the sun', وقال مع ذلك *wa-qāla maʿa dhālika* 'And, moreover, he said . . . '. Frequently, a simultaneous condition is referred to, because of which or despite which something has occurred: قتل مع قوّته *qutila maʿa quwwatihī* 'Despite his strength, he was killed'.

§**299.** من *min* has two distinct uses: 'of, part of, some of' (a–b) and 'from, from the direction of, away from' (c–d).

Note 1. As a result of these two uses, *min* may be employed to paraphrase the genitive, when it is necessary to circumvent the formal requirements of the construct state (§§145 f.): بيت من بيوته *baytun min buyūtihī* 'one of his houses', في الجانب الشّرقيّ من النّهر *fī ʾl-jānibi ʾsh-sharqiyyi min-a ʾn-nahri* 'on the east bank of the river'.

a) *min* 'of, part of, some of' indicates belonging to a larger entity: ليس هذا من عاداته *laysa hādhā min ʿādātihī* 'This is not one of his habits', منهم من تحبّهم *minhum man tuḥibbuhum* 'Among them are those you love', أنت منه *ʾanta minhu* 'You belong to him'. *min* also indicates kind or material: شيء من الخوف *shayʾun min-a ʾl-khawfi* 'some fear', هذا من عيش *hādhā min ʿayshin* 'such a life', عدوّكم من أهل فارس *ʿadūwukum min ʾahli fārisa* 'your enemy from among the Persians', i.e., 'your enemy, the Persians', لباس من الحرير *libāsun min-a ʾl-ḥarīri* 'a garment of silk'. Instead of referring to a whole, it may refer to an entity consisting of more than one part: كلّ من رجال ونساء *kullun min rijālin wa-nisā'in* 'all, namely men and women'. With an indefinite genitive (§141 c), *min* is used in apposition as a means of explication, especially with proper names and personal suffixes: شلّت يدا زيد من قاتل *shallat yadā Zaydin min qātilin* 'May the hands of Zayd (who belongs to the genus "murderer", i.e.), that murderer, wither!', قبحها الله من سيوف *qabaḥahā 'l-lāhu min suyūfin* 'May God ruin them, the swords!', حيّيت من أخ *ḥuyyīta min 'akhin* 'May you, a brother, be greeted!'. See also §421.2.

Note 2. See §425 c on *min* used to supplement a relative.

Note 3. من غير *min ghayri* (§325) means 'without': من غير خلاف *min ghayri khilāfin* 'without contradiction'.

Note 4. In archaic usage, an accusative often replaces the *min* of explication; cf. §§128.2; 263.

b) *min* 'a part of' is used to indicate a partitive relationship, 'some of . . ., someone of . . .': شربت من الماء *sharibtu min-a 'l-mā'i* 'I drank some (of the) water', قد أصاب فؤاده من حبّها *qad 'aṣāba fu'ādahū min ḥubbihā* 'His heart was stricken with (some) love for her', أمرت أن أكون من المؤمنين *'umirtu 'an 'akūna min-a 'l-mu'minīna* 'I was commanded to be one of the believers'; in negative and interrogative sentences: ما نسيت من شيء *mā nasītu min shay'in* 'I have not forgotten any of it', هل لكم من أب *hal lakum min 'abin* 'Do you have a father?'. In combination with terms that denote place and time, *min* refers to a certain segment of the place or time: من فوقه سحاب *min fawqihī saḥābun* '(In the space) above him were clouds', من داخل المسجد *min dākhili 'l-masjidi* '(at a place) within the mosque', من بعد موته *min ba'di mawtihī* 'in the time after his death', من اللّيل *min al-layli* 'in a part of the night,', i.e., 'at night', من الغد *min-a 'l-ghadi* 'the next morning,' رجع من وقته *raja'a min waqtihī* 'He returned (in a part of his time, i.e.) at the same time, immediately'.

c) *min* 'from' indicates the direction from which something comes out: خرج صوت من الباب *kharaja ṣawtun min-a 'l-bābi* 'A voice came out of the gate', دخل من الباب *dakhala min-a 'l-bābi* 'He came in through (from) the gate'; — in constructions with other prepositions: جاء من عند الخليفة *jā-*

ʾa min ʿindi ʾl-khalīfati 'He came from being with the Caliph', من فوق ظهر الفرس min fawqi ẓahri ʾl-farasi 'from (off) the back of the horse' (§291.3); in time: بعد حول من مقتل أخيه baʿda ḥawlin min maqtali ʾakhīhi 'a year since the murder of his brother'. *min* frequently indicates the origin or cause: لقيت منك شرّا laqītu minka sharran 'I felt evil coming from you', هذا منك hādhā minka 'this from you', i.e., 'this as a result of your behavior', من نبأ جاءني min nabaʾin jāʾanī 'because of a report that came to me', من بغضه min bughḍihī 'out of hate for him'; cf. §199.2.

d) In the meaning 'away from', *min* indicates distance: قريب منه qarībun minhu 'near him', يعرف الجيّد من الرّديء yaʿrifu ʾl-jayyida min-a ʾr-radīʾi 'He (knows) can distinguish the perfect from the worthless'; 'in relation to': أين نحن منك ʾayna naḥnu minka 'Where are we in relation to you', i.e., 'how incomparable is our situation to yours!', منزلته من الأمير manzilatuhū min-a ʾl-ʾamīri 'His status in relation to the prince', ما هذا الغلام منك mā hādhā ʾl-ghulāmu minka 'What is this boy in relation to you?'. See §125 on the use of *min* in the comparative elative.

§300. منذ *mundhu*, مذ *mudh* (< **min-dhū* §52.2) 'from ... on,' 'since', 'ago' is treated as both a conjunction and a preposition. According to the rules of Arab grammarians, it should be treated as a preposition only when it refers to an unexpired period of time: منذ السّنة mundhu ʾs-sanati = من السّنة min-a ʾs-sanati 'as of, from this year on, since this year', but منذ سنة mundhu sanatun 'a year ago'. Contrary to this rule, the genitive nevertheless is often used after *mundhu*.

Note 1. A clause usually follows *mundhu* when used as a conjunction: منذ خلقنا mundhu khuliqnā 'since we were created', منذ نحن من الأغنياء mundhu naḥnu min-a ʾl-ʾaghniyāʾi 'since we were counted among the rich'.

§301. a) عن *ʿan* 'from, away from' designates complete removal or departure from: بعيد عن الحقّ baʿīdun ʿan al-ḥaqqi 'far removed from the truth', سكت عنّي sakata ʿannī 'He sat silent opposite (cut off from) me', شغله عن شيء shaghalahū ʿan shayʾin 'He occupied him away from something', i.e., 'he distracted him', مات عن ولد māta ʿan waladin 'He died, leaving behind a child'. Like *min* (§299 c-d), *ʿan* also indicates distance and source: عن شمال ʿan shimālin 'on the left'; 'on the basis of': كان ذلك عن أمرك

kāna dhālika ʿan ʾamrika 'That happened on account of your command', حدّثني هشام عن أبيه *ḥaddathanī Hishāmun ʿan ʾabīhi* 'Hisham related on the authority of his father'.

Note 1. عن يمينه (شماله) 'to his right (left)' *ʿan yamīnihī* (*shimālihī*) may be combined with *min*: من عن يمينه *min ʿan yamīnihī* 'on the right side of him.'

Note 2. In the expression عن قريب (قليل) *ʿan qarībin* (*qalīlin*) or عمّا قريب (قليل) *ʿammā qarībin* (*qalīlin*) 'in a short time, shortly' (cf. §285 c), *ʿan* designates a time interval.

b) عن *ʿan* has numerous lexicalized usages, such as the 'elimination of a condition': أطعمه عن الجوع *ʾaṭʿamahū ʿan-i ʾl-jūʿi* 'He gave him something to eat to dispel his hunger'; 'in defense of': أقاتل عنك *ʾuqātilu ʿanka* 'I fought in your defence'; 'opposition': فسق عن أمر ربّه *fasaqa ʿan ʾamri rabbihī* 'He deviated from the command of his lord'; 'as a substitute for': الإبل الّتي نحرت عنك (ʾa)*l-ʾibilu ʾllatī nuḥirat ʿanka* 'the camels that were slaughtered instead of you': 'incompatibility': ضاق عن السّاق خلخالها *ḍāqa ʿan-i ʾs-sāqi khalkhāluhā* 'Her anklet was too small for her leg'; 'exposing': تبسم عن درّ *tabsimu ʿan durrin* 'She laughed showing [her] pearls (i.e., teeth)'; also to refer to a topic, i.e., 'on, about': سئل عنها *suʾila ʿanhā* 'He was asked about her'.

Note 3. *ʿan* may refer equally to something that has been removed as to that from which it has been removed: عفا عن ذنبه *ʿafā ʿan dhanbihī* 'He forgave his sin' or عفا عنه ذنبه *ʿafā ʿanhu dhanbahū* 'He forgave him his sin'.

§302. على *ʿalā* 'on, above' is used in the following ways:

a) 'on top of', 'above': على وجه الماء *ʿalā wajhi ʾl-māʾi* 'on the surface of the water, over the water', عليه ثوب *ʿalayhi thawbun* 'On him is (i.e., he wore) a garment': to indicate superiority: كان أميرا على العراق *kāna ʾamīran ʿalā ʾl-ʿirāqi* 'He was commander over Iraq'; 'at the front of': لقيهم على ماء *laqiyahum ʿalā māʾin* 'He met them at a watering hole', قرأ على أبيه *qaraʾa ʿalā ʾabīhi* 'He recited (the Koran) before his father, i.e., studied it under his guidance'.

Note 1. Infrequently in expressions of time: على حين *ʿalā ḥīni* 'at the time of ...', على عهد *ʿalā ʿahdi* 'in the era of ...'.

Note 2. *ʿalā* as 'over, higher than' is used for comparison: فضّلنا بعضهم على بعض منهم *faḍḍalnā baʿḍahum ʿalā baʿḍin minhum* (Koran 2:253) 'We preferred some of them to the others'.

b) 'onto, into the presence of, before': سقط على الأرض *saqaṭa ʿalā 'l-ʾarḍi* 'He fell onto the ground', دخل على الملك *dakhala ʿalā 'l-maliki* 'He came into the presence of the king', خاف عليك *khāfa ʿalayka* 'He was fearful in your presence' often to indicate that against which something is directed: تجير عدوّنا علينا *tujīru ʿadūwanā ʿalaynā* 'You defended our enemy against us', دعا علينا *daʿā ʿalaynā* 'He invoked (God) against us', i.e., 'cursed us' as opposed to دعا لهم *daʿā lahum* 'He invoked (God) in favor of them', i.e., 'blessed them'.

c) 'obligation, duty': هذا حرام عليكم *hādhā ḥarāmun ʿalaykum* 'This is forbidden to you', عليك أن تفعل ذلك *ʿalayka ʾan tafʿala dhālika* 'You are obligated (it is your duty) to do that'; cf. §295.5.

Note 3. Similarly in these uses: عليك به *ʿalayka bihī* 'Depend on him!', عليه بي *ʿalayhi bī* 'He must rely on me!'.

d) 'on the basis of', for indicating the basis of a condition or action: ليس حكمه على شيء *laysa ḥukmuhū ʿalā shayʾin* 'His judgment is baseless', هذا على قسمين *hādhā ʿalā qismayni* 'This consists of two parts', هو على دين آبائه *huwa ʿalā dīni ʾābāʾihī* 'He follows the religions of his fathers', ما أنا عليه *mā ʾanā ʿalayhi* 'that (i.e., the condition) in which I am', جاء على أنّه أبي *jāʾa ʿalā ʾannahū ʾabī* 'He came by virtue of his being my father', صالحنا على ألف دينار *ṣālaḥanā ʿalā ʾalfi dīnārin* 'He made peace with us on the condition (that he be paid) 1,000 dinars'; to express a negative pre-condition ('despite'): قتله على صغر سنّه *qatalahū ʿalā ṣighari sinnihī* 'He killed him despite his young age'; — often in the sense of 'following the pattern of, corresponding to, according to': كانت عدّتنا على عدّتهم *kānat ʿiddatunā ʿalā ʿiddatihim* 'Our number corresponds to theirs', هذا على ما ذكرناه *hādhā ʿalā mā dhakarnāhu* 'This is according to what we have reported'.

Note 4. *ʿalā ... min* is used to indicate distance: كان من مكّة على ليلة *kāna min Makkata ʿalā laylatin* 'It was a night('s journey) distant from Mecca', على ستّة أشهر من خلافة عمر *ʿalā sittati ʾa<u>sh</u>hurin min <u>kh</u>ilāfati ʿUmara* 'After six months of the caliphate of Umar'.

Note 5. على يدي *ʿalā yaday*, على أيدي *ʿalā ʾaydī* 'at the hand of' has the sense 'as a result of the act of, through, by'.

§**303.** إلى *ʾilā* 'in the direction of, toward' is used to indicate:

a) a direction, a goal, or an obtainable end: إليك قطعنا الفلاة *ʾilayka qaṭaʿnā 'l-falāta* '(On our way) to you, we traversed the desert', أمر به إلى السجن *ʾamara bihī ʾilā 'l-sijni* 'He ordered him (thrown) into prison'; إلى اليوم *ʾilā 'l-yawmi* 'until today', إلى سنة *ʾilā sanatin* '(after a period) of up to a year', ثمانون دينارا إلى مائة *<u>th</u>amānūna dīnāran ʾilā miʾatin* '80 to 100 dinars'.

Note 1. *ʾilā* may be combined with other prepositions (§291.3).

Note 2. In addition to *min ... ʾilā* 'from ... to', in post-classical Arabic, *min ... wa-ʾilā* sometimes occurs; cf. §308.5.

Note 3. *ʾilā* often occurs for *li-* (§295), when there is ambiguity: هو أحبّ إليّ منك *huwa ʾaḥabbu ʾilayya minka* 'He is dearer to me than you'.

b) a tendency to, belonging to, and the like: لونه إلى السّواد *lawnuhū ʾilā 's-sawādi* 'His color tends toward black', كان إليه الشّرطة *kāna ʾilayhi 's<u>h</u>-<u>sh</u>urṭatu* 'The police were assigned to him', الشأم وما إليه من البلاد (ʾa)*s<u>h</u>-<u>Sh</u>aʾmu wa-mā ʾilayhā min-a 'l-bilādi* 'Damascus and the country that belongs to it'; هو إلى الطّول ما هو *huwa ʾilā 'ṭ-ṭūli mā huwa* 'He tends to be somewhat tall'.

c) the immediate proximity: وجدناهم إلى نهر الأردنّ *wajadnāhum ʾilā nahri 'l-ʾUrdunni* 'We found them at the river Jordan', إلى جانبه *ʾilā jānibihī* 'at his side, next to him'.

Note 4. As an order, إليك *ʾilayka* means 'Keep back!, be off'; in the same way, إليك عنّي *ʾilayka ʿannī* 'Stay away from me!'.

§304. حتّى *ḥattā* 'until, to (cf. §439) is occasionally treated like a preposition: حتّى البحر *ḥattā 'l-baḥri* 'up to the sea', حتّى الممات *ḥattā 'l-mamāti* 'until death'.

Note 1. In cases like دعاهم بأجمعهم حتّى عمرو *daʿāhum bi-ʾajmaʿihim ḥattā ʿAmrin* 'He summoned them all together up to and including Amr', *ḥattā* acquires the meaning 'even' and is treated in post-classical Arabic as a particle: دعاهم بأجمعهم حتّى عمرا *daʿāhum bi-ʾajmaʿihim ḥattā ʿAmran* 'He summoned them all together, even Amr', قد جاء كلّ النّاس حتّى أنت *qad jāʾa kullu 'n-nāsi ḥattā ʾanta* 'All the people have come, even you'.

§305. لدى *ladā* 'at, near': لاقيته لدى الباب *lāqaytuhū ladā 'l-bābi* 'I met him at the door', ما لديّ *mā ladayya* 'What is with me?', i.e., 'What do I have with me?' or 'What do I feel?', لدى القيظ *ladā 'l-qayẓi* 'in summer'; أتى من لديكم *ʾatā min ladaykum* 'He came from you'.

§306. لدن *ladun*, in the construction من لدن *min ladun* 'from' هب لنا من لدنك رحمة *hab lanā min ladunka raḥmatan* (Koran 3:8) 'Give us compassion from You!', من لدن ابتدائه إلى تمامه *min ladun-i 'btidāʾihī ʾilā tamāmihī* 'From its beginning to its end'.

Note 1. Frequently, *ladun*, with or without *min*, is a conjunction 'since': (من) لدن متع الضّحى *(min) ladun mataʿa 'ḍ-ḍuḥā* 'Since the forenoon shone brightly; also لدن غدوة حتّى غابت الشّمس *ladun ghudwatan ḥattā ghābat-i 'sh-shamsu* 'from morning until the sun set' (§439). Also used as conjunctions are (من) لدن أن *(min) ladun ʾan* (*ʾanna*), منذ لدن *mundhu ladun* (§300).

Note 2. من لد *min ladu* occurs as a rare short form.

§307. عند *ʿinda* 'at' indicates that which is present or available: شفعاؤنا عند الله *shufaʿāʾunā ʿinda 'l-lāhi* 'our intercessors with God', عندك لها دواء *ʿindaka lahā dawāʾun* '(With you is, i.e.) you possess a remedy for it', كانت عنده *kānat ʿindahū* 'She was in his possession (i.e., his wife)', الحلم عند الغضب *(ʾa)l-ḥilmu ʿinda 'l-ghaḍabi* 'clemency considering the anger'; in time: عند القحط *ʿinda 'l-qaḥṭi* 'during the famine', عند ذلك *ʿinda dhālika* 'then, thereupon, at the moment'.

Note 1. *ʿinda* frequently means 'in the opinion of': كان عندنا ميّتا *kāna ʿindanā mayyitan* 'He was in our opinion dead', ما عندك *mā ʿindaka* 'What do you think?'.

Note 2. *ʿinda* may occur in constructions with *min* and *ʾilā* in a directional sense; cf. §§291.3; 299 c.

§**308.** a) بين *bayna* 'between, among' indicates both separation and connection between things: جمع بينهم *jamaʿa baynahum* 'He brought them together', يميّز بين وجهين *yumayyizu bayna wajhayni* 'He distinguished (between) the two viewpoints'; in reciprocal relationships: قالت النّساء بينهنّ *qālat-i 'n-nisāʾu baynahunna* 'The women spoke to each other'.

Note 1. In combination with *bayna*, verbal stem III means 'bring about separation or connection': عادى بينهم *ʿādā baynahum* 'He promoted enmity among them', لاءم بينهم *lāʾama baynahum* 'He brought about a reconciliation between them'.

Note 2. بين يدي *bayna yaday* ('between the hands of') means 'before, in the presence of': قام بين يدي الأمير *qāma bayna yaday-i 'l-ʾamīri* 'He stood before the prince', also بين يدي سريره *bayna yaday sarīrihī* 'before his throne'; sometimes with the same meaning بين أيدي *bayna ʾaydī*, بين أرجل *bayna ʾarjuli* (from رجل *rijlun* 'foot').

Note 3. *bayna* may be combined with *min* and *ʾilā* when they designate direction: خرج من بينهم *kharaja min baynihim* 'He departed from their midst' (§291.3).

b) 'Between ... and' is expressed by بين ... و *bayna ... wa-*; when the pronominal suffixes are added or clarification is necessary, it is بين ... وبين *bayna ... wa-bayna*: بيني وبينك *baynī wa-baynaka* 'between you and me'. As a result of contamination from *min ... ʾilā* (*ḥattā*) 'from ... up to', one sometimes encounters بين ... إلى (حتّى) *bayna ... ʾilā* (*ḥattā*): بين الصفا إلى المروة *bayna 'ṣ-Ṣafā ʾilā 'l-Marwata* 'between Ṣafā and Marwa' or 'from Ṣafā to Marwa'.

Note 4. In poetry, with the same meaning, بين ... ف *bayna ... fa-* (§329) is used with terms denoting places.

Note 5. Also as a result of contamination, the expression بين ... وإلى (فإلى) *bayna* ... *wa-ʾilā* (*fa-ʾilā*) occasionally occurs; cf. §303.2.

c) ما بين *mā bayna* ('what is between') occurs instead of *bayna* when the expression is syntactically a nominative or genitive: فرق ما بيننا وبينهم *farqu mā baynanā wa-baynahum* 'the difference between them and us'; *mā bayna* also appears in the position of an accusative: كان ينام ما بين المغرب والعشاء *kāna yanāmu mā bayna 'l-maghribi wa-'l-ʿishāʾi* 'He used to sleep (in the time) between sunset and evening prayer'.

Note 6. فيما بين *fī-mā bayna* is close in meaning to *bayna*: قالوا فيما بينهم *qālū fī-mā baynahum* 'They spoke among themselves'.

Note 7. In pre-classical Arabic, *bayna* may be rendered in the genitive: مودّة بينكم *mawaddatu baynikum* 'the love between you'.

d) With an indefinite genitive singular (§141 c) following, *bayna* ... *wa-* indicates a whole consisting of several parts ("partly ... partly, some ... some"): تراهم بين قائم وقاعد *tarāhum bayna qāʾimin wa-qāʿidin* 'You see them, some standing, some sitting'. In this use, *bayna* may appear with partitive *min*: تأتون من بين تاجر وأجير *taʾtūna min bayni tājirin wa-ʾajīrin* 'You come, some merchants, some workers'. Sometimes, أو *ʾaw* 'or' occurs with the same meaning instead of *wa-*: قوم بين هارب أو قتيل *qawmun bayna hāribin ʾaw qatīlin* 'a people, partly fleeing, partly killed'.

§309. a) دون *dūna* 'beneath' denotes an inferior position: شعب دون القنّة *shiʿbun dūna 'l-qunnati* 'a ravine below the peak'; mostly in reference to rank, value, or weight 'under, short of': النحاس دون الفضّة (*ʾa*)*l-nuḥāsu dūna 'l-fiḍḍati* 'copper is of less value than silver', ليس بدونه *laysa bi-dūnihī* (§291.3) 'He is not beneath him (in rank)'.

b) 'before, on this side', to describe a position that obstructs or protects against something: إنّه لكم دون النّاس *ʾinnahū lakum dūna 'n-nāsi* 'He stood (as protection) for you before the people', أغلق دوني الباب *ʾaghlaqa dūnī 'l-bāba* 'He locked the door on me (closing me in or locking me out)', إنّ دون الغد اللّيلة *ʾinna dūna 'l-ghadi 'l-laylata* 'Before morning is night'.

Note 1. دونك *dūnaka* '(There it is) before you!' as a command 'Seize it!' is used with the accusative: دونك الدّرهم *dūnaka 'd-dirhama* 'Take the dirham!', دونكموها *dūnakumūhā* 'Grab them/her!'. As an interjection *dūnaka* has the sense of 'look out, take care!'.

c) 'Apart from, to the exclusion of, barring, without', as when the hindrance is considered insurmountable: لا يكتسب المال دون مشقّة *lā yuktasabu 'l-mālu dūna* (or بدون *bi-dūni*) *ma<u>sh</u>aqqatin* 'Nothing is acquired without toil' معه ألف عبد دون من كان من عشيرته *maʿahū ʾalfu ʿabdin dūna man kāna min ʿa<u>sh</u>īratihī* 'He has 1,000 slaves, excluding his family members'.

Note 2. In this use, *dūna* is often combined with *min*: يعبدون الاصنام من دون الله *yaʿbudūna 'l-aṣnāma min dūni 'l-lāhi* 'They worship the idols (to the exclusion of God, i.e.), but not God'.

Particles of Exception and Restriction

§310. إلّا *ʾillā* 'except, unless' (< *ʾ*in-lā* 'if not'):

a) In positive sentences, the exception follows in the accusative: قتل كلّهم إلّا أباك *qutila kulluhum ʾillā ʾabāka* 'All were killed except your father', اشتراه بمائة درهم إلّا واحدا (ʾ*i*)*shtarāhu bi-miʾati dirhamin ʾillā wāḥidan* 'He bought it for a hundred dirhams save one (i.e., 99 dirhams)'.

Note 1. ʾ*illā* 'if not' occurs rarely as a conditional (§452).

Note 2. Occasionally in post-classical usage, the personal suffixes are attached directly to the particle: إلّاي *ʾillā-ya*, إلّاك *ʾillā-ka*, etc.

b) In negative sentences, among which may be included interrogative (§335 a) and unreal conditional (§453) sentences, the exception agrees in case with the general term (i.e., that from which the exception is made): ما لنا نصير إلّا الله *mā lanā naṣīrun ʾillā 'l-lāhu* 'We have no helper but God', هل رأيت أحدا إلّا عليّا *hal raʾayta ʾaḥadan ʾillā ʿAlīyan* 'Have you seen anyone but 'Ali?'; لا إله إلّا الله *lā ʾilāha ʾillā 'l-lāhu* 'There is no god other than Allāh' (§318 c), where *lā ʾilāha* is in the position of a nominative. The exception must be in the accusative, however, if it precedes the general term or is of another species: ما لنا إلّا الله نصير *mā lanā ʾillā 'l-lāha naṣīrun* (see above), ما جاءني أحد إلّا حمارا *mā jāʾanī ʾaḥadun ʾillā ḥimāran* 'No one came to me but an ass'. Contrary to these rules, the nominative occurs sometimes instead of the accusative.

c) In negative sentences, frequently only the exception is identified, and thus, a positive restriction ('only') is expressed: ما هذا إلّا لأنفسهم *mā hādhā ʾillā li-ʾanfusihim* 'This is only for themselves', لا يعلم الغيب إلّا هو *lā yaʿlamu ʾl-ghayba ʾillā huwa* 'Only He knows the concealed'. Personal suffixes used as objects after *ʾillā* must be introduced with *ʾiyyā* (§272): ألّا يعبدوا إلّا إيّاه *ʾallā yaʿbudū ʾillā ʾiyyāhu* 'that they worship only Him'.

d) Subordinate clauses may also follow *ʾillā*: ما أظنّه إلّا قد مات *mā ʾaẓunnuhū ʾillā qad māta* 'I can only believe that he died', لا يلقاني إلّا وسيفي في يدي *lā yalqānī ʾillā wa-sayfī fī yadī* 'He will not meet me, unless I have my sword in hand' (§409), لا تسجد إلّا أن تكون طاهرا *lā tasjud ʾillā ʾan takūna ṭāhiran* 'Do not bow down in worship, unless you are pure'. إلّا أنّ *ʾillā ʾanna* (and غير أنّ *ghayru ʾanna* §311) is used in an adversative sense: كان لي ابن إلّا أنّه توفّي *kāna lī ʾbnun ʾillā ʾannahū tuwuffiya* 'I had a son (except that, i.e.), but he died.'

Note 3. *mā huwa ʾillā* is used to introduce surprising events, e.g.: ما هو إلّا أن رآني فعرفني (حتّى عرفني) *mā huwa ʾillā ʾan raʾānī fa-ʿarafanī* (or *ḥattā ʿarafanī*) 'He had hardly (no sooner) seen me, when (than) he recognized me'.

§311. غير *ghayru*, سوى *siwā* 'other than, different from' (§325) and the preposition دون *dūna* (§309 c) also indicate exceptions. They are used either with the genitive or with affixed personal suffixes. The case of *ghayru* is determined according to the rules that hold for substantives after *ʾillā* (§310 a–c): ما وجدت غيرك (سواك) *mā wajadtu ghayraka (siwāka)* 'I found only you', ذهب النّاس غيرنا *dhahaba ʾn-nāsu ghayranā* 'The people went away with the exception of us', من إله غير اللّه *man ʾilāhun ghayru ʾl-lāhi* '...who is a god other than God ...? (Koran 6:46; 28:71, 72).

§312. ما عدا *mā ʿadā*, ما خلا *mā khalā* or عدا *ʿadā*, خلا *khalā* 'what goes beyond ...' are used like particles of exception. Consistent with their origin as verbs, the accusative follows: كلّ شيء ما خلا اللّه باطل *kullu shayʾin mā khalā ʾl-lāha bāṭilun* 'Everything but God is vain'. By analogy with سوى *siwā* (§311), the genitive may also appear after *ʿadā* and *khalā*.

Note 1. Verbal constructions with relative *mā* are also possible: منع ما عدا واجبه *manaʿa mā ʿadā wājibahū* 'He refused to do whatever exceeded the bounds of his duty'.

Note 2. حاشا, حاشى *ḥāshā* 'far be it!' (e.g., حاشا للّه *ḥāshā li-llāhi* 'God forbid!') is used as a particle of exception like *ʿadā, khalā*: حاشى عليّ *ḥāshā ʿAlīyin*, ما حاشى عليّا *mā ḥāshā ʿAlīyan* 'except for Alī'.

§**313.** إنّما *ʾinnamā* is an emphatic and restrictive particle 'only'. While *ʾinnamā* stands at the beginning, that which is affected by it is usually, but not always, placed at the end of the sentence for emphasis: إنّما هي خرقاء حمقاء *ʾinnamā hiya kharqāʾu ḥamqāʾu* 'She is only a slovenly, stupid (woman)', إنّما قال ذلك لأنّه ... *ʾinnamā qāla dhālika li-ʾannahū* ... 'He said that only because ...'; very often adversative 'but, rather': إنّما هو دينار *ʾinnamā huwa dīnārun* 'It is rather a dinar (not a dirham!)'.

Note 1. In pre-classical Arabic, *ʾinnamā* can be understood as *ʾinna* (§339) with relative *mā*: إنّما أبلى عظامي حبّها *ʾinnamā ʾablā ʿiẓāmī ḥubbuhā-* 'What has worn out my bones is (certainly only) my love for her'.

§**314.** إمّالا *ʾimmālā* 'at least': هو إمّالا رجل *huwa ʾimmālā rajulun* 'That is then at least a man!'; to restrict the imperative with a following *fa-* (§222.3) إمّالا فابصروا *ʾimmālā fa-ʾbṣirū* 'At least have patience!'.

Adverbs

§**315.** a) Adverbs denoting conditions have developed from various accusative usages into independent terms (§§373 ff.): جدّا *jiddan* 'very', جميعا *jamīʿan* 'altogether'; definite: الهوينا (*ʾa*)*l-huwaynā* 'leisurely', البتّة (*ʾa*)*l-battata* 'absolutely' (with negatives). Note here also analogical formations like معا *maʿan* 'together' (from *maʿa* §298), أوّلا *ʾawwalan* 'first' (§127 b).

Note 1. كثيرا ما *kathīran mā* 'frequently', قليلا ما *qalīlan mā* 'seldom' with subordinate *mā* are used like *ṭāla-mā, qalla-mā* (§262.1).

b) Terms indicating time in particular appear in the adverbial accusative: يوما *yawman* 'one day', ليلا *laylan* 'at night', غدا *ghadan* 'tomorrow', قدما *qidman* 'once, in olden times'; definite: اليوم (*ʾa*)*l-yawma* 'today', البارحة (*ʾa*)*l-bāriḥata* 'yesterday'; with following genitive: يوم الوغى *yawma 'l-waghā* 'on the day of the uproar', ليالي العيد *layāliya 'l-ʿīdi* 'in the nights of the festival', يومئذ *yawma-ʾidhin* 'then, on that day' (§284.2); see also §§346; 420.

Note 2. Adverbial accusative forms are inflected following prepositions: بعد غد *baʿda ghadin* 'the day after tomorrow', إلى اليوم *ʾilā 'l-yawmi* 'until today'. After *ladun* (§306), the adverb may be uninflected: لدن غدوة *ladun ghudwatan* (or *ghudwatin*) 'from early morning'.

§**316.** a) Accusative adverbs are often used to bid someone (to do) something (§375): مهلا *mahlan* 'slowly' or 'take it easy!', أهلا وسهلا *ʾahlan wa-sahlan* 'Welcome!'.

b) Many adverbs used in this manner take the 2nd person suffix: رويدا *ruwaydan* 'leisurely', رويدك *ruwaydaka* 'take it easy!, شأنك *shaʾnaka* 'It's your business!', i.e., 'Do as you wish!', شأنكها *shaʾnakahā* 'Do with her as you wish!' (§271).

§**317.** Several adverbs have the uninflected ending *-u*: بعد *baʿdu* 'later, afterwards', تحت *taḥtu* 'beneath' فوق *fawqu* 'above', وراء *warāʾu* 'behind' عل *ʿalu* 'above'. These can also be combined with partitive *min* (§299 b); من فوق *min fawqu* '(within the space) above'.

Note 1. Diminutives (§81) also figure among the adverbs: قبيل *qubaylu* 'a little before' from قبل *qablu* 'earlier, before'.

Note 2. The ending *-u* also appears in لا غير *lā ghayru* 'nothing else, no more', فحسب *fa-ḥasbu* 'and that's all, only'.

Note 3. See §§284; 288 on demonstrative and interrogative adverbs.

Negation

§**318.** a) لا *lā* negates the imperfect (§184), the subjunctive (§196), the energetic (§198), the jussive (§195 b), the perfect when it expresses a wish (§182 b), and individual elements of the sentence: ركبت بغلا لا حمارا *rakibtu* *baghlan lā ḥimāran* 'I rode a mule, not an ass', فتى ولا كمالك *fatan wa-lā ka-Mālikin* 'a young man, but not like Mālik'. See §294.4 on بلا *bi-lā* 'without'.

Note 1. *lā* is affixed to particles that introduce clauses: ألّا *ʾallā* = أن لا *ʾan lā* 'that not', إلّا *ʾillā* < *ʾin-lā* 'if not' (§§310; 452), لولا *law-lā* 'if not' (§455), هلّا *hal-lā* 'is not ...?, why not?' (§335), كيلا *kay-lā* 'so that not' (§438), كلّا *kallā* 'not at all, by no means'.

b) *wa-lā* continues the subsequent negation of sentence elements in a series of negatives. لم يجد إنسا ولا جنّا *lam yajid ʾinsan wa-lā jinnan* 'He found neither men nor ghosts', i.e., 'no one', رجل غير طويل ولا قصير *rajulun ghayru ṭawīlin wa-lā qaṣīrin* 'a man neither tall nor short'. In expressions that consist of several elements, *lā ... wa-lā* may be used instead of other negatives in the first element: لا رأى ولا سمع *lā raʾā wa-lā samiʿa* 'He neither saw nor heard', لا هو ذو مال ولا ذو مجد *lā huwa dhū mālin wa-lā dhū majdin* 'He is a man of neither wealth nor nobility'.

c) *lā* is used with a directly following accusative in the definite state (§142) as a general denial: لا شكّ *lā shakka* 'There is no doubt'. This expression appears mostly in the subject position (§§367.2; 369 b): لا لذّات للشّيب *lā ladhdhāti lish-shībi* 'There is no pleasure for old men'; cf. 310 b.

Note 2. أب *ʾabun* 'father, أخ *ʾakhun* 'brother (§150) appear in the construct state: لا أبا لك *lā ʾabā laka* 'May you have no father!' (also on occasion لا أباك *lā ʾabāka*).

Note 3. According to the rules of the Arab grammarians, the substantive should be in the indefinite state if it occurs in combination with a dependent prepositional phrase: لا حاجة إليه عندنا *lā ḥājatan ʾilayhi ʿindanā* 'We have no need for him'.

Note 4. When there is more than one element in the negative phrase, the nominative or accusative of the indefinite state may occur in both elements: لا حسّ (حسّا) له ولا عقل (عقلا) *lā ḥissa* (*ḥissun, ḥissan*) *lahū wa-lā ʿaqlun* (*ʿaqla, ʿaqlan*) 'He has neither feeling nor understanding'.

§**319.** لم *lam* with the jussive denies that an act has been accomplished or something has become a fact (§194); لمّا *lam-mā* negates in a preliminary way ('not yet'): لمّا يمت *lammā yamut* 'He has (had) not yet died'.

Note 1. Instead of *lammā*, *lam ... baʿdu* (§317) may occur: لم يمت بعد *lam yamut baʿdu* 'He did not die — only later, i.e., not yet'.

§**320.** لن *lan* (< **lā-'an*) with the subjunctive negates a future action (§196 c): لن ينجحوا *lan yunjiḥū* 'They will not succeed'.

§**321.** ما *mā* is always at the beginning of the sentence. Unlike *lam* and *lā*, *mā* with the perfect denies the whole fact; with the imperfect, the action or its possibility: ما جعت *mā juʿtu* 'I am not (did not become) hungry' (cf. §189), ما يراك *mā yarāka* 'He does not see you at all, cannot see you'.

Note 1. Typically, *mā* is used after particles expressing oaths and in sentences containing the particle of exception *ʾillā* (§310).

Note 2. See §367 a for *mā* used to negate nominal sentences.

§**322.** إن *ʾin* (§52.1) is functionally equivalent to *mā*: إن أدري *ʾin ʾadrī* 'I do not know', إن الحكم إلّا لله *ʾin-i 'l-ḥukmu ʾillā li-llāhi* (Koran 6:57; 12:40, 67) 'Judgment is God's alone'. This negative particle may be combined with *mā*: ما إن جزعت *mā ʾin jaziʿtu* 'I am not at all worried'.

§**323.** a) ليس *laysa* is an inflected negative (§209) and is used chiefly to negate nominal sentences (§367 a). The predicate is in the accusative or is introduced by *bi-* (§294 d): لست بخيلا *lastu bakhīlan* or لست ببخيل *lastu bi-bakhīlin* 'I am not miserly'. Verbal predicates may also occur: لسنا نصل إليك *lasnā naṣilu ʾilayka* 'We do not come to you' (§§431 f.).

Note 1. أليس *ʾa-laysa* (§335) 'is not?' often introduces negative interrogative sentences: ألست أعطيتك *ʾa-lastu ʾaʿṭaytuka* 'Did I not give you?'.

Note 2. *laysa* may occur in combination with *kāna* when it indicates the past (§190): كان ليس ببخيل *kāna laysa bi-bakhīlin* 'He was not miserly'.

b) Uninflected *laysa* negates single elements of the sentence: ليس عن هذا نسألك *laysa ʿan hādhā nasʾaluka* 'We are not asking you about that', ليس أنا قتلتهم *laysa ʾanā qataltuhum* 'It was not I who killed them'.

In non-classical usage, it also occurs with verbs: ليس نقبل *laysa naqbalu* 'We do not accept'.

§**324.** لات *lāta* 'it is not' is used sporadically in pre-classical Arabic as a negative: لات حين مناص *lāta ḥīna manāṣin* (Koran 38:3) 'But the time is none to escape', لات هنّا *lāta hannā* 'That is not so'.

§**325.** a) غير *ghayru* and سوى *siwā* 'other than, different from' exclude following substantives in the genitive, personal suffixes, or adjectives: زينب وغيرها من النّساء *Zaynabu wa-ghayruhā min-a 'n-nisāʾi* 'Zaynab and other (than her from among the) women', نتوكّل إلى غيرك *natawakkalu ʾilā ghayrika* 'We place our trust in someone other than you', غير أحد *ghayru ʾaḥadin* 'not one, i.e., more than one, several', غير مرّة *ghayru marratin* 'not once, i.e., several times' (§315).

b) *ghayru* negates a nominal predicate and attributive: إنّها غير ملومة *ʾinnahā ghayru malūmatin* 'She is not blameworthy', رجل غير ملوم *rajulun ghayru malūmin* 'a man who is not reprehensible'. When there is more than one element to negate, *lā ... wa-lā* may occur instead of *ghayru ... wa-lā* (§318 b): رجل لا طويل ولا قصير *rajulun lā ṭawīlun wa-lā qaṣīrun* 'a man neither tall nor short'.

Note 1 In post-classical usage, *ghayru* in constructions with attributives may take the article: الأشياء الغير الثّابتة (ʾ*a*)*l-ʾashyāʾu 'l-ghayru 'th-thābitati* 'the impermanent things' (§398.1).

Note 2. بغير *bi-ghayri* (§294.4), من غير *min ghayri* (§299.3) 'without' may also be continued by *lā*: من غير أب ولا أمّ *min ghayri ʾabin wa-lā ʾummin* 'without father or mother'.

Note 3. For *ghayru* used as a particle of exception, see §311; *ghayru mā*, §285 c; *lā ghayru*, §317.2.

§**326.** بل *bal* '(no) rather, on the contrary' counters a preceding proposition and introduces a correction or confirmation: أعطاني درهما بل درهمين *ʾaʿṭānī dirhaman bal dirhamayni* 'He gave me a dirham, no, rather, two dirhams', ما أقمنا هناك يوما بل شهرا *mā ʾaqamnā hunāka yawman bal shahran* 'We sojourned there not just a day, but a month'.

Note 1. Introducing an answer to a double question (§333): قال أذكر أم أنثى فقلت بل أنثى *qāla ʾa-dhakarun ʾam ʾunthā fa-qultu bal ʾunthā* 'He said, male or female? I then answered, but female (i.e., not male, but female)'.

§**327.** Peculiarities in the use of negatives:

a) Negative particles sometimes become redundant: لم أسمع بمثلك لا حلما ولا جودا *lam ʾasmaʿu bi-mithlika lā ḥilman wa-lā jūdan* 'I have never heard from anyone like you about gentleness or generosity'. Negation in main and secondary clauses comes to mean affirmation: لم نأمن أن لا نجد أمنا *lam naʾman ʾan lā najida ʾamnan* 'We were (not) certain that we would (not) find security'.

b) A negative declaration is produced in pre-classical Arabic after an oath without the use of a negative: بالله أفعل *bi-'l-lāhi ʾafʿalu* 'By God, I would not do that'.

Coordinating Conjunctions

§**328.** a) و *wa-* (§23) joins equivalent sentences and clauses (§§401; 404 ff.). Frequently *wa-* connects the statement to the context (§276.1) or given situation, e.g., when a question is offered in reply to another: أوأنت تكذّبني *ʾa-wa-ʾanta tukadhdhibunī* 'Are you calling me a liar?'.

Note 1. *wa-* introduces coordinated circumstantial clauses (§§407 ff.); with the subjunctive, see §410.1; with the particle expressing oaths with the genitive, §294.2; before a genitive introducing a condition, §389.

b) و *wa-* 'with' and the accusative following joins a substantive to the subject, less frequently to an object, in a verbal sentence. The personal pronoun is introduced by *ʾiyyā-* (§272) after *wa-*: كان وأباه على ما قد علمنا *kāna wa-ʾabāhu ʿalā mā qad ʿalimnā* 'He was (i.e., stood) with his father as far as we know', ما صنعت وإيّاه *mā ṣanaʿta wa-ʾiyyāhu* 'What have you done with him?', سرنا والنّيل *sirnā wa-'n-Nīla* 'We traveled with the Nile, i.e., along the Nile', دعنا وأمرنا *daʿnā wa-ʾamranā* 'Let us alone with our business!'.

Note 2. The Arab grammarians call this *wa-* with accusative واو المعيّة *wāw al-maʿiyyah*, "*wa-* meaning *maʿa*".

Note 3. *wa-* with the accusative does not occur in nominal sentences: أنت وأبوك على ما نعلم *ʾanta wa-ʾabūka ʿalā mā naʿlamu* 'you and your father are in such a relationship, as far as we know'. Yet the accusative may be used after *wa-* in certain nominal phrases: أنت وذاك *ʾanta wa-dhāka* 'you and that!', i.e., 'It is your thing!', ما أنا والأمر *mā ʾanā wa-'l-ʾamra* 'What do I have to do with this affair?', إيّاك والحيّة *ʾiyyāka wa-'l-ḥayyata* 'Watch out for the snake!' (§272.2), شأنكم والرّحيل *shaʾnakum wa-'r-raḥīla* 'You may leave at your discretion' (§316 b).

§**329.** ف *fa-* 'and then, and so, and consequently, for' (§23) indicates a sequence: تغتسل فتطهّر ثوبيك *taghtasilu fa-tuṭahhiru thawbayka* 'You are to wash yourself and then to clean both your garments', جاءوا واحدا فواحدا *jāʾū wāḥidan fa-wāḥidan* 'They came one after the other', من الآن فصاعدا *min-a 'l-ʾāna fa-ṣāʿidan* 'From now on and beyond'; it designates what follows as a result of the preceding statement: ضربته فبكى *ḍarabtuhū fa-bakā* 'I struck him so he cried'; cf. §402.1.

Note 1. On *fa-* after *'ammā*, see §336; *fa-* introducing the apodosis, §§447; 443.1; *fa-'inna-* 'then', §404 b; *fa-* with the subjunctive, §410; with the imperative, §222.3.

Note 2. In poetry, places are presented in sequence by *fa-*: غشيت ديارا بالبقيع فثهمد *ghashītu diyāran bi-'l-Baqīʿi fa-Thahmadin* 'I came to dwellings in al-Baqīʿ and then in Thahmad'.

Note 3. After verbs expressing commands, decisions, and the like, the clause containing the statement of resulting action begins with *fa-*: أمر بالباب فأغلق *ʾamara bi-'l-bābi fa-ʾughliqa* 'He commanded the door to be closed', بدا له فابتنى مسجدا *badā lahū fa-'btanā masjidan* 'It came into his mind to build a mosque' (cf. §359).

Note 4. *fa-* links the verb to a verbal complement: سكت سكتة فأطالها *sakata saktatan fa-ʾaṭālahā* 'He was completely silent and was so for a long time', تكلّم النّاس فأكثروا *takallama 'n-nāsu fa-ʾaktharū* 'The people spoke and did so at length'.

§330. ثمّ *thumma* 'then, thereupon, next, furthermore' joins both sentences and words: إنّه أقام على ذلك أربعين يوما ثمّ طلّقها *ʾinnahū ʾaqāma ʿalā dhālika ʾarbaʿīna yawman thumma ṭallaqahā* 'He passed forty days in this way, then he granted her the divorce'; sometimes in an intensifying sense: قد جرّبوني ثمّ جرّبوني *qad jarrabūnī thumma jarrabūnī* 'They tested me, and then they tested me some more'. Sometimes *thumma* indicates transition from general to specific: جاءنا فتى من قريش ثمّ أحد بني عبد المطّلب *jāʾanā fatan min Qurayshin thumma ʾaḥadu banī ʿAbdi 'l-Muṭṭalibi* 'A young man came to us from the Quraysh, in fact, one of the Banū ʿAbd al-Muṭṭalib'.

Note 1. An alternative form, ثمّت *thummata*, also occurs.

§331. أو *ʾaw* 'or' (§54.1) introduces alternatives: رمى بسهم أو سهمين *ramā bi-sahmin ʾaw sahmayni* 'He shot an arrow or two'.

Note 1. See §411 for *ʾaw* with the subjunctive; in disjunctive conditional clauses, §459 a; cf. also §§308 d; 333.1.

§332. إن *ʾin* and إمّا *ʾimmā* (§459) are used to express alternatives: إمّا ... وإمّا *ʾimmā ... wa-ʾimmā*, إمّا ... أو *ʾimmā ... ʾaw*, and less often إن ... وإن *ʾin ... wa-ʾin*, إن ... أو *ʾin... ʾaw* 'either ... or', e.g., إنّني رجل إمّا محمود وإمّا ذميم *ʾinnanī rajulun ʾimmā maḥmūdun wa-ʾimmā dhamīmun* 'I am a man who is either praiseworthy or blameworthy'.

§333. أم *ʾam* 'or' in questions offering a choice: أ ... أم *ʾa ... ʾam*, on occasion هل ... أم *hal ... ʾam* (§335), e.g., أذلك من عندك أم من عند الله *ʾa-dhālika min ʿindaka ʾam min ʿindi 'l-lāhi* 'Does this come from you or from God?'. The interrogative particle may be lacking following another question or in indirect questions: لا أدري خرج إليهم أم لا *lā ʾadrī kharaja ʾilayhim ʾam lā* 'I do not know, did he depart in their direction, or not?'. The alternative question may come after the statement: صدقت أم أنا مخطئ *ṣadaqta ʾam ʾanā mukhṭiʾun* 'You have spoken the truth, or am I in error?'.

Note 1. *ʾaw* is on occasion used in alternative questions: أعربيّ أنت أو مولى *ʾa-ʿarabiyyun ʾanta ʾaw mawlan* 'Are you an Arab or a client?'.

Note 2. On *ʾam* in disjunctive conditional clauses, see §459.1.

Particles Introducing the Main Clause

§**334.** لَ *la-* (§§22; 23) 'truly, verily' confirms a statement and, as a rule, marks the beginning of a sentence; and almost always it occurs with an elative in the predicate position: للموت خير من حياة على غمض *lal-mawtu khayrun min ḥayātin ʿalā ghamḍin* 'Death is truly better than life in gloom'; cf. also §198. In conditional clauses, *la-* may come before the protasis and apodosis (*la-ʾin* ... *la-* and *law* ... *la-* §447 b). On *la-* after *ʾinna*, see §339 b.

Note 1. In pre-classical Arabic, *la-* sometimes is used with *mā* (§285 c): لما *lamā, lammā* (§339.2). The latter is used, for example, to introduce oaths: أقسم عليك لمّا فعلت ذلك *ʾuqsimu ʿalayka lammā faʿalta dhālika* 'I beseech you, truly, not to do this!' (§456.1).

§**335.** a) أ *ʾa-* (§41 c) and هل *hal* begin interrogative sentences. *ʾa-* is used mainly when the question is left open, and *hal* is used mostly when a negative answer is anticipated and when the question is rhetorical: أعلمت أنّي قد أسلمت *ʾa-ʿalimta ʾannī qad ʾaslamtu* 'Do you know that I have become a Muslim?', هل تذكرني *hal tadhkurunī* 'Then do you remember me?'. Sentences introduced with *hal* are treated like negated sentences (§§294 d; 299 b; 310 b). See §333 on alternative questions.

Note 1. *ʾa-* comes before *wa-*, *fa-*, *thumma* (§§328 ff.); *hal* comes after. — On هل لك في *hal laka fī* ..., see §296.3.

Note 2. *ʾa-* sometimes is lacking: معكم منه شيء *maʿakum minhu shayʾun* 'Do you have any of it with you?'.

b) Negative particles follow immediately after *ʾa-* and *hal*: ألا *ʾa-lā*, أما *ʾa-mā*, أليس *ʾa-laysa* (§323.1), هلّا *hal-lā*, e.g.: فهلّا تشكر لي *fa-hal-lā tashkuru lī* 'Why would you not then give me thanks?'; often as an exclamation: ألا أرسلت إليّ *ʾa-lā ʾarsalta ʾilayya* 'Why have you not sent [it] to me?!'. — On *ʾalā, ʾamā* as interjections, see §347.

Note 3. ألا ترى أنّ *ʾa-lā tarā ʾanna* 'Do you not see that' presents a confirmation: 'After all, it is true that ..., Certainly, ...'.

§336. أمّا *ʾammā* 'as for, regarding' with a nominative following as a subject of a copulative sentence (§§368 ff.). The predicate clause is always joined with *fa-* (§329): أمّا أخوك فاعلم أنّه قد مات *ʾammā ʾakhūka fa-ʿlam ʾannahū qad māta* 'As for your brother, know that he has died'. Adverbial sentence elements and clauses may be set apart by *ʾammā*: أمّا بعد ف *ʾammā baʿdu fa-* ... 'Now then on to ...' (a formula for introducing the main topic).

§337. ربّ *rubba* 'many a' with the indefinite genitive following (§389) is mostly the subject of a copulative sentence (§§389 ff.): ربّ رجل كريم قد لقيت *rubba rajulin karīmin qad laqītu* 'Many a noble man have I met'.

Note 1. Often *yā* (§347) is used before *rubba*.

Note 2. In pre-classical Arabic, the feminine ربّت *rubbata* appears on rare occasion. Sometimes, *rubba, rubbata* occur in combination with *mā* (§285 c): ربّتما غارة *rubbata-mā ghāratin* 'Many a raid'.

Note 3. ربّما *rubba-mā* (with subordinating *mā* §416) 'many a time, sometimes, perhaps': ربّما أكفّ يدي عنكم *rubba-mā ʾakuffu yadī ʿankum* 'Sometimes I restrained my hand from (striking) you'.

§338. After the particles إنّ *ʾinna*, لكنّ *lākinna*, ليت *layta*, لعلّ *laʿalla*, the subject of a nominal or copulative sentence (§§360 ff.; 368 ff.) in the accusative or a personal suffix (§268.1) follows. If the subject does not immediately follow, the 3rd masc. personal suffix appears as the "pronoun of the fact" (ضمير الشّأن *ḍamīr ash-shaʾn*) and represents or anticipates the subject: إنّه لا يفلح المجرمون *ʾinnahū lā yufliḥu 'l-mujrimūna* (Koran 10:17) 'Surely the sinners do not prosper'.

Note 1. أنّ *ʾanna* (§415) 'that', the subordinate clause particle corresponding to *ʾinna*, is also followed by the accusative.

Note 2. *ʾinna* and *lākinna* with the suffixes of the 1st person (*-nī, -nā*) are frequently shortened (§49 c): إنّي *ʾinnī*, إنّا *ʾinnā* = إنّني *ʾinna-nī*, إنّنا *ʾinna-nā*; لكنّي *lākinnī*, لكنّا *lākinnā* = لكنّني *lākinna-nī*, لكنّنا *lākinna-nā*. In combination with *laʿalla*, the 1st person suffix *-ī* occurs in place of *-nī*: لعلّي *laʿallī* rather than لعلّني *laʿalla-nī*.

§339. a) إنّ *ʾinna* in the meaning 'verily, truly' indicates that the following statement is remarkable: إنّ اللّه على كلّ شيء قدير *ʾinna 'l-lāha ʿalā kulli shayʾin qadīrun* (Koran 2:20, 106, 109, etc.) 'Truly, God is powerful over everything'. According to nominal sentence word order (§366), a prepositional phrase as predicate appears between *ʾinna* and the accusative: إنّ في القلعة سجنا *ʾinna fī 'l-qalʿati sijnan* 'Surely, in the fortress is a prison'.

Note 1. إنّما *ʾinna-mā* has a restrictive sense (§313).

b) The predicate after *ʾinnā* is often marked by *la-* (§334): إنّي بك لعارف *ʾinnī bika la-ʿārifun* 'I know you'. When the word order is predicate–subject (§366), *la-* may also come before the subject: إنّ في ذلك لعبرة *ʾinna fī dhālika la-ʿibratan* (Koran 3:13; 24:44; 79:26) 'Surely, in that is a lesson'.

Note 2. The closely related pre-classical particle إن *ʾin* is not followed by the accusative, and the predicate is often marked by *la-* (§334.1): إن كادت لتقتلني *ʾin kādat la-taqtalunī* 'She had nearly killed me', واللّه إن كان لبادنا *wa-'l-lāhi ʾin kāna la-bādinan* 'By God, he was corpulent', إن كلّ نفس لما (لمّا) عليها حافظ *ʾin kullu nafsin lamā (lammā) ʿalayhā ḥāfiẓun* (Koran 86:4) 'Over every soul there is a watcher', which could also be interpreted as 'There is not any soul, but a watcher is above it'.

§340. لكنّ *lākinna*, ولكنّ *wa-lākinna* 'but, yet': ولكنّ كثيرا منهم فاسقون *wa-lākinna kathīran minhum fāsiqūna* (Koran 5:81) 'But many of them are ungodly'. If no substantive or personal suffix follows, (و) لكن (*wa-*) *lākin* or (و) لكنّما (*wa-*) *lākinna-mā* (§416) occurs: لكن ضربته *lākin ḍarabtahū* 'But you struck him'.

Note 1. In pre-classical Arabic, the subject in the nominative may follow *lākin* (cf. §339.2).

§341. ليت *layta* 'if only, would that', frequently with يا *yā* or ألا *ʾalā* (§347), introduces a sentence expressing a wish: ليتني بعيد عنك *laytanī baʿīdun ʿanka* 'If only I were far from you!', يا ليته لم يفعل *yā laytahū lam yafʿal* 'If only he had not done it!'. Rather than the accusative, a clause introduced by *ʾanna* (§415) may follow: ليت أنّه شاعر *layta ʾannahū shāʿirun* 'Would that he were a poet!'.

Note 1. The predicate appears on occasion as a predicate accusative (§§381 f.): ليت زيدا شاخصا *layta Zaydan shākhiṣan* 'If only Zayd would start out!'.

§**342.** لعلّ *la‘alla* 'perhaps' (§338.2): لعلّها سترحمني *la‘allahā sa-tarḥamunī* 'Perhaps she will take pity on me'. Verbal predicate clauses are often introduced by أن *ʼan* 'that' (§414): لعلّ صاحبنا أن يهلك *la‘alla ṣāḥibanā ʼan yahlika* 'Perhaps our companion has perished'.

Note 1. *la-* (§334) has become an inseparable component of *la‘alla.* The form *‘alla* without *la-* does occur in pre-classical Arabic.

Note 2. Verbal عسى *‘asā* 'it could be' (with أن *ʼan* 'that') is occasionally treated like a particle and appears with the personal suffixes: عساه الّذي يسمّيه العرب سولان *‘asāhu ʼlladhī yusammīhi ʼl-‘arabu sūlān* 'Perhaps this is what the Arabs call Sūlān'.

Subordinating Conjunctions

§**343.** a) For conditional particles: إن *ʼin,* إمّا *ʼimmā,* لو *law* 'if', see §§450ff.

b) Temporal particles: إذ *ʼidh,* إذا *ʼidhā* (§280) 'if, when', لمّا *lammā* 'when, after', ما *mā* 'as long as'; see §§442 f.; 462; 464.

Note 1. *mā* is often added to *ʼidhā*, and *ʼan* is often added to *lammā*: إذاما *ʼidhā-mā* 'if, when' (§465), لمّا أن *lammā ʼan* 'after, when'.

§**344.** أن *ʼan* (§196 b), أنّ *ʼanna* (§338.1) 'that' and subordinating ما *mā* 'the fact that' introduce subordinate clauses which occupy the position of substantives in the sentence; see §§414 ff. These particles make subordinate clauses dependent on prepositions and adverbs: بأن *bi-ʼan,* بأنّ *bi-ʼanna* 'by (followed by a gerund), by means of the fact that ...', إلى أن *ʼilā ʼan* 'until, up to the point that', مع أن *ma‘a ʼan* 'although', لأنّ *li-ʼanna* 'because', كأن *ka-ʼan,* كأنّ *ka-ʼanna* 'as if, as though', كما *ka-mā* 'as', فيما *fī-mā* 'during, while', بينما *bayna-mā* > بينا *baynā* 'during, while' (§49.1), بعدما *ba‘da-mā,* بعد أن *ba‘da ʼan* 'after', قبل أن *qabla ʼan,* قبل ما *qabla mā* 'before' (§346.1), كلّما *kulla-mā* 'whenever', the more ..., أوّل ما *ʼawwala mā* 'the moment when, just when', etc.

Note 1. Subordinating *mā* often occurs instead of a substantive which would be dependent on a particle introducing the clause: *rubba-mā* (§337.3), *lākinna-mā* (§340), rarely also *layta-mā* (341), *laʿallā-mā* (§342); also at times *mā* is joined to *ʾanna* and *ka-ʾanna*: أنّما *ʾanna-mā* 'that', كأنّما *ka-ʾanna-mā* 'as if'.

Note 2. A clause introduced with *ʾidh* (§343 b) may also be dependent on *baʿda* 'after': بعد إذ *baʿda ʾidh* 'after'.

§345. The following may function sometimes as prepositions and at other times as conjunctions: لِ *li-* 'so that, in order to' (§§196 b; 295), حتّى *ḥattā* 'until, so that' (§§196 b; 304), منذ *mundhu*, مذ *mudh* 'since' (§300), لدن *ladun*, من لدن *min ladun* 'since' (§306). The following are used only as conjunctions: كي *kay*, لكي *li-kay* 'so that, in order to' (§196 b), حيث *ḥaythu* 'where, inasmuch as' (§441).

Note 1. These conjunctions sometimes occur in constructions with *ʾan* or *mā*: منذ أن *mundhu ʾan*, من لدن أن *min ladun ʾan*, كيما *kay-mā*, لكيما *li-kay-mā*.

Note 2. Interrogative particles used as relatives may also begin subordinate clauses: *kayfa, ʾayna, matā* (§289).

§346. Substantives expressing time in the adverbial accusative (§315 b) may be followed by a dependent clause in the role of a genitive (§420): حين *ḥīna* 'at the time when', يوم *yawma* 'on the day when', ليالي *layāliya* 'on the nights when', ريث *raytha* 'while', etc.

Note 1. In post-classical Arabic, *mā* frequently occurs with these adverbs: حينما *ḥīna-mā*, ريثما *raytha-mā*. On the other hand, *qabla*, instead of *qabla-mā* 'before' (§344), sometimes behaves like a conjunction: قبل أسافر *qabla ʾusāfiru* 'before I travel'.

Note 2. After the preposition *ʿalā* (§302.1), *ḥīna* may be uninflected: على حين *ʿalā ḥīna* or *ʿalā ḥīni*.

Vocative Particles (Interjections)

§347. يا *yā* 'O, oh' (vocative §§157 ff.; imperative §221.1; cf. §§263; 337; 341) — وا *wā* 'oh, ah' (§158) — ها *hā* 'ha, oh' (cf. §279 b); as oath particles:

ها اللّه *hā 'l-lāhi* 'O God!' (§294.2) — أيّها *ʾayyuhā*, يا أيّها *yā ʾayyuhā* 'O' (vocative §157) — أ *ʾa*, أيا *ʾayā* 'ah, oh' (vocative §157.4) — ألا *ʾalā*, أما *ʾamā* 'oh no, ah, ah yes' (§335 b): ألا ليت شعري *ʾalā layta shiʿrī* 'Ah, if I only knew!' (§341).

Note 1. يا ل *yā la-* with the genitive is used to call out or call for help: يا للرّجال *yā lar-rijāli* 'O men (come)!', يال تميم (Note the orthography!) *yā-la Tamīmin* 'O you Tamim, (help)!', يا للّه للعدوّ *yā la-llāhi lil-ʿadūwi* 'O God, (help us) against the enemy!'; with personal suffixes referring to the one called and the indefinite accusative or *min* (§299.4) as an interjection of astonishment: يا له من رجل (رجلا) *yā lahū min rajulin* (or *rajulan*) 'O, what a man!', يا لك من ليلة *yā laki min laylatin* 'O, what a night!'.

§**348.** Interjections bemoaning misfortune: وي *way* 'woe'; mostly with *la-* and personal suffixes: ويلي *waylī* 'woe is me!', ويلك *waylaka* 'woe to you!' (see also *waylun* §350; *waylummi* §349.1) — ويح *wayḥa* with the genitive or personal suffixes: ويحنا *wayḥanā* 'woe to us!' — هيهات *hayhāta/i/u* (§53.2) 'far from it!'.

§**349.** Several interjections take on the inflection of the imperative or the endings of the 2nd pers. personal pronoun: تعال *taʿāla* 'Come on!', fem. تعالي *taʿālay*, dual تعاليا *taʿālayā*, masc. pl. تعالوا *taʿālaw*, fem. تعالين *taʿālayna*. — هات *hāti* 'Give here!', fem. هاتي *hātī*, dual هاتيا *hātiyā*, masc. pl. هاتوا *hātū*, fem. هاتين *hātīna*. هاك *hāka* 'Here, take it!', هاكها *hākahā* 'Take her, you've got her!', fem. هاك *hāki*, dual هاكما *hākumā*, masc. pl. هاكم *hākum*, fem. هاكنّ *hākunna*. هاء *hāʾa* 'Take!', fem. هاء *hāʾi*, dual هاؤما *hāʾumā*, masc. pl. هاؤم *hāʾum*, fem. هاؤنّ *hāʾunna*, or with the imperative inflection: masc. sing. هأ *haʾ*, هاء *hāʾi*, fem. هائي *hāʾī*, dual هاءا *hāʾā*, هائيا *hāʾiyā*, masc. pl. هاؤوا *hāʾū*, fem. هائين *hāʾīna*. هلمّ *halumma* 'Get up, forward, come on!' (with accusative 'bring here!'), fem. هلمّي *halummī*, dual هلمّا *halummā*, masc. pl. هلمّوا *halummū*, fem. هلممن *halmumna*.

Note 1. Uninflected *-umm* also appears in the interjection أللّهمّ *ʾal-lā-humma* 'O God!' and in ويلمّ or ويل امّ *waylummi*; with the 3rd person suffix and indefinite accusative (§384) as an interjection expressing horror or wonder: ويلمّها حربا *waylummihā ḥarban* 'What a horrible war!', ويلمّه مالا *waylummihī mālan* 'What a wonderful possession!'.

Particles as Substantives

§**350.** Particles may be treated like substantives (on gender, see §112). As such, either they are cited without modification or they take nominal inflectional endings: مضى يوم بليت ولو أنّي *maḍā yawmun bi-layta wa-law ʾannī* 'A day passed with an "Oh would that" and an "If only I"'; in poetry, they are inflected: ما ليت بنافعة *mā laytun bi-nāfiʿatin* 'An "if only" is of no use'. ويل *waylun* 'woe, affliction', ويلة *waylatun* 'an expression of woe' are formed from *wayla-* (§348). From these derive adverbial accusative ويلا *waylan* 'Woe!', ويلا لك *waylan laka* 'Woe to you!'

Syntax

Syntax: Sentences

Subject and Predicate

§351. Classical Arabic has three kinds of sentences:

a) Verbal sentence: The predicate is a verb. The word order is predicate–subject (§§355 ff.).

b) Nominal sentence: The predicate is a noun or a pronoun. The word order is subject–predicate or predicate–subject (§§360 ff.).

c) Compound sentence: The predicate is a verbal or nominal clause connected to the subject by a copulative pronoun (personal pronoun or suffix, subject pronoun incorporated into the verb). The subject comes at the beginning of the sentence (§§368 ff.)

Note 1. Prepositional phrases sometimes function as sentences; see §§294.5; 302.3; 303.4; 309.1. Interrogative particles also occur in such uses: كَيْفَ لِي بِهِ 'How can I get in touch with him?', أَيْنَ بِكَ 'Where can one meet you?', ... هَلْ لَكَ فِي 'Do you feel a desire to? ...' (§296.3).

§352. a) The subject is in the nominative. It is a substantive or a pronoun. Non-substantive nominal forms like adjectives and numbers function as substantives when in the subject position: جَاءَ مِنْهُمْ ثَلَاثَةٌ 'three of them came'. In addition, non-substantive nominal forms like numbers, *kullun* (§136), *g͟hayru-* (§325) and other similar forms, as well as those prepositions which may serve as substantives like *ka-* (§297 b) and *min* (§299 b) in constructions with the dependent genitive, may also be used as subjects: فِي كَبِدِي كَالنَّفْطِ 'There is something (burning) like oil in my liver', جَاءَ غَيْرُكَ 'Someone other than you came'. Relative clauses and substantive clauses (§§414 ff.; 421 ff.) may also appear in subject position.

Note 1. The pronominal subject is incorporated in the verb (§355).

Note 2. After the introductory particles mentioned in §§338 ff., the subject is in the accusative. After *rubba* (§337) and other particles, the subject is in the introductory genitive (§389).

b) As a rule the predicate agrees with the subject in gender. Terms that refer to persons agree *ad sensum* also in number. Nominal predicates follow essentially the same rules of agreement as attributes (§§113 f.; 362). Terms that indicate quantity not infrequently agree *ad sensum* rather than grammatically (§§353 f.). See §§356 f. on the details of verbal predicate agreement.

§**353.** Terms indicating totality (§§136 ff.) and words like *ʾayyu-* (§286), *g͟hayru-* (§325), *mit͟hlu* (§297 c) and other similar terms with the genitive following are considered masc. sing.: كُلُّنَا قَتَلَهُ ‘All of us killed him’, كُلُّهُمْ شَاعِرٌ ‘They are all poets’. Yet, often the predicate agrees with the genitive *ad sensum*: أَيُّ بُشْرَى أَتَتْنِي ‘What good news reached me?’, كُلُّهُمْ سَيَغْضَبُونَ ‘All of them will be angry’.

Note 1. Similarly, when *ka-* and *min* function as substantives (§352), the agreement is with the word in the genitive: مَا حَمَلَتْ مِنْ نَاقَةٍ ‘No camel carried anything’ (§299 b).

§**354.** The numbers from 3 to 10 are treated like feminine plurals, if the objects to which they refer are things: لِثَلَاثٍ لَيَالٍ خَلَوْنَ مِنْ رَجَبٍ ‘When three nights of the month of Rajab have passed’ (§295.1), ثَلَاثٌ لَا بُدَّ مِنْهُنَّ ‘Three (things) are unavoidable’. Numbers over 10 in such cases are treated like feminine singulars: لِأَرْبَعَ عَشْرَةَ لَيْلَةً بَقِيَتْ مِنْ رَمَضَانَ ‘When 14 nights in Ramadan remained’ (i.e., on the 16th of Ramadan). Numbers referring to persons have predicates *ad sensum* in the masculine or feminine plural: أَرْبَعَةٌ قَامُوا إِلَيْهِ ‘Four (people) came up to him’, هٰؤُلَاءِ ٱثْنَا عَشَرَ رَجُلًا ‘These are 12 men’. Cf. §399.

Note 1. *Ad sensum* agreement may occur even when a verbal predicate comes first (§356): تَمَاشَوْا إِلَيْهِ ثَلَاثَتُهُمْ ‘Three of them went to him’.

Note 2. Numbers in the abstract are feminine singular: اَلسَّبْعَةُ تُعْجِزُ عَنِ ٱلثَّمَانِيَةِ وَاحِدًا ‘Seven is one short of eight’; in post-classical Arabic, however, it is usually masculine singular: سَبْعَةٌ نَاقِصٌ ثَلَاثَةً يُسَاوِي أَرْبَعَةً ‘Seven minus three is four’ (§129.5).

Verbal Sentences

§355. The pronominal subject is incorporated in the verb: لَعِبَ 'He played', يَلْعَبُ 'He plays'. The substantive subject follows the 3rd person masculine or feminine singular (§356); likewise, a personal pronoun follows the verb for emphasis (§266). Other sentence elements may intervene between the verb and subject: إِنْتَهَى إِلَى ٱلْخَلِيفَةِ ٱلْخَبَرُ 'The news reached the Caliph'. If the subject has more than one verbal predicate, the subject comes after the first verb: صَلَّى ٱللّٰهُ عَلَيْهِ وَسَلَّمَ 'May God bless him and grant him salvation'.

Note 1. When the subject is placed before the verbal predicate, the sentence is considered compound (§368 ff.).

Note 2. See §§318–323 on the negation of verbal predicates.

§356. Agreement between verbal predicate and subject:

a) The 3rd masculine singular of the verb comes before masculine subjects, regardless of whether it is sing., dual, or plural: جَاءَ سَارِقٌ 'A thief came', جَاءَ سَارِقَانِ 'Two thieves came', جَاءَ سَارِقُونَ 'Thieves came'. Frequently, the 3rd masc. sing. also precedes feminine subjects (sing. or plural), especially if other sentence elements intervene between subject and predicate: أَتَى ٱلْقَاضِيَ رِسَالَةٌ 'A message came to the judge', تَغَيَّرَ ٱلْأُمُورُ 'The circumstances changed'.

b) The 3rd fem. sing. usually precedes feminine subjects (§§110 ff.); the 3rd masc. sing. may appear instead, except before sing. terms that refer to female persons and the fem. dual: جَاءَتْ سَارِقَةٌ 'A thief (fem.) came', جَاءَتْ سَارِقَتَانِ 'Two thieves (fem.) came'.

Note 1. Before the names of clans (§86 b), including those consisting of بنو *banū* 'sons of ...' (§385.3), the predicate is usually in the 3rd. fem. sing.: قَالَتِ ٱلْيَهُودُ 'The Jews said'.

Note 2. Agreement *ad sensum* in number in verbal sentences is attested only exceptionally: إِحْمَرَّتَا عَيْنَاهُ 'Both his eyes turned red'.

§357. Agreement of a succeeding verbal predicate with a subject already mentioned in the sentence is strict, and agreement in number is, as a rule, *ad sensum* with terms referring to persons (cf. §114): جَاءَ زَيْدٌ وَأَبُوهُ فَقَالَا

'Zayd and his father came, and then they said', كَانَ ٱلنَّاسُ يَقُولُونَ 'The people used to say', بَكَتِ ٱلنِّسْوَةُ وَعَوَّلْنَ 'The women cried and wailed'; but also سَمِعَتْ قُرَيْشٌ فَغَضِبَتْ 'The Quraysh (§86 b) heard (it) and became angry'.

Note 1. After place names, the inhabitants are frequently referred to without explicitly naming them: أَتَى ٱلْيَمَنَ فَحَارَبُوهُ 'He came to the Yemen and there they (i.e., the Yemenis) fought with him'; also outside the subject–predicate context: نَزَلَ بِحِصْنِ حُواثَى فَقَاتَلَهُمْ 'He stopped at the fortress of Ḥuwāthā and fought them (the garrison)'.

§**358.** An unspecified subject may be expressed—more frequently than by such terms as رَجُلٌ, إِمْرُؤٌ 'man', أَحَدٌ 'one', among others—in the following ways:

a) With the 2nd masc. sing. (less often the plural): تَخَالُ 'You think', i.e., 'It is thought, one thinks, they think'; with the 3rd masc. plural: سَمِعُوا صَوْتًا 'They heard, i.e., one heard a voice'; sometimes with 3rd masc. sing.: إِذَا مَاتَ ظَهَرَتْ لَهُ ٱلْأَشْيَاءُ عَلَى خِلَافِ مَا يُشَاهِدُهُ ٱلْآنَ 'When someone dies, things seem to him different from how he now sees them'; with the passive without a subject, see §199 b.

Note 1. Similarly, in nominal constructions with the personal suffixes: كَقَوْلِكَ 'like your speech', or كَقَوْلِهِمْ 'like their speech', i.e., 'as they say, as it is said, as one says'.

b) With the active participle of the verb which forms the predicate; as a singular, the participle is usually indefinite, as a plural, definite: قَالَ قَائِلٌ 'Someone said', لَا يَشْغُلْكَ عَنْهُ شَاغِلٌ 'Don't let anything distract you!', لَمْ يَرَ ٱلرَّاؤُونَ مِثْلَهُ 'No one ever saw anyone like him.'

Note 2. Likewise, with nominal constructions: لَوْمَةُ لَائِمٍ 'someone's blame'.

§**359.** The absence of the subject occurs with the passive of intransitive and, occasionally, transitive verbs (§199 b): غُشِيَ عَلَيْهِ 'There was a covering thrown over him, i.e., he fainted'. There are only a few other cases of the unmentioned subject, e.g.: كَفَى بِٱللّٰهِ شَهِيدًا 'God is a sufficient witness'

(Koran 4:79, 166; 10:29, etc.), بَدَا لَهُ 'It seemed good to him', i.e., 'He decided' (as in the example cited in §329.3).

Note 1. When the subject can be determined from the context, it is not a case of a truly lacking subject: لَوْ أَقَمْتَ لَسَرَّنَا 'If you would remain, it would make us happy', فَذَهَبَتْ مَثَلًا Then it (what was told) became a proverb', لَمَّا كَانَ فِي ٱلْيَوْمِ ٱلرَّابِعِ 'when it was [on] the fourth day'.

Note 2. Observe that verbs which incorporate an element of time always take a personal subject: لَمَّا أَصْبَحْنَا ٱنْصَرَفْنَا 'When we woke up in the morning', i.e., 'when it was morning, we left.'

Nominal Sentences

§**360.** The nominal sentence describes a condition which exists or a desired one: أَلسَّلَامُ عَلَيْكُمْ 'Peace be on you!' (a Muslim greeting). To refer to a past and future condition, a verbal sentence with كَانَ 'was' or يَكُونُ 'will be' is used (§§382 a; 190.2).

Note 1. Terms referring to time are sometimes the subject of a nominal sentence: نَهَارُهُ صَائِمٌ وَلَيْلُهُ قَائِمٌ 'His day is fasting, and his night is standing', i.e., 'Daytime he fasts, and nighttime he is awake'.

§**361.** The predicate of a nominal sentence may be a noun, pronoun, prepositional phrase (§293), or adverb (§§315 ff.), e.g.: هُمْ فَوْقُ 'They are above', كَيْفَ حَالُكَ 'How are you?'. In addition, relative clauses (§§421 ff.) and subordinate clauses beginning with *ʾan, ʾanna, mā* (§§414 ff.) may be predicates. Adjectival predicates are as a rule asyndetically coordinated, i.e., without a conjunction: إِنَّ ٱللّٰهَ غَفُورٌ رَحِيمٌ 'God is forgiving and merciful'.

Note 1. See §202 on the use of the predicative participle.

§**362.** Adjectives in the predicate are in the nominative of the indefinite state and agree with the subject (§§113 f.): أَلْوَلَدُ صَغِيرٌ 'The boy is small', أَلنَّاقَةُ كَوْمَاءُ 'The camel is big-humped', أَلْأَلْوَانُ مُخْتَلِفَةٌ 'The colors are diverse', هُمْ نِيَامٌ 'They are sleeping' (§122). On agreement in cases like: كُلُّ حِزْبٍ بِمَا لَدَيْهِمْ فَرِحُونَ 'Each party is rejoicing in what is with them' (Koran 23:53; 30:32), see §353.

§363. a) Substantives in the predicate are in the nominative of the indefinite state and, as such, have a qualifying sense: هُوَ رَجُلٌ 'He is a man', نَحْنُ حَرْبٌ لَكُمْ 'We are war (i.e., hostile) to you', ثَوْبُهُ حَرِيرٌ 'His garment is silk (i.e., made of silk)', أَنْتَ ثِقَةٌ 'You are reliability (i.e., reliable)', أَمْرُكَ طَاعَةٌ 'Your order means obedience', اَلدَّهْرُ يَوْمٌ وَلَيْلَةٌ 'Time consists of day and night'.

b) A definite substantive or a predicate that serves as a substantive has an identifying sense: هٰذِهِ ٱلْفَرَسُ فَرَسُكَ 'This horse is your horse', أَنْتَ أَمِيرُ ٱلْمُؤْمِنِينَ 'You are the commander of the faithful'. If a predicate substantive is made definite with the article, a compound sentence with a copulative subject pronoun (§370 a) results: أُولٰئِكَ هُمُ ٱلْكَافِرُونَ 'Those are the unbelievers'.

Note 1. In pre-classical Arabic, the definite predicate is occasionally introduced by *bi-* (§294 d): هُوَ بِهِ 'He is it'.

Note 2. Matching subject and predicate are used to emphasize an identity: أَنْتَ أَنْتَ 'You are really you', أَرْضُكَ أَرْضُكَ 'Your land is really yours'.

§364. The 3rd person pronoun in the predicate always refers to a person; neuter "it" does not exist in Arabic: أَنْتَ هُوَ 'You (masc.) are it' (literally 'you are he'), أَنْتِ هِيَ 'You (fem.) are it' (literally 'you are she'), أَنْتُمْ هُمْ 'You (pl.) are it', إِنَّهُ هُوَ هُوَ 'Verily, he is it', هٰذَا هُوَ 'This is it, there it is', هٰذِهِ عَجُوزٌ 'This is an old woman', 'There is an old woman'.

§365. a) The 3rd person pronoun is often lacking in the subject or predicate position, especially after *ʾidhā* (§280) and *fa-* (§329): إِلْتَفَتُّ فَإِذَا ٱلْوَزِيرُ 'I turned around, and there (it) was the vizier', إِنْ كَانَ مَعْبَدٌ فِي ٱلدُّنْيَا فَهٰذَا 'If there is a Maʿbad in the world, then this one is it' (§448).

b) In the following formulas, the 3rd person pronoun is regularly lacking: حَسْبُكَ '(It is) enough for you!', قَدِي or قَدْنِي 'Enough for me!', قَدْكَ 'Enough for you!', etc., كَأَنَّ (§§415; 418 b) 'It is as if . . . ', e.g., وَكَأَنِّي أَمْشِي فِي جَنَّةٍ 'And it is as if I were walking in a garden'.

Note 1. *ka-ʾanna* may occur with predicate *bi-* (§294 d): كَأَنِّي بِكَ 'It is as if I had something to do with you', 'It is as if I saw you before me'. It is often augmented by a circumstantial accusative (§383) or a circumstantial clause

(§436): كَأَنَّكَ بِهِ قَدْ أَدْرَكَكَ 'It is as if you had something to do with him as he has already met you', i.e., 'It seems that he has already met you'.

§366. The word order is usually subject–predicate. Definite predicates, however, may come at the beginning of the sentence: أَلْجَارِيَةُ فِي ٱلْبَيْتِ 'The maid is in her chamber', but فِي ٱلْبَيْتِ جَارِيَةٌ 'In her chamber is the maid'. Likewise, sentence elements called into question appear at the beginning: أَحَقٌّ مَا تُخْبِرُنِي 'Is it true what you reported to me?'; مَنْ فِي ٱلْبَيْتِ 'Who is in the room?' and analogously in the reply: جَارِيَةٌ فِي ٱلْبَيْتِ 'A maid is in the room'.

Note 1. The introductory particle *ʾinna* (§339) has no influence on the position of words in the nominal sentence: إِنَّ فِي ٱلْبَيْتِ جَارِيَةً 'Verily, in the room is a slave-girl'.

§367. a) A nominal sentence is negated with *mā*, *ʾin*, and *laysa* (§§321ff.). After *mā* and *ʾin* the predicate is in the nominative; after *laysa*, in the accusative. The predicate may also be introduced with *bi-* (§294 d): مَا أَنْتَ بَخِيلٌ or مَا أَنْتَ بِبَخِيلٍ and لَسْتَ بَخِيلًا or لَسْتَ بِبَخِيلٍ 'You are not miserly'. An indefinite subject is frequently introduced with partitive *min* (§299 b): مَا لَكُمْ مِنْ دُونِ ٱللّٰهِ مِنْ وَلِيٍّ 'You have no protector apart from God' (Koran 2:107; 9:116; 29:22; etc.); cf. §318 b.

Note 1. The use of so-called مَا ٱلْحِجَازِيَّةُ "the Ḥijāzī *mā*", according to which the predicate follows in the accusative, as with *laysa*, is limited to pre-classical Arabic: مَا هٰذَا بَشَرًا 'This is no mortal' (Koran 12:31).

Note 2. The subject may be negated with the particle of general denial *lā* (§318 c): لَا شَاعِرَ مِثْلُهُ 'There is no poet like him'.

b) Nominal predicates may be negated with *ghayru* (§325 b). In this case, agreement of the adjective is unaffected: دِيَارُنَا غَيْرُ بَعِيدَةٍ 'Our dwellings are not far'.

Compound Sentences

§368. The subject of a compound sentence is always at the beginning. Any nominal or pronominal part of the sentence may become the subject of a copulative sentence by being placed at the beginning for emphasis. In the predicate clause, then, a copulative personal pronoun or personal suffix appears for the subject: زَيْدٌ مَاتَ أَبُوهُ 'Zayd, his father died' as opposed to مَاتَ أَبُو زَيْدٍ 'The father of Zayd died'. If the subject of a copulative sentence is also a subject in the predicate clause, the subject pronoun that is incorporated in the verb functions as a copulative pronoun, provided there is a verbal clause. According to §357, there is strict agreement between verb and subject: مَعْصِيَةُ ٱلْعَاقِلِ تُورِثُ ٱلْحَسْرَةَ 'The disobedience of the sensible one engenders sadness'.

§**369.** a) The subject may come at the beginning of the sentence for reasons of context and prominence and usually in connection with the use of demonstrative and interrogative pronouns: أَيُّ رَجُلٍ جَاءَ 'Which man came?'. The same also occurs with the introductory particles *ʾidhā* (§280), *ʾammā* (§336), and *ʾinna, lākinna, laʿalla, layta* (§§338 ff.). The introductory genitive (§389) after *wa-* and *rubba* regularly appears at the beginning of the sentence and is the subject of a compound sentence.

b) Spontaneous placement of the subject at the beginning of the sentence is used to emphasize contrasts: أَلشَّاهِدُ يَرَى مَا لَا يَرَى ٱلْغَائِبُ 'The eyewitness sees what the one who is absent does not'. Similarly: لَنِعْمَ ٱلْفَتَى طَعَنْتَ عَلَيْهِ 'What an excellent youth you have slandered!' (§§259 ff.), ثِنْتَانِ لَا بُدَّ مِنْهُمَا 'Two (things) are unavoidable', أَمْرٌ أَنَا فِي طَلَبٍ مِنْهُ مُنْذُ عِشْرِينَ سَنَةً 'A certain thing I have been seeking for twenty years'.

Note 1. See §§409 a; 433 ff.; 428 ff. on copulative subordinate clauses.

§**370.** The predicate of a compound sentence is a verb or a nominal clause in which a copulative pronoun refers to the subject.

a) The copulative pronoun is the subject of the predicate clause: أُولَائِكَ هُمُ ٱلْكَافِرُونَ 'Those are the unbelievers' (§363 b), أَلْعَاقِلُ لَا يُصَاحِبُ ٱلْأَشْرَارَ 'The sensible one does not associate with the evil ones'.

Note 1. The copulative personal pronoun may be lacking before an indefinite nominal predicate: أَمَّا ثِيَابُهُمْ فَبِيضٌ 'As for their garments, they are white'.

b) The copulative pronoun is the object of a predicate clause: إِنِّي ٱلْهَوَى قَدْ غَلَبَنِي 'Look at me! Passion has conquered me'. In these examples, the copulative pronoun may be lacking, unless ambiguity results: رُبَّ كَأْسٍ شَرِبْتَ many a cup have you drunk' (rather than شَرِبْتَهَا).

Note 2. In these cases, a substantive which becomes prominent by its placement at the beginning of the sentence appears on occasion in the accusative as a result of prolepsis: وَٱلْقَمَرَ قَدَّرْنَاهُ مَنَازِلَ 'And the moon — we have determined for it stations' (Koran 36:39).

c) The copulative pronoun occupies the position of the genitive in the predicate clause: وَٱلظُّلْمُ مَرْتَعُهُ وَخِيمٌ 'And tyranny, its pasturing ground is unhealthy'.

Predicate Complements

§371. a) Nominal, prepositional, and verbal complements may be added to the verbal predicate. The nominal predicate complement is in the accusative (§§372 ff.). See §293 on the use of prepositional predicate complements. Verbal predicate complements are termed circumstantial clauses (§§431 ff.).

b) In nominal sentences, prepositional phrases (§293) or circumstantial expressions of adverbial origin (§§315 ff.) may be appended to the predicate: إِنَّ ٱلْمُلُوكَ عِنْدَ ٱللّٰهِ تُرَابٌ 'Kings are (no more than) dust before God', هُوَ أَسَدٌ يَوْمَ ٱلْوَغَى 'He is a lion on the day of the battle'.

Uses of the Accusative

§372. When it is governed by a verb, the accusative is the object, inner (absolute) object, or predicate accusative. Additional uses of the accusative, namely, adverbial expressions describing circumstances and denominal expressions indicating conditions, have developed from the accusative and assumed a status of their own. The accusative governed by the verb as a rule follows the verb; placement of the accusative first for emphasis does, however, occasionally occur (§370.2).

Note 1. On the accusative as vocative, §§157 f.; with the general negation, §318 c; after *wa-* 'with', §328 b; with numbers, §§130 f.; after particles of exception, §§310 a; 312; after introductory particles, §§338 ff.; in negative nominal sentences, §367.

Accusative as Object

§**373.** The accusative indicates the direct object on which an action is effected: يَطْلُبُ آلْعِلْمَ 'He seeks knowledge', قَدِمَ آلْبَصْرَةَ 'He reached Basra', تَبِعَ أَبَاهُ 'He followed his father', أَتَاهُ 'He came to him'.

Note 1. One must determine from the lexicon which verbs are used with the object accusative. Occasionally, either the accusative or a preposition is used: ذَهَبَ آلشَّأْمَ or ذَهَبَ إِلَى آلشَّأْمِ 'He went to Syria'.

Note 2. Pronominal object complements may be omitted from verbs that appear in quick succession: قُلْتُ لَهُ حَدِّثْنِي فَفَعَلَ 'I said to him: Report to me. He did (it)'.

Note 3. An unspecified object may be expressed with a verbal adjective of the same verbal stem: قَتَلَ قَتِيلًا 'He killed someone'.

§**374.** a) Causative verbs and those with related meanings may take an additional object accusative referring to a person: عَلَّمَهُ آلْقِرَاءَةَ 'He taught him reading', أَعْطَى آبْنَتَهُ نِطَاقًا 'He gave his daughter a girdle', أَلْبَسَنِي ثِيَابَهُ 'He clothed me in his garments', قُوا أَنْفُسَكُمْ وَأَهْلِيكُمْ نَارًا وَقُودُهَا آلنَّاسُ 'Guard yourselves and your families against a fire whose fuel is men ...' (Koran 66:6). Cf. also §§271 f.

Note 1. With certain verbs, the second accusative is a predicate accusative (§§380 ff.).

b) If verbs like these appear in the passive (§§199 f.), the personal object becomes the subject, while the second accusative remains unaffected: أُعْطِيَتْ نِطَاقًا 'She was given a girdle', 'She received a girdle', أُوتِينَا كِتَابًا 'We received a letter', passive formation of آتَانَا كِتَابًا 'He sent us a letter'.

Note 2. The intransitive basic stem is treated like a passive: لَبِسْتُ ثِيَابَهُ 'I dressed in his clothes', مَلِئَ آلدَّلْوُ مَاءً 'The bucket was filled with water', intransitive of مَلَأَ آلدَّلْوَ مَاءً 'He filled the bucket with water'.

§**375.** The accusative may refer to a perceived or intended object, even if it is not governed by a verb: أَلْهِلَالَ وَآللّٰهِ '(Look) the new moon, by God!', سَمْعًا وَطَاعَةً 'Hearing and obeying', i.e., 'I am ready to obey', أَتَوَانِيًا وَقَدْ عَلَاكَ آلْمَشِيبُ 'Is there hesitancy now that gray hairs cover you?'; often as an exclamation or warning: أَلْحَدِيثَ 'Please, the story!', أَلْأَسَدَ ٱلْأَسَدَ 'Watch out, the lion!', رِجْلَكَ 'Careful, your foot', مَكَانَكَ 'Stay where you are!' (cf. §379.1). Cf. also §§272.2; 316.

Note 1. Verbal substantives used in exclamations have the sense of imperatives: فَإِذَا لَقِيتُمُ ٱلَّذِينَ كَفَرُوا فَضَرْبَ ٱلرِّقَابِ 'When you meet the unbelievers, then smite them on their necks' (Koran 47:4), أَلْأَسْرَ ٱلْأَسْرَ 'Take prisoners!'. On the accusative used with the vocative, see §§157 f.

Inner (Absolute) Object

§376. Any verb, even intransitive and passive, may occur in conjunction with the accusative of the inner object, with the effect of confirming or strengthening the action. As a rule, the inner object is the verbal substantive of the main verb: ضَرَبَهُ ضَرْبًا 'He hit him hitting, i.e., really', ضُرِبَ ضَرْبًا 'He was struck with a blow, i.e., was really hit'. Even verbal substantives of another verb stem of the same root, a *nomen vicis* (§232), or a *nomen speciei* (§77), may be an inner object: إِقْتَتَلُوا قِتَالًا شَدِيدًا 'They fought each other in a violent fighting', رَمَى رَمْيَتَيْنِ 'He shot two shots, i.e., twice', قَتَلُوهُمْ كُلَّ قِتْلَةٍ 'They killed them with every way of killing, i.e., in every conceivable way'.

Note 1. Sometimes a verbal substantive with a related meaning occurs as the inner object: شَدُّوهُ رِبَاطًا 'They bound him really tight.'

Note 2. The inner object may be represented by the personal suffix: فَرْحَتَانِ يَفْرَحُهُمَا 'Two joys that he feels'.

§377. Most of the time, the inner object appears with an attribute or genitive that further specifies the action and is used to qualify the verb: أَدَّبَهُ تَأْدِيبًا حَسَنًا 'He educated him really well', إِطَّلَعْتُ عَلَيْهِ ٱطِّلَاعًا لَمْ أَشُكَّ فِيهِ 'I found out enough about him that I had no more doubts'; — it appears with the genitive often to offer comparison: خَافَ خَوْفَ ٱلْجَبَانِ 'He was frightened like a coward', سُقْنَاهُمْ سَوْقَ ٱلْبِكَارِ 'We drove them like camels', أَحْكُمُ عَلَى ذٰلِكَ حُكْمَكَ عَلَيْهِ 'I judge it as you do'.

Note 1. Sometimes the adjective appears alone and thus assumes the role of an adverb: كَانَ يَأْتِي كَثِيرًا 'He came often (much)'. The verbal substantive is usually lacking when numbers are cited: شَتَمْتَهُ أَلْفًا 'You have insulted him a thousand times', ضَرَبَهُ سِتِّينَ 'He struck him 60 (blows)'.

Adverbial Accusative

§**378.** Verbal substantives that are not related in meaning to their respective verbal predicates are used as inner objects to describe circumstances, i.e., the kind and manner or the cause of the action: ذَهَبُوا جَمْزًا 'They ran away taking great leaps', أَخَذَهُ غَصْبًا 'He seized him by force', يَسْكُتُ جَهْلًا 'He remained silent out of ignorance', قُمْتُ إِكْرَامًا لَهُ 'I stood up in honor of him'.

Note 1. Adverbs like عَلَانِيَةً 'openly', عَمْدًا 'deliberately', among others, have developed into independent expressions from this usage.

§**379.** The accusative is used to indicate extent and direction, as well as duration and points in time: سَارَ فَرْسَخَيْنِ 'He traveled two parsangs', رَفَعْنَا بَعْضَهُمْ فَوْقَ بَعْضٍ دَرَجَاتٍ 'We raised some of them above the others by several steps' (Koran 43:32), تَبَدَّدُوا شَرْقًا وَغَرْبًا 'They scattered east and west', كَانَ ذٰلِكَ مَرْجِعَهُ مِنَ ٱلْكُوفَةِ 'This happened on his return from Kufa' (§382.2), أَقَامَ بِمَكَّةَ عَامَ ٱلْفَتْحِ نِصْفَ شَهْرٍ 'During the year of the conquest, he spent a half month in Mecca'; cf. §315 b.

Note 1. This kind of accusative sometimes occurs with terms indicating places: إِجْلِسُوا مَكَانَكُمْ 'Remain sitting in your place!'.

Note 2. The personal suffixes may substitute for this accusative: لَيَالٍ مَرِضْتُهَا 'Nights during which I was ill'.

Circumstantial Accusative

§**380.** The circumstantial accusative functions as a predicate to a verb and indicates a simultaneous condition (حَالٌ). As such, these predicatives are treated as nominal predicates (§§361 f.): They can be nouns or adjectives, are usually indefinite, and agree grammatically with the subject (§§113 f.): جَاءَ رَاكِبًا 'He came riding', قَامَتِ ٱبْنَتُهُ إِلَيْهِ بَاكِيَةً 'His sister, crying, went up to him', خَرَجْنَا مُتَوَجِّهِينَ إِلَى ٱلْيَمَنِ 'We departed in the direction of Yemen', طَلَعَ ٱلْقَمَرُ بَدْرًا 'The moon rose full', تَأْتُونَ أَفْوَاجًا 'You come in droves'. Adjectival predicate elements follow one another asyndetically (§361): أُخْرُجْ مِنْهَا مَذْءُومًا مَدْحُورًا 'Go forth from it (from Paradise), despised and banished!' (Koran 7:18).

Note 1. As a circumstantial accusative, the participle may be imperfective or perfective (§202 c): خَرَجَ هَارِبًا 'He went out, with the intent of fleeing', جَاءَ هَارِبًا 'He came in flight'.

Note 2. The predicative may precede an indefinite subject: إِذَا جَاءَهُ مُرْتَغِبًا سَائِلٌ 'If a beggar, with a wish, comes to him ...'.

Note 3. The predicative adjective may have its own subject with which it agrees: أَمْسَتِ ٱلْآفَاقُ غُبْرًا جُنُوبُهَا 'In the evening the horizon appeared dust-colored at its edges' (§435).

§**381.** When used with verbs conveying the ideas of "inducing ..., considering as ..., finding as ...", and the like, the circumstantial accusative refers to the object and agrees with it as need be: أَرَانِي أَكْبَرَ مِنْكَ 'I see myself as larger than you' (i.e., 'that I am larger than you'), جَعَلَ لَكُمْ ٱلْأَرْضَ قَرَارًا '(It is God who) made for you the earth as a resting place' (Koran 40:64), غَادَرَ أَقْرَانَهُ أَمْوَاتًا 'He left his opponents for dead', وَجَدْتُ ٱلنِّسَاءَ مُغْشِيًّا عَلَيْهِنَّ 'I found the women unconscious' (§204). If a causative governs two accusatives (§374), the circumstantial accusative refers to the second object: يُرِيكُمْ أَعْمَالَكُمْ خَبِيثَةً 'He showed them that their deeds were evil'.

Note 1. If the circumstantial accusative refers to subject and object, it appears in the dual as the occasion arises: مَتَى مَا تَلْقَنِي فَرْدَيْنِ 'whenever you meet me so that we are both alone'.

Note 2. According to §363 b, a personal pronoun may come before a definite predicate: جَعَلْنَا ذُرِّيَّتَهُ هُمُ ٱلْبَاقِينَ 'We caused his descendants to be the unending ones', إِذَا كَانَ ٱلْوَاجِبُ هُوَ ٱلْعُنْفَ 'If violence is the obligation' (§382).

§**382.** a) Nominal predicates coming after كَانَ (يَكُونُ) 'be' (§360) may be considered to be in the circumstantial accusative: كَانَ أَخًا لِي 'He was a brother of mine', أَلشَّيْءُ ٱلْوَاحِدُ لَا يَكُونُ مَوْجُودًا مَعْدُومًا 'A single thing cannot (at the same time) exist and be non-existent'. Any other predicate in a nominal sentence (§361) may also occur with *kāna*, e.g., كَانَ لِي أَخٌ 'A brother was mine', i.e., 'I have a brother', يَكُونُ رَجْعَتُهُ غَدًا 'His return will be tomorrow'. See §381.2 on the definite predicate.

Note 1. Although the personal suffixes do not occur in place of the circumstantial accusative, *kāna* may appear with predicate personal suffixes: إِيَّاكَ أَنْ تَكُونَهُ 'Watch out that you are not it!'.

Note 2. Without a predicate, *kāna* has the meaning 'exist, occur': كَانَ تَاجِرٌ 'There was once a merchant'. See §§190 ff., on *kāna* in complex verbal constructions.

b) In the same manner, accusative predicates may occur with such semantically related verbs as صَارَ (يَصِيرُ) 'become', مَا زَالَ (لَا يَزَالُ) 'not cease', i.e., 'continue being, still . . . ', among others: صَارَتِ ٱلْأَرْضُ خَصِيبَةً 'The earth became fertile', لَمْ يَزَلْ قَوِيًّا 'He was still strong'. In place of the circumstantial accusative, there may be a circumstantial clause (§432): لَا يَزَالُ دَائِرًا or لَا يَزَالُ يَدُورُ 'He is still turning', صَارَ لَا يَتَكَلَّمُ 'He became so that he did not speak', i.e., 'He became speechless'.

§**383.** a) A substantive or personal pronoun (personal suffixes) may be followed by an appositional circumstantial accusative which indicates the immediate condition of the substantive or the pronoun: مَا لِجِسْمِكَ شَاحِبًا 'What's with your body, being (so) emaciated', i.e., Why is your body so emaciated?', هُوَ حِسُّ ٱلْحُمُرِ وَارِدَةً 'It is the sound of the wild asses going to drink', إِنْتَهَوْا إِلَيْهِ جَالِسًا قُدَّامَ بَيْتِهِ 'They reached him just as he was sitting before his house'.

b) Substantives in the appositional accusative most often have an explicative sense: دَعَوْتُ ٱللّٰهَ سَمِيعًا 'I called to God to hear (my prayers)', هٰذَا عِنَبًا أَطْيَبُ مِنْهُ زَبِيبًا 'This is more tasty as fresh grapes than it is as raisins'. The appositional accusative of pronouns of the 1st and 2nd persons is, as a rule, definite: أَنْتُمُ ٱلْمُؤْمِنِينَ 'You, as believers', نَحْنُ مَعَاشِرَ ٱلْأَنْبِيَاءِ 'We, the multitude of prophets'.

Note 1. The explicative accusative is for the most part replaceable with *min* (§299.4): يَا لَهُ رَجُلًا or يَا لَهُ مِنْ رَجُلٍ 'Oh, what a man!' (§347.1).

Note 2. The explication may consist of a distributive pair (§402): سَمَّاهُمْ رَجُلًا رَجُلًا 'He named them man for man', كَذٰلِكَ ٱلدَّهْرُ حَالًا بَعْدَ حَالٍ 'So is time one state after another'.

Note 3. In pre-classical Arabic, substantives occur on occasion in the definite appositional accusative: إِمْرَأَتُهُ حَمَّالَةَ ٱلْحَطَبِ 'his wife, the carrier of the firewood' (Koran 111:4), بِنَعْلَيْهِ ٱلْعُتُقَ 'with his sandals, the old ones'.

Accusative of Specificity

§**384.** The indefinite accusative is used to specify (§141 c). It occurs with verbs: تَزِيدُ عِشْقًا 'You increase in love', i.e., 'You love more', لَنْ تَبْلُغَ ٱلْجِبَالَ طُولًا 'You will not reach the mountains in tallness'; with adjectives in the predicate and, especially, with the elative (§124.3): أَحْدَثُنَا سِنًّا 'the youngest among us in age', هُوَ أَكْثَرُ قَوْمِهِ مَالًا 'He is the most of his people in possessions', i.e., 'He is the most wealthy of his people'. This accusative is also used to indicate content and material: جُبَّتُكَ خَزًّا 'your *jubbah* of silk', مِثْقَالُ ذَرَّةٍ خَيْرًا 'an atom's weight of good' (Koran 99:7); cf. §§261 b; 262; 287.

Nominal Constructions

Genitive Constructions

§**385.** a) A substantive that is dependent on a noun is in the genitive. The noun on which the genitive depends is in the construct state (§§145 f.). Additional genitives may be dependent on a genitive: أَسْمَاءُ خَيْلِ رَسُولِ ٱللّٰهِ 'The names of the horses of the Messenger of God'.

Note 1. Personal pronouns in genitive position appear as personal suffixes (§269). All prepositions govern the genitive (§§291 ff.). See §§129; 132 on the use of the genitive after numerals.

Note 2. Relative clauses as well as subordinate clauses introduced by *ʾan*, *ʾanna*, or *mā* (§§414 ff.) may appear in the position of a genitive. Only with substantives referring to time (§420) may clauses follow the construct state without a subordinating particle.

b) The genitive construction, which consists of the construct state (*regens*, i.e., governing) and the *rectum* (i.e., governed) in the genitive, normally indicates the connection of the *regens* to the *rectum*: رَأْسُ زَيْدٍ 'the head of Zayd'. The genitive construction, however, also involves the relationship of the *rectum* to the *regens*: أَرْضُ جَدْبٍ 'Earth with barrenness', i.e., 'infertile earth' (§§391 ff.).

c) In genitive constructions which represent lexical unities, e.g., personal names like عَبْدُ ٱلرَّحْمَانِ ('slave of the Merciful'), شَمْسُ ٱلدِّينِ ('sun of the religion'), أَبُو بَكْرٍ ('father of Bakr') or the constructions mentioned in §391, the construct state retains its grammatical independence: يَا أَبَا بَكْرٍ 'Oh, Abu Bakr'. If such constructions occur in the plural, as a rule both members become plurals: أُمَرَاءُ ٱلْجُيُوشِ from أَمِيرُ ٱلْجَيْشِ 'commander of the army', إِخْوَانُ ثِقَاتٍ from أَخُو ثِقَةٍ 'trustworthy' (§391).

Note 3. If the *regens* indicates only a formal connection, gender agreement is sometimes determined by the genitive (§353). Like other names of clans, even those formed with بَنُو 'sons of ...' are regularly feminine (§86b).

Note 4. In post-classical Arabic, compound names are treated as units, so that forms like عَبَادِلَةٌ (§96), عَبْدَلِيٌّ (§116) from عَبْدُ ٱللّٰهِ ʿAbd Allāh ('slave of God') make their way into classical texts.

§**386.** a) The genitive is used to express various kinds of relationships: possession or being part of, belonging to a space, a time, and so forth, e.g., قَلَمُ ٱلْكُتَّابِ 'the pen of the scribes', سُوقُ عُكَاظٍ 'the market of Ukāẓ', طَرِيقُ ٱلشَّأْمِ 'the way to Syria', مَطَرُ ٱلشِّتَاءِ 'the rain in winter'. If the meanings of both members together imply no particular relationship, the genitive construction indicates a simple belonging together: ثَلَاثُ لَيَالٍ وَأَيَّامُهَا 'three nights and their (proper) days'.

Note 1. Proper names also may be in the genitive: نَابِغَةُ ذُبْيَانَ 'Nābighah of (the clan of) Dhubyān', طَرَابُلُسُ ٱلشَّأْمِ 'Tripoli of Syria'.

Note 2. Expressions of time often receive a genitive personal suffix that refers to the appropriate person: مَضَى لَيْلَتَهُ 'He spent his night (i.e., the night as it concerned him at the time)', رَجَعَ مِنْ وَقْتِهِ 'He returned at his time, i.e., at once'. Demonstratives in the genitive refer, however, to a situation or event: يَوْمَ ذٰلِكَ 'on the day of that', i.e., 'on the day when that occurred'.

b) The genitive may appear in a subject or object relationship with a verbal substantive (*genitivus subjectivus, gen. objectivus*): حُبُّ لَيْلَى 'the love of Laylā', i.e., 'Laylā's loving' or 'loving Laylā', حَدِيثُ عُمَرَ 'the report 'Umar gave' or 'the report about 'Umar'; see also §206.

Note 3. The object genitive may appear with active participles: مُؤَلِّفُ ٱلْكِتَابِ 'the author of the book'; see also §146 c. The subject genitive may appear with passive verbal adjectives: قَتِيلُ ٱلْجُوعِ 'killed by starvation'.

§**387.** a) When dependent on an elative (§124), كُلٌّ (§136), أَيٌّ (§286), كَمْ (§287), مِنْ (§299.4), and a few others, the indefinite genitive indicates the overall class to which the preceding word belongs: كُلُّ رَجُلٍ 'every man', أَفْضَلُ رَجُلٍ 'the most excellent man', أَيُّ رِجَالٍ 'what men'. This kind of genitive (which may be termed the generic genitive) may also be used with adjectives functioning as substantives: كَبِيرُ شَيْءٍ 'important of matter', i.e., 'something important', نَجِيعُ دَمٍ 'curdled with blood'.

b) The definite genitive in such constructions indicates a totality, and so the *regens* functions in a partitive relationship with the *rectum*: أَفْضَلُ ٱلرِّجَالِ 'the most excellent of the men', أَحْسَنُ صُنْعِهِ 'the best of his work', i.e., 'his best work', كُلُّ ٱلْقَوْلِ 'the entire speech', أَيُّ ٱلْعَمَلِ 'which part of the (whole) action'. Adjectives functioning as substantives also work in a similar way: كَرِيمُ خُلْقِهِ 'the noble side of his character', فِي قَدِيمِ ٱلزَّمَانِ 'in olden times'.

Note 1. Partitive genitive constructions often have a superlative sense: قَاضِي ٱلْقُضَاةِ 'judge of judges', i.e., 'chief judge', دَقِيقُ ٱلْإِشَارَاتِ 'the subtleness of the signs', i.e., 'the especially subtle signs'.

Note 2. أَلنَّاسُ 'the people', as a partitive genitive, is sometimes treated as an indefinite like a generic genitive: كَانَ أَوَّلَ ٱلنَّاسِ ضَرَبَهُ 'He was the first (of the people) to hit him'.

§**388.** a) Adjectives may govern the genitive of specificity. This genitive is always definite in the generic sense (§144), but it does not make the adjective definite ("improper annexation" §146 c): حَسَنُ ٱلْوَجْهِ 'pretty with respect to the face, pretty-faced', إِمْرَأَةٌ سَوْدَاءُ ٱلشَّعْرِ 'a black-haired woman', أَلْمَرْأَةُ ٱلسَّوْدَاءُ ٱلشَّعْرِ 'the black-haired woman'. This genitive may be replaced with the personal suffixes: كَانَ يَزِيدُ حَسَنَ ٱللِّحْيَةِ خَفِيفَهَا 'Yazid was handsome of beard but thin of it', i.e., 'had a handsome but thin beard' (§§145 c; 380).

Note 1. This genitive also occurs in pre-classical Arabic in *nisbah*-adjectives referring to clan-names: أَلتَّيْمِيُّ تَيْمِ عَدِيٍّ 'belonging to the clan of Taym, namely Taym (ibn) ʿAdī'.

b) Terms of comparison like مِثْلٌ (§297 d), نَظِيرٌ, شِبْهٌ 'resembling', عِدْلٌ, قَدْرٌ, شَرْوَى 'equivalent', غَيْرٌ, سِوَى 'other than' (§325) may also appear, usually defined in the generic sense, with the genitive. The *regens*, however, is considered indefinite (§146 b): صَنَمٌ قَدْرُ ٱلرَّجُلِ ٱلْمُعْتَدِلِ ٱلْخِلْقَةِ 'an idol the size of a man of medium stature', شِبْهُ ٱلْفِعْلِ 'something verb-like'.

§389. The introductory genitive presents a new subject. It is always indefinite and as a rule singular. It appears with *rubba* 'many a' (§337) and, in poetry, with *wa-* (§328). The introductory genitive is usually the subject of a copulative sentence: يَا رُبَّ مَكْرُوبٍ كَرَرْتُ وَرَاءَهُ 'Oh, behind many an overburdened one have I ridden'. While the genitive after *rubba* refers to a plurality of subjects, after *wa-*, the plural is not necessarily implied: وَكَأْسٍ شَرِبْتُ 'Many a cup have I quaffed' (§370 b), وَدَارٍ تُؤَدَّبُ فِيهَا ٱلْبُزَاةُ '(I will speak about) a house in which the falcons were trained', وَذِي رِجْلَيْنِ لَا يَمْشِي عَلَيْهِمَا 'I know of one with two legs who does not walk on them' (§391 a).

Note 1. The plural may follow *wa-*: وَأَيَّامٍ عَصَيْنَا ٱلْمَلْكَ فِيهَا '(I remember) the days when we defied the king'.

Note 2. On rare occasion, this genitive may follow *fa-* (§329), *bal* (§326), or there may be no particle at all: بَلْ بَلَدٍ مِلْءُ ٱلْفِجَاجِ قَتَمُهُ 'But (now I think of) a place where the paths are filled with dust'.

§390. a) The qualifying genitive indicates something by which the *regens* is characterized: يَمِينُ صِدْقٍ 'an oath of sincerity', 'a sincere oath', أَقْوَالُ ٱلضَّلَالِ 'the words of error', 'false statements'; also with proper names: عَلْقَمَةُ ٱلنَّدَى ''Alqamah of generosity', i.e., 'the generous ʿAlqamah', عُوَيْفُ ٱلْقَوَافِي ''Uwayf with the rhymes'.

b) It is also used to indicate dimension, content, or material: سَنَةَ خَمْسٍ وَسَبْعِينَ 'in the year 75' (§379), كَأْسُ مَاءٍ 'a cup of water', مَلِكُ شَهْرٍ 'king of a month (for a month)', بُيُوتُ ٱلرُّخَامِ 'houses made of marble'.

Note 1. In addition, materials may be indicated by apposition (§394 a), the indefinite accusative (§384), or *min* (§299 a).

Note 2. In fixed expressions, adjectival qualification in the genitive is also used on occasion: رَبِيعُ ٱلْأَوَّلِ 'Rabīʿ I', رَبِيعُ ٱلثَّانِي 'Rabīʿ II' (names of months), عَامُ ٱلْأَوَّلِ 'the previous year', عَامُ ٱلْقَابِلِ 'the next year', مَسْجِدُ ٱلْجَامِعِ 'the main mosque'.

§**391.** a) The nominal demonstrative ذُو (§283) followed by substantives or adjectives in the genitive is used to form qualifying expressions: ذُو ٱلْقَرْنَيْنِ 'the one with the two horns' (proper name), ذُو ٱلْعِلْمِ 'the one with knowledge, the knowing', إِمْرُؤٌ ذُو مَالٍ 'a wealthy man' (§398.1).

Note 1. Only the dual and plural of <u>dh</u>*ū* are combined with personal suffixes: ذَوُوكَ 'your relatives/family'.

b) Terms referring to relationship are often used as substantives indicating a connection or affinity, as are also صَاحِبٌ 'companion', أَهْلٌ 'people', and words of like meaning, e.g.: أَبُو ٱلضَّيْفِ 'the father of the guest, the host', إِبْنُ حَرْبٍ 'son of war, warrior', إِبْنُ ٱلْخَمْسِينَ 'the son of fifty, the fifty-year-old', أَخُو ثِقَةٍ 'a trustworthy person', صَاحِبُ شَرَابٍ 'a drinker', أَهْلُ ٱلسُّنَّةِ 'the followers of the Sunnah'.

Note 2. Such constructions are sometimes used for the names of things or animals: بَنَاتُ ٱلدَّهْرِ 'daughters of time, blows of fate', أَبُو ٱلْحُصَيْنِ 'father of the small fortress', i.e., 'fox'.

§**392.** Proper names follow in the genitive (*genitivus epexegeticus*) the appropriate terms that identify them: شَهْرُ رَمَضَانَ 'the month (called by the name of) Ramadan', سُورَةُ فَاتِحَةِ ٱلْكِتَابِ 'the Surah (called) the Opening of the Book', مَدِينَةُ بَغْدَادَ 'the city of Baghdad', يَوْمُ ٱلْأَحَدِ 'the day one', i.e., 'Sunday'.

Note 1. Personal names are not in the genitive but follow in apposition (§394 b) to the term referring to the person.

Note 2. In analogy to proper names, terms indicating specific things are sometimes expressed in the genitive after a term referring to something generic: آفَةُ ٱلْمَحْلِ 'the plague of famine'; in the same way with grammatical terms: كَلِمَةُ كَانَ 'the word *kāna*'.

Apposition

§393. All nominal forms that appear as predicates in nominal sentences (§361), and including prepositions (§293 b), may clarify, emphasize, or qualify in apposition. Apposition follows the substantive, which functions as a *regens*, and agrees with it in case: كَابُولُ مَدِينَةٌ مَعْرُوفَةٌ فِي بِلَادِ ٱلتُّرْكِ 'Kabul, a famous city in the land of the Turks', إِلَى صِرَاطٍ مُسْتَقِيمٍ صِرَاطِ ٱللّٰهِ 'to a straight path, the path of God'.

Note 1. When the *regens* is dependent on a preposition, that preposition may be repeated in the apposition: إِنَّا مِنْ هٰذَا ٱلْحَيِّ مِنْ رَبِيعَةَ 'We belong to this clan, Rabīʿah'. Personal suffixes may at times carry over into the term in apposition: مَعَ أَخِيهِ صَغِيرِهِ 'with his brother, the younger one'.

Note 2. A substantive in apposition may also appear after the personal pronouns of the 3rd person and demonstratives (§277). After the 1st and 2nd persons, the term in apposition is in the accusative (§383 b).

Note 3. After the personal suffixes, the apposition may appear in the accusative (§383) or with the preposition *min* (§299 a): ضَرَبَهُ ٱلْوَجْهَ 'He struck him, namely his face', 'He struck him in the face'.

§394. a) A substantive in apposition may be used, like the genitive (§390 b), to indicate material or content and to denote dimension, weight, or price: أَلْخَاتَمُ ٱلْحَدِيدُ 'the sealing ring (of) iron', جُبَّةٌ لِي صُوفٌ 'a jacket of mine (made of) wool', صُرَّةٌ مِائَةٌ دِينَارٍ, 'a purse (containing) 100 dinars', جَزِيرَةٌ خَمْسَةُ فَرَاسِخَ فِي خَمْسَةٍ 'an island (measured) five by five parsangs', مُصَنَّفَاتٌ عِدَّةٌ 'systematic works (in) large quantity'.

Note 1. Prepositional apposition may occur instead: لِحْيَةٌ ذِرَاعٌ 'a beard (of) a cubit' or لِحْيَةٌ بِطُولِ ذِرَاعٍ 'a beard the length of a cubit'; cf. also §299 a.

b) Personal names follow what they qualify in apposition; however, the qualified may also follow in apposition: أَخُوكَ زَيْدٌ 'your brother Zayd' or زَيْدٌ أَخُوكَ 'Zayd, your brother', أَلْإِمَامُ مَالِكٌ 'the Imam Mālik', مُوسَى ٱلنَّبِيُّ 'the prophet Moses'.

§**395.** a) Permutative apposition makes it possible to put the second member of a genitive construction first. The prominent member is represented in the appositional term by a personal suffix: أَعْجَبَنِي عَمْرٌو حُسْنُهُ ''Amr, his handsomeness astonished me' = حُسْنُ عَمْرٍو 'the handsomeness of 'Amr', قَوْمُكَ أَكْثَرُهُمْ 'your people, most of them' = أَكْثَرُ قَوْمِكَ 'most of your people'.

Note 1. This apposition may in special cases occur with the preposition *bi-*: أَلْأَمِيرُ بِنَفْسِهِ 'the prince himself', جَارِيَتِي بِعَيْنِهَا 'my slave-girl herself', رَجُلٌ بِعَيْنِهِ 'a certain man'.

b) Permutative apposition is the preferred construction in expressions that indicate totality and identity: أَلنِّسَاءُ كُلُّهُنَّ 'all women' (§136), إِبْنَاهُ كِلَاهُمَا 'both his sons' (§109), قَامَ هُوَ نَفْسُهُ (عَيْنُهُ) 'He himself stood up'.

§**396.** Appositional repetition is used for emphasis: إِذَا ٱلْحَبْلُ حَبْلُ ٱلْوَصْلِ لَمْ يَتَصَرَّمْ 'if the cord, the cord of union, is not torn', إِذَا دُكَّتِ ٱلْأَرْضُ دَكًّا دَكًّا 'When the earth is totally demolished' (Koran 89:21).

Note 1. Repetition also has a strengthening effect with other kinds of words: أَفِيقُوا أَفِيقُوا 'Wake up, wake up!', رَجُلٌ أَمِينٌ حَقُّ أَمِينٍ 'a reliable, truly reliable man'. See §402 on other uses of repetition.

§**397.** Abstracts denoting attributes also appear in apposition in an adjectival function. Here, the apposition agrees not only in case, but also in definiteness, with its *regens*: مَوْضِعٌ قُرْبٌ 'a close-by place', أَلرَّأْيُ ٱلْخَطَأُ 'the mistaken opinion', قِسْمَةٌ تَشْعِيبٌ 'a subdivided distribution', خُلُقٌ عَادَةٌ 'a character trait acquired by habit', أَلْمَوَازِينُ ٱلْقِسْطُ 'the correct (just) scales'.

Note 1. Terms of comparison (§388 b) usually come after an indefinite *regens*: شَخْصٌ كَٱلْجَبَلِ 'a shape like a mountain'.

Attributives

§**398.** Attributive adjectives agree with governing substantives in case and definiteness, as well as in gender (number) according to the rules given in §§113 f.: رَجُلٌ صَادِقٌ 'an honest man', أَلْجَارِيَةُ ٱلصَّادِقَةُ 'the honest slave-girl',

ثِيَابُكَ ٱلْبِيضُ 'your white garments' (§119.2). The attribute of the *regens* in a genitive construction follows after the genitive; §§145 b; 146 a.

Note 1. Negative *g͟hayru* (§325) agrees in case with the governing substantive,with the adjective following in the genitive in gender and in definiteness: أَلرَّجُلُ غَيْرُ ٱلصَّادِقِ 'the dishonest man'. The genitive of specification (§388 a) has no effect on whether the adjective is definite or indefinite; see §146c. Whether adjectival *d͟hū* is definite or indefinite is determined by the genitive (§391 a): رَجُلٌ ذُو حِلْمٍ 'a man of reason', أَلرَّجُلُ ذُو ٱلْحِلْمِ 'the man of reason'.

Note 2. Attributes are asyndetically coordinated (§400). Prepositional phrases and attributive clauses (§§428 ff.) may precede an attributive adjective: بَلَاءٌ مِنْ رَبِّكُمْ عَظِيمٌ 'a grievous trial from your Lord' (Koran 2:49; 7:141; 14:6), خَبَرٌ ذَكَرَهُ طَوِيلٌ 'a long report which he gave'.

§**399.** Attributive adjectives that appear with numerals are, irrespective of the number of the object counted, very often construed *ad sensum* in the plural: مِائَةٌ مِنَ ٱلْإِبِلِ عِشَارٌ 'one hundred she-camels pregnant in the tenth month', أَرْبَعُونَ رَجُلًا مُرَاقِبِينَ 'forty observant men', سِتُّونَ بُرْجًا كِبَارًا 'sixty large towers'; cf. §354.

Coordination of Parts of the Sentence

§**400.** a) Appositional and attributive expressions are as a rule asyndetically coordinated: عَدُوٌّ مُضِلٌّ مُبِينٌ 'an enemy misleading, manifest' (Koran 28:15), أَللّٰهُ ٱلْعَلِيُّ ٱلْكَبِيرُ 'the exalted and great God'. Dissimilar qualifications are identified as belonging together by means of *wa-* 'and': أَهْلُ ٱلْعِرَاقِ خَوَاصُّهَا وَعَوَامُّهَا 'the people of Iraq, the eminent and the ordinary of them'.

Note 1. Parts that are asyndetically coordinated may appear next to each other in an adversative relationship: مَدِينَةٌ جَبَلِيَّةٌ بَرِّيَّةٌ 'a city, part mountainous, part flat', رَجُلٌ دَمِيمٌ حَسَنُ ٱللِّمَّةِ 'a homely, but in hair growth handsome, man'.

b) Several adjectival predicates may be asyndetically coordinated; see §§361; 380. Other nominal predicates are usually coordinated with conjunctions, for the most part with *wa-* (§§328 ff.): هُوَ أَشْعَرُ مِنْكَ وَأَشْرَفُ 'He is a greater poet and more honorable than you'.

§**401.** More than one substantive referring to different things and identified as parallel parts of the sentence are always coordinated by conjunctions, usually *wa-* (§§328 ff.): ذٰلِكَ عَارٌ وَسُبَّةٌ عَلَيْنَا 'This is a shame and disgrace for us', مَرُّ ٱلْأَيَّامِ وَٱللَّيَالِي 'the passing of the days and the nights'.

Note 1. *wa-* coordinates approximate numbers in a range: طُولُهُ مِائَةُ بَاعٍ وَمِائَتَا بَاعٍ 'Its length is 100 to 200 fathoms'.

§**402.** To illustrate distributive enumeration, two asyndetically coordinated substantives may be cited, e.g.: فَأَعْطَى إِخْوَتَهُ نَاقَةً نَاقَةً وَشَاتَيْنِ شَاتَيْنِ 'And so he gave his brothers each a camel and two sheep', جَعَلَ يَسْأَلُنِي عَنْ وَادٍ وَادٍ 'He began to ask me about each individual valley'; cf. §383.2.

Note 1. In distributive pairs, coordination with *fa-* has the sense of a sequence: عَامًا فَعَامًا 'year by year, every year' (§329); with *wa-*, a sum: شَرٌّ وَشَرٌّ 'one evil after (added to, on top of) another', مِئُونَ وَمِئُونَ 'hundreds and hundreds more'.

§**403.** If a complement belongs to all of the coordinated parts of a sentence, the complement is usually mentioned only once. If the complement goes with the first part, the coordinated parts follow without the complement: كَانَ ذَا شَرَفٍ فِي ٱلْقَوْمِ وَفَضْلٍ 'He was a man of distinction and standing among the people', كُلُّ خَيْرٍ رَأَيْتُهُ وَشَرٍّ 'all the good and bad that I have seen', كَمْ نَاقِمٍ مِنَّا عَلَيْكُمْ وَنَاقِمَةٍ 'Indeed, there are so many (masc. and fem.) among us who take revenge on you'; — with verbs: نَمُوتُ مَعَكَ وَنَحْيَا 'We shall die and live with you'.

Note 1. In the coordination of the construct state, the genitive must be repeated as personal suffix; see §145 c.

Syntax: Clauses

Coordinate Clauses

§**404.** a) Independent clauses or subordinate clauses of equal status are coordinated by coordinating conjunctions (§§328 ff.), for the most part by *wa-* or *fa-*: قَدْ وَٱللّٰهِ رَابَنِي أَمْرُ هٰذَا ٱلْغُلَامِ وَلَا آمَنُهُ 'The behavior of this boy has, by God, filled me with suspicion, and I do not trust him' (§189.1). A change in subject is often indicated by *fa-*: أَتَى عُمَرُ أَعْرَابِيًّا فَقَالَ لَهُ 'Umar came to a Bedouin, and he (the Bedouin) said to him ...'.

b) The coordinate clause is not always parallel to the preceding clause but can be adversative: وَٱللّٰهُ يَعْلَمُ وَأَنْتُمْ لَا تَعْلَمُونَ 'And God knows it, but you do not' (Koran 2:216, 232; 3:66, etc.). Clauses that justify are often coordinated with *fa-* or *fa-ʾinna* (§339), especially following exclamations and the like: هَلُمَّ أَرْكَبْ مَعَكَ إِلَى يُوسُفَ فَإِنَّهُ صَدِيقِي 'Come on, I will ride to Joseph with you, for he is my friend' (§412).

Note 1. Coordination of a pair of clauses is sometimes expressed by placing parallel parts directly before and after *wa-*: تُلْحِمُ أَمْرًا وَأُمُورًا تُسْدِي 'With one thing you make the weft, and with others you make the warp'.

§**405.** a) Asyndetic coordination of clauses occurs only in lively conversation, e.g., introducing direct discourse and a reply: قَالَ ... قُلْتُ ... 'He said ..., I replied ...'.

b) An asyndetically coordinated clause may follow another in apposition as an explanatory postscript: قَتَلُوا عَبْدَ ٱللّٰهِ ذَبَحُوهُ ذَبْحًا 'They killed Abdallah, indeed, they really slaughtered him'. The agent of the action may be appended after a passive verb in this way: أُسِرَ ٱبْنُ عَمِّكَ أَسَرَتْهُ بَنُو فَزَارَةَ 'Your cousin was taken prisoner, that is, by the Banū Fazārah'.

Note 1. An explanatory afterthought may also be introduced by *wa-* or *fa-*: قَالُوا وَٱللّٰهِ مَا عَرَفْنَاهُ وَصَدَقُوا 'They said, By God, we did not recognize him, and they were speaking the truth'.

Note 2. Sometimes, verbs are coordinated asyndetically and form a semantic unit: أَرْسِلْ أَعْلِمْنِي 'Send, inform me!'; also in the standard phrase introducing a tradition: حَدَّثَنِي فُلَانُ بْنُ فُلَانٍ قَالَ 'So-and-so reported to me, he said'.

§**406.** In coordinate clauses which have one or more components in common, the shared one is usually mentioned only once: أَذُو نَسَبٍ أَمْ أَنْتَ بِٱلْحَيِّ عَارِفٌ 'Are you related or are you merely familiar with the clan?' (§333), نَحْنُ بِمَا عِنْدَنَا وَأَنْتَ بِمَا عِنْدَكَ رَاضٍ 'We are content with what we have, and you are with what you have', لَا سُوقَةٌ يَبْقَى وَلَا مَلِكٌ 'No subject and no king will be left alive' (§318 b).

Coordinate Circumstantial Clauses

§**407.** A circumstantial clause relates a condition or action simultaneous with an event. The verb assumes its aspect capacity in the circumstantial clause, while tense is determined by the preceding independent clause: مَاتَتْ آمِنَةُ وَهِيَ رَاجِعَةٌ إِلَى مَكَّةَ 'Aminah died while she was returning to Mecca', قَدْ أَغْتَدِي وَٱلطَّيْرُ فِي وُكُنَاتِهَا 'Sometimes I go out early in the morning, while the birds are still in their nests'.

Note 1. The coordinate particle *wa-* also connects adversative conditions (§404 b): كَيْفَ نَرْهَنُكَ نِسَاءَنَا وَأَنْتَ أَشَبُّ أَهْلِ يَثْرِبَ 'How can we pledge our women to you, when you are Yathrib's most renowned celebrator of women in verse'.

Note 2. Although *wa-* coordinates the clauses, the circumstantial clause is nevertheless a dependent clause. Its dependency is formally marked by the subject–predicate word order in the verbal clause and functionally indicated by the verb in its aspect capacity. Pre-classical Arabic still has an independent circumstantial clause after *ʾinna*, which is always followed by a clause introduced by *ʾidh* or *ʾidhā* (§280): إِنَّا لَنَتَرَحَّلُ إِذْ أَقْبَلْتُمْ 'We were just about to set out on the journey, when you suddenly approached', إِنِّي لَفِي أَيْدِيهِمْ إِذْ طَلَعَ عَلَيْهِمْ نَفَرٌ 'I was in their hands, when a group of people came suddenly upon them'. In classical usage, the conjunction that introduces the subordinate clause is *bayna-mā, baynā* (§444), rather than *ʾinna*.

§**408.** If the action or condition mentioned in the circumstantial clause represents an event independent of the main clause, the circumstantial clause is coordinated with *wa-* 'and': أَقْبَلَتْ عِيرٌ وَنَحْنُ نُصَلِّي 'A caravan approached, just as we were praying'. Conversely, a predicate circumstantial clause (§§413 ff.), which occupies the position of a circumstantial accusative and is not coordinated by a conjunction, designates that the action or condition is incorporated in the action of the main clause and specifies it: أَقْبَلُوا تُعْنِقُ بِهِمْ خَيْلُهُمْ 'They approached while their horses galloped with them'.

Note 1. When the subjects are the same in the main and the circumstantial clauses, predicate circumstantial clauses and coordinate circumstantial clauses are often equivalent. This is because it is not clear whether both actions are mutually independent or mutually inclusive, e.g., أَتَى عُمَرُ وَهُوَ يُعْطِي ٱلْمَسَاكِينَ مِنَ ٱلصَّدَقَةِ "'Umar came, and as he did, he gave the poor some of the alms tax at the same time', for which أَتَى عُمَرُ يُعْطِي ... "'Umar came, while he gave ...' is also possible. Still another interpretation (§431 b, 'came in order to give') is ruled out with coordinate circumstantial clauses.

Note 2. On occasion, coordinate circumstantial clauses may also come after *kāna* 'be' and verbs with related meanings (cf. §382): كُنَّا وَمَا نُصَلِّي 'We were, and at the same time, we were not praying', i.e., 'At that time, we were not praying'.

§**409.** Coordinate circumstantial clauses may occur as follows:

a) with the imperfect indicating simultaneous action; the subject always comes immediately after *wa-*: مَرَّ بِي وَأَصْحَابِي يَنْظُرُونَ إِلَيْهِ 'He passed by me, and my companions were looking at him at that same time'. A pronominal subject appears as an independent personal pronoun: لَقِيتُ أَحْمَدَ وَهُوَ يَطُوفُ بِٱلْبَيْتِ 'I met Ahmad just as he was circumambulating the (holy) house', إِجْتَازَ أَخُوهَا وَهِيَ لَا تَعْرِفُهُ 'Her brother passed by, but she did not recognize him'.

b) with the perfect and *qad* (§189 a) indicating an action already completed; the subject always follows the verb: فَٱنْتَبَهَ وَقَدْ شَدُّوهُ 'Then he woke up, to find that they had tied him up'. In the negative, these clauses take *mā* with the perfect (§321) to indicate a negative condition, or *lam* with the jussive (§319) to indicate a condition that does not exist: جَاءَ زَيْدٌ وَمَا رَكِبَ 'Zayd came, but he was not mounted', مَاتَ وَلَمْ يُعْقِبْ 'He died, without having left behind descendants', نَجَوْتُ وَلَمْ يَنْزِعُوا سَلَبِي 'I escaped, before they could strip me of my arms (i.e., what would have been their booty)'.

Note 1. The perfect without *qad* is very rare: أَنُؤْمِنُ لَكَ وَٱتَّبَعَكَ ٱلْأَرْذَلُونَ 'Shall we believe you, though the vilest followed you?' (Koran 26:111).

c) with nominal clauses; there is nothing peculiar about the word order (§366): قُلْتُ مَتَى تَزَوَّجْتَهَا قَالَ وَأَنَا بِعَدَنَ 'I said, when did you marry her? He replied, when I was in Aden', أَبَى أَنْ يَدْخُلَ ٱلْبَيْتَ وَفِيهِ ٱلْآلِهَةُ 'He did not want to enter the house while there were idols in it'; cf. also the examples in §407.

Note 2. Coordinated circumstantial sentences may follow ʾ*illā* (§310 d).

Coordinate Clauses with the Subjunctive

§410. Clauses coordinated with the main clause by *fa-* 'and then' (§329) which indicate a possible result have the subjunctive, provided the head clause is not a statement of fact, but a wish, question, condition, negation, and the like; *fa-* has the meaning 'so that' and, after negatives, 'lest' in these constructions: أَلَا تَجِيءُ فَأُطْعِمَكَ تَمْرًا 'Will you not come, so that I might give you dates to eat?', لَا تُقَدِّرْ عَظَمَةَ ٱللّٰهِ عَلَى قَدْرِ عَقْلِكَ فَتَكُونَ مِنَ ٱلْهَالِكِينَ 'Do not judge the majesty of God according to your intellect, lest you then be among the doomed'; cf. §197.

Note 1. The subjunctive occurs occasionally after *wa-* and other particles (§196.2) under similar conditions: يَا لَيْتَنَا نُرَدُّ وَلَا نُكَذِّبَ بِآيَاتِ رَبِّنَا 'O, that we would be brought back (from Hell), then we would not disbelieve the signs of our Lord' (Koran 6:27).

§411. After ʾ*aw* 'or' (§331), the subjunctive presents a possible alternative ('unless, until'): لَأَضْرِبَنَّهُ أَوْ يَقُومَ 'I will really strike him, unless he stands up', لَا نَسْتَطِيعُ أَوْ نَمْضِيَ 'We can do nothing else other than go away'.

Asyndetic Result Clauses with the Jussive

§412. A clause expressing the result of an imperative in the main clause has the verb in the jussive and is asyndetically joined to the main clause: سَمِّنْ كَلْبَكَ يَأْكُلْكَ 'Fatten your dog, and he will devour you', إِرْحَمْ تُرْحَمْ 'Be compassionate, and someone will show compassion for you' (conditional implication: 'if you show compassion . . . '; see §460). The jussive, as a rule, also follows when the result clause suggests the intent of the command or request: مُرْهُ يَأْتِ 'Order him, he should come!', دَعْنِي أَذْهَبْ 'Let me go away!', إِئْذَنْ لِي أَضْرِبْ عُنُقَهُ 'Allow me to decapitate him!'.

Note 1. Similarly, following particles of exclamation: إِيَّاكَ لَا أَقْذِفْكَ 'Watch out, lest I hit you!' (§272.2)

Subordinate Clauses as Parts of the Main Clause

§**413.** Some subordinate clauses may appear in the same syntactic positions in which nominal forms function as parts of the clause. Substantive clauses introduced by ᵓ*an,* ᵓ*anna, mā*, clauses functioning as substantives, or relative clauses may function syntactically as substantives. Attributive and circumstantial clauses may occupy the position of adjectives. Still other subordinate clauses may appear where circumstantial adverbial phrases are otherwise found.

Substantive Clauses

§**414.** أَنْ 'that' introduces a verbal clause whose predicate is either in the subjunctive (§§196 f.), if the action is expected, or in the perfect, if the action has taken place: يَنْبَغِي أَنْ تَحْذَرَ مِنَ ٱلْفَوَاحِشِ 'It is proper that you beware of abominations', قَضَى ٱللّٰهُ أَنْ كُسِرَتِ ٱلنَّصَارَى 'God has foreordained that the Christian (power) be broken'. Usually, ᵓ*anna* (§415) occurs instead of ᵓ*an* with the imperfect (§196.1): أَعْلَمُ أَنْ يَنَامُ = أَعْلَمُ أَنَّهُ يَنَامُ 'I know that he is sleeping'. The future particle *sa-* with the imperfect may also occur: زَعَمَ أَنْ سَيَزُورُكَ 'He claimed that he would visit you'.

Note 1. ᵓ*an* is used to introduce direct discourse, if it is not indicated by قَالَ 'say' (§419 a): أَشْهَدُ أَنْ لَا إِلٰهَ إِلَّا ٱللّٰهُ 'I attest, there is no god but the (one) God', أَرْسَلُوا إِلَيْهِمْ أَنْ رُدُّوا عَلَيْنَا إِبِلَنَا 'They sent them word, give us back our camels!', نَادَى مُنَادِي ٱلْقَوْمِ أَنْ قَدْ أُتِيتُمْ 'One of the people called, they have come to you'.

Note 2. In pre-classical Arabic, ᵓ*an* occurs where in classical Arabic only ᵓ*anna* may, especially before a nominal clause which does not begin with the subject: تَعْلَمُ أَنْ مَا لَنَا ذَنْبٌ 'You know that we are without guilt'; but also وَٱعْلَمْ بِأَنْ كُلُّ عَيْشٍ صَالِحٍ فَانٍ 'And know that every fortunate life is transitory'.

§**415.** أَنَّ 'that' introduces a nominal or a copulative clause. The subject follows in the accusative (§338): حُكِيَ أَنَّ مَلِكًا مِنَ ٱلْهِنْدِ كَانَتْ لَهُ زَوْجَةٌ 'It is told that one of the kings of India had a wife', يَرَى أَنَّ بَعْدَ ٱلْعُسْرِ يُسْرًا 'He thinks that after adversity comes ease', ذٰلِكَ أَنَّكَ ٱطَّلَعْتَ عَلَى أَسْرَارِنَا 'That is a result of your having found out our secrets'.

Note 1. After *ʾanna-mā* (§416.2), the structure of the clause is free: بَدَا لِي أَنَّمَا هُوَ فَارِسٌ 'It was clear to me that he was a horseman'.

Note 2. In post-classical Arabic, *ʾanna* may introduce an indirect question: لَا يَدْرِي أَنَّهُ كَيْفَ ٱنْتَهَى إِلَيْنَا 'He does not know how he reached us' (see §338 on the use of أَنَّهُ with the "pronoun of the fact").

§**416.** Subordinating مَا 'the fact that' (§289) introduces a verbal clause: لَا أَعْرِفَنَّ مَا أَخَّرْتَ 'I will certainly not acknowledge that you delayed the matter', يَسُرُّ ٱلْمَرْءَ مَا ذَهَبَ ٱللَّيَالِي 'It makes a person (§358) happy that the nights pass by', عَجِبْتُ مِمَّا ضَرَبْتَهُ 'I was amazed that you hit him'.

Note 1. The Arab grammarians called this *mā* مَا ٱلْمَصْدَرِيَّةُ *mā al-maṣdariyyah*, because this *mā* and following verb are always replaceable by a verbal substantive (*maṣdar*): عَجِبْتُ مِنْ ضَرْبِكَ إِيَّاهُ.

Note 2. Wherever particles introducing a clause are of the type that occur in constructions with a substantive, *mā* may replace that substantive and permit any kind of following clause; see §§337.3; 344.1; cf. also §§261 f. On أَلَّذِي 'that', see §426.1.

Note 3. كَوْنٌ 'being' is used in post-classical Arabic to embed clauses in complex sentences. The subject of the subordinate clause appears as a genitive of كَوْنٌ, and the predicate follows in the accusative (§382) or as a predicate circumstantial clause (§431): مَنَعَهُ عَنِ ٱلرِّحْلَةِ كَوْنُهُ جَبَانًا 'The fact that he is a coward prevented him from making the journey', جَاءَ ٱلنَّاسُ إِلَيْهِ لِلْهَنَاءِ لِكَوْنِ ٱلْوَزِيرِ كَلَّمَهُ 'The people came to congratulate him, because the vizier had spoken to him'.

§**417.** Although substantive clauses (clauses beginning with 'that') function mostly as subjects or objects, they may also serve as predicates or in apposition: ظَنِّي أَنْ تَعُودَ 'My assumption is that you will return', لَيْسَ هٰذَا بِرَأْيٍ أَنْ تَنْطَلِقَ 'This, namely that you go away, is not a good idea'. They may also appear in the position of adverbial accusatives (§378): إِسْتَأْجَرَ قَوْمًا أَنْ يَعْمَلُوا لَهُ 'He hired people to work for him', أَمَرَ رَسُولُ ٱللّٰهِ بِقَتْلِهِ أَنَّهُ كَانَ قَدْ أَسْلَمَ فَٱرْتَدَّ مُشْرِكًا 'The Messenger of God ordered him killed, because (of the fact that) he became a Muslim and then returned to polytheism'.

Note 1. In pre-classical Arabic, after verbs expressing a negative intent, the adverbial "that"-clause has a negative sense without being explicitly negative: تَرَكَ ٱلْأَحِبَّةَ أَنْ يُقَاتِلَ عَنْهُمْ 'He abandoned his loved ones lest he have to fight for them'.

Note 2. Clauses with *ʾanna* in the object position or which are dependent on a preposition governed by a verb tend to be abbreviated. Accordingly, the subject of the *ʾanna* clause is added directly to the main clause, and the predicate follows as if it were a predicate circumstantial clause (§434): أَرَى أَنَّ ٱلسُّيُوفَ... = أَرَى ٱلسُّيُوفَ سَتُسَلُّ 'I see that the swords will one day be drawn', أَبْكِي عَلَى أَنَّ خَبَرَ... = أَبْكِي عَلَى خَبَرِ ٱلسَّمَاءِ ٱنْقَطَعَ 'I am crying because the news from heaven has been cut off'.

Note 3. Clauses with *ʾan, ʾanna, mā* may function as genitives after verbal substantives : بِشَرْطِ أَنَّ 'on the condition that', طُولَ مَا 'while'; clauses with *ʾan* may function as genitive or accusative: مَخَافَةَ أَنْ or مَخَافَةً أَنْ 'out of fear that'.

§**418.** a) *ʾan, ʾanna,* and *mā* may occur in constructions with all prepositions, e.g.: فَفَعَلُوا ذٰلِكَ إِلَى أَنْ مَاتُوا 'Then they did this until they died', لَمْ يُشَكَّ فِي أَنَّهُ أَعْمَى 'There was no doubt that he was blind'; see §437.

Note 1. Sometimes, the preposition is lacking before *ʾan* and *ʾanna* as long as there is no ambiguity: إِسْتَعْجَمَتْ أَنْ تَكَلَّمَ 'She was too mute to have been able to speak' (for عَنْ أَنْ §301), لَوْ نَظَرْتَ إِلَيْهَا فَإِنَّهُ أَحْرَى أَنْ يُؤْدَمَ بَيْنَكُمَا 'If you regarded her (with the intent of marriage), that would be most appropriate that a good relationship develop between you two' (for بِأَنْ), إِنَّ ٱللّٰهَ لَا يَسْتَحِي أَنْ يَضْرِبَ مَثَلًا 'God is not ashamed to strike a similitude' (Koran 2:26; for مِنْ أَنْ).

b) Certain prepositional constructions with *ʾanna* and *mā* may assume an independent role and function as conjunctions (§344), e.g.: كَمَا, مِثْلَ مَا 'as', كَأَنَّ 'as if': أَرَى ٱلْأَمْرَ كَمَا تَرَى 'I regard the affair as you do', هَرَبَ كَأَنَّهُ نَعَامَةٌ 'He fled as if he were an ostrich', غُلَامٌ كَأَنَّ لِسَانَهُ لِسَانُ ثَوْرٍ 'A boy whose tongue is as it were a bull's tongue'; cf. also §365 b.

Note 2. In pre-classical Arabic, *ka-mā* also has the meaning 'so that' and occurs with the subjunctive: إِسْمَعْ حَدِيثًا كَمَا يَوْمًا تُحَدِّثَهُ 'Listen to an account so that you can report it some day!'; cf. §438.1.

Clauses Functioning as Substantives

§419. a) When elements of a sentence in the form of direct or indirect speech need to be inserted, they appear without an introductory particle in the position of a substantive: أَلْمُرُوءَةُ إِذَا أُعْطِيتَ شَكَرْتَ 'Manliness consists of this: if you are given something, you are thankful', تَسْمَعُ بِٱلْمُعَيْدِيِّ خَيْرٌ لَكَ مِنْ أَنْ تَرَاهُ 'It is better for you to hear about the Muʿaydī than to see them', لَقَدْ عَلِمْتُمْ مَا جِئْنَا لِنُفْسِدَ ٱلْأَرْضَ 'You know, we did not come to ruin the land', بَدَا لَهُمْ ... لَيَسْجُنُنَّهُ 'It seemed good to them ...they should imprison him' (Koran 12:35). Similarly, direct speech always follows قَالَ 'say': قَالَ لَنَا إِنَّ ٱلنَّاسَ نِيَامٌ 'He said to us, the people are sleeping'.

Note 1. ʾ*anna* may come after قَالَ only when it has the sense of 'suppose': مَتَى تَقُولُ أَنَّهُ مُنْطَلِقٌ 'When would you say he would go away', or when the direct speech is not the object of قَالَ: أَوَّلُ مَا أَقُولُ أَنِّي أَحْمَدُ ٱللّٰهَ 'The first thing I shall say is that I praise God'; cf. §414.1.

b) Likewise, indirect interrogative clauses are added without conjunctions: فَنَظَرَتْ هَلْ تَرَى أَحَدًا 'Then she looked there to determine whether she saw anyone', مُشِتٌّ عَلَيْنَا ٱلْأَمْرُ أَيْنَ يَرُومُ 'It is clear to us where the matter is headed', سَأَلَهُ عَنِ ٱلْأَضْحِيَّةِ أَوَاجِبَةٌ أَمْ لَا 'He asked him about the sacrifice, whether or not it was obligatory' (§333).

Note 2. Notice the different possible treatments of ʾ*ayyun* (§286) as subject of the interrogative clause, depending on whether it is classified as part of the main clause or remains in the nominative as part of the interrogative clause: لَمْ يَتَّفِقُوا عَلَى أَيُّهُمْ أَشْعَرُ or لَمْ يَتَّفِقُوا عَلَى أَيِّهِمْ أَشْعَرُ 'They did not agree on which of them was the better poet'.

§420. Substantives referring to time are followed by substantivized clauses without subordinating particles in the position of a genitive: ذَاكَ أَوَانُ أَبْصَرْتَ ٱلطَّرِيقَ 'That was the right time that you saw the road', بَعْدَ عَامِ لَقِيتُهُمْ 'after the year in which I met them'. The unrestricted use of such constructions in all syntactic positions is possible in early stages of the language. Later, usage was restricted to the adverbial accusative: أَخْطَأَهُ سَهْمِي حِينَ رَمَيْتُ 'My arrow missed him when I shot it'; see §346.

Relative Clauses as Substantives

§421. Relative clauses functioning as substantives are introduced by مَنْ 'who' ('one who', people who'), مَا 'what' ('something that'), or أَلَّذِي 'the one who, one which' (§§289; 281). The relative pronoun appears in the sentence where a substantive would be and may function as subject or predicate, as object, and may occupy the position of a genitive: إِنَّ أَوْسًا مَنْ قَدْ عَرَفْتَ 'Aws is one whom you know', يَقُولُونَ بِأَفْوَاهِهِمْ مَا لَيْسَ فِي قُلُوبِهِمْ 'They say with their mouths what is not in their hearts' (Koran 3:167), إِصْنَعْ مَا بَدَا لَكَ 'Do what seems good to you!'; also in the vocative: يَا أَيُّهَا ٱلَّذِينَ آمَنُوا 'O you who believe'.

Note 1. ذُو (§281.2) may also be a relative pronoun: كُنْ ذُو يَتَأَخَّرُ 'Be the one who falls behind'.

Note 2. In pre-classical Arabic, *man* and *mā* may stand in apposition: وَٱلْمُسْلِمُونَ مَنْ تَبِعَ رَسُولَ ٱللّٰهِ كَثِيرٌ 'And the Muslims, the ones who follow the Messenger of God, are many'. In constructions with *min*, relative pronouns are used for appositional clarification (§299 a): ثَلَاثُونَ رَجُلًا مِمَّنْ أَخْرَجَهُ ٱلْحَاجَةُ 'Thirty men, driven out by poverty', مُدَامَةٌ مُعَتَّقَةٌ مِمَّا يَجِيءُ بِهِ ٱلتُّجُرُ 'Aged wine, what the merchants bring'.

§422. The relative pronoun is always the subject of a compound clause (§368), which, as a relative clause, has a copulative personal pronoun like the predicate of a compound sentence: يَعْلَمُ ٱللّٰهُ مَنْ هُوَ فِي ضَلَالٍ مُبِينٍ 'God knows who has strayed into unmistakable error', إِتَّفَقَ عَلَى مَا تَطْلُبُهُ ٱلنَّاسُ 'He agreed as to what the people asked', مَا وَجَدْتُ مَرْكَبًا قَبْلَ ٱلَّذِي أَتَيْتُ بِهِ 'I did not find any ship before the one in which I came'. The copulative pronoun may also appear in a subordinate clause governed by the relative clause: فَٱلَّتِي يَقُولُ أَنَّهَا ٱلْجَنَّةُ هِيَ ٱلنَّارُ 'Therefore that which he says would be Paradise is (in reality) Hellfire'. The copulative pronoun may be lacking according to the conditions mentioned in §370: هُوَ ٱلَّذِي فِي ٱلسَّمَاءِ إِلٰهٌ وَفِي ٱلْأَرْضِ إِلٰهٌ 'He is the one who is God in heaven and God on earth'

(Koran 43:84), أَأَسْجُدُ لِمَنْ خَلَقْتَ طِينًا 'Shall I bow myself to the one You have created of clay?' (Koran 17:61).

Note 1. If the relative clause is dependent on a preposition which must be repeated in the relative clause in combination with the copulative pronoun, the prepositions together with the personal suffix may be omitted in the relative clause: أُطْلُبِ ٱلْقَوْمَ بِٱلَّذِي أُصِبْتَ 'Seek revenge on those people for what happened to you' (where بِهِ is omitted).

Note 2. If the copulative pronoun refers to a 1st or 2nd person in the main clause, this person also appears frequently in the relative clause: نَحْنُ ٱلَّذِينَ إِذَا زُجِرْنَا ٱسْتَقْدَمْنَا 'We are the ones who, if driven back, moved forward'; cf. also §429.2.

§**423.** مَنْ 'who' is used to refer to persons and is usually treated as a masculine singular, even when it refers to a female or to several people: كَانَتْ إِحْدَى مَنِ ٱتَّهَمَ بِهِ مِنَ ٱلْجَوَارِي 'She was one of the slave-girls whom he suspected' (§425 c), مِنْهُمْ مَنْ يُؤْمِنُ بِهِ 'Among them was one who believed in him', مَنْ تَبِعَ هُدَايَ فَلَا خَوْفٌ عَلَيْهِمْ 'Whoever follows my guidance has nothing to fear'. Nevertheless, the construction may have *ad sensum* agreement: كَانَتْ فِيمَنْ ضُرِبَ عَلَيْهَا ٱلْحِجَابُ 'She was among those before whom the screen was erected', مِنْهُمْ مَنْ يَسْتَمِعُونَ إِلَيْكَ 'Among them there are some who listen to you' (Koran 10:42).

§**424.** مَا 'what' is used for things and is masculine singular: هٰذَا مَا كَنَزْتُمْ لِأَنْفُسِكُمْ 'This is what you have amassed for yourselves'. Sometimes it is used to refer to groups of people: مَا قَتَلَ ٱلْأَمِيرُ صَبْرًا 'That which (i.e., those whom) the prince had killed in captivity' (cf. 425 c).

Note 1. See §416 on subordinating *mā* 'the fact that'.

Note 2. In pre-classical Arabic, *mā* is used for emphasis. The emphasized word comes at the beginning of the sentence and is followed by a clause introduced by *mā*: فَارِسٌ مَا غَادَرُوهُ 'It is a horseman that they have left behind', لِلْجَدِّ مَا خُلِقَ ٱلْإِنْسَانُ 'It is for good luck that man was created'. In many cases, however, *mā* is syntactically unimportant and is placed before the emphasized word as an expletive: فَٱذْهَبِي مَا إِلَيْكِ 'So go away!' (§303.4), إِنْ أَكُ مَا شَيْخًا كَبِيرًا 'if I became, so to speak, a very old man'.

§**425.** a) Relative clauses with مَنْ and مَا are as a rule indefinite. As such, they may occur in the position of a generic genitive (§387 a): كُلُّ مَا يَتَغَيَّرُ 'all that changes', شَرُّ مَنْ خَلَقَ ٱللّٰهُ 'the most evil one that God has created', كَثِيرُ مَا وَهَبُوا 'much of what they gave'. They also appear as qualifying genitives: مَا تَرَى رَأْيَ مَا نَرَى 'You do not think what we think', أَمْرَ مَا تَحْذَرُ 'the matter of which you are wary' (§392.2).

b) Relative *man* and *mā* are used in paronomastic constructions to express uncertainty: جَمَعْتُ مَا جَمَعْتُ 'I gathered what I gathered, i.e., a certain quantity', هُمْ مَا هُمْ 'They are what they are', i.e., 'they represent something', نَزَلَ مَنْ نَزَلَ مِنْهُمْ 'Some of them came down', فَمَكُثَ مَا شَاءَ ٱللّٰهُ أَنْ يَمْكُثَ 'Then he dwelled for as long as God willed'.

c) Frequently, partitive *min* (§299 b) is added to relative *man* and *mā*: فَأَعْطَانِي مَا كَانَ عِنْدَهُ مِنْ خُبْزٍ 'Then he gave me what he had of bread', i.e., 'the bread that he had', مَنْ دَخَلَ ٱلشَّأْمَ مِنَ ٱلْعَرَبِ 'Those Arabs who entered Syria'. In this case, *mā* often refers to groups of people: فَٱنْكِحُوا مَا طَابَ لَكُمْ مِنَ ٱلنِّسَاءِ 'So marry such women as seem good to you' (Koran 4:3).

Note 1. On relative clauses with conditional implication, see §461.

§**426.** أَلَّذِي introduces definite relative clauses. According to the subject referred to, the relative pronoun may be singular, dual, or plural and masculine or feminine (§281): قَدْ بَلَغَنَا ٱلَّذِي قُلْتُمْ 'What you said reached our ears', أَحْسَبُ أَنَّهَا ٱلَّتِي ذَكَرَهَا 'I think that it is she whom he mentioned', نَحْنُ ٱلَّذِينَ بَكَوْا لَهُ 'We are the ones who cried for him'.

Note 1. On occasion, أَلَّذِي occurs in the role of introductory *mā* (§416), especially in constructions with *ka-* (§297): فَصَلَّوْا كَٱلَّذِي كَانُوا يَفْعَلُونَ 'Then they prayed as they used to do', as well as in the post-classical phrase: أَلْحَمْدُ لِلّٰهِ ٱلَّذِي 'Thank God that ...'.

§**427.** Other interrogatives (§289) are also used as relatives: عَرَفَ ٱلْمَكِيدَةَ وَكَيْفَ كَانَ ٱلْمَلِكُ أَوْقَعَهَا 'He knew the trick and how the king employed it', وَٱللّٰهِ مَا نُبَالِي أَيْنَ ذَهَبَ 'By God, we do not care where he went'; cf. also §419b.

Attributive Relative Clauses

§**428.** An attributive relative clause occupies the position of an attributive adjective (§398). In attributive relative clauses, the governing substantive (*regens*) replaces the relative pronoun: رَجُلٌ قَدْ ضَرَبَنِي 'a man who struck me' (cf. مَنْ قَدْ ضَرَبَنِي 'one who struck me'). Like the attributive, the clause agrees with the *regens* in (in)definiteness. أَلَّذِي (§281) is used to make the clause definite. For its part, أَلَّذِي agrees with respect to gender (number) and case with the *regens*: أَلرَّجُلُ ٱلَّذِي قَدْ ضَرَبَنِي 'the man who struck me', قَوْمٌ يُؤْمِنُونَ 'people who believe', definite أَلْقَوْمُ ٱلَّذِينَ يُؤْمِنُونَ 'the people who believe', ثُمَّ إِنَّ وَلَدَيْهِ ٱللَّذَيْنِ قَتَلَاهُ هَرَبَا إِلَى ٱلْجِبَالِ 'Thereupon his two sons, who had murdered him, fled into the mountains'.

Note 1. When there is generic definiteness, the attributive clause is not always explicitly defined: أَنْتَ ٱلْوَزِيرُ لَا يُعْصَى 'You are the vizier who is not disobeyed', هُمُ ٱلْفَوَارِسُ يَحْمُونَ ٱلنِّسَاءَ 'They are the horsemen who protect the women'.

§**429.** In an attributive relative clause, the copulative personal pronoun refers to the *regens*. In an indefinite relative clause, the pronoun appears as a rule; in a definite relative clause, it may, under the circumstances mentioned in §370, be dropped: لَمَّا كَانَ بِٱلْكُوفَةِ بَنَى مَسْجِدًا هُوَ بِهَا إِلَى ٱلْيَوْمِ 'When he was in Kufah, he built a mosque, which stands there even today', رَأَيْتُ رَجُلًا أَعْمَى يَقُودُهُ شَابٌّ 'I saw a blind man whom a youth was leading', إِنَّ ٱلرَّجُلَ ٱلَّذِي طَلَبْتَ بِٱلْبَابِ 'The man whom you seek is at the door'.

Note 1. The copulative pronoun may also appear in a clause subordinate to a relative clause: قَدْ قَرُبَ إِلَيْهِ ٱلْجَيْشُ ٱلَّذِي ظَنَّ أَنَّهُ بَعِيدٌ 'The army that he thought was distant drew near him'.

Note 2. The 1st and 2nd persons appearing in the main clause may reappear in indefinite relative clauses and sometimes in definite relative clauses (§422.2): أَنْتُمْ قَوْمٌ تَجْهَلُونَ 'You are people who are ignorant', أَنْتَ آدَمُ ٱلَّذِي أَغْوَيْتَ ٱلنَّاسَ 'You are Adam, who misled mankind'.

§**430.** a) In an attributive relative clause with an adjectival predicate, the adjective immediately follows the *regens* and agrees with it in case and definiteness; however, it agrees in gender (number) with the appropriate subject coming afterward. That subject takes a copulative pronoun: رَأَيْتُ ٱمْرَأَةً حَسَنًا وَجْهُهَا 'I saw a woman whose face was pretty', قَوْمٌ شَدِيدَةٌ نِكَايَتُهُمْ 'people whose harmfulness is severe', أَلتَّوَارِيخُ ٱلْآتِي ذِكْرُهَا 'the to-be-mentioned chronicles'.

Note 1. At times, the copulative pronoun appears with another part of the clause: هُوَ ٱلْحَجَرُ ٱلرَّامِي بِهِ ٱللّٰهُ مَنْ رَمَى 'That is the stone which God throws at the one whom he wishes to throw it at'.

b) This kind of relative clause may also function as a substantive: مُحْمَرَّةٌ عَيْنُهُ 'one whose eyes are reddened', إِنَّمَا ٱلصَّدَقَاتُ لِلْفُقَرَاءِ ... وَٱلْمُؤَلَّفَةِ قُلُوبُهُمْ 'The alms are only for the poor ... and those whose hearts should be made to tend (to Islam)' (Koran 9:60).

Predicate Circumstantial Clauses

§**431.** a) Circumstantial clauses, which modify and complement the governing verb (cf. §§202 c; 408), occupy the position of the circumstantial accusative (§§380 ff.): بَعَثَ إِلَى مُعَاوِيَةَ يَطْلُبُ ٱلصُّلْحَ 'He sent to Muʿāwiyah to ask for peace', دَخَلَ ٱلْبَيْتَ لَا تُسَلِّمُ عَلَيَّ 'He entered the room without greeting me'.

b) With the imperfect, the circumstantial clause indicates action or intent that is conceived to be simultaneous with or following the action expressed by the governing verb: ثُمَّ نَزَعَتْ ثِيَابَهَا تَغْتَسِلُ 'Then she removed her garments in order to bathe', خَرَجْتُ أَنَا وَأَبِي نَتَصَيَّدُ 'I went out with my father with the intention of hunting'. — The perfect, sometimes with *qad*, indicates a condition that already obtains: جَاؤُوكُمْ حَصِرَتْ صُدُورُهُمْ 'They came to you with their breasts constricted' (Koran 4:90). See §435 on nominal clauses.

c) If the subject of the circumstantial clause is different from that of the main clause, a copulative personal pronoun refers to the subject of the main clause: أَقْبَلُوا تُعْنِقُ بِهِمْ خَيْلُهُمْ 'They approached while their horses galloped with them'.

§**432.** Very often circumstantial clauses are governed by verbs whose literal meanings have faded and which have come to indicate merely *Aktionsarten*, or modes of action (§190).

a) 'begin': جَعَلْتُ أُحَذِّرُهُمْ 'I began to warn them', أَخَذَ يُعَاتِبُهُ 'He began to blame him', طَفِقَ ٱلْقَوْمُ يَرْجِعُونَ 'Suddenly the people returned'.

b) 'become': فَأَصْبَحَ ٱلنَّاسُ يَضْحَكُونَ بِهِ 'Then it came to the point that the people laughed at him', أُمْسِي قَدِ ٱنْقَطَعَ ٱلْحَبْلُ بَيْنِي وَبَيْنَهُ 'I shall end up such that the bond between him and me will have been severed'.

c) 'persist': يَظَلُّ يَتْبَعُهَا 'He persisted in following her', مَكَثَ عُثْمَانُ ثَلَاثَةَ أَيَّامٍ لَمْ يُدْفَنْ 'Uthman remained for three days without being buried'.

d) 'repeat': لَمْ يَعُودُوا يَعْرِفُونَهُ 'They no longer recognized him'; cf. also §446.2.

Note 1. This kind of construction is extended to some other semantically related verbs, which occur in combination with *ʾan* clauses (§414), so that both constructions may be used interchangeably: كَادَ ٱلنَّعَامُ أَنْ يَطِيرَ or كَادَ ٱلنَّعَامُ يَطِيرُ 'The ostrich can almost fly', أَرَادُوا أَنْ يَقْتُلُوهُ or أَرَادُوا يَقْتُلُونَهُ 'They wanted to kill him'.

§**433.** A predicate circumstantial clause following the verb may refer to the object, just as a circumstantial accusative in the same position refers to the object (§381): أَظُنُّنِي قَدْ صَدَقْتُ 'I consider myself to have spoken the truth', لَا نَدَعُكَ تَخْرُجُ 'We will not let you go out', وَجَدَ ٱلْبَابَ قَدْ فُتِحَ 'He found the door already opened', شَهِدْتُ رَسُولَ ٱللّٰهِ يَقْرَأُ 'I witnessed the Messenger of God reading', أَبْعَثُ إِلَيْكَ أُخْتَنَا تَكُونُ مَعَكَ 'I shall send our sister so that she will be with you'.

Note 1. The subject of the circumstantial clause may also in this case be different from the object of the main clause: تَرَى رَأْسِي تَغَيَّرَ لَوْنُهُ شَمَطًا 'You see that the color of my head has changed to gray'.

Note 2. The verb of the circumstantial clause may refer to two nouns and, as such, is in the dual: تَرَكَ عُرْوَةَ مَعَ عَفْرَاءَ يَتَحَدَّثَانِ 'He left Urwah with Afra chatting with each other'.

§**434.** After verbs of sense perception or intellectual activity, substantive clauses which describe an event take the form of a circumstantial clause, and introductory *ʾanna* is dropped (§417.2): سَمِعْتُ مَوْلَاكَ قَالَ لَكَ بَأْسًا 'I heard that your client said something bad to you', رَأَيْتُ عَمْرًا فِي ٱلْمَنَامِ كَسَانِي رِدَاءَهُ

'I saw in the dream that Amr covered me in his robe', نَعْلَمُ عَدُوَّ ٱللّٰهِ قَدْ مَاتَ 'We know that the enemy of God died', خُبِّرْتُهَا قَالَتْ 'It was reported to me that she said . . . '.

Note 1. After *mā li-* (§285.1) and *mā bālu-* 'why . . . ?', an asyndetic clause follows instead of the circumstantial accusative: مَا لِي لَمْ أَسْمَعْ بِكَ 'Why did I not hear of you?', مَا بَالُ عَيْنِكَ مِنْهَا ٱلْمَاءُ يَنْسَكِبُ 'Why is water pouring down from your eye?'.

§435. a) Predicate nominal clauses describe the condition of the subject or object: كُنْتُ أَمْشِي مَعَهُ يَدُهُ فِي يَدِي 'I used to walk with him, while his hand was in mine'; referring to the object: لَقِيتُهُ عَلَيْهِ جُبَّةُ وَشْيٍ 'I met him when he was wearing an ornate jacket'.

Note 1. Nominal clauses may appear in apposition to a circumstantial accusative: إِنَّ ٱلْمَمْلَكَةَ تَصِيرُ مُخْتَلِفَةً بَعْضُهَا قَوِيٌّ وَبَعْضُهَا ضَعِيفٌ 'The kingdom will become diverse, partly strong and partly weak'.

b) If it comes at the beginning of the clause, the subject of the predicate nominal clause may appear in the circumstantial accusative: كُنْتُ أَمْشِي مَعَهُ يَدَهُ فِي يَدِي 'I used to walk with him hand in hand'. Similarly, an adjectival predicate tends to come at the beginning and then is inserted as a circumstantial accusative in the main clause (§380): رَأَيْتُ عَمْرًا مَجْمُوعَةً يَدَاهُ إِلَى عُنُقِهِ بِحَبْلٍ 'I saw Amr, his hands tied with a rope to his neck' (§356 b), نَظَرَ إِلَيْهِ بِمُؤَخَّرِ عَيْنِهِ مَصْرُوفًا عَنْهُ وَجْهُهُ 'He looked at him out of the corner of his eye with his face turned away', إِنَّ حَاجَتَكَ تُقْضَى كَائِنَةً مَا كَانَتْ 'Your request will be fulfilled, whatever it be'.

Appositional Circumstantial Clauses

§436. In apposition, a circumstantial clause indicates a temporary condition of the *regens*: لِمَنِ ٱلدِّيَارُ غَشِيتُهَا 'Whose are the dwellings that I have come to?' (Beginning of an old Arabic *qaṣīdah*), كَمَثَلِ ٱلْحِمَارِ يَحْمِلُ أَسْفَارًا 'like the ass that is carrying books' (Koran 62:5).

Adverbial Clauses

§437. Numerous subordinate clauses occupy the position of circumstantial adverbial expressions. Among them are substantive clauses that are dependent on prepositions or adverbial accusatives; e.g.: مَا رَأَيْنَاهُ لِأَنَّهُ مَاتَ مِنْ قَبْلُ 'We did not see him any more, because he had died before', بَاكَرْتُهَا قَبْلَ مَا بَدَا ٱلصَّبَاحُ لَنَا 'I came to her early, before morning appeared to us', أُذِينَا مِنْ قَبْلِ أَنْ تَأْتِيَنَا وَمِنْ بَعْدِ مَا جِئْتَنَا 'We were tormented before you came and after you came', رَبَّنَا لَا تُزِغْ قُلُوبَنَا بَعْدَ إِذْ هَدَيْتَنَا 'Our Lord, do not cause our hearts to stray after you have guided us right!' (Koran 3:8) (§344.2), شَدُّوهُ رِبَاطًا أَوَّلَ مَا ٱنْتَبَهَ 'They bound him tight as soon as he woke up'; cf. §418.

Note 1. See §§346; 420 on the adverbial accusative with genitive clauses. On *mundhu, mudh* 'since' §300, *ladun* (*ʾan*) 'since' §306, *qabla* 'before' §346.1.

§438. Clauses expressing intent or purpose are introduced by *li-, li-ʾan* (§295) or *kay, li-kay* 'so that, in order to' and the subjunctive (§196): لَمْ آخُذْكَ لِأَقْتُلَكَ 'I did not seize you with the intent of killing you', أَرَادَ أَنْ يُخِيفَنِي لِئَلَّا أَرْجِعَ 'He wanted to frighten me, so that I would not return', يَتُوقُ قَلْبِي إِلَيْكُمْ كَيْ يُلَاقِيَكُمْ 'My heart longs for you, in order to meet with you'.

Note 1. In pre-classical Arabic, the imperfect sometimes comes after *kay-mā* (§345.1) and *ka-mā* (§418.2) 'so that, in order to': لِكَيْمَا تَقُولُ 'so that she says'.

Note 2. It may happen that a clause expressing intent is coordinated with a circumstantial accusative (§380.1): إِنَّمَا خَرَجَ رَسُولُ ٱللّٰهِ مُرْهِبًا لِلْعَدُوِّ وَلِيُبَلِّغَهُمْ 'The Messenger of God went out only to threaten the enemy and to let them know ...'.

Note 3. مَا كَانَ لِ or لَمْ يَكُنْ لِ means 'not inclined to, not apt to, not in a position to do something, not capable of doing something': لَمْ أَكُنْ لِأَمَسَّهَا 'I was incapable of touching her'.

§439. a) حَتَّى (§304) 'until, as long as': سَارُوا حَتَّى طَلَعَتِ ٱلشَّمْسُ 'They traveled until the sun came up', بَقِيَ حَتَّى أَدْرَكَ خِلَافَةَ أَبِي بَكْرٍ 'He remained alive until he reached the caliphate of Abū Bakr', i.e., 'He lived to see the caliphate of Abū Bakr'; 'to the extent that, so much that': غَمَّهُ ذٰلِكَ حَتَّى ٱمْتَنَعَ مِنَ ٱلْغَدَاءِ 'That saddened him so much that he refused to eat breakfast', مَا فَعَلَتْ حَتَّى ٱسْتَوْجَبَتِ ٱلْقَتْلَ 'What did she do to deserve to be killed?'; sometimes the consecutive 'so that': رَأَيْتُ ٱلسَّمَاءَ أُفْرِجَتْ لِي حَتَّى دَخَلْتُهَا 'I saw that Heaven was parted for me so that I could enter it'. Frequently, *ḥattā* leads up to a concluding action, 'until eventually, thereupon, finally': لَمْ يَفْعَلْ حَتَّى أَغْلَقَ بَابَهُ فِي وَجْهِهِ 'He did nothing, until finally he closed the door in his face', خَرَجَ حَتَّى قَعَدَ لِلنَّارِ 'He came out and thereupon sat at the fire'.

Note 1. After negative clauses, *ḥattā* has the sense of 'before, not even ...when': لَمْ آتِكُمْ حَتَّى أَتَتْنِي كُتُبُكُمْ 'I had not come to you before your letters reached me'. It is also used to introduce a sudden occurrence: مَا بَلَغْتُ ٱلْبَابَ حَتَّى سَمِعْتُ 'I had not yet reached the door when I heard ...'.

b) Statements of fact follow *ḥattā* in the perfect, infrequently in the imperfect or as nominal clauses: يُغْشَوْنَ حَتَّى لَا تَهِرُّ كِلَابُهُمْ 'They are visited so often that their dogs do not snarl'. Expected or intended actions are described in the subjunctive (§196): فَٱصْبِرُوا حَتَّى يَحْكُمَ ٱللَّهُ بَيْنَنَا 'Be patient until God will judge between us' (Koran 7:87), لَا بُدَّ مِنَ ٱلتَّأَمُّلِ قَبْلَ ٱلْكَلَامِ حَتَّى يَكُونَ صَوَابًا 'We must meditate before we speak, in order that our words may be appropriate'.

Note 2. A clause introduced by *ʾinna* (§339) and by *kaʾanna* (§365) may follow *ḥattā*.

§440. a) حَتَّى إِذَا: *ḥattā* frequently precedes a clause introduced by *ʾidhā* (§464): لَيْسَتِ ٱلتَّوْبَةُ لِلَّذِينَ يَعْمَلُونَ ٱلسَّيِّئَاتِ حَتَّى إِذَا حَضَرَ أَحَدَهُمُ ٱلْمَوْتُ قَالَ إِنِّي تُبْتُ 'There is no repentence for those who do evil deeds until, when one of them is visited by death, he says, indeed I repent' (Koran 4:18). *ʾidhā* after *ḥattā* usually has a temporal function without the conditional implication common in *ʾidhā*-clauses (§445); as a rule, the perfect comes after *ḥattā ʾidhā*: لَمْ تَزَلْ سَلْمَى مُغَاضِبَةً لِسَعْدٍ حَتَّى إِذَا أَصْبَحَتْ أَتَتْهُ وَصَالَحَتْهُ 'Salmā remained angry at Saʿd; finally, however, when morning came, she went to him and reconciled', إِنْصَرَفَ إِلَى مَنْزِلِهِ حَتَّى إِذَا كَانَ مِنَ ٱلْغَدِ خَرَجَ 'He went to his dwelling and, when the next morning arrived, came back out'.

Note 1. *ʾidhā-mā* (§465) may also follow *ḥattā*.

b) Often the continuation of the *ḥattā* clause is lacking after the *ʾidhā*-clause. As a result, *ḥattā ʾidhā* as a fixed construction has the meaning 'until finally': فَخَرَجُوا حَتَّى إِذَا كَانُوا عَلَى ٱلرَّجِيعِ فَغَدَرُوا فِيهِ 'Then they went out until at last they were before al-Rajīʿ, and then they betrayed him', ذَهَبَ حَتَّى إِذَا كَانَ ٱلْيَوْمُ ٱلثَّالِثُ 'They went away until the third day arrived', لَقَدْ صَدَقَكُمُ ٱللّٰهُ وَعْدَهُ... حَتَّى إِذَا فَشِلْتُمْ 'God has been true in his promise towards you, ... until you finally lost heart' (Koran 3:152).

§**441.** حَيْثُ 'where' begins adverbial subordinate clauses: رَمَى بِسَهْمٍ حَيْثُ سَمِعَ ٱلْحِسَّ 'He shot the arrow where he had heard the sound'; — to substantiate or restrict, 'such that, as, inasmuch as': غَضِبَ ٱللّٰهُ عَلَيْهِمْ حَيْثُ لَمْ يَتَّعِظُوا 'God was angry at them inasmuch as they would not be admonished'. Prepositions like *bi-, min, ʾilā*, among others, come before *ḥaythu* for clarity: حَدَوْتُ بِحَيْثُ يُسْتَمَعُ ٱلْحُدَاءُ 'I provoked where it was listened to', ٱلْجِسْمُ مِنْ حَيْثُ هُوَ جِسْمٌ 'the body insofar as it is a body', i.e., 'the body as body, the body *qua* body'.

Note 1. As with relative clauses (§§421 ff.), a copulative personal pronoun may on rare occasion come after *ḥaythu*, or *ḥaythu* may appear with partitive *min* (§425 c): أَرَدْتُ ٱلْٱنْصِرَافَ إِلَى حَيْثُ أَقْبَلْتُ مِنْهُ 'I wanted to go back to where I had come from', إِرْعَوْا مِنْ أَرْضِنَا حَيْثُ شِئْتُمْ 'Graze in our land wherever you wish' (with conditional implication: §461.1).

Note 2. In post-classical Arabic, the subordinate clause is at times reduced to just a subject: دَخَلْتُ حَيْثُ ٱلْقَبْرُ 'I went into where the grave was', مِنْ حَيْثُ ٱلصُّورَةُ 'from there where the form is', i.e., 'as to, with respect to, concerning the form'.

§**442.** a) إِذْ 'when, as' (§280), as a conjunction, indicates a particular time, usually in the past: قَدْ ظَلَمْتَهُمْ إِذْ حَبَسْتَهُمْ 'You treated them wrongly when you imprisoned them', إِذْ يَتَّقُونَ بِي ٱلْأَسِنَّةَ لَمْ أَخِمْ 'As (while) they protected themselves with me from the spear-tips, I did not recoil like a coward'; — sometimes also in the future or present: هَلْ يَسْمَعُونَكُمْ إِذْ تَدْعُونَ 'Do they hear you when you call?', يَا لَيْتَنِي أَكُونُ حَيًّا إِذْ يُخْرِجُكَ قَوْمُكَ 'If only I could be alive when your people drive you out'.

b) Not infrequently, especially in post-classical Arabic, *ʾiḏ* expresses a reason and means 'since, because': أَنْتِ إِذْ لَمْ تُصْلِحِي لِأَبِيكِ لَا تُصْلِحِينَ لِي 'You, since you did not treat your father kindly, will not treat me kindly'.

Note 1. In the Koran (2:126; 14:35), *ʾiḏ* sometimes begins a main clause and indicates a time in the past, 'once, at one time': وَإِذْ قَالَ إِبْرَاهِيمُ رَبِّ ٱجْعَلْ هٰذَا ٱلْبَلَدَ آمِنًا 'And once Abraham said: My Lord, make this place safe!'.

§**443.** لَمَّا or لَمَّا أَنْ 'when, after' followed by the perfect introduces an action that is a precondition of what takes place in the main clause: لَمَّا رَمَتْنِي أَقْصَدَتْنِي بِسَهْمِهَا 'When she shot at me, she hit me with her arrow', لَمَّا دَنَا مِنِّي رَفَعَ يَدَهُ فَلَطَمَنِي 'After he had drawn near me, he raised his hand and slapped me'; — sometimes giving a reason: لَمَّا لَمْ يَكُنْ لِبَحْثِهِ مَقْصُودٌ لَمْ يَبْلُغْ فِيهِ ٱلْغَايَةَ ٱلْقُصْوَى 'Since (because) his searching had no aim, he did not reach with it the final objective'.

Note 1. The main clause sometimes begins with *ʾiḏā* (§280) or *fa-* (§329): لَمَّا بَرَزُوا إِذَا هُمْ يَفْقِدُونَ سَبْعِينَ رَجُلًا 'When they emerged, they were missing seventy men'.

§**444.** بَيْنَمَا, بَيْنَا 'while' begins a circumstantial clause (§§407.2; 409). The subject comes immediately after *bayna-mā, baynā*; the subsequent main clause is often introduced by *ʾiḏ*, and occasionally by *fa-* or *fa-ʾiḏā* (§280): بَيْنَا أَنَا ذَاتَ يَوْمٍ جَالِسٌ أَقْبَلَتْ عَلَيَّ 'While I sat there one day, she approached me', بَيْنَمَا نَحْنُ نَمْشِي إِذْ عَرَضَ رَجُلٌ 'While we were walking along, a man suddenly appeared', بَيْنَا ٱلنَّاسُ قَدْ أَجْمَعُوا لِلْحَرْبِ تَدَاعَوْا إِلَى ٱلصُّلْحِ 'While they resolved to go to war, they suddenly called upon one another for peace'.

Note 1. The subordinate clause is sometimes reduced to just a subject: بَيْنَمَا صَلَاةُ ٱلْعَصْرِ إِذْ أَبْصَرْتُ ٱلْمِسْكِينَ 'While it was afternoon prayer, I caught sight of the poor man', بَيْنَمَا ذَاكَ 'meanwhile'.

Note 2. In pre-classical Arabic, the suffix of the 3rd masculine is occasionally added: بَيْنَاهُ 'while he ...', بَيْنَاهُمْ 'while they ...'.

Note 3. In post-classical Arabic, the perfect (without *qad*) occurs.

Conditional Sentences

§445. a) There are two types of conditional sentences in Arabic: 1. real (or valid) conditional sentences, in which the protasis presents a statement of fact that is believed to be generally valid and realizable at any time as the precondition or premise (introductory particle *ʾin* §§450 ff.); 2. unreal (or unfulfilled, hypothetical) conditional sentences, in which the protasis presents a specific hypothetical situation or action as the presupposition (introductory particle *law* §§453 ff.). To be included among the former type are also sentences with conditional implication (§§460 ff.), in which again a statement of fact that is universally accepted as such is given as the premise.

b) As a rule, the protasis precedes the apodosis (main clause). Variations from this order are, however, not unusual: لَا نَجَوْتُ إِنْ نَجَا 'May I not be saved, if he is saved!', إِنِّي أَجَبْتُ لَوْ سَأَلْتَنِي 'I would have answered, if you had only asked me'.

Note 1. When dependent on introductory particles like *ʾinna* (§338), the subject of the protasis may appear before the conjunction at the beginning of the sentence: إِنِّي كُلَّمَا دَعَوْتُهُمْ لِتَغْفِرَ لَهُمْ جَعَلُوا أَصَابِعَهُمْ فِي آذَانِهِمْ 'Whenever I call them that You might forgive them, they put their fingers into their ears' (Koran 71:7). The subject of the apodosis may also come before the conjunction: أَنَا لَوْ ذَهَبَ مَالِي لَجَلَسْتُ قَاصًّا 'Should my possessions disappear, I would sit down as a story teller'.

§446. a) In conditional sentences and sentences with conditional implication, the statement of fact in the premise (i.e., in the protasis), as it is generally valid and not restricted in time, is described in the jussive or perfect. In the apodosis, the verb is also in the jussive or perfect, insofar as it contains a generally valid result: مَتَى تَعْجَلْ تَنْدَمْ 'Whenever you are hasty, you will regret it', مَنْ جَالَ نَالَ 'He who roams will reach something'. For negative sentences, *lam* with the jussive is used: إِنْ لَمْ يَبْرَحْ لَمْ أَرْضَ 'If he does not vanish, I shall not be content'.

b) In sentences with conditional implication, *kāna*, indicating the past, usually appears at the beginning of the sentence before the conjunction and indicates that the entire sentence is in the past. As a rule, *kāna* agrees with the subject of the protasis: كُنْتَ مَتَى تُجْهِلْ خَصِيمَكَ يَجْهَلْ 'Whenever you considered your adversary stupid, he was'; see also §464 b. Sometimes *kāna* indicating the past appears before *ʾin*.

Note 1. Verbs that indicate mode of action (§432) are also used on occasion to indicate the past; in the apodosis the general perfect appears instead of the predicate imperfect: فَجَعَلَ كُلَّمَا مَرَّ بِحَيٍّ مِنَ ٱلْعَرَبِ بِطَرِيقِ ٱلشَّأْمِ أَخَذَ مِنْ أَشْرَافِهِمْ 'Then he began, whenever he passed by a tribe of the Arabs on the road to Syria, to enter into a relationship with the distinguished among them'.

§**447.** The apodosis, which follows the protasis, is introduced by particles under the following specific circumstances:

a) *fa-* (§329) begins the apodosis after *ʾin* and after clauses with conditional implication, if the apodosis does not contain a generally valid statement in the jussive, perfect, or imperfect; i.e., *fa-* comes: 1. before nominal and copulative clauses (§§360 ff.): إِنْ تَسْخَرُوا مِنَّا فَإِنَّا نَسْخَرُ مِنْكُمْ كَمَا تَسْخَرُونَ 'If you scoff at us, we shall surely scoff at you, as you scoff' (Koran 11:38), إِذَا أَتَيْنَا سَائِلِينَ فَلَيْسَ مِنَ ٱلْأَشِحَّاءِ 'When we come asking, he is not among the stingy', إِنْ فَعَلْتَ ذٰلِكَ فَنِعْمَ ٱلْفَتَى أَنْتَ 'If you do that, you are an admirable young man indeed' (§§259 f.); 2. before clauses containing commands and prohibitions: إِذَا رَأَيْتَنِي أَرْمِزُ فَلَا تَدْخُلْ 'If you see me making a sign, do not enter!', فِي أَيِّ أَرْضٍ شِئْتَ فَٱنْزِلْ 'In whatever land you wish, settle!'; 3. before the future particles *sawfa, sa-, lan* (§187): إِنْ عَادَ فَلَنْ يَلْقَانِي 'If you return, you will not encounter me'; 4. before the verbal particle *qad* (§189) and عَسَى 'it could be, perhaps' (§342.2): إِنْ أَسْلَمُوا فَقَدِ ٱهْتَدَوْا 'If they become Muslims, they are rightly guided'; 5. before an abbreviated apodosis (§448) and in most cases before an apodosis that does not contain a direct logical conclusion (§449).

b) *la-* (§334) generally begins the apodosis of an unreal conditional sentence: لَوْ لَمْ أَعْرِفْهُ لَسَأَلْتُ عَنْهُ 'If I had not known him, I would have asked about him', لَوْ أَنَّنِي فِيكُمْ لَرَأَيْتُ مِنْكُمْ شَرًّا 'Had I been with you, I would have experienced your evilness'. In real conditional clauses, *la-* tends to be used in both the protasis and the apodosis, and *fa-* is not used to introduce the apodosis: لَئِنْ كُنْتَ صَادِقًا لَقَدْ قَتَلْتَنِي وَإِنْ كُنْتَ كَاذِبًا لَقَدْ فَضَحْتَنِي 'If you are truthful, you have killed me; but if you are a liar, you have exposed me'.

Note 1. Sometimes ʾ*idhan* 'then' (§284 b) introduces the apodosis: لَوْ خَلَدَ ٱلْمُلُوكُ إِذًا خَلَدْنَا 'If kings lived forever, so would we'. It is typically also found in the apodosis of a sentence with an unspoken protasis: لَا أَتَّبِعُ أَهْوَاءَكُمْ قَدْ ضَلَلْتُ إِذًا 'I do not follow your caprices; (if I did,) I would fall into error'.

§448. The apodosis may be abbreviated, if the missing component of the clause can be inferred from the protasis (cf. §406). It is then introduced by *fa-*: إِنْ يَكُنْ فِي أَحَدٍ مِنْكُمْ خَيْرٌ فَفِي هٰذَا 'If there is to be found good in any of you, then (it is to be found) in this one', مَنْ عَمِلَ صَالِحًا فَلِنَفْسِهِ 'He who does a good deed, (does it) for himself' (Koran 41:46; 45:15).

§449. The apodosis of real conditional sentences and sentences with conditional implication does not always contain an immediate logical conclusion, but a reply, assessment, or confirmation of the assumption made in the protasis: "If this is so, well, such and such is the case", e.g., إِنْ يَسْرِقْ فَقَدْ سَرَقَ أَخٌ لَهُ مِنْ قَبْلُ 'If he is a thief, well, a brother of his was already a thief before' (Koran 12:77), إِنْ قُلْتُمْ إِنَّا ظَلَمْنَا فَلَمْ نَكُنْ ظَلَمْنَا 'If you declare that we did wrong, well, we had never done wrong', إِمَّا تَرَيْنَا لَا تَزَالُ دِمَاؤُنَا فَإِنَّا لَحْمُ ٱلسَّيْفِ 'If ever you (fem.) see that our blood does not cease (flowing), well, we are just flesh for the sword.'

§450. a) إِنْ 'if, in case' introduces real conditional sentences. The apodosis for the most part is a generally valid and always realizable statement of fact. The verb is in the jussive or perfect: إِنْ تَصْبِرُوا يُمْدِدْكُمْ رَبُّكُمْ 'If you are patient, your Lord will help you', إِنْ نَفَعَنِي غَنَائِي يَوْمًا نَفَعَنِي ٱلْيَوْمَ 'If my wealth one day serves me, it benefits me today'.

Note 1. In poetry, the imperfect or energetic occurs in isolated cases: إِنْبِذِ ٱلْهُمُومَ إِنْ تَضِيقُ بِهَا 'Banish your cares, if you feel anguish because of them'.

b) If the protasis puts into question a specific fact, *kāna* (or *yakun*) is used with the perfect or imperfect. The perfect then indicates a fact that could have already been realized, while the imperfect indicates an expected action: إِنْ كَانَ قَمِيصُهُ قُدَّ مِنْ قُبُلٍ فَصَدَقَتْ 'If his shirt has been torn from the front, then she has spoken the truth' (Koran 12:26), لَئِنْ كَانَ يَسْمَعُ بَعْضَهُ لَقَدْ يَسْمَعُ كُلَّهُ 'If he hears part of it, then perhaps he hears all of it'.

c) Any clause structure is possible (see §447 a) in the apodosis, provided it is not a generally valid conclusion. In pre-classical Arabic, the imperfect may appear along with the jussive and perfect (§446 a) even in a generally valid sense: وَهُوَ يَرِثُهَا إِنْ لَمْ يَكُنْ لَهَا وَلَدٌ 'And he is her heir, if she has no children' (Koran 4:176).

Note 2. In a negative apodosis, *lam* appears with the jussive. In pre-classical Arabic, *lā* may occur with the jussive: إِنْ تَدْعُوهُمْ إِلَى ٱلْهُدَى لَا يَتَّبِعُوكُمْ 'If you call them to the guidance, they do not heed you' (Koran 7:193).

Note 3. See §§456 ff. on *ʾin* in disjunctive, concessive, and oath clauses.

§**451.** إِمَّا 'if, if ...ever' (< *ʾin-mā* §290) functions like *ʾin*: إِمَّا تَعُدُّوا ٱلصَّالِحَاتِ فَإِنَّنِي أَقُولُ بِهَا 'If you ever count the good deeds, I shall also speak about them'. Relatively frequently, the energetic follows: إِمَّا تَرَيِنَّ مِنَ ٱلْبَشَرِ أَحَدًا فَقُولِي 'If you (fem.) ever see any mortal, then say ...' (Koran 19:26).

Note 1. On disjunctive *ʾimmā*, see §459; on *ʾimmā-lā*, see §314.

§**452.** a) إِلَّا 'if not, unless' (§45) is used only in pre-classical Arabic to introduce negative conditional clauses. The jussive always follows: إِلَّا تَفْعَلُوهُ تَكُنْ فِتْنَةٌ فِي ٱلْأَرْضِ وَفَسَادٌ كَبِيرٌ 'Unless you do this, there will be upheaval in the land and a great corruption' (Koran 8:73).

b) وَإِلَّا 'and if not, otherwise' occurs as a negative alternative to a positive *ʾin*-clause whose apodosis ('then it is good, all well and good' فَبِهَا) is usually left unexpressed. In the apodosis, the perfect expressing a generally valid conclusion follows *wa-ʾillā*: إِنْ تَمَمْتَ عَلَى مَوَاعِيدِكَ وَإِلَّا ضَرَبْتُ عُنُقَكَ 'If you keep your promises (that is good), and if not, I shall knock off your head'. With a similar meaning, *wa-ʾillā* comes after a command: أَطِعْنِي وَإِلَّا فَإِنِّي تَارِكُكَ 'Obey me, otherwise I will abandon you!'.

Note 1. See §310 for *ʾillā* as a particle of exception. See also §456.

§**453.** a) لَوْ 'if' introduces an unreal or potential conditional sentence which contains a hypothetical presumption of a specific unrealized event. The apodosis is as a rule introduced by *la-*. Earlier stages of Arabic used the perfect and imperfect with their aspect function after *law* (§§180 ff.): لَوْ نَعْلَمُ قِتَالًا لَٱتَّبَعْنَاكُمْ 'If we knew how to fight, we would follow you', لَوْ قَدْ أَصَابُونِي لَهَوْا عَنْ طَلَبِ غَيْرِي 'If they had caught me, they would have given up the pursuit of someone else', إِنْ تَدْعُوهُمْ لَا يَسْمَعُوا دُعَاءَكُمْ وَلَوْ سَمِعُوا مَا ٱسْتَجَابُوا لَكُمْ 'If you call upon them, they will not hear your call; and if they had heard, they would not have answered you' (Koran 35:14).

b) Frequently in classical Arabic and regularly in post-classical, the perfect is used in a generally valid sense (§446 a): لَوْ كَانَ عَاشِقًا لَمْ يَكُنْ يَخْتَلِفُ 'If he had (were to have) loved passionately, he would not waver (have wavered)'. To express the past explicitly, *kāna* may be used with the perfect: لَوْ كُنْتُمْ دَعَوْتُمُونَا أَطَعْنَاكُمْ 'If you had called us, we would have heeded you'.

Note 1. To express an absurdly unreal condition, *law* is sometimes strengthened through the addition of *ʾin*: إِنْ لَوْ جَاءَكَ عَمُّ مُوسَى مُسْلِمًا مَا كُنْتَ صَانِعًا بِهِ 'If ever it were to happen that the uncle of Moses came to you as a convert to Islam, what would you do to him?'.

Note 2. See §§457 f. on *law* in wish and concessive sentences.

§**454.** لَوْ أَنَّ occurs in place of *law* when a nominal or copulative clause follows (§§360 ff.): لَوْ أَنِّي جِئْتُ فُلَانًا ٱلْخَمَّارَ لَعَلِّي أَجِدُ عِنْدَهُ خَمْرًا 'If I would come to so-and-so, the wine-merchant, maybe I could find some wine with him'.

Note 1. In poetry, *law ʾanna* occurs as لَوَآنَّ *law-anna.*

§**455.** لَوْلَا 'if not' in classical Arabic is always followed by a noun in the nominative: لَوْلَا حُبُّ أَهْلِكَ مَا أَتَيْتُ 'If it were not for the love of your people, I would not have come'. A substantive clause (§§414 f.) introduced by *ʾan* or *ʾanna* may also follow: لَوْلَا أَنْ تُفْسِدَ بِأَلْفَاظِكَ أَكْثَرَ رَعِيَّتِي مَا حَبَسْتُكَ 'If you were not perverting most of my subjects with your words, I would not have imprisoned you', لَوْلَا أَنَّ لِسَانَ ٱلْفِيلِ مَقْلُوبٌ لَتَكَلَّمَ 'If the tongue of the elephant were not turned upside down, he would speak'.

Note 1. The personal pronoun in the form of either an independent pronoun or a personal suffix may follow: لَوْلَا أَنْتَ or لَوْلَاكَ 'if it were not for you, but for you'.

Defective Conditional Sentences

§**456.** Sentences containing oaths are usually introduced by *ʾin, ʾillā*; *ʾin* for negative, *ʾillā* for positive oaths: بِحَيَاتِي إِلَّا أَنْشَدْتَنِي ٱلْبَيْتَ 'By my life, if you do not recite the verse for me!', i.e., 'Recite the verse for me!'; frequently, after verbs expressing oaths: نَشَدْتُكَ ٱللّٰهَ إِنْ رِمْتَ هٰذَا ٱلْمَكَانَ أَبَدًا 'I swear to you by God that you shall never leave this place!'.

Note 1. *lammā* may appear in place of *ʾillā*; again, the perfect follows: أَسْأَلُكَ لَمَّا أَخْبَرْتَنِي 'I ask you not to inform me' (§334.1).

§**457.** Sentences expressing wishes are frequently introduced by *law*: لَوْ أَنِّي أَعْرِفُهُ 'If I only knew him!', لَوْ كُنْتَ أَسْوَدَ ٱللِّحْيَةِ وَٱلرَّأْسِ 'If only you had a black beard and head!', لَوْ سَأَلْتَهُ أَنْ يُقِيمَ عِنْدَنَا 'If you had asked him to stay with us!' (i.e., Ask him to ...'), يَوَدُّ لَوْ أَنَّ بَيْنَهُ وَبَيْنَهَا أَمَدًا بَعِيدًا 'He would like there to be a wide space between him and her'.

Note 1. In pre-classical Arabic, *law-lā* and *law-mā* in interrogative sentences have the meaning 'why not ...?': لَوْمَا تَأْتِينَا بِٱلْمَلَائِكَةِ إِنْ كُنْتَ مِنَ ٱلصَّادِقِينَ 'Why do you not bring the angels to us, if you speak truly?' (Koran 15:7), لَوْلَا دَفَعَ عَنْهُ 'Why did he not defend him?'.

§**458.** *ʾin* and *law* clauses coordinated by *wa-* function as concessive clauses. The verb is in the perfect, and in pre-classical Arabic at times in the jussive: هَدَاكُمْ وَإِنْ كُنْتُمْ مِنْ قَبْلِهِ لَمِنَ ٱلضَّالِينَ 'He has guided you, though formerly you were gone astray' (Koran 2:198), لَوْ عَلِمْتُ لَأَقْحَمْتُ خَلْفَهُ وَلَوْ دَخَلَ ٱلنَّارَ 'Had I known (it), I would have rushed after him, even if he had gone into Hellfire'. Often, only components of the sentence that supplement the main clause follow *wa-law*: فَأَمَرَ ٱلْأَمِيرُ بِإِحْضَارِهِ وَلَوْ مَحْمُولًا 'Then the prince commanded him to be brought in, even though he had to be carried', كُونُوا قَوَّامِينَ بِٱلْقِسْطِ وَلَوْ عَلَى أَنْفُسِكُمْ 'Be steadfast in fairness, even if it goes against yourselves!'.

§**459.** a) Disjunctive conditional clauses are introduced by *ʾin ... wa-ʾin* or *ʾimmā ... wa-ʾimmā*: إِنْ كَانَ قَمِيصُهُ قُدَّ مِنْ قُبُلٍ فَصَدَقَتْ وَإِنْ كَانَ قَمِيصُهُ قُدَّ مِنْ

دُبُرٍ فَكَذَبَتْ 'If his shirt has been torn from the front, then she has spoken the truth ...If his shirt is torn from behind, then she has lied' (Koran 12:26–27) (§450 b). Before the second part of the sentence, *wa-ʾin, wa-ʾimmā* may be replaced by *ʾaw* (§331): إِنْ تُقْبِلُوا نُعَانِقْ أَوْ تُدْبِرُوا نُفَارِقْ 'If you draw near, we shall embrace (you), or if you turn away, we shall withdraw', i.e., 'Either you approach, then we embrace you, or you turn away, then we withdraw'.

b) Disjunctive sentences beginning with *ʾin ... wa-ʾin/ʾaw* and *ʾimmā ... wa-ʾimmā/ʾaw* may appear instead of alternative conditional sentences (§452 b). Accordingly, the verb is in the generally valid perfect: إِمَّا جِئْتَنِي آللَّيْلَةَ أَوْ فَعَلْتُ 'Either you come to me tonight, or I will do it (i.e., will come to you)'. Frequently, an *ʾan*-clause follows *ʾimmā* (§414) in such alternative disjunctive sentences: أَرْسَلَ إِلَيْهِمْ إِمَّا أَنْ تَضَعُوا آلسِّلَاحَ وَإِمَّا أَنْ تُؤْذِنُوا بِحَرْبٍ 'He sent to them: Either lay down your arms or declare war'.

Note 1. Consistent with the conditional implication in alternative sentences, the perfect usually also appears with *ʾaw* (§331) or *ʾam* (§333) in disjunctive sentences: سَوَاءٌ عَلَيْهِمْ أَأَنْذَرْتَهُمْ أَمْ لَمْ تُنْذِرْهُمْ 'It is all the same for them, if you warn them or do not warn them' (Koran 2:6; 36:10), سَوَاءٌ شَاءُوا أَوْ أَبَوْا 'It does not matter whether they want or do not want', نُخْرِجُكَ كَاذِبًا كُنْتَ أَوْ صَادِقًا 'We shall drive you away, whether you are a liar or speak the truth'.

c) As disjunctive particles, *ʾin* and *ʾimmā* (§332) may also join alternative elements of the sentences: قَدْ قِيلَ مَا قِيلَ إِنْ صِدْقًا وَإِنْ كَذِبًا 'What is said is said, be it truth or be it falsehood', وَآخَرُونَ مُرْجَوْنَ لِأَمْرِ آللّٰهِ إِمَّا يُعَذِّبُهُمْ وَإِمَّا يَتُوبُ عَلَيْهِمْ 'And others are deferred to God's commandment, whether He chastises them, or turns toward them' (Koran 9:106).

Sentences with Conditional Implication

§460. In sentences in which the relationship of the protasis and the apodosis constitutes a generally valid condition (§445), the verb as a rule, according to §446, is in the jussive or perfect, regardless of what formal structure they have. Thus, it can be said also for clauses expressing commands, questions, or wishes that if the apodosis follows them, their verb will be in the jussive (cf. §412): عِشْ قَنِعًا تَكُنْ مَلِكًا 'Live with contentment, and you will be a king', هَلْ لَكُمْ بِسَيِّدِ أَهْلِ ٱلشَّأْمِ تُحْبَوْا 'Do you wish to go to the leader of the Syrians? Then you will be given gifts' (cf. §296.3), لَيْتَ لِي مَالًا أُنْفِقْ مِنْهُ 'If only I had wealth, then I could spend it!'.

§**461.** a) Relative particles (§289) often begin generalizing sentences with conditional implication: *mā* 'whatever (else)', *man* 'whoever', etc. In the protasis and the apodosis, the verb is always in the jussive or perfect: مَا أَنْسَ لَا أَنْسَ وَجْهَكِ 'Whatever else I forget, I shall not forget your face' (§450.2), أَيَّهُمَا شِئْتُمْ فَبَايِعُوا 'Whichever of those two you wish to, pay homage to him!' (§447 a), مَنْ نَامَ عَنْ حَقِّهِمْ لَمْ أَنَمْ 'If anyone overlooks what is due him, I shall not overlook it' (§449), مَتَى تَسْأَلْنِي عَنْ شَرِّ ٱلنَّاسِ أَقُلْ 'If (whenever) you ask me about the most evil of mankind, I would say ...'.

> **Note 1.** After *ḥaythu* (§441), the conditional implication is expressed by the perfect: لِيَذْهَبْ حَيْثُ أَحَبَّ 'May he go wherever he desires!'.

> **Note 2.** On rare occasion, *ʾin* may be used as an indication of conditional implication with relatives: إِنْ مَنْ 'If anyone'.

b) In constructions with conditional implication, the relative may often appear with generalizing *mā* (§290): مَهْمَا تَأْتِنَا بِهِ مِنْ آيَةٍ لِتَسْحَرَنَا بِهَا فَمَا نَحْنُ لَكَ بِمُؤْمِنِينَ 'Whatever miraculous sign you might bring to enchant us with, we will not believe you' (Koran 7:132), أَيْنَمَا أَتَوَجَّهْ أَلْقَ سَعْدًا 'Wherever I go, I meet Saʿd'.

> **Note 3.** In constructions with other particles, *mā* also has a generalizing function: *ḥaythu-mā* 'wherever' (§441). The imperfect may also come after seldom-used *ʾidh-mā* 'then whenever' (§442).

§**462.** مَا 'while', occasionally also 'as often as', is followed as a rule by the perfect: أَلْهَمُّ مَا دَعَوْتَهُ أَجَابَ 'Anxiety answers as often as you call it'. The structure of the main clause is arbitrary: مَا أَنْسَى بُكَاءَكُمْ مَا مَشَيْتُ عَلَى ٱلْأَرْضِ 'I shall not forget your crying as long as I walk on the earth', أَغُضُّ طَرْفِي مَا بَدَتْ لِي جَارَتِي 'I lower my eyes while my neighbor (fem.) appears before me'.

Note 1. Sometimes, *mahmā* (§290) may be used in this function: مَهْمَا تَصْلُحْ فَلَنْ نَعْزِلَكَ 'As long as you do good, we shall not dismiss you', مَهْمَا نَظَرَ شَيْئًا مِنَ ٱلْمَوْجُودَاتِ عَرَفَ رَحْمَةَ خَالِقِهَا 'Whenever he looks at any of the things in existence, he recognizes the mercy of their creator'.

Note 2. In post-classical Arabic, this use of *mā* is clarified by the addition of دَامَ 'last, continue'. After مَا دَامَ 'as long as', the predicate follows as a predicate circumstantial clause or as a circumstantial accusative (§§382 b; 432).

§463. كُلَّمَا 'every time that, whenever, as often as' as a rule occurs with the perfect: كُلَّمَا (كُلَّ مَا) جَاءَ أُمَّةً رَسُولُهَا كَذَّبُوهُ 'Whenever its messenger came to a nation, they called him a liar' (Koran 23:44). When the elative follows (§§124 ff.), *kulla-mā* with the appropriate apodosis corresponds to the use of 'the more ... the more': كُلَّمَا كَانَ ٱلْخَبَرُ أَغْرَبَ كَانُوا بِهِ أَشَدَّ عَجَبًا 'The more strange the news was, the more they were astounded by it', كَانَ كُلَّمَا أَكْثَرَ كَانَ أَجْوَدَ كَلَامًا 'The more he spoke, the better he got' (§446 b).

§464. a) إِذَا 'then when, if' begins temporal adverbial clauses (cf. §442) with conditional implication. The always possible stated fact may occur once ('as soon as') or several times ('as often as'). As a rule, the perfect appears in the protasis, while the structure of the apodosis is free. When the statement is conceived of as generally valid, the perfect may also occur in the apodosis rather than the imperfect: إِنَّمَا ٱلْمُؤْمِنُونَ ٱلَّذِينَ إِذَا ذُكِرَ ٱللّٰهُ وَجِلَتْ قُلُوبُهُمْ 'The believers are only those whose hearts are filled with fear whenever God is mentioned' (Koran 8:2), إِذَا فَعَلَ ذٰلِكَ رَأَيْنَا رَأْيَنَا 'As soon as he does this, we will form our opinion', إِذَا شِئْتُمْ فَأَعْطُوهُمْ مَا يُرِيدُونَ 'If you wish, give them what they desire' (§447a). In pre-classical Arabic, the subject frequently comes immediately after the conjunction: إِذَا ٱلْكَوَاكِبُ ٱنْتَثَرَتْ 'When the stars are scattered' (Koran 82:2).

Note 1. In pre-classical Arabic, the imperfect, and rarely the jussive, may appear in the protasis: إِنَّ ٱلْكَرِيمَ إِذَا يُحَرَّبُ يَغْضَبُ 'As soon as the noble one is irritated, he becomes angry'.

Note 2. In pre-classical Arabic, ʾ*i͟dhā* is sometimes used without conditional implication. ʾ*i͟dhā* then has the sense of ʾ*i͟dh*. In classical Arabic, ʾ*i͟dhā* coming after *ḥattā* also has the same meaning. See §440.

b) *kāna* is regularly used before the conjunction (§446 b) to indicate the past tense: كُنْتُ إِذَا ٱشْتَكَيْتُ رَحِمَنِي ‘Whenever I complained, he showed me compassion’. It may happen that *kāna*, when it comes first, agrees with the subject of the apodosis: كُنْتُ إِذَا قَوْمٌ غَزَوْنِي غَزَوْتُهُمْ ‘When people attacked me, I attacked them’. This is the rule when the imperfect follows in the apodosis (§192): كَانَتِ ٱلْعَجُوزُ إِذَا كَلَّمَهَا تَسْكُتُ عَنْهُ ‘The old woman used to be silent before him whenever he spoke to her’.

§**465.** إِذَامَا ‘when, while’ is treated like ʾ*i͟dhā* and occurs instead of ʾ*i͟dhā*, if the events described in the protasis and apodosis occur simultaneously: إِذَامَا رُحْنَ يَمْشِينَ ٱلْهُوَيْنَى ‘When they (fem.) go away, they walk at a leisurely pace’, قُلْتُ لَهُ ٱرْتَحِلْ إِذَامَا ٱلنُّجُومُ أَعْرَضَتْ ‘I said to him, leave, while the stars are out!’, لَا يَأْبَ ٱلشُّهَدَاءُ إِذَامَا دُعُوا ‘The witnesses should not refuse, when they are called’.

Paradigms

1. Nouns with Pronominal Suffixes

	Masculine			Feminine		
Singular	Nom.	Gen.	Acc.	Nom.	Gen.	Acc.
Sg. 1. Pers.	سَارِقِي	سَارِقِي	سَارِقِي	سَارِقَتِي	سَارِقَتِي	سَارِقَتِي
2. m.	سَارِقُكَ	سَارِقِكَ	سَارِقَكَ	سَارِقَتُكَ	سَارِقَتِكَ	سَارِقَتَكَ
2. f.	سَارِقُكِ	سَارِقِكِ	سَارِقَكِ	سَارِقَتُكِ	سَارِقَتِكِ	سَارِقَتَكِ
3. m.	سَارِقُهُ	سَارِقِهِ	سَارِقَهُ	سَارِقَتُهُ	سَارِقَتِهِ	سَارِقَتَهُ
3. f.	سَارِقُهَا	سَارِقِهَا	سَارِقَهَا	سَارِقَتُهَا	سَارِقَتِهَا	سَارِقَتَهَا
Du. 2.	سَارِقُكُمَا	سَارِقِكُمَا	سَارِقَكُمَا	سَارِقَتُكُمَا	سَارِقَتِكُمَا	سَارِقَتَكُمَا
3.	سَارِقُهُمَا	سَارِقِهِمَا	سَارِقَهُمَا	سَارِقَتُهُمَا	سَارِقَتِهِمَا	سَارِقَتَهُمَا
Pl. 1.	سَارِقُنَا	سَارِقِنَا	سَارِقَنَا	سَارِقَتُنَا	سَارِقَتِنَا	سَارِقَتَنَا
2. m.	سَارِقُكُمْ	سَارِقِكُمْ	سَارِقَكُمْ	سَارِقَتُكُمْ	سَارِقَتِكُمْ	سَارِقَتَكُمْ
2. f.	سَارِقُكُنَّ	سَارِقِكُنَّ	سَارِقَكُنَّ	سَارِقَتُكُنَّ	سَارِقَتِكُنَّ	سَارِقَتَكُنَّ
3. m.	سَارِقُهُمْ	سَارِقِهِمْ	سَارِقَهُمْ	سَارِقَتُهُمْ	سَارِقَتِهِمْ	سَارِقَتَهُمْ
3. f.	سَارِقُهُنَّ	سَارِقِهِنَّ	سَارِقَهُنَّ	سَارِقَتُهُنَّ	سَارِقَتِهِنَّ	سَارِقَتَهُنَّ

Dual	Nom.	Obl.	Nom.	Obl.
Sg. 1. Pers.	سَارِقَايَ	سَارِقَيَّ	سَارِقَتَايَ	سَارِقَتَيَّ
2. m.	سَارِقَاكَ	سَارِقَيْكَ	سَارِقَتَاكَ	سَارِقَتَيْكَ
3. m.	سَارِقَاهُ	سَارِقَيْهِ	سَارِقَتَاهُ	سَارِقَتَيْهِ

Plural	Nom.	Obl.	Nom.	Obl.
Sg. 1. Pers.	سَارِقِيَّ	سَارِقِيَّ	سَارِقَاتِي	سَارِقَاتِي
2. m	سَارِقُوكَ	سَارِقِيكَ	سَارِقَاتُكَ	سَارِقَاتِكَ
3. m.	سَارِقُوهُ	سَارِقِيهِ	سَارِقَاتُهُ	سَارِقَاتِهِ

2. Nouns Ending in -ā

	Sg.	Du. Nom.	Obl.	Pl. Nom.	Obl.
Sg. 1. Pers.	مُلْقَايَ	مُلْقَيَايَ	مُلْقَيَّ	مُلْقَيَّ	مُلْقَيَّ
2. m.	مُلْقَاكَ	مُلْقَيَاكَ	مُلْقَيَيْكَ	مُلْقَوْكَ	مُلْقَيْكَ
3. m.	مُلْقَاهُ	مُلْقَيَاهُ	مُلْقَيَيْهِ	مُلْقَوْهُ	مُلْقَيْهِ

3. Nouns Ending in -ī

	Sg. Nom./Gen.	Acc.	Du. Nom.	Obl.	Pl. Nom.	Obl.
Sg. 1. Pers.	دَاعِيَّ	دَاعِيَّ	دَاعِيَايَ	دَاعِيَيَّ	دَاعِيَّ	دَاعِيَّ
2. m.	دَاعِيكَ	دَاعِيَكَ	دَاعِيَاكَ	دَاعِيَيْكَ	دَاعُوكَ	دَاعِيكَ
2. f.	دَاعِيهِ	دَاعِيَهُ	دَاعِيَاهُ	دَاعِيَيْهِ	دَاعُوهُ	دَاعِيهِ

4. Basic Stem of the 3-Radical Verb (Active)

	Perf. (a)	Imperf. (a)	Subj.	Juss.	Energ. I	Energ. II
Sg. 3. m.	فَعَلَ	يَفْعَلُ	يَفَلَ	يَفْعَلْ	يَفْعَلَنَّ	يَفْعَلَنْ
3. f.	فَعَلَتْ	تَفْعَلُ	تَفْعَلَ	تَفْعَلْ	تَفْعَلَنَّ	تَفْعَلَنْ
2. m.	فَعَلْتَ	تَفْعَلُ	تَفْعَلَ	تَفْعَلْ	تَفْعَلَنَّ	تَفْعَلَنْ
2. f.	فَعَلْتِ	تَفْعَلِينَ	تَفْعَلِي	تَفْعَلِي	تَفْعَلِنَّ	تَفْعَلِنْ
1.	فَعَلْتُ	أَفْعَلُ	أَفْعَلَ	أَفْعَلْ	أَفْعَلَنَّ	أَفْعَلَنْ
Du. 3. m.	فَعَلَا	يَفْعَلَانِ	يَفْعَلَا	يَفْعَلَا	يَفْعَلَانِّ	
3. f.	فَعَلَتَا	تَفْعَلَانِ	تَفْعَلَا	تَفْعَلَا	تَفْعَلَانِّ	
2.	فَعَلْتُمَا	تَفْعَلَانِ	تَفْعَلَا	تَفْعَلَا	تَفْعَلَانِّ	
Pl. 3. m.	فَعَلُوا	يَفْعَلُونَ	يَفْعَلُوا	يَفْعَلُوا	يَفْعَلُنَّ	يَفْعَلُنْ
3. f.	فَعَلْنَ	يَفْعَلْنَ	يَفْعَلْنَ	يَفْعَلْنَ	يَفْعَلْنَانِّ	
2. m.	فَعَلْتُمْ	تَفْعَلُونَ	تَفْعَلُوا	تَفْعَلُوا	تَفْعَلُنَّ	تَفْعَلُنْ
2. f.	فَعَلْتُنَّ	تَفْعَلْنَ	تَفْعَلْنَ	تَفْعَلْنَ	تَفْعَلْنَانِّ	
1.	فَعَلْنَا	نَفْعَلُ	نَفْعَلَ	نَفْعَلْ	نَفْعَلَنَّ	نَفْعَلَنْ

Imperative					
	Sg. m.	*f.*	*Du.*	*Pl. m.*	*f.*
(*a*)	اِفْعَلْ	اِفْعَلِي	اِفْعَلَا	اِفْعَلُوا	اِفْعَلْنَ
(*i*)	اِفْعِلْ	اِفْعِلِي	اِفْعِلَا	اِفْعِلُوا	اِفْعِلْنَ
(*u*)	اُفْعُلْ	اُفْعُلِي	اُفْعُلَا	اُفْعُلُوا	اُفْعُلْنَ

Active Participle			
Sg. m.	*Pl. m.*	*Sg. f.*	*Pl. f.*
فَاعِلٌ	فَاعِلُونَ	فَاعِلَةٌ	فَاعِلَاتٌ

5. Basic Stem of the 3-Radical Verb (Passive)

	Perf.	Imperf.	Subj.	Juss.	Energ. I.
Sg. m.	فُعِلَ	يُفْعَلُ	يُفْعَلَ	يُفْعَلْ	يُفْعَلَنَّ
3. f.	فُعِلَتْ	تُفْعَلُ	تُفْعَلَ	تُفْعَلْ	تُفْعَلَنَّ
2. m.	فُعِلْتَ	تُفْعَلُ	تُفْعَلَ	تُفْعَلْ	تُفْعَلَنَّ
2. f.	فُعِلْتِ	تُفْعَلِينَ	تُفْعَلِي	تُفْعَلِي	تُفْعَلِنَ
1.	فُعِلْتُ	أُفْعَلُ	أُفْعَلَ	أُفْعَلْ	أُفْعَلِنَّ
Du. 3. m.	فُعِلَا	يُفْعَلَانِ	يُفْعَلَا	يُفْعَلَا	يُفْعَلَانِّ
3. f.	فُعِلَتَا	تُفْعَلَانِ	تُفْعَلَا	تُفْعَلَا	تُفْعَلَانِّ
2.	فُعِلْتُمَا	تُفْعَلَانِ	تُفْعَلَا	تُفْعَلَا	تُفْعَلَانِّ
Pl. 3. m.	فُعِلُو	يُفْعَلُونَ	يُفْعَلُوا	يُفْعَلُوا	يُفْعَلُنَّ
3. f.	فُعِلْنَ	يُفْعَلْنَ	يُفْعَلْنَ	يُفْعَلْنَ	يُفْعَلْنَانِّ
2. m.	فُعِلْتُمْ	تُفْعَلُونَ	تُفْعَلُوا	تُفْعَلُوا	تُفْعَلُنَّ
2. f.	فُعِلْتُنَّ	تُفْعَلْنَ	تُفْعَلْنَ	تُفْعَلْنَ	تُفْعَلْنَانِّ
1.	فُعِلْنَا	نُفْعَلُ	نُفْعَلَ	نُفْعَلْ	نُفْعَلَنَّ

Passive Participle			
Sg. m.	*Pl. m.*	*Sg. f.*	*Pl. f.*
مَفْعُولٌ	مَفْعُولُونَ	مَفْعُولَةٌ	مَفْعُولَاتٌ

6. 3-Radical Derived Verbs

	Basic stem (I)			Form II	Form III	Form IV
Perf. act.	فَعَلَ	فَعِلَ	فَعُلَ	فَعَّلَ	فَاعَلَ	أَفْعَلَ
Perf. pass.		فُعِلَ		فُعِّلَ	فُوعِلَ	أُفْعِلَ
Imperf. act.	يَفْعَلُ	يَفْعِلُ	يَفْعُلُ	يُفَعِّلُ	يُفَاعِلُ	يُفْعِلُ
Imperf. pass.		يُفْعَلُ		يُفَعَّلُ	يُفَاعَلُ	يُفْعَلُ
Juss. act.	يَفْعَلْ	يَفْعِلْ	يَفْعُلْ	يُفَعِّلْ	يُفَاعِلْ	يُفْعِلْ
Juss. pass.		يُفْعَلْ		يُفَعَّلْ	يُفَاعَلْ	يُفْعَلْ
Imper.	اِفْعَلْ	اِفْعِلْ	اُفْعُلْ	فَعِّلْ	فَاعِلْ	أَفْعِلْ
Act. part.		فَاعِلٌ		مُفَعِّلٌ	مُفَاعِلٌ	مُفْعِلٌ
Pass. part.		مَفْعُولٌ		مُفَعَّلٌ	مُفَاعَلٌ	مُفْعَلٌ
Verbal subst.		فَعْلٌ		تَفْعِيلٌ	فِعَالٌ	إِفْعَالٌ

	Form V	Form VI	Form VII	Form VIII	Form X
Perf. act.	تَفَعَّلَ	تَفَاعَلَ	اِنْفَعَلَ	اِفْتَعَلَ	اِسْتَفْعَلَ
Perf. pass.	تُفُعِّلَ	تُفُوعِلَ	اُنْفُعِلَ	اُفْتُعِلَ	اُسْتُفْعِلَ
Imperf. act.	يَتَفَعَّلُ	يَتَفَاعَلُ	يَنْفَعِلُ	يَفْتَعِلُ	يَسْتَفْعِلُ
Imperf. pass.	يُتَفَعَّلُ	يُتَفَاعَلُ	يُنْفَعَلُ	يُفْتَعَلُ	يُسْتَفْعَلُ
Juss. act.	يَتَفَعَّلْ	يَتَفَاعَلْ	يَنْفَعِلْ	يَفْتَعِلْ	يَسْتَفْعِلْ
Juss. pass.	يُتَفَعَّلْ	يُتَفَاعَلْ	يُنْفَعَلْ	يُفْتَعَلْ	يُسْتَفْعَلْ
Imper.	تَفَعَّلْ	تَفَاعَلْ	اِنْفَعِلْ	اِفْتَعِلْ	اِسْتَفْعِلْ
Act. part.	مُتَفَعِّلٌ	مُتَفَاعِلٌ	مُنْفَعِلٌ	مُفْتَعِلٌ	مُسْتَفْعِلٌ
Pass. part.	مُتَفَعَّلٌ	مُتَفَاعَلٌ	مُنْفَعَلٌ	مُفْتَعَلٌ	مُسْتَفْعَلٌ
Verb. subst.	تَفَعُّلٌ	تَفَاعُلٌ	اِنْفِعَالٌ	اِفْتِعَالٌ	اِسْتِفْعَالٌ

	IX Form			XI Form		
	Perf.	Imperf.	Juss.	Perf.	Imperf.	Juss.
Sg. 3. m.	اِفْعَلَّ	يَفْعَلُّ	يَفْعَلِلْ /يَفْعَلَّ /يَفْعَلِّ	اِفْعَالَّ	يَفْعَالُّ	يَفْعَالِلْ /يَفْعَالَّ /يَفْعَالِّ
3. f.	اِفْعَلَّتْ	تَفْعَلُّ	تَفْعَلِلْ /تَفْعَلَّ /تَفْعَلِّ	اِفْعَالَّتْ	تَفْعَالُّ	تَفْعَالِلْ /تَفْعَالَّ /تَفْعَالِّ
2. m.	اِفْعَلَلْتَ	تَفْعَلُّ	تَفْعَلِلْ / تَفْعَلَّ /تَفْعَلِّ	اِفْعَالَلْتَ	تَفْعَالُّ	تَفْعَالِلْ / تَفْعَالَّ /تَفْعَالِّ
2. f.	اِفْعَلَلْتِ	تَفْعَلِّينَ	تَفْعَلِّي	اِفْعَالَلْتِ	تَفْعَالِّينَ	تَفْعَالِّي
1.	اِفْعَلَلْتُ	أَفْعَلُّ	أَفْعَلِلْ /أَفْعَلَّ /أَفْعَلِّ	اِفْعَالَلْتُ	أَفْعَالُّ	أَفْعَالِلْ /أَفْعَالَّ /أَفْعَالِّ
Du. 3. m.	اِفْعَلَّا	يَفْعَلَّانِ	يَفْعَلَّا	اِفْعَالَّا	يَفْعَالَّانِ	يَفْعَالَّا
3. f.	اِفْعَلَّتَا	تَفْعَلَّانِ	تَفْعَلَّا	اِفْعَالَّتَا	تَفْعَالَّانِ	تَفْعَالَّا
2.	اِفْعَلَلْتُمَا	تَفْعَلَّانِ	تَفْعَلَّا	اِفْعَالَلْتُمَا	تَفْعَالَانِ	تَفْعَالَّا
Pl. 3. m.	اِفْعَلُّوا	يَفْعَلُّونَ	يَفْعَلُّوا	اِفْعَالُّوا	يَفْعَالُّونَ	يَفْعَالُّوا
3. f.	اِفْعَلَلْنَ	يَفْعَلِلْنَ	يَفْعَلِلْنَ	اِفْعَالَلْنَ	يَفْعَالِلْنَ	يَفْعَالِلْنَ
2. m.	اِفْعَلَلْتُمْ	تَفْعَلُّونَ	تَفْعَلُّوا	اِفْعَالَلْتُمْ	تَفْعَالُّونَ	تَفْعَالُّوا
2. f.	اِفْعَلَلْتُنَّ	تَفْعَلِلْنَ	تَفْعَلِلْنَ	اِفْعَالَلْتُنَّ	تَفْعَالِلْنَ	تَفْعَالِلْنَ
1.	اِفْعَلَلْنَا	نَفْعَلُّ	نَفْعَلِلْ /نَفْعَلَّ /نَفْعَلِّ	اِفْعَالَلْنَا	نَفْعَالُّ	نَفْعَالِلْ /نَفْعَالَّ /نَفْعَالِّ
Imperative *sg. m.* اِفْعَلِلْ /اِفْعَلَّ /اِفْعَلِّ *f.* اِفْعَلِّي				*Sg. m.* اِفْعَالِلْ /اِفْعَالَّ /اِفْعَالِّ *f.* اِفْعَالِّي		
Participle *sg. m.* مُفْعَلٌّ *f.* مُفْعَلَّةٌ				*Sg. m.* مُفْعَالٌّ *f.* مُفْعَالَّةٌ		
Verbal subst. اِفْعِلَالٌ				اِفْعِيلَالٌ		

	XII Form	XIII Form	XIV Form	XV Form
Perf.	اِفْعَوْعَلَ	اِفْعَوَّلَ	اِفْعَنْلَلَ	اِفْعَنْلَى
Imperf.	يَفْعَوْعِلُ	يَفْعَوِّلُ	يَفْعَنْلِلُ	يَفْعَنْلِي
Juss.	يَفْعَوْعِلْ	يَفْعَوِّلْ	يَفْعَنْلِلْ	يَفْعَنْلِ
Act. part.	مُفْعَوْعِلٌ	مُفْعَوِّلٌ	مُفْعَنْلِلٌ	مُفْعَنْلٍ
Verbal subst.	اِفْعِيعَالٌ	اِفْعِوَّالٌ	اِفْعِنْلَالٌ	اِفْعِنْلَاءٌ

7. II-Geminate Verbs

Basic Stem (I)						
	Active			Passive		
	Perf.	Imperf.	Juss.	Perf.	Imperf.	Juss.
Sg. 3. m.	رَدَّ	يَرُدُّ	يَرْدُدْ/يَرُدَّ /يَرُدِّ/يَرُدُّ	رُدَّ	يُرَدُّ	يُرْدَدْ/يُرَدَّ /يُرَدِّ
3. f.	رَدَّتْ	تَرُدُّ	تَرْدُدْ/تَرُدَّ /تَرُدِّ/تَرُدُّ	رُدَّتْ	تُرَدُّ	تُرْدَدْ/تُرَدَّ /تُرَدِّ
2. m.	رَدَدْتَ	تَرُدُّ	تَرْدُدْ/تَرُدَّ /تَرُدِّ/تَرُدُّ	رُدِدْتَ	تُرَدُّ	تُرْدَدْ/تُرَدَّ /تُرَدِّ
2. f.	رَدَدْتِ	تَرُدِّينَ	تَرُدِّي	رُدِدْتِ	تُرَدِّينَ	تُرَدِّي
1.	رَدَدْتُ	أَرُدُّ	أَرْدُدْ/ أَرُدَّ/أَرُدِّ/أَرُدُّ	رُدِدْتُ	أُرَدُّ	أُرْدَدْ/ أُرَدَّ/أُرَدِّ
Du. 3. m.	رَدَّا	يَرُدَّانِ	يَرُدَّا	رُدَّا	يُرَدَّانِ	يُرَدَّا
3. f.	رَدَّتَا	تَرُدَّانِ	تَرُدَّا	رُدَّتَا	تُرَدَّانِ	تُرَدَّا
2.	رَدَدْتُمَا	تَرُدَّانِ	تَرُدَّا	رُدِدْتُمَا	تُرَدَّانِ	تُرَدَّا
Pl. 3. m.	رَدُّوا	يَرُدُّونَ	يَرُدُّوا	رُدُّوا	يُرَدُّونَ	يُرَدُّوا
3. f.	رَدَدْنَ	يَرْدُدْنَ	يَرْدُدْنَ	رُدِدْنَ	يُرْدَدْنَ	يُرْدَدْنَ
2. m.	رَدَدْتُمْ	تَرُدُّونَ	تَرُدُّوا	رُدِدْتُمْ	تُرَدُّونَ	تُرَدُّوا
2. f.	رَدَدْتُنَّ	تَرْدُدْنَ	تَرْدُدْنَ	رُدِدْتُنَّ	تُرْدَدْنَ	تُرْدَدْنَ
1.	رَدَدْنَا	نَرُدُّ	نَرْدُدْ /نَرُدَّ/نَرُدِّ/نَرُدُّ	رُدِدْنَا	نُرَدُّ	نُرْدَدْ /نُرَدَّ/نُرَدِّ/نُرَدُّ
Imperative *Sg. m.* أُرْدُدْ/رُدَّ/رُدِّ/رُدُّ *f.* رُدِّي *Du.* رُدَّا *Pl. m.* رُدُّوا *f.* أُرْدُدْنَ						
Act. part. *Sg. m.* رَادٌّ *f.* رَادَّةٌ Pass. part. *Sg. m.* مَرْدُودٌ *f.* مَرْدُودَةٌ						

Form II						
	Perf.	Imperf.	Juss.	Imperat.	Part.	Verb. Subst.
Active	رَدَّدَ	يُرَدِّدُ	يُرَدِّدْ	رَدِّدْ	مُرَدِّدٌ	تَرْدِيدٌ
Passive	رُدِّدَ	يُرَدَّدُ	يُرَدَّدْ		مُرَدَّدٌ	

Form V						
	Perf.	Imperf.	Juss.	Imperat.	Part.	Verb. Subst.
Active	تَرَدَّدَ	يَتَرَدَّدُ	يَتَرَدَّدْ	تَرَدَّدْ	مُتَرَدِّدٌ	تَرَدُّدٌ
Passive	تُرُدِّدَ	يُتَرَدَّدُ	يُتَرَدَّدْ		مُتَرَدَّدٌ	

	Form IV	Form III	Form VI	Form VII	Form VIII	Form X
Perf. act.						
Sg. 3. m.	أَرَدَّ	رَادَّ	تَرَادَّ	اِنْرَدَّ	اِرْتَدَّ	اِسْتَرَدَّ
2. m.	أَرْدَدْتَ	رَادَدْتَ	تَرَادَدْتَ	اِنْرَدَدْتَ	اِرْتَدَدْتَ	اِسْتَرْدَدْتَ
Perf. pass.						
Sg. 3. m.	أُرِدَّ	رُودِدَ	تُرُودِدَ	اُنْرُدَّ	اُرْتُدَّ	اُسْتُرِدَّ
2. m.	أُرْدِدْتَ	رُودِدْتَ	تُرُودِدْتَ	اُنْرُدِدْتَ	اُرْتُدِدْتَ	اُسْتُرْدِدْتَ
Imperf. act.						
Sg. 3. m.	يُرِدُّ	يُرَادُّ	يَتَرَادُّ	يَنْرَدُّ	يَرْتَدُّ	يَسْتَرِدُّ
Pl. 3. m.	يُرِدُّونَ	يُرَادُّونَ	يَتَرَادُّونَ	يَنْرَدُّونَ	يَرْتَدُّونَ	يَسْتَرِدُّونَ
3. f.	يُرْدِدْنَ	يُرَادِدْنَ	يَتَرَادَدْنَ	يَنْرَدِدْنَ	يَرْتَدِدْنَ	يَسْتَرْدِدْنَ
Imperf. pass.						
Sg. 3. m.	يُرَدُّ	يُرَادُّ	يُتَرَادُّ	يُنْرَدُّ	يُرْتَدُّ	يُسْتَرَدُّ
Pl. 3. m.	يُرَدُّونَ	يُرَادُّونَ	يُتَرَادُّونَ	يُنْرَدُّونَ	يُرْتَدُّونَ	يُسْتَرَدُّونَ
3. f.	يُرْدَدْنَ	يُرَادَدْنَ	يُتَرَادَدْنَ	يُنْرَدَدْنَ	يُرْتَدَدْنَ	يُسْتَرْدَدْنَ
Juss. act.						
Sg. 3. m.	يُرْدِدْ/يُرِدَّ/يُرِدِّ	يُرَادِدْ /يُرَادَّ/يُرَادِّ	يَتَرَادَدْ/يَتَرَادَّ/يَتَرَادِّ	يَنْرَدِدْ/يَنْرَدَّ /يَنْرَدِّ	يَرْتَدِدْ/يَرْتَدَّ/يَرْتَدِّ	يَسْتَرْدِدْ/يَسْتَرِدَّ/يَسْتَرِدِّ
Pl. 3. m.	يُرِدُّوا	يُرَادُّوا	يَتَرَادُّوا	يَنْرَدُّوا	يَرْتَدُّوا	يَسْتَرِدُّوا
3. f.	يُرْدِدْنَ	يُرَادِدْنَ	يَتَرَادَدْنَ	يَنْرَدِدْنَ	يَرْتَدِدْنَ	يَسْتَرْدِدْنَ
Juss. pass.						
Sg. 3. m.	يُرْدَدْ/يُرَدَّ/يُرَدِّ	يُرَادَدْ/ يُرَادَّ/يُرَادِّ	يُتَرَادَدْ/يُتَرَادَّ/يُتَرَادِّ	يُنْرَدَدْ/يُنْرَدَّ/ يُنْرَدِّ	يُرْتَدَدْ/يُرْتَدَّ/يُرْتَدِّ	يُسْتَرْدَدْ/يُسْتَرَدَّ/يُسْتَرَدِّ
Pl. 3. m.	يُرَدُّوا	يُرَادُّوا	يُتَرَادُّوا	يُنْرَدُّوا	يُرْتَدُّوا	يُسْتَرَدُّوا
3. f.	يُرْدَدْنَ	يُرَادَدْنَ	يُتَرَادَدْنَ	يُنْرَدَدْنَ	يُرْتَدَدْنَ	يُسْتَرْدَدْنَ
Imperat. *Sg. m.*	أَرْدِدْ/أَرِدَّ/أَرِدِّ	رَادِدْ/رَادَّ/رَادِّ	تَرَادَدْ/تَرَادَّ/تَرَادِّ	اِنْرَدِدْ/اِنْرَدَّ/اِنْرَدِّ	اِرْتَدِدْ/اِرْتَدَّ/اِرْتَدِّ	اِسْتَرْدِدْ/اِسْتَرِدَّ /اِسْتَرِدِّ
f.	أَرِدِّي	رَادِّي	تَرَادِّي	اِنْرَدِّي	اِرْتَدِّي	اِسْتَرِدِّي
Part. act.	مُرِدٌّ	مُرَادٌّ	مُتَرَادٌّ	مُنْرَدٌّ	مُرْتَدٌّ	مُسْتَرِدٌّ
Part. pass.	مُرَدٌّ	مُرَادٌّ	مُتَرَادٌّ	مُنْرَدٌّ	مُرْتَدٌّ	مُسْتَرَدٌّ
Verb. subst.	إِرْدَادٌ	رِدَادٌ	تَرَادٌّ	اِنْرِدَادٌ	اِرْتِدَادٌ	اِسْتِرْدَادٌ

8. I-*hamzah* and I-Weak Verbs

	I-ʾ Roots		I-*w* Roots		I-*y* Roots	
	Form I	Form IV	Form I	Form IV	Form I	Form IV
Perf. act.						
Sg. m.	أَثَرَ	آثَرَ	وَصَلَ	أَوْصَلَ	يَسَرَ	أَيْسَرَ
Perf. pass.						
Sg. 3. m.	أُثِرَ	أُوثِرَ	وُصِلَ	أُوصِلَ	يُسِرَ	أُوسِرَ
Imperf. act.						
Sg. 3. m	يَأْثِرُ	يُؤْثِرُ	يَصِلُ	يُوصِلُ	يَيْسِرُ	يُوسِرُ
1.	آثِرُ	أُوثِرُ	أَصِلُ	أُوصِلُ	أَيْسِرُ	أُوسِرُ
Imperf. pass.						
Sg. 3. m.	يُؤْثَرُ	يُؤْثَرُ	يُوصَلُ	يُوصَلُ	يُوسَرُ	يُوسَرُ
1.	أُوثَرُ	أُوثَرُ	أُوصَلُ	أُوصَلُ	أُوسَرُ	أُوسَرُ
Subj. act.						
Sg. 3. m.	يَأْثِرَ	يُؤْثِرَ	يَصِلَ	يُوصِلَ	يَيْسِرَ	يُوسِرَ
1.	آثِرَ	أُوثِرَ	أَصِلَ	أُوصِلَ	أَيْسِرَ	أُوسِرَ
Subj. pass.						
Sg. 3. m	يُؤْثَرَ	يُؤْثَرَ	يُوصَلَ	يُوصَلَ	يُوسَرَ	يُوسَرَ
1.	أُوثَرَ	أُوثَرَ	أُوصَلَ	أُوصَلَ	أُوسَرَ	أُوسَرَ
Imperat. *sg.*	آئْثِرْ/إِيثِرْ	آثِرْ	صِلْ	أَوْصِلْ	إِيسِرْ	أَيْسِرْ
Part. act.	آثِرٌ	مُؤْثِرٌ	وَاصِلٌ	مُوصِلٌ	يَاسِرٌ	مُوسِرٌ
Verb. subst.	أَثْرٌ	إِيثَارٌ	صِلَةٌ	إِيصَالٌ	يَسْرٌ	إِيسَارٌ

	I-ʾ Roots		I-*w* Roots	
	VIII Form		VIII Form	
	Act.	Pass.	Act.	Pass.
Perf. *Sg. 3. m.*	آئْتَثَرَ/إِيتَثَرَ	آؤْتُثِرَ/أُوتُثِرَ	اِتَّصَلَ	أُتُّصِلَ
Imperf. *Sg. 3. m.*	يَأْتَثِرُ	يُؤْتَثَرُ	يَتَّصِلُ	يُتَّصَلُ
1.	آتَثِرُ	أُوتَثَرُ	أَتَّصِلُ	أُتَّصَلُ
Subj. *Sg. 3. m.*	يَأْتَثِرَ	يُؤْتَثَرَ	يَتَّصِلَ	يُتَّصَلَ
1.	آتَثِرَ	أُوتَثَرَ	أَتَّصِلَ	أُتَّصَلَ
Imperat. *Sg.*	آئْتَثِرْ/إِيتَثِرْ		اِتَّصِلْ	
Part.	مُؤْتَثِرٌ	مُؤْتَثَرٌ	مُؤْتَصِلٌ	مُؤْتَصَلٌ
Verb. subst.	آئْتِثَارٌ/إِيتِثَارٌ		اِتِّصَالٌ	

9. The Verb رَأَى 'see'

Active

	Form I			Form IV		
	Perf.	Imperf.	Juss.	Perf.	Imperf.	Juss.
Sg. 3. m.	رَأَى	يَرَى	يَرَ	أَرَى	يُرِي	يُرِ
3. f.	رَأَتْ	تَرَى	تَرَ	أَرَتْ	تُرِي	تُرِ
2. m.	رَأَيْتَ	تَرَى	تَرَ	أَرَيْتَ	تُرِي	تُرِ
2. f.	رَأَيْتِ	تَرَيْنَ	تَرَيْ	أَرَيْتِ	تُرِينَ	تُرِي
1.	رَأَيْتُ	أَرَى	أَرَ	أَرَيْتُ	أُرِي	أُرِ
Du. 3. m.	رَأَيَا	يَرَيَانِ	يَرَيَا	أَرَيَا	يُرِيَانِ	يُرِيَا
3. f.	رَأَتَا	تَرَيَانِ	تَرَيَا	أَرَتَا	تُرِيَانِ	تُرِيَا
2.	رَأَيْتُمَا	تَرَيَانِ	تَرَيَا	أَرَيْتُمَا	تُرِيَانِ	تُرِيَا
Pl. 3. m.	رَأَوْا	يَرَوْنَ	يَرَوْا	أَرَوْا	يُرُونَ	يُرُوا
3. f.	رَأَيْنَ	يَرَيْنَ	يَرَيْنَ	أَرَيْنَ	يُرِينَ	يُرِينَ
2. m.	رَأَيْتُمْ	تَرَوْنَ	تَرَوْا	أَرَيْتُمْ	تُرُونَ	تُرُوا
2. f.	رَأَيْتُنَّ	تَرَيْنَ	تَرَيْنَ	أَرَيْتُنَّ	تُرِينَ	تُرِينَ
1.	رَأَيْنَا	نَرَى	نَرَ	أَرَيْنَا	نُرِي	نُرِ
Imperative *Sg. m.* رَهْ		*Pl. m.* رَوْا	*Sg. m.* أَرِ		*Pl. m.* أَرُوا	
	Du. رَيَا			*Du.* أَرِيَا		
f. رَيْ		*f.* رَيْنَ	*f.* أَرِي		*f.* أَرِينَ	

Passive

	Form I Perf.	Form IV Perf	Form I & IV Imperf.	Form I & IV Juss.
Sg. 3. m.	رُئِيَ	أُرِيَ	يُرَى	يُرَ
3. f.	رُئِيَتْ	أُرِيَتْ	تُرَى	تُرَ
2. f.	رُئِيتِ	أُرِيتِ	تُرَيْنَ	تُرَيْ
Du. 3. m.	رُئِيَا	أُرِيَا	تُرَيَانِ	تُرَيَا
Pl. 3. m.	رُءُوا	أُرُوا	يُرَوْنَ	يُرَوْا
3. f.	رُئِينَ	أُرِينَ	يُرَيْنَ	يُرَيْنَ

10. II-Weak Verbs

Basic Stem (I)				
	Perfect Active			Perf. Passive
Sg. 3. m.	قَامَ	صَارَ	نَامَ	قِيمَ
3. f.	قَامَتْ	صَارَتْ	نَامَتْ	قِيمَتْ
2. m	قُمْتَ	صِرْتَ	نِمْتَ	قِمْتَ
2. f.	قُمْتِ	صِرْتِ	نِمْتِ	قِمْتِ
1.	قُمْتُ	صِرْتُ	نِمْتُ	قِمْتُ
Du. 3. m.	قَامَا	صَارَا	نَامَا	قِيمَا
3. f.	قَامَتَا	صَارَتَا	نَامَتَا	قِيمَتَا
2.	قُمْتُمَا	صِرْتُمَا	نِمْتُمَا	قِمْتُمَا
Pl. 3. m.	قَامُوا	صَارُوا	نَامُوا	قِيمُوا
3. f.	قُمْنَ	صِرْنَ	نِمْنَ	قِمْنَ
2. m.	قُمْتُمْ	صِرْتُمْ	نِمْتُمْ	قِمْتُمْ
2. f.	قُمْتُنَّ	صِرْتُنَّ	نِمْتُنَّ	قِمْتُنَّ
1.	قُمْنَا	صِرْنَا	نِمْنَا	قِمْنَا
	Imperfect Active			Imperf. Passive
Sg. 3. m.	يَقُومُ	يَصِيرُ	يَنَامُ	يُقَامُ
3. f.	تَقُومُ	تَصِيرُ	تَنَامُ	تُقَامُ
2. m.	تَقُومُ	تَصِيرُ	تَنَامُ	تُقَامُ
2. f.	تَقُومِينَ	تَصِيرِينَ	تَنَامِينَ	تُقَامِينَ
1.	أَقُومُ	أَصِيرُ	أَنَامُ	أُقَامُ
Du. 3. m.	يَقُومَانِ	يَصِيرَانِ	يَنَامَانِ	يُقَامَانِ
3. f.	تَقُومَانِ	تَصِيرَانِ	تَنَامَانِ	تُقَامَانِ
2.	تَقُومَانِ	تَصِيرَانِ	تَنَامَانِ	تُقَامَانِ
Pl. 3. m.	يَقُومُونَ	تَصِيرُونَ	يَنَامُونَ	يُقَامُونَ
3. f.	يَقُمْنَ	يَصِرْنَ	يَنَمْنَ	يُقَمْنَ
2. m.	تَقُومُونَ	تَصِيرُونَ	تَنَامُونَ	تُقَامُونَ
2. f.	تَقُمْنَ	تَصِرْنَ	تَنَمْنَ	تُقَمْنَ
1.	نَقُومُ	نَصِيرُ	نَنَامُ	نُقَامُ

بِيعَ بُعْتُ، خِيفَ خُفْتُ Passive – بَاعَ بِعْتُ، خَافَ خِفْتُ

	Subjunctive Active			Subj. Passive
Sg. 3. m.	يَقُومَ	يَصِيرَ	يَنَامَ	يُقَامَ
3. f.	تَقُومَ	تَصِيرَ	تَنَامَ	تُقَامَ
2. m.	تَقُومَ	تَصِيرَ	تَنَامَ	تُقَامَ
2. f.	تَقُومِي	تَصِيرِي	تَنَامِي	تُقَامِي
1.	أَقُومَ	أَصِيرَ	أَنَامَ	أُقَامَ
Du. 3. m.	يَقُومَا	يَصِيرَا	يَنَامَا	يُقَامَا
3. f.	تَقُومَا	تَصِيرَا	تَنَامَا	تُقَامَا
2.	تَقُومَا	تَصِيرَا	تَنَامَا	تُقَامَا
Pl. 3. m.	يَقُومُوا	يَصِيرُوا	يَنَامُوا	يُقَامُوا
3. f.	يَقُمْنَ	يَصِرْنَ	يَنَمْنَ	يُقَمْنَ
2. m.	تَقُومُوا	تَصِيرُوا	تَنَامُوا	تُقَامُوا
2. f.	تَقُمْنَ	تَصِرْنَ	تَنَمْنَ	تُقَمْنَ
1.	نَقُومَ	نَصِيرَ	نَنَامَ	نُقَامَ

	Jussive Active			Juss. Passive
Sg. 3. m.	يَقُمْ	يَصِرْ	يَنَمْ	يُقَمْ
3. f.	تَقُمْ	تَصِرْ	تَنَمْ	تُقَمْ
2. m.	تَقُمْ	تَصِرْ	تَنَمْ	تُقَمْ
2. f.	تَقُومِي	تَصِيرِي	تَنَامِي	تُقَامِي
1.	أَقُمْ	أَصِرْ	أَنَمْ	أُقَمْ
Du. 3. m.	يَقُومَا	يَصِيرَا	يَنَامَا	يُقَامَا
3. f.	تَقُومَا	تَصِيرَا	تَنَامَا	تُقَامَا
2.	تَقُومَا	تَصِيرَا	تَنَامَا	تُقَامَا
Pl. 3. m.	يَقُومُوا	تَصِيرُوا	يَنَامُوا	يُقَامُوا
3. f.	يَقُمْنَ	يَصِرْنَ	يَنَمْنَ	يُقَمْنَ
2. m.	تَقُومُوا	تَصِيرُوا	تَنَامُوا	تُقَامُوا
2. f.	تَقُمْنَ	تَصِرْنَ	تَنَمْنَ	تُقَمْنَ
1.	نَقُمْ	نَصِرْ	نَنَمْ	نُقَمْ

Imperative			
Sg. m.	قُمْ	صِرْ	نَمْ
f.	قُومِي	صِيرِي	نَامِي
Du.	قُومَا	صِيرَا	نَامَا
Pl. m.	قُومُوا	صِيرُوا	نَامُوا
f.	قُمْنَ	صِرْنَ	نَمْنَ

	Active Participle			Passive Participle		
Sg. m.	قَائِمٌ	صَائِرٌ	نَائِمٌ	مَقُومٌ	مَصِيرٌ	مَنُومٌ
f.	قَائِمَةٌ	صَائِرَةٌ	نَائِمَةٌ	مَقُومَةٌ	مَصِيرَةٌ	مَنُومَةٌ

Form II						
	Active			Passive		
Perf.	قَوَّمَ	صَيَّرَ	نَوَّمَ	قُوِّمَ	صُيِّرَ	نُوِّمَ
Imperf.	يُقَوِّمُ	يُصَيِّرُ	يُنَوِّمُ	يُقَوَّمُ	يُصَيَّرُ	يُنَوَّمُ
Juss.	يُقَوِّمْ	يُصَيِّرْ	يُنَوِّمْ	يُقَوَّمْ	يُصَيَّرْ	يُنَوَّمْ
Imperat.	قَوِّمْ	صَيِّرْ	نَوِّمْ			
Part.	مُقَوِّمٌ	مُصَيِّرٌ	مُنَوِّمٌ	مُقَوَّمٌ	مُصَيَّرٌ	مُنَوَّمٌ
Verb. subst.	تَقْوِيمٌ	تَصْيِيرٌ	تَنْوِيمٌ			

	Form III		Form V		Form VI	
	Active	Passive	Active	Passive	Active	Passive
Perf.	قَاوَمَ	قُووِمَ	تَقَوَّمَ	تُقُوِّمَ	تَقَاوَمَ	تُقُووِمَ
	صَايَرَ	صُويِرَ	تَصَيَّرَ	تُصُيِّرَ	تَصَايَرَ	تُصُويِرَ
Imperf.	يُقَاوِمُ	يُقَاوَمُ	يَتَقَوَّمُ	يُتَقَوَّمُ	يَتَقَاوَمُ	يُتَقَاوَمُ
	يُصَايِرُ	يُصَايَرُ	يَتَصَيَّرُ	يُتَصَيَّرُ	يَتَصَايَرُ	يُتَصَايَرُ
Juss.	يُقَاوِمْ	يُقَاوَمْ	يَتَقَوَّمْ	يُتَقَوَّمْ	يَتَقَاوَمْ	يُتَقَاوَمْ
	يُصَايِرْ	يُصَايَرْ	يَتَصَيَّرْ	يُتَصَيَّرْ	يَتَصَايَرْ	يُتَصَايَرْ
Imperat.	قَاوِمْ		تَقَوَّمْ		تَقَاوَمْ	
	صَايِرْ		تَصَيَّرْ		تَصَايَرْ	
Part.	مُقَاوِمٌ	مُقَاوَمٌ	مُتَقَوِّمٌ	مُتَقَوَّمٌ	مُتَقَاوِمٌ	مُتَقَاوَمٌ
	مُصَايِرٌ	مُصَايَرٌ	مُتَصَيِّرٌ	مُتَصَيَّرٌ	مُتَصَايِرٌ	مُتَصَايَرٌ
Verb. subst.	قِوَامٌ		تَقَوُّمٌ		تَقَاوُمٌ	
	صِيَارٌ		تَصَيُّرٌ		تَصَايُرٌ	

	IV Form	IV Form	VII Form	VIII Form	X Form
Perf. act.					
Sg. 3. m.	أَقَامَ	أَصَارَ	اِنْقَامَ	اِقْتَامَ	اِسْتَقَامَ
1.	أَقَمْتُ	أَصَرْتُ	اِنْقَمْتُ	اِقْتَمْتُ	اِسْتَقَمْتُ
Perf. pass.					
Sg. 3. m.	أُقِيمَ	أُصِيرَ	أُنْقِيمَ	أُقْتِيمَ	أُسْتُقِيمَ
1.	أُقِمْتُ	أُصِرْتُ	أُنْقِمْتُ	أُقْتِمْتُ	أُسْتُقِمْتُ
Imperf. act.	يُقِيمُ	يُصِيرُ	يَنْقَامُ	يَقْتَامُ	يَسْتَقِيمُ
pass.	يُقَامُ	يُصَارُ	يُنْقَامُ	يُقْتَامُ	يُسْتَقَامُ
Juss. act.	يُقِمْ	يُصِرْ	يَنْقَمْ	يَقْتَمْ	يَسْتَقِمْ
pass.	يُقَمْ	يُصَرْ	يُنْقَمْ	يُقْتَمْ	يُسْتَقَمْ
Imperat. *Sg. m.*	أَقِمْ	أَصِرْ	اِنْقَمْ	اِقْتَمْ	اِسْتَقِمْ
f.	أَقِيمِي	أَصِيرِي	اِنْقَامِي	اِقْتَامِي	اِسْتَقِيمِي
Active part.	مُقِيمٌ	مُصِيرٌ	مُنْقَامٌ	مُقْتَامٌ	مُسْتَقِيمٌ
pass.	مُقَامٌ	مُصَارٌ	مُنْقَامٌ	مُقْتَامٌ	مُسْتَقَامٌ
Verbal subst.	إِقَامَةٌ	إِصَارَةٌ	اِنْقِيَامٌ	اِقْتِيَامٌ	اِسْتِقَامٌ

11. III-Weak Verbs

	Basic Stem (I)				
	Perfect Active				Perf. Passive
Sg. 3. m.	رَمَى	دَعَا	لَقِيَ	سَرُوَ	دُعِيَ
3. f.	رَمَتْ	دَعَتْ	لَقِيَتْ	سَرُوَتْ	دُعِيَتْ
2. m.	رَمَيْتَ	دَعَوْتَ	لَقِيتَ	سَرُوتَ	دُعِيتَ
2. f.	رَمَيْتِ	دَعَوْتِ	لَقِيتِ	سَرُوتِ	دُعِيتِ
1.	رَمَيْتُ	دَعَوْتُ	لَقِيتُ	سَوُوتُ	دُعِيتُ
Du. 3. m.	رَمَيَا	دَعَوَا	لَقِيَا	سَرُوَا	دُعِيَا
3. f.	رَمَتَا	دَعَتَا	لَقِيَتَا	سَرُوَتَا	دُعِيَتَا
2.	رَمَيْتُمَا	دَعَوْتُمَا	لَقِيتُمَا	سَرُوتُمَا	دُعِيتُمَا
Pl. 3. m.	رَمَوْا	دَعَوْا	لَقُوا	سَرُوا	دُعُوا
3. f.	رَمَيْنَ	دَعَوْنَ	لَقِينَ	سَرُونَ	دُعِينَ
2. f.	رَمَيْتُمْ	دَعَوْتُمْ	لَقِيتُمْ	سَرُوتُمْ	دُعِيتُمْ
2. f.	رَمَيْتُنَّ	دَعَوْتُنَّ	لَقِيتُنَّ	سَرُوتُنَّ	دُعِيتُنَّ
1.	رَمَيْنَا	دَعَوْنَا	لَقِينَا	سَرُونَا	دُعِينَا

	Imperfect Active				Imperf. Pass.
Sg. 3. m.	يَرْمِي	يَدْعُو	يَلْقَى	يَسْرُو	يُدْعَى
3. f.	تَرْمِي	تَدْعُو	تَلْقَى	تَسْرُو	تُدْعَى
2. m.	تَرْمِي	تَدْعُو	تَلْقَى	تَسْرُو	تُدْعَى
2. f.	تَرْمِينَ	تَدْعِينَ	تَلْقَيْنَ	تَسْرِينَ	تُدْعَيْنَ
1.	أَرْمِي	أَدْعُو	أَلْقَى	أَسْرُو	أُدْعَى
Du. 3. m.	يَرْمِيَانِ	يَدعُوَانِ	يَلْقَيَانِ	يَسرُوَانِ	يُدْعَيَانِ
3. f.	تَرْمِيَانِ	تَدعُوَانِ	تَلْقَيَانِ	تَسرُوَانِ	تُدْعَيَانِ
2.	تَرْمِيَانِ	تَدعُوَانِ	تَلْقَيَانِ	تَسرُوَانِ	تُدْعَيَانِ
Pl. 3. m.	يَرْمُونَ	يَدْعُونَ	يَلْقَوْنَ	يَسْرُونَ	يُدْعَوْنَ
3. f.	يَرْمِينَ	يَدْعُونَ	يَلْقَيْنَ	يَسْرُونَ	يُدْعَيْنَ
2. m.	تَرْمُونَ	تَدْعُونَ	تَلْقَوْنَ	تَسْرُونَ	تُدْعَوْنَ
2. f.	تَرْمِينَ	تَدْعُونَ	تَلْقَيْنَ	تَسْرُونَ	تُدْعَيْنَ
1.	تَرْمِي	نَدْعُو	نَلْقَى	نَسْرُو	نُدْعَى

	Subjunctive Active			Subj. Pass.
Sg. 3. m.	يَرْمِيَ	يَدْعُوَ	يَلْقَى	يُدْعَى
3. f.	تَرْمِيَ	تَدْعُوَ	تَلْقَى	تُدْعَى
2. m.	تَرْمِيَ	تَدْعُوَ	تَلْقَى	تُدْعَى
2. f.	تَرْمِي	تَدْعِي	تَلْقَيْ	تُدْعَيْ
1.	أَرْمِيَ	أَدْعُوَ	أَلْقَى	أُدْعَى
Du. 3. m.	يَرْمِيَا	يَدعُوَا	يَلْقَيَا	يُدْعَيَا
3. f.	تَرْمِيَا	تَدعُوَا	تَلْقَيَا	تُدْعَيَا
2. f.	تَرْمِيَا	تَدعُوَا	تَلْقَيَا	تُدْعَيَا
Pl. 3. m.	يَرْمُوا	يَدْعُوا	يَلْقَوْا	يُدْعَوْا
3. f.	يَرْمِينَ	يَدْعُونَ	يَلْقَيْنَ	يُدْعَيْنَ
2. m.	تَرْمُوا	تَدْعُوا	تَلْقَوْا	تُدْعَوْا
2.	تَرْمِينَ	تَدْعُونَ	تَلْقَيْنَ	تُدْعَيْنَ
1.	نَرْمِيَ	نَدْعُوَ	نَلْقَى	نُدْعَى

	Jussive Active			Juss. Pass.
Sg. 3. m.	يَرْمِ	يَدْعُ	يَلْقَ	يُدْعَ
3. f.	تَرْمِ	تَدْعُ	تَلْقَ	تُدْعَ
2. m.	تَرْمِ	تَدْعُ	تَلْقَ	تُدْعَ
2. f.	تَرْمِي	تَدْعِي	تَلْقَيْ	تُدْعَيْ
1.	أَرْمِ	أَدْعُ	أَلْقَ	أُدْعَ
Du. 3. m.	يَرْمِيَا	يَدْعُوَا	يَلْقَيَا	يُدْعَيَا
3. f.	تَرْمِيَا	تَدْعُوَا	تَلْقَيَا	تُدْعَيَا
2.	تَرْمِيَا	تَدْعُوَا	تَلْقَيَا	تُدْعَيَا
Pl. 3. m.	يَرْمُوا	يَدْعُوا	يَلْقَوْا	يُدْعَوْا
3. f.	يَرْمِينَ	يَدْعُونَ	يَلْقَيْنَ	يُدْعَيْنَ
2. m.	تَرْمُوا	تَدْعُوا	تَلْقَوْا	تُدْعَوْا
2.	تَرْمِينَ	تَدْعُونَ	تَلْقَيْنَ	تُدْعَيْنَ
1.	نَرْمِ	نَدْعُ	نَلْقَ	نُدْعَ

	Energetic I Active			Energ. I Pass.
Sg. 3. m.	يَرْمِيَنَّ	يَدْعُوَنَّ	يَلْقَيَنَّ	يُدْعَيَنَّ
3. f.	تَرْمِيَنَّ	تَدْعُوَنَّ	تَلْقَيَنَّ	تُدْعَيَنَّ
2. f.	تَرْمِنَّ	تَدْعِنَّ	تَلْقَيِنَّ	تُدْعَيِنَّ
Du. 3. m.	يَرْمِيَانِّ	يَدْعُوَانِّ	يَلْقَيَانِّ	يُدْعَيَانِّ
Pl. 3. m.	يَرْمُنَّ	يَدْعُنَّ	يَلْقَوُنَّ	يُدْعَوُنَّ
3. f.	يَرْمِينَانِّ	يَدْعُونَانِّ	يَلْقَيْنَانِّ	يُدْعَيْنَانِّ

	Form II	Form III	Form IV	Form V	Form VI
Perf. act.					
Sg. 3. m.	لَقَّى	لَاقَى	أَلْقَى	تَلَقَّى	تَلَاقَى
1.	لَقَّيْتُ	لَاقَيْتُ	أَلْقَيْتُ	تَلَقَّيْتُ	تَلَاقَيْتُ
Perf. pass.	لُقِّيَ	لُوقِيَ	أُلْقِيَ	تُلُقِّيَ	تُلُوقِيَ
Imperf. act.	يُلَقِّي	يُلَاقِي	يُلْقِي	يَتَلَقَّى	يَتَلَاقَى
pass.	يُلَقَّى	يُلَاقَى	يُلْقَى	يُتَلَقَّى	يُتَلَاقَى
Subj. act.	يُلَقِّيَ	يُلَاقِيَ	يُلْقِيَ	يَتَلَقَّى	يَتَلَاقَى
Juss. act.	يُلَقِّ	يُلَاقِ	يُلْقِ	يَتَلَقَّ	يَتَلَاقَ
pass.	يُلَقَّ	يُلَاقَ	يُلْقَ	يُتَلَقَّ	يُتَلَاقَ
Active part.	مُلَقٍّ	مُلَاقٍ	مُلْقٍ	مُتَلَقٍّ	مُتَلَاقٍ
pass.	مُلَقًّى	مُلَاقًى	مُلْقًى	مُتَلَقًّى	مُتَلَاقًى
Imperat.	لَقِّ	لَاقِ	أَلْقِ	تَلَقَّ	تَلَاقَ
Verbal subst.	تَلْقِيَةٌ	لِقَاءٌ	إِلْقَاءٌ	تَلَقٍّ	تَلَاقٍ

	Form VII	Form VIII	Form IX	Form X
Perf. act.				
Sg. 3. m.	اِنْلَقَى	اِلْتَقَى	اِرْعَوَى	اِسْتَلْقَى
1.	اِنْلَقَيْتُ	اِلْتَقَيْتُ	اِرْعَوَيْتُ	اِسْتَلْقَيْتُ
Imperf. act.	يَنْلَقِي	يَلْتَقِي	يَرْعَوِي	يَسْتَلْقِي
pass.	يُنْلَقَى	يُلْتَقَى	يُرْعَوَى	يُسْتَلْقَى
Subj. act.	يَنْلَقِيَ	يَلْتَقِيَ	يَرْعَوِيَ	يَسْتَلْقِيَ
Juss. act.	يَنْلَقِ	يَلْتَقِ	يَرْعَوِ	يَسْتَلْقِ
pass.	يُنْلَقَ	يُلْتَقَ	يُرْعَوَ	يُسْتَلْقَ
Active part.	مُنْلَقٍ	مُلْتَقٍ	مُرْعَوٍ	مُسْتَلْقٍ
pass.	مُنْلَقًى	مُلْتَقًى	مُرْعَوًى	مُسْتَلْقًى
Imperat.	اِنْلَقِ	اِلْتَقِ	اِرْعَوِ	اِسْتَلْقِ
Verbal subst.	اِنْلِقَاءٌ	اِلْتِقَاءٌ	اِرْعِوَاءٌ	اِسْتِلْقَاءٌ

Imperative			
Sg. m.	اِرْمِ	أُدْعُ	اِلْقَ
f.	اِرْمِي	أُدْعِي	اِلْقَيْ
Du.	اِرْمِيَا	أُدْعُوَا	اِلْقَيَا
Pl. m.	اِرْمُوا	أُدْعُوا	اِلْقَوْا
f.	اِرْمِينَ	أُدْعُونَ	اِلْقَيْنَ

Participle						
	Active			Passive		
Sg. m.	رَامٍ	دَاعٍ	لَاقٍ	مَرْمِيٌّ	مَدْعُوٌّ	مَلْقِيٌّ
f.	رَامِيَةٌ	دَاعِيَةٌ	لَاقِيَةٌ	مَرْمِيَّةٌ	مَدْعُوَّةٌ	مَلْقِيَّةٌ

12. I-*w* – III-Weak Verbs

Basic Stem (I)						
	Active			Passive		
	Perf.	Imperf.	Juss.	Perf.	Imperf.	Juss.
Sg. 3. m.	وَفَى	يَفِي	يَفِ	وُفِيَ	يُوفَى	يُوفَ
3. f.	وَفَتْ	تَفِي	تَفِ	وُفِيَتْ	تُوفَى	تُوفَ
2. m.	وَفَيْتَ	تَفِي	تَفِ	وُفِيتَ	تُوفَى	تُوفَ
2. f.	وَفَيْتِ	تَفِينَ	تَفِي	وُفِيتِ	تُوفَيْنَ	تُفَيْ
1.	وَفَيْتُ	أَفِي	أَفِ	وُفِيتُ	أُوفَى	أُوفَ
Du. 3. m.	وَفَيَا	يَفِيَانِ	يَفِيَا	وُفِيَا	يُوفَيَانِ	يُوفَيَا
3. f.	وَفَتَا	تَفِيَانِ	تَفِيَا	وُفِيَتَا	تُوفِيَانِ	تُوفِيَا
2.	وَفَيْتُمَا	تَفِيَانِ	تَفِيَا	وُفِيتُمَا	تُوفَيَانِ	تُوفَيَا
Pl. 3. m.	وَفَوْا	يَفُونَ	يَفُوا	وُفُوا	يُوفَوْنَ	يُوفَوْا
3. f.	وَفَيْنَ	يَفِينَ	يَفِينَ	وُفِينَ	يُوفَيْنَ	يُوفَيْنَ
2. m.	وَفَيْتُمْ	تَفُونَ	تَفُوا	وُفِيتُمْ	تُوفَوْنَ	تُوفَوْا
2. f.	وَفَيْتُنَّ	تَفِينَ	تَفِينَ	وُفِيتُنَّ	تُوفَيْنَ	تُوفَيْنَ
1.	وَفَيْنَا	نَفِي	نَفِ	وُفِينَا	نُوفَى	نُوفَ
Imperative *Sg. m.* فِهْ *f.* فِي *Du.* فِيَا *Pl. m.* فُوا *f.* فِينَ						
Act. part. *Sg. m.* وَافٍ *f.* وَافِيَةٌ Pass. part. *Sg. m.* مَوْفِيٌّ *f.* مَوْفِيَّةٌ						

13. II-*y* – III-Weak Verbs

Basic Stem (Active)			
	Perfect	Imperfect	Jussive
Sg. 3. m.	حَيِيَ/حَيَّ	يَحْيَا/يَحَيُّ	يَحْيَ
Sg. m.	حَيِيَتْ/حَيَّتْ	تَحْيَا/تَحَيُّ	تَحْيَ
2. m.	حَيِيتَ	تَحْيَا/تَحَيُّ	تَحْيَ
2. f.	حَيِيتِ	تَحْيَيْنَ/تَحَيِّينَ	تَحَيِّي/تَحْيَيْ
1.	حَيِيتُ	أَحْيَا/أَحَيُّ	أَحْيَ
Du. 3. m.	حَيِيَا/حَيَّا	يَحَيَّانِ	يَحَيَّا
3. f.	حَيِيَتَا/حَيَّتَا	تَحَيَّانِ	تَحَيَّا
2.	حَيِيتُمَا	تَحَيَّانِ	تَحَيَّا
Pl. 3. m.	حَيُوا/حَيُّوا	يَحَيُّونَ/يَحْيَوْنَ	يَحَيُّوا / يَحْيَوْا
3. f.	حَيِينَ	يَحْيَيْنَ	يَحْيَيْنَ
2. m.	حَيِيتُمْ	تَحَيُّونَ/تَحْيَوْنَ	تَحَيُّوا / تَحْيَوْا
2. f.	حَيِيتُنَّ	تَحْيَيْنَ	تَحْيَيْنَ
1.	حَيِينَا	نَحْيَا/نَحَيُّ	نَحْيَ
Participle *Sg. m.* حَيٌّ *f.* حَيَّةٌ			
Imperat. *Sg. m.* إِحْيَ *f.* إِحْيَيْ *Du.* إِحْيَيَا *Pl. m.* إِحْيَوْا *f.* إِحْيَيْنَ			

14. 4-Radical Verbs

Active				
	Form I	Form II	Form III	Form IV
Perf.	خَرْطَمَ	تَخَرْطَمَ	اِخْرَنْطَمَ	اِخْرَطَمَّ
Imperf.	يُخَرْطِمُ	يَتَخَرْطَمُ	يَخْرَنْطِمُ	يَخْرَطِمُّ
Juss.	يُخَرْطِمْ	يَتَخَرْطَمْ	يَخْرَنْطِمْ	يَخْرَطْمِمْ / يَخْرَطِمِّ / يَخْرَطِمَّ
Imperat.	خَرْطِمْ	تَخَرْطَمْ	اِخْرَنْطِمْ	اِخْرَطْمِمْ / اِخْرَطِمِّ / اِخْرَطِمَّ
Part.	مُخَرْطِمٌ	مُتَخَتْطِمٌ	مُخْرَنْطِمٌ	مُخْرَطِمٌّ
Verb. subst.	خَرْطَمَةٌ	تَخَرْطُمٌ	اِخْرِنْطَامٌ	اِخْرِطْمَامٌ

Form IV (Active)			
	Perf.	Imperf.	Juss.
Sg. 3. m.	اِخْرَطَمَّ	يَخْرَطِمُّ	يَخْرَطْمِمْ / يَخْرَطِمِّ / يَخْرَطِمَّ
1.	اِخْرَطْمَمْتُ	أَخْرَطِمُّ	أَخْرَطْمِمْ / أَخْرَطِمِّ / أَخْرَطِمَّ
Pl. 3. m.	اِخْرَطَمُّوا	يَخْرَطِمُّونَ	يَخْرَطِمُّوا
3. f.	اِخْرَطْمَمْنَ	يَخْرَطْمِمْنَ	يَخْرَطْمِمْنَ

Passive				
	Form I	Form II	Form III	Form IV
Perf.	خُرْطِمَ	تُخُرْطِمَ	أُخْرُنْطِمَ	أُخْرُطِمَّ
Imperf.	يُخَرْطَمُ	يُتَخَرْطَمُ	يُخْرَنْطَمُ	يُخْرَطَمُّ
Juss.	يُخَرْطَمْ	يُتَخَرْطَمْ	يُخْرَنْطَمْ	يُخْرَطْمَمْ / يُخْرَطَمِّ / يُخْرَطَمَّ
Part.	مُخَرْطَمٌ	مُتَخَرْطَمٌ	مُخْرَنْطَمٌ	مُخْرَطَمٌّ

Selective Bibliography of Arabic Grammar and Linguistics†

1. General and Reference Works

Salih J. Altoma: Modern Arabic Literature: A bibliography of articles, books, dissertations and translations in English. Bloomington 1975 (Asian Studies Research Institute. Occasional Papers; 3)

Julia Ashtiany, ed. ... [et al.] ʿAbbasid belles-lettres. Cambridge ; New York 1990 (The Cambridge History of Arabic Literature)

M. H. Bakalla: Arabic Linguistics. An introduction and bibliography. London 1983

Erika Bär: Bibliographie zur deutschsprachigen Islamwissenschaft und Semitistik vom Anfang des 19. Jahrhunderts bis heute. 3 Bde. Wiesbaden 1985–1994

A. F. L. Beeston, T. M. Johnstone, R. B. Sergeant, G. R. Smith [ed.]: Arabic Literature to the End of the Umayyad Period. Cambridge 1983 (The Cambridge history of Arabic literature)

Max van Berchem: Matériaux pour un Corpus Inscriptionum Arabicorum. I 1.2 Egypte. II a 1–3. Syrie du Nord II b 1–3. Syrie du Sud. III Asie Mineure. Cairo 1894–1956 (Mémoires publiés par les membres de la Mission archéologique française du Caire 19. 25. 29. 43–45. 52. 76–78

Gotthelf Bergsträßer: اصول نقد النصوص ونشر الكتب: محاضرات بكلّيّة الآداب سنة ١٩٣١-١٩٣٢. Cairo 1969

Bibliographie der Deutschsprachigen Arabistik und Islamkunde : von den Anfängen bis 1986 nebst Literatur über die arabischen Länder der Gegenwart hrsg. von Fuat Sezgin; in Zusammenarbeit mit Gesine Degener... [et al.]. Frankfurt am Main 1990–1995. (Veröffentlichungen des Institutes für Geschichte der Arabisch-Islamischen Wissenschaften. Reihe A, Texte und Studien; 21 Bd.)

† Superscript numbers joined to publication dates or titles indicate editions; e.g., ^{3}1945 signifies the third edition.

Régis Blachère: Histoire de la littérature Arabe des origines à la fin du XVe siècle de J.-C. Paris 1952–1966

Régis Blachère et Jean Sauvaget: Règles pour éditions et traductions de textes arabes. Paris 1953 (Collection arabe publiée sous le patronage de l'Association Guillaume Budé)

Carl Brockelmann: Geschichte der Arabischen Litteratur, zweite den Supplementbänden angepaßte Auflage, 2 Bde., 3 Supplementbände. Leiden 1937–1949

Louis Cheikho: Les savants arabes chrétiens en Islam (622–1300). Texte établi et augmenté avec introduction, notes et index par Camille Héchaimé. Rom 1983

The Encyclopædia of Islam: A Dictionary of the geography, ethnography and biography of the Muhammadan peoples. Leiden 1913–1938. Reprint as: Brill's First Encyclopædia of Islam 1913–1936, 1993

The Encyclopædia of Islam: New edition prepared by a number of leading orientalists. Leiden/London 1954–

The Encyclopædia of Islam on CD-ROM. Vol. 1–9. Leiden 1999

Enzyklopaedie des Islam, geographisches, ethnographisches und biographisches Wörterbuch der muhammedanischen Völker, hrsg. von M. Th. Houtsma, T. W. Amold, R. Basset und R. Hartmann, 4 Bde. Leiden/Leipzig 1913–1934, Ergänzungsband 1938

Johann Fück: Die Arabischen Studien in Europa bis in den Anfang des 20. Jahrhunderts. Leipzig 1955

Hamilton A. R. Gibb and Jacob M. Landau: Arabische Literaturgeschichte. Zürich-Stuttgart 1968 (Die Bibliothek des Morgenlandes)

Georg Graf: Geschichte der Christlichen Arabischen Literatur, Bd. 1–5. Città del Vaticano 1944–1953

Diana Grimwood-Jones, Derek Hopwood, J. D. Pearson [ed.]: Arab Islamic Bibliography. Atlantic Highlands 1977

Adolf Grohmann: Arabic Papyri in the Egyptian Library. 6 vol. Cairo 1934–1962

—: Einführung und Chrestomathie zur Arabischen Papyruskunde. Bd. 1. Einführung. Prag 1954 (Československý Ústav Orientální v Praze. Monografie Archivu Orientálního; 13,1)

—: Arabische Papyruskunde. Handbuch der Orientalistik. Abt. 1. Ergänzungsband 2,1. Leiden 1966

Grundriß der Arabischen Philologie. Bd. 1: Sprachwissenschaft. Hrsg. von W. Fischer. Wiesbaden 1982. Bd. 2: Literaturwissenschaft. Hrsg. von H. Gätje. Wiesbaden 1987. Bd. 3: Supplement Hrsg. von W. Fischer. Wiesbaden 1992.

Gustave Edmund von Grunebaum: Kritik und Dichtkunst: Studien zur arabischen Literaturgeschichte. Wiesbaden 1955

Handwörterbuch des Islam, hrsg. von Arent Jan Wensinck und J. Kramers. Leiden 1941

Index Islamicus, 1906–1955. London 1956/60. The Quarterly Index Islamicus. London, v. 1– 1977– . Index Islamicus (East Grinstead, England) no. 1– 1994– . Index Islamicus, 1665–1905 ... compiled by W. H. Behn. Millersville, Pa. 1989. Index Islamicus. Supplement, 1665–1980 ... by W. H. Behn. Millersville, Pa. 1995– . Index Islamicus on CD-ROM: a Bibliography of publications on Islam and the Muslim world since 1906[–1997].

ʿUmar Riḍā Kahhāla: أعلام النّساء في عالمي العرب والإسلام. 5 vol. Damascus [2]1958–1959

—: معجم المؤلّفين. 15 vol. Damascus 1376/1957–1380/1961

—: معجم قبائل العرب القديمة والحديثة. 5 vol. Beirut [3]1402/1982

Reynold A. Nicholson: A Literary History of the Arabs. London 1907

Theodor Nöldeke: Geschichte des Qorans. 2. Aufl. bearbeitet von Friedrich Schwally. 1. Teil: Über den Ursprung des Qorans. Leipzig 1909. 2. Teil: Die Sammlung des Qorans. Leipzig 1919. 3. Teil: Die Geschichte des Korantextes. Von G. Bergsträßer und O. Pretzl. Leipzig 1938. Neudruck 1961

Rudi Paret: Arabistik und Islamkunde an Deutschen Universitäten. Deutsche Orientalisten seit Theodor Nöldeke. Wiesbaden 1966

Répertoire chronologique d'épigraphie arabe. Publié par M. Cohen (et al.) sous la direction de Et. Combe, J. Sauvaget et G. Wiet. 16 vol. Cairo 1931–1964. Index géographique du répertoire chronologique d'épigraphie arabe. Cairo 1975

Oskar Rescher: Abriß der arabischen Literaturgeschichte. Bd. 1. 2. Stuttgart 1925. 1933 — Neudruck mit Nachträgen. Osnabrück 1983

Rudolf Sellheim: Materialien zur Arabischen Literaturgeschichte. T. 1. Wiesbaden 1976 (Verzeichnis der Orientalischen Handschriften in Deutschland; Bd. XVII. Reihe A. T. 1)

Fuat Sezgin: Geschichte des arabischen Schrifttums ... bis ca. 430 H. Bd. 1: Qur'ānwissenschaften, Ḥadīṯ, Geschichte, Fiqh, Dogmatik, Mystik. Leiden 1967, Bd. 2: Poesie, Philologie, Unterhaltungsliteratur und erbauliche Schriften. Leiden 1975, Bd. 3: Medizin, Pharmazie, Zoologie, Tierheilkunde. Leiden 1970, Bd. 4: Alchemie, Chemie, Botanik, Agrikultur. Leiden 1971, Bd. 5: Mathematik. Leiden 1974, Bd. 6: Astronomie. Leiden 1978, Bd. 7: Astrologie und Meteorologie. Leiden 1979, Bd. 8: Lexikographie. Leiden 1982, Bd. 9: Grammatik. Leiden 1984

Moritz Steinschneider: Die arabische Literatur der Juden: Ein Beitrag zur Literaturgeschichte der Araber, großentheils aus handschriftlichen Quellen. Frankfurt/Main 1902. Neudruck 1964

Manfred Ullmann: Untersuchungen zur Ragazpoesie: Ein Beitrag zur arabischen Sprach- und Literaturwissenschaft. Wiesbaden 1966

M. J. L. Young, J. D. Latham, and R. B. Serjeant [ed.]: Religion, Learning, and Science in the Abbasid Period. Cambridge; New York 1990 (The Cambridge History of Arabic Literature)

Khayr ad-Dīn Ziriklī: الاعلام: قاموس تراجم لاشهر الرّجال والنّساء من العرب والمستعربين والمشتقرقين. 13 vol. Beirut 1389/1969 3. ed.

2. Historical Linguistics

Semitics

K. Ahrens: Der Stamm der schwachen Verba in den semitischen Sprachen. ZDMG 64 (1910) 161–194

Jussi Aro: Die Vokalisierung des Grundstammes im Semitischen Verbum. Helsinki 1964 (Studia orientalia, ed. Societas orientalis fennica; vol. XXXI)

—: Jacob Barth: Die Nominalbildung in den semitischen Sprachen. 2. Ausg. Leipzig 1894

—: Die Pronominalbildung in den semitischen Sprachen. Leipzig 1913

—: Sprachwissenschaftliche Untersuchungen zum Semitischen I. II. Leipzig 1907. 1911

Hans Bauer: Die Tempora im Semitischen und ihre Ausgestaltung in den Einzelsprachen. Leipzig 1910 (Beiträge zur Assyriologie und semitischen Sprachwissenschaft; VIII, 1)

Patrick R. Bennett: Comparative Semitic Linguistics : A Manual. Winona Lake, Ind. 1998

Gotthelf Bergsträßer: Einführung in die Semitischen Sprachen. Sprachproben und grammatische Skizzen. München 1928 — Im Anhang: Zur Syntax der Sprache von Ugarit von Carl Brockelmann. (Neudruck) Darmstadt 1963

—: [Einführung in die Semitischen Sprachen. English. 1995] Introduction to the Semitic Languages [2nd ed.]. Translated with notes and bibliography and an appendix on the scripts by Peter T. Daniels. Winona Lake, Ind. 1995

J. Blau: On Pseudo-Corrections in Some Semitic Languages. Jerusalem 1970 (Publications of the Israel Academy of Sciences and Humanities. Section of Humanities)

Klaus Boekels: Quadriradikalia in den semitischen Sprachen: unter besonderer Berücksichtigung des Arabischen (Thesis (doctoral)–Freie Universität Berlin, 1990)

G. J. Botterweck: Der Triliterismus im Semitischen. Bonn 1952 (Bonner Biblische Beiträge)

Meïr Max Bravmann: Genetic Aspects of the Genitive in the Semitic Languages. JAOS 81 (1961) 386–394

—: Some Aspects of the Development of Semitic Diphthongs. Orientalia N. S. 8 (1939) 244–253; 9 (1940) 45–60

—: On a Case of Quantitative Ablaut in Semitic. Orientalia N. S. 22 (1953) 1–24

Carl Brockelmann: Grundriß der vergleichenden Grammatik der semitischen Sprachen I–II. Berlin 1908–1913. Reprint: Hildesheim 1961

—: Deminutiv und Augmentativ im Semitischen. ZS 6 (1928) 109–134

—: Semitische Reimwortbildungen. ZS 5 (1927) 6–38

—: Die "Tempora" des Semitischen. Zeitschrift für Phonetik und allgemeine Sprachwissenschaft 5 (1951) 133–154

Jean Cantineau: La notion de "schème" et son altération dans diverses langues sémitiques. Semitica 3 (1950) 73–83

V. S. Chračkovskij: O charaktere oppozicii form *kataba/yaktubu* v arabskom jazyke. Kratkie soobščenija Instituta Vostokovedenija 86 (1965) 115–163

Viktor Christian: Das Wesen der semitischen Tempora. ZDMG 81 (1927) 232–258

David Cohen: Remarques sur la derivation nominale par affixes dans quelques langues sémitiques. Semitica 14 (1964) 73–92

Marcel Cohen: Essai comparatif sur le vocabulaire et la phonétique du Chamito-Sémitique. Paris 1947

—: Le Système verbal sémitique et l'expression du temps. Paris 1924

Federico C. Corriente: Introducción a la gramática comparada del semítico meridional. Madrid 1996 (Lenguas y culturas del antiguo Orient Próximo ; no. 1 Colección Textos universitarios. Consejo Superior de Investigaciones Científicas Spain; no. 25.)

—: On the Functional Yield of Some Synthetic Devices in Arabic and Semitic Morphology. Jewish Quarterly Review N. S. 62 (1971) 20–50

—: Again on the Functional Yield of some Synthetic Devices in Arabic and Semitic Morphology. Jewish Quarterly Review N. S. 64 (1973–1974) 154-163

Adolf Denz: Strukturanalyse der pronominalen Objektsuffixe im Altsyrischen und Klassischen Arabisch. Diss. München 1962

Développements récents en linguistique arabe et sémitique organisé et par Georges Bohas. – Damas 1993. (Publication de l'I.F.E.A.D.; no 142)

Y. M. Diakonoff: Afrasian Languages. Moscow 1988 (Languages of Asia and Africa)

—: Semito-Hamitic Languages. Moscow 1965

Werner Diem: Suffixkonjugation und Subjektspronomina: Ein Beitrag zur Rekonstruktion des Ursemitischen und zur Geschichte der Semitistik ZDMG 147 (1997) 10–76

Michel Féghali - Albert Cuny: Du genre grammatical en sémitique. Paris 1924

August Fischer: Ursemit. *e*, zum Demonstrativ *ḏ, tī*, und Verwandtes. ZDMG 59 (1905) 644–671

Wolfdietrich Fischer: K > Š in den südlichen Semitischen Sprachen (Kaškaša). Münchener Studien zur Sprachwissenschaft 8 (1956) 25–38

—: Die Position von ض im Phonemsystem des Gemeinsemitischen. Studia Orientalia in Memoriam Caroli Brockelmann, Halle (Saale) 1968, 55–63

Henri Fleisch: Introduction à l'étude des langues sémitiques: Eléments de bibliographie. Paris 1947

—: Les verbes à allongement vocalique interne sémitique: Études de grammaire comparée. Paris 1944

—: *yaqtula* cananéen et subjonctif arabe. Studia Orientatia in Memoriam Caroli Brockelmann, Halle (Saale) 1968, 65–76

—: Sur le système verbal du sémitique commun et son évolution dans les langues sémitiques anciennes. MUSJ 27 (1947/48) 36–60

Amikam Gai: The Category 'Adjective' in Semitic Languages. JSS 40 (1995) 1–9

Giovanni Garbini – Olivier Durand: Introduzione alle lingue semitiche. Brescia 1994. (Studi sul vicino oriente antico; 2)

Gideon Goldenberg: Studies in Semitic Linguistics: Selected writings. Jerusalem 1998

Joseph H. Greenberg: The Patterning of Root Morphemes in Semitic. Word 6 (1950) 162–181

Handbuch der Orientalistik, hrsg. von B. Spuler. Band III Semitistik. Mit Beiträgen von A. Baumstark, C. Brockelmann, E. L. Dietrich, J. Fück, M. Höfner, E. Littmann, A. Rücker, B. Spuler. Leiden 1952–1954

S. T. H. Hurwitz: Root-Determinatives in Semitic Speech. New York 1913

P. Joüon: Études de philologie sémitique. MUSJ 5 (1911) 355–404

—: Sémantique des verbes statifs de la forme *qatila* (*qatel*) en arabe, hebreu et araméen. MUSJ 15 (1930) 1–32

Geoffrey Khan: Studies in Semitic Syntax. Oxford 1988 (London Oriental Series; v. 38)

Burkhardt Kienast: Das Punktualthema *yaprus* und seine Modi. Orientalia N.S. 29 (1960) 151–167

August Klingenheben: Die Tempora Westafrikas und die Semitischen Tempora. Zeitschrift für Eingeborenen-Sprachen 19 (1928/29) 241–268

—: Die Präfix- und die Suffixkonjugation des Hamitosemitischen. Mitteilungen des Instituts für Orientforschung 4 (1950) 211–277

J. Kuryłowicz: L'apophonie en sémitique. Warszawa 1961

—: Esquisse d'une théorie de l'apophonie en sémitique. BSL 53 (1957/58) 1–38

—: Studies in Semitic Grammar and Metrics. Warszawa 1972 (Polska Akad. Nauk. Kom. język, prace język. 67)

—: Le système verbal du sémitique. BSL 45 (1949) 47–56

Paul de Lagarde: Obersicht über die im Aramäischen, Arabischen und Hebräischen übliche Bildung der Nomina, Göttingen 1889

Edward Lipiński: Semitic Languages: Outline of comparative grammar. Leuven 1997 (Orientalia lovaniensia analecta; 80)

De Lacy O'Leary: Comparative Grammar of the Semitic Languages. London 1923

Giorgio Levi Della Vida: Linguistica Semitica: presente e futuro ... studi di H. Cazalles, E. Cerulli, G. Garbini, W. von Soden, A. Spitaler, E. Ullendorff. Roma 1961

A. Martinet: Remarques sur le consonantisme sémitique. BSL 49 (1953) 67–78

Carl Meinhof: Was sind emphatische Laute und wie sind sie entstanden? Zeitschrift für Eingeborenensprachen 9 (1920/21) 81–106

Sabatino Moscati, Edward Ullendorff, Anton Spitaler, Wolfram von Soden: An Introduction to the Comparative Grammar of the Semitic Languages: Phonology and Morphology. Wiesbaden 1964

Sabatino Moscati: Il biconsonantismo nelle lingue semitiche. Biblia 28 (1947) 113–135

—: Il sistema consonantico delle lingue Semitiche. Roma 1954

Theodor Nöldeke: Beiträge zur semitischen Sprachwissenschaft. Straßburg 1904

—: Neue Beiträge zur semitischen Sprachwissenschaft. Straßburg 1910

—: Beiträge und Neue Beiträge zur semitischen Sprachwissenschaft: Achtzehn Aufsätze und Studien, teilweise in 2. verbesserter und vermehrter Aufl. Mit einem Nekrolog von C. Snouck Hurgronje. Straßburg 1904–1910. Neudruck 1982.

Henrik Samuel Nyberg: Zur Entwicklung der mehr als dreikonsonantischen Stämme in den semitischen Sprachen. Westöstliche Abhandlungen Rudolf Tschudi zum 70. Geburtstag (Wiesbaden 1954) 127–136

—: Wortbildung mit Präfixen in den semitischen Sprachen. MO 14 (1920) 177–272

Vladimir E. Orel, Olga V. Stolbova: Hamito-Semitic Etymological Dictionary: Materials for a reconstruction. Leiden; New York (Handbuch der Orientalistik. Erste Abteilung, der Nahe und Mittlere Osten; 18. Bd.)

K. Petráček: Die innere Flexion in den semitischen Sprachen. ArOr 28 (1960) 547–606; 29 (1961) 513–545; 30 (1962) 361–408; 31 (1963) 577–624; 32 (1964) 185–222

Robert R. Ratcliffe: The Broken Plural Problem in Arabic and Comparative Semitic: Allomorphy and analogy in non-concatenative morphology. Philadelphia 1998. (Amsterdam Studies in the Theory and History of Linguistic Science. Series IV, Current Issues in Linguistic Theory; v. 168)

—: Defining Morphological Isoglosses : The 'Broken' plural and Semitic subclassification. JNES 57 (1998) 81–23

H. Reckendorf: Über Paranomasie in den Semitischen Sprachen: Ein Beitrag zur Allgemeinen Sprachwissenschaft. Gießen 1909

Jan Retsö: Diathesis in the Semitic languages : A Comparative morphological study. Leiden; New York 1989 (Studies in Semitic languages and linguistics; 14)

Nikolaus Rhodokanakis: Reduplikation und Vokaldehnung, Druck und Ton in der semitischen Nominalbildung. WZKM 29 (1915) 60–73

André Roman: De la langue arabe comme un modèle de la formation des langues sémitiques et de leur évolution. Arabica 28 (1981) 127–161

Otto Rössler: Verbalbau und Verbalflexion in den Semitohamitischen Sprachen: Vorstudien zu einer vergleichenden Semitohamitischen Grammatik. ZDMG 100 (1950) 461–514

—: Akkadisches und libysches Verbum I. Orientalia N. S. 20 (1951) 101–107

Frithjof Rundgren: Ablaut und Apothematismus im Semitischen. Orientalia Suecana 13 (1964) 48–83

—: Semitische Wortstudien. Orientalia Suecana 10 (1961) 99–136

R. Růžička: Konsonantische Dissimilation in den semitischen Sprachen. Leipzig 1909 (Beiträge zur Assyriologie und semitischen Sprachwissenschaft; VII)

—: L'alternance de ʿain-ghain en arabe d'aprés les témoignages des grammairiens et lexicographes arabes. JA 221 (1932) 67–115

—: Quelques cas du ghain secondaire en arabe. JA 238 (1950) 269–318

—: Un cas de préfixe verbal ʿain-ghain en arabe. JA 227 (1935) 177–217

C. Sarauw: Über Akzent und Silbenbildung in den älteren semitischen Sprachen. Kopenhagen 1939

The Semitic Languages ed. Robert Hetzron. New York 1997 (Routledge Language Family Descriptions)

Semitic Studies : In Honor of Wolf Leslau on the occasion of his eighty-fifth birthday, November 14th, 1991 ed. Alan S. Kaye. Wiesbaden 1991

Ur Shlonsky: Clause Structure and Word Order in Hebrew and Arabic: An essay in comparative Semitic syntax. New York 1997 (Oxford Studies in Comparative Syntax)

J. M. Solá-Solé: L'Infinitiv sémitique: Contribution à 1'étude des formes et des fonctions des noms d'action et des infinitifs sémitiques. Paris 1961

Anton Spitaler: Zur Frage der Geminatendissimiiation im Semitischen. Zugleich ein Beitrag zur Kenntnis der Orthographie des Reichsaramäischen. Indogermanische Forschungen 61 (1954) 257–266

C. Tagliavini: Alcune osservazioni sul primitive valore della mimazione e nunazione nelle lingue semitiche: Donum natalicum Schrijnen (Chartres 1929) 240–290

Tempus und Aspekt in den semitischen Sprachen: Jenaer Kolloquium zur semitischen Sprachwissenschaft. Herausgeben von Norbert Nebes. Wiesbaden, 1999 (Jenaer Beiträge zum Vorderen Orient; 1.)

David Testen: Parallels in Semitic Linguistics: The Development of Arabic *la-* and related Semitic particles. Leiden; Boston 1998. (Studies in Semitic Languages and Linguistics; v. 26)

T. W. Thacker: The Relationship of the Semitic and Egyptian Verbal Systems. Oxford 1954

N. H. Torczyner: Die Entstehung des semitischen Sprachtypus, I. Wien 1916

Edward Ullendorff: The Form of the Definite Article in Arabic and other Semitic Languages. In: Arabic and Islamic Studies in Honor of Hamilton A. R. Gibb (Leiden 1965) 631–637

Rainer Maria Voigt: Die infirmen Verbaltypen des Arabischen und das Biradikalismus-Problem. Stuttgart; Wiesbaden 1988. (Veröffentlichungen der Orientalischen Kommission. Akademie der Wissenschaften und der Literatur, Mainz; Bd. 39)

-: Inkompatibilitäten und Diskrepanzen in der Sprache und das erste phonologische Inkompatibilitätsgesetz des Semitischen. Wirkendes Wort 38 (1988) 136–172

Karl Vollers: Arabisch und Semitisch: Gedanken über eine Revision der semitischen Lautgesetze. ZA 9 (1894) 165–217

Ewald Wagner: Der Übergang von Fragewörtern zu Negationen in den semitischen Sprachen. Mitteilungen des Instituts für Orientforschung 10 (1964) 261–274

Arent Jan Wensinck: Some Aspects of Gender in the Semitic Languages (Verhandlingen der Koninkl. Akademie van Wetenschappen Amsterdam, Afdeeling Letterkunde; XXVI, 3). Amsterdam 1926

William Wright: Lectures on the Comparative Grammar of the Semitic Languages. Cambridge 1890

Andrzej Zaborski: The Position of Arabic within the Semitic Dialect Continuum. The Arabist: Budapest Studies in Arabic 3–4 (1991) 365–375 (Proceedings of the Colloquium on Arabic Grammar, Budapest, 1–7 September 1991)

Old North Arabic

A. F. L. Beeston: Languages of Pre-Islamic Arabia. Arabica 28 (1981) 178–186

James A. Bellamy: A New Reading of the Namarah Inscription. JAOS 105 (1985) 31-48

A. van den Branden: Les inscription thamoudéennes. Louvain 1950 (Bibliothèque du Muséon Vol.; 25)

—: Les textes thamoudéns de Philby. 2 vol. Louvain 1956 (Bibliothèque du Muséon; Vol. 40. 41)

Jean Cantineau: Nabatéen et Arabe. AJEO 1 (1934/35) 77–97

Werner Caskel: Die Inschrift von en-Nemāra – neu gesehen. Mélanges de l'Université Saint-Joseph 45 (1969) 367–379

Corpus Inscriptionum Semiticarum. Pars V. Inscriptiones saracenicas continens, ed. G. Ryckmanns. Paris 1950

—: Lihyan und Lihyanisch. Köln-Opladen 1954 (Arbeitsgemeinschaft für Forschung des Landes Nordrhein-Westfalen. Geisteswissenschaften Heft 4)

Werner Diem: Die nabatäischen Inschriften und die Frage der Kasusflexion im Altarabischen. ZDMG 123 (1973) 227–237

René Dussaud: L'inscription nabatéo-arabe d'en-Nemāra. Revue Archéologique (1902) 409–421

G. Lancaster Harding: An Index and Concordance of Pre-Islamic Arabian Names and Inscriptions. Toronto 1971 (Near and Middle East Series; 8)

—: Preliminary Survey in N. W. Arabia 1968. Part II. Epigraphy. The Thamudic and Lihyanite Texts. Bulletin of the Institute of Archaeology 10 (1972) 36–52

Enno Littmann: Thamūd und Ṣafā: Studien zur altnordarabischen Inschriftenkunde (Abhandlungen für die Kunde des Morgenandes; XXV, 1). Leipzig 1940

—: Safaitic Inscriptions (Syria IV C). Leiden 1943

Hans P. Roschinski: Sprachen, Schriften und Inschriften in Nordwestarabien. Bonner Jahrbücher 180 (1980) 155–180

J. K. Stark: Personal Names in Palmyrene Inscriptions. Oxford 1971

Fredrick Victor Winnett: Safaitic Inscriptions from Jordan. Toronto 1957 (Near and Middle East Series; 2)

—: A Study of the Lihyanite and Thamudic Inscriptions. Toronto 1937

Classical Arabic, Middle Arabic, Arabic Dialects

Arne A. Ambros: Beobachtungen zu Aufbau und Funktionen der gereimter klassisch-arabischen Buchtitel WZKM 80 (1990) 13–57

ʿArabiyya [various authors: C. Rabin, M. Khalafallah, J. Fück, H. Wehr, H. Fleisch, Ph. Marçais, H. A. R. Gibb, et al.] Encyclopædia of Islam. New Ed. Vol. 1 561–603

E. Beck: ʿArabiyya, Sunna und ʿĀmma in der Koranlesung des zweiten Jahrhunderts. Orientalia N.S. 15 (1946) 180–224

R. Kirk Belnap, John Gee: Classical Arabic in Contact: The transition to near categorical agreement patterns. Perspectives on Arabic Linguistics VI (1994) 121-49: Papers from 6th Annual Symposium on Arabic

Linguistics (Amsterdam Studies in the Theory and History of Linguistic Science Series IV: Current Issues in Linguistic Theory, 115)

Joshua Blau: L'apparition du type linguistique néo-arabe. Revue des Études Islamique 38 (1969) 191-201

—: Die arabischen Dialekte der Juden des Mittelalters im Spiegel der jüdisch-arabischen Texte. Orbis 7 (1958) 159–167

—: The Beginnings of the Arabic Digiossia: A study of the origins of Neoarabic. Afroasiatic Linguistics 4 (Malibu 1977) 175–202

—: The Emergence and Linguistic Background of Judaeo-Arabic: A study of the origins of Middle Arabic. Oxford 1965. 2. ed. Jerusalem 1981

—: The Importance of Middle Arabic Dialects for the History of Arabic. In: Studies in Islamic history and civilization (Scripta Hierosolymitana 9, 1960) 206–228

—: Judaeo-Arabic in Its Linguistic Setting. Proceedings of the American Academy for Jewish Research 36 (1968) 1–12

—: On the Problem of the Synthetic Character of Classical Arabic as against Judaeo-Arabic (Middle Arabic). Jewish Quarterly Review N.S. (1972) 29–38

—: The Role of the Beduins as Arbiters in Linguistic Questions and the *Masʾala az-Zunbūriyya.* JSS 8 (1963) 42–51.

—: The State of Research in the Field of the Linguistic Study of Middle Arabic. Arabica 28 (1981) 187–203

—: Studies in Middle Arabic and Its Judaeo-Arabic Variety. Jerusalem 1988

—: Vernacular Arabic as Reflected by Middle Arabic (including Judæo-Arabic). The Arabist: Budapest Studies in Arabic 15–16 (1995) 11–15 (Proceedings of the 14th Congress of the Union Européenne des Arabisants et Islamisants II, Budapest 29th Aug.–3rd Sept. 1988)

Carl Brockelmann: Das Arabische und seine Mundarten. In: Handbuch der Orientalistik. Hrsg. von Bertold Spuler. Band 3. Semitistik. (Leiden 1954) 207–245

Frederic J. Cadora: Linguistic Change and the Bedouin-Sedentary Dichotomy in Old Arabic Dialects. Anthropological Linguistics 31 (1989) 264–84

Jean Cantineau: La dialectologie arabe. Orbis 4 (1955) 149–169

David Cohen: Koiné, langues communes et dialectes arabes. Arabica 9 (1962) 119–144

Federico C. Corriente: Marginalia on Arabic Diglossia and Evidence thereof in the Kitāb al-Aġānī. JSS 20 (1975) 38–61

—: From Old Arabic to Classical Arabic through the Pre-lslamic Koine. Some notes on the native grammarians' sources, attitudes and goals. JSS 21 (1976) 62–98

Werner Diem: Hochsprache und Dialekt im Arabischen: Untersuchungen zur heutigen arabischen Zweisprachigkeit. Wiesbaden 1974 (Abhandlungen f. d. Kunde des Morgenlandes; XLI, 1)

—: *Kawnahū rasūlan* (weil er Bote ist) und Verwandtes: Ein Beitrag zur Syntax des nachklassischen Arabisch. ZDMG 145 (1995) 49–105

Charles Ferguson: The Arabic Koine. Language 35 (1959) 616–630

Wolfdietrich Fischer: Die Perioden des Klassischen Arabisch. Abr-Nahrain 12 (1972) 15–18

Wolfdietrich Fischer und Otto Jastrow: Handbuch der Arabischen Dialekte. Mit Beiträgen von P. Behnstedt, H. Grotzfeld, B. Ingham, A. Sabuni, P. Schabert, H.-R. Singer, L. Tsotskhadze und M. Woidich. Wiesbaden 1980 (Porta linguarum Orientalium, N.S.; 16)

Georg Wilh. Freytag: Einführung in das Studium der arabischen Sprache. Bonn 1861.

Johann Fück: Arabiya. Untersuchungen zur arabischen Sprach- und Stilgeschichte. Berlin 1950 (Abhandlungen der Sächsischen Akademie der Wissenschaften zu Leipzig, Phil.-hist. Kl. Bd.; 45, 1)

Georg Graf: Der Sprachgebrauch der ältesten christlich-arabischen Literatur: Ein Beitrag zur Geschichte des Vulgär-Arabisch. Leipzig 1905

Jacques Grand'Henry: Quelques proto-formes nominales et verbales en Arabe Maghrébin. Studia Orientalia 75 (1995) 95–100

Benjamin H. Hary: Multiglossia in Judeo-Arabic: With an edition, translation and grammatical study of the Cairene Purim scroll. Leiden; New York 1992. (Études sur le judaïsme médiéval; t. 14)

Aḥmad ʿAlam ad-Dīn al-Jundī: أللّهجات العربيّة في التّراث. 2 vol. Cairo 1974

Paul Kahle: The Qurʾān and the ʿArabīya. Ignace Goldziher Memorial Volume. Vol. l. (Budapest 1948) 163–182

—: The Arabic Readers of the Koran. JNES 8 (1949) 65–71

Alan S. Kaye: Modern Standard Arabic and the Colloquials. Lingua 24 (1969/70) 374–391

K. Knutsson: Studies in the Text and Language of Three Syriac-Arabic Versions of the Book of Judicum with Special Reference to the Middle Arabic Elements. Leiden 1974

Hans Kofler: Reste altarabischer Dialekte. WZKM 47 (1940) 61–130, 233–262; 48 (1941) 52–88, 247–274; 49 (1942) 15–30; 734–256

Carlo de Landberg: La langue arabe et ses dialectes. Communication faite au XIVe Congrès International des Orientalistes à Alger. Leiden 1905

Enno Littmann: Survivals of the Arabic Dialects in the Arabic Literature. BFA 10 (1948) 1–58

August Müller: Über Text und Sprachgebrauch von Ibn Abî Uṣeibiʿa's Geschichte der Ärzte. Sitzungsberichte der K. bayer. Akad. der Wiss. 1884 853–977

Ghālib Fāḍil al-Muṭṭalibī: لهجة تميم وأثرها في العربيّة الموحّدة. Baghdad 1978

Karel Petráček: Material zum altarabischen Dialekt von al-Madīna. ArOr 22 (1954) 460–466

Chaim Rabin: The Beginnings of Classical Arabic. Studia Islamica 4 (1955) 19–37

—: Ancient West-Arabian. London 1951

ʿAbduh ar-Rājiḥī: اللّهجات العربيّة في القراءات القرآنيّة. Cairo 1968

Brigitte Reichel-Baumgartner: Parameter des Idiolekts des Propheten Muḥammad auf Grundlage des Ṣaḥīḥ von al-Buḫārī. WZKM 78 (1988) 121–159

André Roman: Étude de la phonologie et de la morphologie de la Koinè arabe. Tome I. II. Aix en Provence 1983

—: Les faits coranique poétique, prosodique et la stabilité de la koïnè arabe. Mélanges offerts au R. P. Henri Fleisch. Bd. l. Beirut 1976 = MUSJ 43 (1973/74) 217–230

Chr. Sarauw: Die altarabische Dialektspaltung. ZA 21 (1908) 31–49

J. Schen: Usama Ibn Munqidh's Memoirs. Some further light on Muslim Middle Arabic. JSS 17 (1972) 218–236; 18 (1973) 64–97

Harvey Sobelman: Arabic Dialect Studies: A selected bibliography. Washington D.C. 1962

David Testen: On the Arabic of the En Avdat Inscription. JNES 55 (1996) 281–292

J. Vilenčik: Zur Genesis der arabischen Zweisprachigkeit. OLZ 38 (1935) 721–727

Karl Vollers: Volkssprache und Schriftsprache im alten Arabien. Straßburg 1906

Michael Zwettler: The Oral Tradition of Classical Poetry: Its character and implications. Columbus (Ohio) 1978

Modern Written Arabic

Salih J. Altoma: The Problem of Diglossia in Arabic: A comparative study of classical and Iraqi Arabic. Cambridge, Mass. 1969 (Harvard Middle Eastern Monographs; XXI)

Mary Catherine Bateson: Arabic Language Handbook. Washington 1967

Anwar G. Chejne: The Arabic language: Its role in history. Minneapolis 1969

Rachad Hamzaoui: L'Académie Arabe de Damas et le problème de la modernisation de la langue arabe. Leiden 1965

Pierre Larcher: Passif grammatical, passif périphrastique et catégorie d'auxiliaire en arabe classique moderne. Arabica 37 (1990) 137–150

Jean Lecerf: L'arabe contemporain comme langue de civilisation. BEO 2 (1932) 179–258; 3 (1933) 43–175

Vincent Monteil: L'arabe moderne. Paris 1960 (Études et documents 3)

Hans Wehr: Entwicklung und traditionelle Pflege der arabischen Schriftsprache in der Gegenwart. ZDMG 97 (1943) 16–46

The Arabic Writing System

Nabia Abbott: Arabic Paleography. The development of early Islamic scripts. Ars Islamica 8 (1941) 65–104

—: The Rise of the North Arabic Script and Its Kur'anic Development with a Full Description of the Kur'an Manuscripts in the Oriental Institute. Chicago 1938 (Oriental Institute Publications; 50)

ALA-LC Romanization Tables: Transliteration schemes for non-roman scripts; approved by the Library of Congress and the American Library Association; tables compiled and ed. Randall K. Barry. 1997 ed. (Washington 1997) Arabic: 10–19

Werner Diem: Some Glimpses at the Rise and Early Development of the Arabic Orthography. Orientalia 45 (1976) 251–261

—: Untersuchungen zur frühen Geschichte der arabischen Orthographie. Orientalia 48 (1979) 207–257; 49 (1980) 67–106; 50 (1981) 332–383; 52 (1983) 367–404

Anīs Furaiḥa [Frayha]: حروف الهجاء العربيّة نشأتها تطوّرها مشاكلها. الابحاث 5 (Beirut 1952) 1–32

Adolf Grohmann: Arabische Paläographie. T. 1 (Einleitung. Die Beschreibstoffe. Die Schreibgeräte. Die Tinte). T. 2. Das Schriftwesen. Die Lapidarschrift. Wien 1967. 1971 (Forschungen zur islamischen Philologie und Kulturgeschichte 1, 2 = Österreichische Akademie der Wissenschaften. Phil.-hist. Klasse. Denkschriften; Bd. 94, 1.2)

—: The Problem of Dating Early Qur'āns. Der Islam 33 (1958) 213–231. Taf. I-V

Beatrice Gruendler: The Development of the Arabic Scripts: From the Nabatean era to the first Islamic century according to dated texts. Atlanta, Ga. 1993. (Harvard Semitic Studies; no. 43)

Suhaylah Yāsīn al-Jubūrī: أصل الخطّ العربي وتطوّره حتّى نهاية العصر الأموي. Baghdad 1977

Arthur Jeffery and J. Mendelsohn: The Orthography of the Samarqand Qur'an Codex. JAOS 62 (1942) 175–195

Ernst Kühnel: Islamische Schriftkunst. Berlin 1942 — Reprint: Graz 1975

Michael V. McDonald: The Order and Phonetic Value of Arabic Sibilants in the "Abjad". JSS 19 (1974) 36–46

T. F. Mitchell: Writing Arabic: A practical introduction to Ruqʿah script. London 1953

Shelomo Morag: The Vocalization System of Arabic, Hebrew and Aramaic: Their phonetic and phonemic principles. s'Gravenhage 1962 (Janua Linguarum; 13)

Bernd Moritz: Arabic Palaeography: A collection of Arabic texts from the first century of the Hidjra till the year 1000. Cairo 1905 (Publications of the Khedivial Library; 16)

Ṣalāḥ ad-Dīn al-Munajjid: دراسات في تاريخ الخطّ العربي منذ بدايته إلى نهاية العصر الأموي. Beirut 1972 (Études de paléographie arabe)

Salahuddin al-Munajjed: Le manuscrit Arabe jusqu'au Xe siècle de l'H., Tome I, Specimens. Le Caire 1960

Khalil Yahya Nami: The Origins of Arabic Writing and Its Historical Evolution before Islam. BFA 3 (1935) 1–112

Nāṣir an-Naqshbandī: منشأ الخطّ العربي وتطوّره لغاية عهد الخلفاء الرّاشدين. Sumer 3 (Baghdad 1947) 129–142; Tab. 1–4

E. J. Revell: The Diacritical Dots and the Development of the Arabic Alphabet. JSS 20 (1975) 178–190

Frank A. Rice: The Classical Arabic Writing System. Cambridge, Mass. 1959

Annemarie Schimmel: Islamic Calligraphy. Leiden 1970 (Iconography of Religions Section XXII: Islam, Fasc. 1)

P. Schwarz: Die Anordnung des arabischen Alphabets. ZDMG 69 (1915) 59–62

Khalil I. H. Semaan: A Linguistic View of the Development of the Arabic Writing System. WZKM 61 (1967) 22–40; Taf. 1–4

Moshe Sharon: Waqf Inscription from Ramla c. 300/912–13. BSOAS 60 (1997) 100–108

Hans-Rudolf Singer: Die arabische Schrift: Ihre Herkunft und Entwicklung. Studium Generale 18 (1965) 769–778

Anton Spitaler: واو عمرو und Verwandtes. In: Die islamische Welt zwischen Mittelalter und Neuzeit: Festschrift für Hans Robert Roemer (Beirut 1979) 591–608.

—: Die Schreibung des Typus صلوة im Koran. Ein Beitrag zur Erklärung der koranischen Orthographie. WZKM 56 (1960) 212–226.

Yasser Tabbaa: The Transformation of Arabic Writing: Part I, Qur'anic calligraphy. Ars Orientalis 21 (1991) 119–148

—: The Transformation of Arabic Writing. 2: The public text. Ars Orientalis 24 (1994) 119–147

Die Transliteration der arabischen Schrift in ihrer Anwendung auf die Hauptliteratursprachen der islamischen Welt. Denkschrift dem 19. Internationalen Orientalistenkongreß in Rom vorgelegt von der Transkriptionskommission der Deutschen Morgenländischen Gesellschaft: Carl Brockelmann, August Fischer, W. Heffening und Franz Taeschner mit Beiträgen von Ph. S. van Ronkel und Otto Spies. Leipzig 1935 (cf. also Aldo Mieli, H. P. J. Renaud, F. Taeschner in: Archeion 14 (1932) 436–444; Julius Ruska in: Archeion 17 (1935) 410–412; Franz Taeschner in: Atti del 19. Congresso Internazionale degli Orientalisti 1935. Roma 1938, 555–556)

Georges Vajda: Album de paléographie arabe. Paris 1958

Anthony Welch: Caligraphy in the Arts of the Muslim World. Austin 1979

3. Arabic Grammar

Grammars, Monographs

Arne A. Ambros: Einführung in die moderne arabische Schriftsprache. München 1969

A. F. L. Beeston: Written Arabic: An approach to the basic structures. Cambridge 1968

Joshua Blau: A Grammar of Christian Arabic: Based mainly on South-Palestinian texts from the first millennium. 3 vol. Louvain 1966–1967 (Corpus Scriptum Christianorum Orientalium Vol. 267, 276, 279)

—: Diḳduḳ ha-ʿArvit-ha-Yehudit shel yeme-ha-benayim (Grammar of mediæval Judaeo-Arabic). Hadpasah ḥozeret. Yerushalayim, 1995

Alfred Bloch: Vers und Sprache im Altarabischen: Metrische und syntaktische Untersuchungen. Basel 1946

Max Meïr Bravmann: Studies in Arabic and General Syntax. Cairo 1953 (Publications de l'Institut Français d'Archéologie Orientale du Caire)

Carl Brockelmann: Arabische Grammatik: Paradigmen, Literatur, Übungsstücke und Glossar. 23. Aufl. – ed. Manfred Fleischhammer. München 1987

Vincente Cantarino: Syntax of Modern Arabic Prose. 3 vol. Bloomington-London 1974–1975

Dr. C. P. Caspari's Arabische Grammatik, 5. Aufl. bearbeitet von August Müller. Halle 1887

Georg Henr. Aug. Ewald: Grammatica critica linguae arabicae cum brevi metrorum doctrine, 1. I. III. Lipsiae 1831–1833

Wolfdietrich Fischer: Classical Arabic. In: The Semitic Languages. Ed. Robert Hetzron (London 1997) 187–219 (Routledge Language Family Descriptions)

Wolfdietrich Fischer and Otto Jastrow: Lehrgang für die Arabische Schriftsprache der Gegenwart. 2 vol. Wiesbaden 1976. 1986

Henri Fleisch: L'arabe classique: Esquisse d'une structure linguistique. Nouv. éd. Beyrouth 1968

—: Traité de philologie arabe. 2 Vol. Beirut 1961. 1979 (Recherches. Collection publiée sous la direction de la Faculté des Lettres et des Sciences Humaines de l'Université Saint-Joseph)

Maurice Gaudefroy-Demombynes - Régis Blachère: Grammaire de l'arabe classique. Paris 1937 — 3e éd. 1952

Ernst Harder – Annemarie Schimmel: Arabische Sprachlehre (Methode Gaspey-Otto Sauer), 11. Auflage. Heidelberg 1968

Regina Hartmann: Untersuchungen zur Syntax der Arabischen Schriftsprache. Wiesbaden 1974

ʿAbbās Ḥasan: النّحو الوافي مع ربطه بالاساليب الرفيعة والحياة اللّغويّة المتجدّدة. 4 Vol. Cairo [4]1971

John A. Haywood and H. M. Nahmad: A New Arabic Grammar of the Written Language. London 1962

—: Key to a New Arabic Grammar of the Written Language. London 1964

Simon Hopkins: Studies in the Grammar of Early Arabic: Based upon papyri datable to before A.H. 300/A.D. 912. Oxford 1984. (London Oriental Series; Vol. 37)

Mortimer Sloper Howell: A Grammar of the Classical Arabic Language: Translated and compiled from the works of the most approved native or naturalized authorities, I–IV. Allahabad 1880–1911. Reprint (with a new preface by Satkari Mukhopadhyaya) Delhi 1986

N. V. Jušmanov: Grammatika literaturnogo arabskogo jazyka pod redakciej i s predisloviem J. J. Kračkovskogo. Leningrad 1928. 3. ed. Moscow 1985.

Theodor Nöldeke: Zur Grammatik des Classischen Arabisch. Wien 1896 (Denkschriften der Kaiserl. Akademie der Wissenschaften, Phil.-hist. Cl.; Bd. 45, Abh. 2)

—: Zur Grammatik des Classischen Arabisch. Im Anhang: Die handschriftlichen Ergänzungen in dem Handexemplar Theodor Nöldekes, bearbeitet und mit Zusätzen versehen von Anton Spitaler. Darmstadt 1963

Hermann Reckendorf: Arabische Syntax. Heidelberg 1921

—: Die syntaktischen Verhältnisse des Arabischen, Tl. 1. 2. Leiden 1895–1898. Reprint in 1 vol. Leiden 1967

W. Reuschel und G. Krahl: Lehrbuch des Modernen Arabisch. Teil I von G. Krahl u. W. Reuschel. Leipzig 1976. 2. ed. Teil II von Dieter Blohm, Wolfgang Reuschel und Abed Samarraie. Leipzig 1981

Abdulghafur Sabuni: Arabische Grammatik: Ein Lernbuch anhand moderner Lektüre. Hamburg 1987

Anton Schall: Elementa arabica: Einführung in die klassische Sprache. Wiesbaden 1988

Antoine Issac Silvestre de Sacy: Grammaire arabe à l'usage des élèves de l'école spéciale des langues orientales vivantes. Sec. éd. I. II. Paris 1831 – 3. éd. revue par L. Machuel. Paris 1904

D. V. Semënov: Sintaksis sovremennogo arabskogo literaturnogo jazyka. Moskva/Leningrad 1941

Wheeler Thackston: An Introduction to Koranic and Classical Arabic: An Elementary grammar of the language. Bethesda, Md. 1994

Manfred Ullmann: Adminiculum zur Grammatik des klassischen Arabisch. Wiesbaden 1989

Laura Veccia Vaglieri: Grammatica teorico-pratica della Lingua Araba, I. II. Roma 1937. 4 éd. 1959–1961

P. Donat Vernier: Grammaire arabe composé d'après les sources primitives I. II. Beyrouth 1891–1892

William Wright: A Grammar of the Arabic Language: Translated from the German of Caspari and edited, with numerous additions and corrections. 3. ed. revised by W. Robertson Smith and M. J. de Goeje, I. II. Cambridge 1896–1898 — Reprint: 1991

Metrics, Prosody

Jean-Pierre Angoujard: Metrical Structure of Arabic. Dordrecht; Providence, RI 1990. (Publications in language sciences 35)

A. F. L. Beeston: A Matter of Length. JSS 34 (1989) 347–354

—: Antecedents of Classical Arabic Verse? In: Festschrift Ewald Wagner zum 65. Geburtstag, I: Semitische Studien unter besonderer Berücksichtigung der Südsemitistik, (Stuttgart 1994) 234–243 (Beiruter Texte und Studien; 54)

Georg Wilh. Freytag: Darstellung der arabischen Verskunst ... nach handschriftlichen Quellen bearbeitet. Bonn 1830

Johann Fück: Bemerkungen zur altarabischen Metrik. ZDMG 111 (1961) 464–469

Chris Golston – Thomas Riad: The Phonology of Classical Arabic Meter. Linguistics 35 (1997) 111–132

Gustav Hölscher: Arabische Metrik. ZDMG 74 (1920) 359–416

Aug. Friedr. Mehren: Die Rhetorik der Araber nach den wichtigsten Quellen dargestellt und mit angeführten Textauszügen nebst einem literaturgeschichtlichen Anhang versehen. Kopenhagen 1853

J. Vadet: Contribution à l'histoire de la métrique arabe. Arabica 2 (1955) 312–321

Gotthold Weil: ʿArūḍ. Encyclopædia of Islam, New Edition, vol. 1 667–677 (1954–)

—: Grundriß und System der altarabischen Metren. Wiesbaden 1958

—: Das metrische System des al-Ḫalīl und der Iktus in den altarabischen Versen. Oriens 7 (1954) 304–321

Native Arabic Grammar

Aḥmad b. ʿAlī b. Masʿūd on Arabic Morphology = مراح الارواح. ed. with translation, commentary, and introduction by Joyce Åkesson. Leiden; New York 1990– (Studia orientalia lundensia; v. 4)

Nadia Anghelescu: Les Éléments du métalangage dans un chapitre d'Ibn Ǧinni. The Arabist: Budapest Studies in Arabic, 6–7 (1993) 205–213 (Proceedings of the Colloquium on Arabic Lexicology and Lexicography (C.A.L.L.) Budapest, 1–7 September 1993)

Georgine Ayoub: La Forme du sens: Le Cas du nom et le mode du verbe. The Arabist: Budapest Studies in Arabic 3–4 (1991) 37–87 (Proceedings of the Colloquium on Arabic Grammar, Budapest, 1–7 September 1991)

—: De ce qui 'ne se dit pas' dans le Livre de Sībawayhi: La Notion de *tamṯīl*. In: Studies in the History of Arabic Grammar II: Proc. of the 2nd Symposium on the Hist. of Arabic Grammar, Nijmegen, 27 Apr.–1 May 1987. (Amsterdam; Philadelphia 1990) 1–15 (Amsterdam Studies in the Theory and History of Linguistic Science Series III: Studies in the History of the Language Sciences 56)

Ramzi Baalbaki: *Iʿrāb* and *Bin* from Linguistic Reality to Grammatical Theory. In Studies in the History of Arabic Grammar II: Proc. of the 2nd Symposium on the Hist. of Arabic Grammar, Nijmegen, 27 Apr.–1 May 1987 (Amsterdam; Philadelphia 1990) 17–33 (Amsterdam Studies in the Theory and History of Linguistic Science Series III: Studies in the History of the Language Sciences, 56)

—: Reclassification in Arab Grammatical Theory. JNES 54 (1995) 1–13

Monique Bernards: Changing Traditions: Al-Mubarrad's refutation of Sībawayh and the subsequent reception of the Kitab. Leiden; New York 1997 (Studies in Semitic Languages and Linguistics; 23)

Georges Bohas, J.-P. Guillaume, D. E. Kouloughli. The Arabic Linguistic Tradition. London; New York 1990. (Arabic Thought and Culture)

—: L'Analyse linguistique dans la tradition arabe. In: Philosophie et langage: Histoire des idées linguistiques, I: La Naissance des métalangages en Orient et en Occident, 260–82 (Liege 1989)

M. G. Carter: Arab Linguistics. An introductory classical text with translation and notes. Amsterdam 1981 (Amsterdam Studies in the Theory and History of Linguistic Sciences III 24)

—: *Qāḍī, Qāḍi, Qāḍ*: Which is the odd man out? In: Studies in the History of Arabic Grammar II: Proc. of the 2nd Symposium on the Hist. of Arabic Grammar, Nijmegen, 27 Apr.–1 May 1987, (Amsterdam; Philadelphia 1990) 73–90 (Amsterdam Studies in the Theory and History of Linguistic Science Series III: Studies in the History of the Language Sciences, 56)

—: When Did the Word 'Naḥw' Come to Denote Grammar? Amsterdam Studies in the Theory and History of Linguistic Science. Studies in the History of the Language Science 38 (1987) 85–96

—: Writing the History of Arabic Grammar. Historiographia Linguistica 21 (1994) 385–414

Janusz Danecki: Al-Mubarrad's Place in the History of Arabic Grammar. In: History and Historiography of Linguistics: Papers from the Fourth International Conference on the History of the Language Sciences (ICHoLS IV), Trier, 24–28 August 1987. Vol. I 135–146 (Amsterdam 1990) (Amsterdam Studies in the Theory and History of Linguistic Science. Series III: Studies in the History of the Language Sciences, 51)

—: The Category of Gender in the Arabic Grammatical Tradition. Rocznik Orientalistyczny 48 (1993) 57–67

—: The Notion of *Tamakkun* in Sībawayhi's Grammar. Rocznik Orientalistyczny 48 (1993) 121-130

—: The Phonetical Theory of Mubarrad. In: Studies in the History of Arabic Grammar II: Proc. of the 2nd Symposium on the Hist. of Arabic Grammar, Nijmegen, 27 Apr.–1 May 1987 (Amsterdam; Philadelphia 1990) 91–99 (Amsterdam Studies in the Theory and History of Linguistic Science Series III: Studies in the History of the Language Sciences, 56)

Kinga Dévényi: Explaining *Iʿrāb* and Analysing Text: On *madḥ* and *taṭāwul* in early Arabic grammar. The Arabist: Budapest Studies in Arabic, 15–16 (1995) 17–26 (Proceedings of the 14th Congress of the Union Européenne des Arabisants et Islamisants, II, Budapest, 29th Aug.–3rd Sept. 1988)

—: The Treatment of Conditional Sentences by the Mediaeval Arabic Grammarians: Stability and change in the history of Arabic grammar. The Arabist: Budapest Studies in Arabic I (1988) 11–42

Werner Diem: Bibliography/Bibliographie: Sekundärliteratur zur einheimischen arabischen Grammatikschreibung. In: The History of Linguistics in the Near East. Amsterdam 1983. 195–250 (Amsterdam Studies in the Theory and History of Linguistic Science. Series III Studies in the History of Linguistics 28)

—: Sekundärliteratur zur einheimischen arabischen Grammatikschreibung. Historiographia Linguistica 8 (1981) 431–486.

Early Medieval Arabic: Studies on al-Khalīl ibn Aḥmad. Ed. Karin C. Ryding. Washington, DC 1998.

Abdelali Elamrani-Jamal: Verbe, copule, nom dérivé (*fiʿl, kalima, ism muštaqq*) dans les commentaires arabes du *Peri Hermeneias* d'Aristote (avec un texte inédit d'Ibn Rušd). In: Studies in the History of Arabic Grammar II: Proc. of the 2nd Symposium on the Hist. of Arabic Grammar, Nijmegen, 27 Apr.–1 May 1987 (Amsterdam; Philadelphia 1990) 151–164 (Amsterdam Studies in the Theory and History of Linguistic Science Series III: Studies in the History of the Language Sciences 56)

Essam Abdel Aziz Fayez: Siibawaih's Linguistic Analysis of the Diminutive in Classical Arabic and Its Subsequent Developments. (Ph.D. Dissertation: Georgetown University 1990)

Henri Fleisch: Arabic Linguistics. In: [Storia della linguistica. English] History of linguistics. ed. Giulio Lepschy. I: The Eastern Traditions of Linguistics 164–84 (London 1994) (Longman Linguistics Library)

—: Esquisse d'une histoire de la grammaire arabe. Arabica 4 (1957) 1–22

Gustav Flügel: Die grammatischen Schulen der Araber. Leipzig 1862 (Abhandlungen der Deutschen Morgenländischen Gesellschaft; 114)

Christiane Gille: Das Kapitel Al-Mauṣūl ("Das Relativum") aus dem Manhağ as-sālik des Grammatikers Abū Ḥaiyān al-Ġarnaṭī (1256–1344). Hildesheim; New York 1995 (Arabistische Texte und Studien; Bd. 7)

Gideon Goldenberg: *Allaḏī al-Maṣdariyyah* in Arab Grammatical Tradition. ZAL 28 (1994) 7–35

Ignác Goldziher: On the History of Grammar among the Arabs: An essay in literary history. trans. and ed. by Kinga Dévényi, Tamás Iványi. Amsterdam; Philadelphia 1994 (Amsterdam Studies in the Theory and History of Linguistic Science. Series III: Studies in the History of the Language Sciences v. 73)

Jean-Patrick Guillaume: Le Discours tout entier est nom, verbe et particule: Elaboration et constitution de la théorie des parties du discours dans la tradition grammaticale arabe. Langages 92 (1988) 25–36

—: Sībawayhi et l'énonciation: Une proposition de lecture. Histoire, Epistémologie Langage 8 (1986) 53–62

Adrian Gully: Grammar and Semantics in Medieval Arabic: A study of Ibn-Hishām's 'Mughnī l-Labīb'. Richmond 1995

Hassan Hamzé: La coordination à un pronom 'conjoint' dans la tradition grammaticale. Arabica 36 (1989) 249–271

—: Les parties du discours dans la tradition grammaticale arabe. Linguistique et sémiologie (Lyon) 1994 93–115

Ibn al-Anbārī: Die grammatischen Streitfragen der Basrer und Kufer, herausgegeben, erklärt und eingeleitet von Gotthold Weil. Leiden 1913

Ibn ʿAqīl: Ibn ʿAḳīl's Commentar zur Alfijja des Ibn Mālik. Aus dem Arabischen zum ersten Male übersetzt von F. Dieterici. Berlin 1852

Boubker Intissar: L'Accord verbal dans le discours de la tradition grammaticale arabe: Esquisse d'une lecture. Faits de Langues: Revue de Linguistique 8 (1996) 25–32

Tamás Iványi: The Term *ḥadd* at Sībawayhi: A list and a contextual analysis. The Arabist: Budapest Studies in Arabic, 15–16 (1995) 57–68 (Proceedings of the 14th Congress of the Union Européenne des Arabisants et Islamisants II, Budapest, 29th Aug.–3rd Sept. 1988)

Naphtali Kinberg: 'Clause' and 'Sentence' in *Maʿānī l-Qurʾān* by al-Farrāʾ: A Study of the term *kalām*. The Arabist: Budapest Studies in Arabic, 3–4 (1991) 239–246 (Proceedings of the Colloquium on Arabic Grammar, Budapest, 1–7 September 1991)

—: The Concepts of Elevation and Depression in Medieval Arabic Phonetic Theory. ZAL 17 (1987) 7–20

Pierre Larcher: Les ʾAmâlî de ibn al-Ḥâĝib ou les "annales" d'un grammairien. Arabica 41 (1994) 273–280

—: La particule *lâkinna* vue par un grammairien arabe du XIII siècle ou comment une description de détail s'inscrit dans une 'théorie pragmatique'. Historiographia Linguistica 19 (1992) 1–24

Abdulmunim Abdulamir Al-Nassir: Sībawayh the Phonologist: A critical study of the phonetic and phonological theory of Sībawayh as presented in his treatise Al-Kitāb. London 1993. (Library of Arabic Linguistics)

E. Y. Odisho: Sībawayhi's Dichotomy of *majhūra/mahmūsa* Revisited. Al-ʿArabiyya 21 (1988) 81–91

El-Sayed Ahmed Osman: The Phonological Theory of Si:bawaihi: An eighth century Arab grammarian (Ph.D. Dissertation: Georgetown University, 1988)

Jonathan Owens: The Foundations of Grammar. An introduction to medieval Arabic grammatical theory. Amsterdam; Philadelphia 1988. (Amsterdam Studies in the Theory and History of Linguistic Science. Series III. Studies in the History of the Language Science v. 45)

—: Early Arabic Grammatical Theory: Heterogeneity and standardization. Amsterdam ; Philadelphia 1990 (Amsterdam Studies in the Theory and History of Linguistic Science. Series III, Studies in the History of the Language Sciences v. 53)

Yishai Peled: Aspects of Case Assignment in Medieval Arabic Grammatical Theory. WZKM 84 (1994) 133–158

Franz Praetorius: Die grammatische Rektion bei den Arabern. ZDMG 63 (1909) 495–503

Oskar Rescher: Studien über Ibn Ǧinnī und sein Verhältnis zu den Theorien der Baṣrī und Baġdādī. ZA 29 (1909) 1–54

Abū 'l-Ḥasan ar-Rummānī: Sieben Kapitel des Šarḥ Sibawaihi. Edition und Übersetzung von E. Ambros. Wien 1979 (Beihefte zur Wiener Zeitschrift für die Kunde des Morgenlandes; 9)

Solomon I. Sara: Al-Xaliil: The first theoretical statement on Arabic phonetics. In: Actes du XVe Congrès International des Linguistes, Quebec, Université Laval, 9–14 aout 1992: Les Langues menacées/Endangered Languages = Proceedings of the XVth International Congress of Linguists, Quebec, Université Laval, 9–14 August 1992, II, 103-06 (Sainte-Foy PU Laval 1993)

—: The Beginning of Phonological Terminology in Arabic. The Arabist: Budapest Studies in Arabic, 6–7 (1993) 181-94 (Proceedings of the Colloquium on Arabic Lexicology and Lexicography (C.A.L.L.), I, Budapest, 1–7 September 1993)

Sībawaih: Sībawaih's Buch über die Grammatik nach der Ausgabe von H. Derenbourg und der Kommentar des Sīrāfī übersetzt und erklärt von G. Jahn, 3 Vol. Berlin 1884–1900

M. Y. Suleiman: Sībawaihi's 'Parts of Speech' according to Zajjājī: A new interpretation. JSS 35 (1990) 245–263

Zeinab A. Taha: Issues of Syntax and Semantics: A comparative study of Sibawayhi, al-Mubarrad, and Ibn as-Sarraj (Ph.D. Dissertation: Georgetown University, 1995)

—: The Term *ṣila* in Early Arab Grammatical Theory: The case of Ibn as-Sarrāǧ. The Arabist: Budapest Studies in Arabic, 6–7 (1993) 233–244 (Proceedings of the Colloquium on Arabic Lexicology and Lexicography (C.A.L.L.) I, Budapest, 1–7 September 1993)

Rafael Talmon: Arabic Grammar in Its Formative Age : Kitāb al-ʿAyn and its attribution to Ḫalīl b. Aḥmad. Leiden; New York 1997 (Studies in Semitic languages and Linguistics; 25)

—: *Ḥattā* + Imperfect and Chapter 239 in Sībawayhī's *Kitāb*: A study in the early history of Arabic grammar. JSS 38 (1993) 71–95

—: *Musnad, musnad ilayhi* and the Early History of Arabic Grammar: A Reconstruction. JRAS 2 (1987) 208–222

Naḥwiyyūn in Sībawayhi's *Kitāb* ZAL 8 (1982) 14 38

—: Two Early 'Non-Sībawaihian' Views of *ʿamal* in Kernel-Sentences. ZAL 25 (1993) 278–288

Gérard Troupeau: Lexique-index du Kitāb Sībawaihi. Paris 1976 (Études arabes et islamiques; III 7)

C. (Kees) H. M. Versteegh: Arabic Grammar and Qurʾanic Exegesis in Early Islam. Leiden; New York 1993 (Studies in Semitic Languages and Linguistics; 19)

—: The Arabic Tradition. In: The Emergence of Semantics in Four Linguistic Traditions: Hebrew, Sanskrit, Greek, Arabic (Amsterdam 1997) 225–283 (Amsterdam Studies in the Theory and History of Linguistic Science III, 82)

—: Current Bibliography on the History of Arabic Grammar. ZAL 10 (1983) 86–89; 11 (1983) 84–86; 12 (1984) 86–89; 14 (1985) 79–81; 16 (1987) 130–133

—: 'Early' and 'Late' Grammarians in the Arab Tradition: The morphonology of the hollow verbs. ZAL 20 (1989) 9–22

—: The Explanation of Linguistic Causes: Az-Zaǧǧāǧī's theory of grammar: Introduction, translation, commentary. Amsterdam 1995 (Amsterdam Studies in the Theory and History of Linguistic Science Series III: Studies in the History of the Language Sciences; 75)

—: Freedom of the Speaker? The term *Ittisāʿ* and related notions in Arabic grammar. In: Studies in the History of Arabic Grammar II: Proc. of the 2nd Symposium on the Hist. of Arabic Grammar, Nijmegen, 27 Apr.–1 May 1987 (Amsterdam; Philadelphia 1990) 281–293 (Amsterdam Studies in the Theory and History of Linguistic Science Series III: Studies in the History of the Language Sciences, 56)

—: Greek Elements in Arabic Linguistic Thinking. Leiden 1977 (Studies in Semitic Languages and Linguistics; 7)

—: Landmarks in Linguistic Thought III: The Arabic linguistic tradition. London 1997

—: The Notion of 'Underlying Levels' in the Arabic Grammatical Tradition. Historiographia Linguistica 21 (1994) 271–296

4. Detailed Treatises on Arabic Linguistics

General

Salman H. Al-Ani [ed.]: Readings in Arabic Linguistics. Bloomington 1978

Salman H. Ani – Dilworth D. Parkinson: Arabic Linguistics Bibliography, Bloomington, Ind. 1996 (Indiana University Linguistics Club Publications)

Muhammad Hasan Bakalla: Arabic Linguistics: An introduction and bibliography. London 1983

—: Bibliography of Arabic Linguistics. London 1975

Jean Cantineau: Études de linguistique arabe: Mémorial J. Cantineau. Paris 1960

Heinrich Leberecht Fleischer: Kleinere Schriften I–III. Leipzig 1886–1888

Richard S. Harrell – Haim Blanc: Contributions to Arabic Linguistics. Ed. Charles A. Ferguson. Cambridge, Mass. 1960 (Harvard Middle Eastern Monographs; 3)

Carolyn G. Killean: Classical Arabic. In: Current Trends in Linguistics vol. 6. (Den Haag – Paris 1970) 413–438.

Karl Petráček: A Study in the Structure of Arabic. Acta Universitatis Carolinae Philologica 1 (1960), Orientalia Pragensia 1, 33–39

B. Hunter Smeaton: Some Problems in the Description of Arabic. Word 12 (1956) 357–368

A. Spitaler: Arabisch. In: G. Levi Della Vida: Linguistica semitica Presente e futuro. Rom 1961 (Università di Roma. Istitutio di Studi del Vicino Oriente. Centro di Studi Semitici. Studi Semitici; no. 4)

C. (Kees) M. H. Versteegh: The Arabic Language. New York 1997

N. V. Yushmanov: The Structure of the Arab Language, Translated from the Russian by Moshe Perlmann. Washington 1961

Phonology

Hassan R. S. Abdel-Jawad – Mohammad Awwad: Reflexes of Classical Arabic Interdentals: A study in historical sociolinguistics. Linguistische Berichte 122 (1989) 259–282

Salman H. Al Ani: Arabic Phonology: An accoustical and physiological investigation. The Hague 1970 (Janua Linguarum 61)

—: Lexical Stress Variation in Arabic: An acoustic spectographic analysis. The Arabist: Budapest Studies in Arabic 3–4 (1991) 9–27 (Proceedings of the Colloquium on Arabic Grammar, Budapest, 1–7 September 1991)

—: Phonology of Contemporary Standard Arabic. Indiana University diss. 1963

Muhammad Hasan Bakalla: A Chapter from the History of Arabic Linguistics: Ibn Jinnī, an early Arab Muslim phonetician. London-Taipei 1982

—: Sibawaihi's Constribution to the Study of Arabic Phonetics. Al-ʿArabiyya 12 (1979) 68–76

A. F. L. Beeston: Arabian Sibilants. JSS 7 (1962) 222–233

Harris Birkeland: Stress Patterns in Arabic. Oslo 1954 (Skrifter utg. av det Norske Videnskaps-Akademi i Oslo, Hist.-filos. kl. 1954, no. 3)

Haim Blanc: The 'Sonorous' vs. 'Muffled' Distinction in Old Arabic Phonology. In: To Honor Roman Jakobson (The Hague 1967) 295–308

(Meïr) Max Bravmann: Materialien und Untersuchungen zu den Phonetischen Lehren der Araber. (Dissertation Breslau) Göttingen 1934

A. Bricteux: Le hamza, étude de phonétique et de grammaire arabes. Muséon N. S. 35 (1922) 109–130

Wolfdietrich Fischer: Silbenstruktur und Vokalismus im Arabischen. ZDMG 117 (1967) 30–77

Henri Fleisch: Études de Phonétique arabe. MUSJ 28 (1949/1950) 78–94

—: Mağhūra, Mahmūsa: Examen critique. MUSJ 28 (1958) 193–234

W. H. T. Gairdner: The Phonetics of Arabic: A phonetic inquiry and practical manual for the pronunciation of classical Arabic and of one colloquial (the Egyptian). London 1925

Max T. Grünert: Die Imala, der Umlaut im Arabischen. Wien 1876

Isḥāq Mūsā al-Ḥusainī: المقطعيّة في اللّغة العربيّة. MMLA 5 (1962) 24–56

Roman Jakobson: Mufaxxama: The 'Emphatic' Phonemes in Arabic. In: Studies presented to J. Whatmough (1957) 105–115

Otto Jastrow: Zur Entwicklung des Wortakzents im Arabischen. Forum Phoneticum 47 (1991) 37–54

Georg Kampffmeyer: Untersuchungen über den Ton im Arabischen I. MSOS 11 (1908), 2. Abt., 1–59

Hartmut Kästner: Phonetik und Phonologie des modernen Hocharabisch. Leipzig 1981

Georg Krotkoff: Nochmals: mağhūra, mahmūsa. WZKM 59/60 (1963/64) 147–153

Mayer Lambert: De l'accent en arabe. JA IX 10 (1897) 402-413

A. Martinet: La palatalisation spontanée de *g* en arabe. BSL 54 (1959) 90–102

—: L'élif wesla. JA IX 5 (1895) 224–234

D. H. Obrecht: Three Experiments in the Perception of Geminate Consonants in Arabic. Language and Speech 8 (1965) 31–41

Karl Petráček: Der doppelte phonologische Charakter des Ghain im Klassischen Arabisch. ArOr 21 (1953) 240–262

P. Philippi: Das Alifu l-Waṣli: Eine Erwiderung. ZDMG 49 (1895) 187–209

André Roman: Le système consonantique de la Koinè arabe au VIIIe siècle d'après le Kitab de Sibawayhi. CLOS 9 (1977) 63–98

—: Les zones d'articulation de la Koinè arabe d'après l'enseignement d'al-Ḫalīl. Arabica XXIV (1977) 58–65

Jean Rousseau: La découverte de la racine trilatère en sémitique par l'idéologue Volney. Historiographia Linguistica 14 (1987) 341–365

Arthur Schaade: Sībawaihi's Lautlehre. Leiden 1911

Khalil I. H. Semaan: Arabic Phonetics: Ibn Sīnā's Risālah on the points of articulation of the speechsounds translated. Lahore 1963

—: Linguistics in the Middle Ages: Phonetic studies in early Islam. Leiden 1968

Arnold Steiger: Contribución a la fonética del hispano-árabe y de los arabismos en el ibero-románico y el siciliano. Madrid 1932 (Revista de filologia española, Anejo 17)

Jacques Thiry: Les Consonnes faibles de l'arabe: Maintiens et mutations. Rapport d'Activités de l'Institut des Langues Vivantes et de Phonétique 23–24 (1989) 139–185

Karl Vollers: The System of Arabic Sounds as Based upon Sibawaih and Ibn Yaish. Transactions of the 9th International Congress of Orientalists, London 1893, II 130–154

Georg Wallin: Über die Laute des Arabischen und ihre Bezeichnung. ZDMG 9 (1855) 1–69; 12 (1858) 599–655

Gotthold Weil: Die Behandlung des Hamza-Alif im Arabischen. ZA 19 (1906) 1–63

Petr Zemanek: A propos de la pharyngalisation et la glottalisation en arabe. ArOr 58 (1990)125 134

—: The Role of *q* in Arabic. ArOr 65 (1997) 143–158

Morphology and Syntax

Kjell Aartun: Zur Frage altarabischer Tempora. Oslo 1963

Mohamad Z. Abd-Rabbo: Some Morphological Constraints in Classical Arabic (Ph.D. Dissertation: Stanford University 1988)

—: Sound Plural and Broken Plural Assignment in Classical Arabic. Perspectives on Arabic Linguistics I (1990) 55–93: Papers from First Annual Symposium on Arabic Linguistics (Amsterdam Studies in the Theory and History of Linguistic Science Series IV: Current Issues in Linguistic Theory, 63)

Joyce Åkesson: Anomalous Elision and Addition of a Vowel in Classical Arabic. ZAL 39 (1999) 21–31

Arne A. Ambros: Beobachtungen zu *fiʿl* der Paarigkeit/Äquivalenz. ZAL 19 (1988) 27–31

—: Haplologie und Assimilation im V. und VI. Verbstamm im Koran. ZAL 25 (1993) 1–16

—: *Lākin und lākinna* im Koran. ZAL 17 (1987) 21–30

—: Syntaktische und stilistische Funktionen des Energikus im Koran. WZKM 79 (1989) 35–56

Anas Hasan Abu-Mansour: The Interface Between Morphology and Phonology: The case of broken plurals in Arabic. The LACUS Forum 22 (1995) 320–339

I. M. Abu-Salim: Consonant Assimilation in Arabic: An autosegmental perspective. Lingua 74 (1988) 45–66

Joyce Åkesson: Conversion of the *yāʾ* into an *alif* in Classical Arabic. ZAL 31 (1996): 27–33

—: The Strong Verb and Infinitive Noun in Arabic. Acta Orientalia (Societates Orientales Danica, Fennica, Norvegica, Svecica) 52 (1991) 35–48

N. Anghelescu: Les désinences casuelles en Arabe: pourquoi? Revue roumaine de linguistique 38 (1993) 19–22

Ibrāhīm Anīs: دراسة في صيغة فِعِّيل كَشِرِّيب وَسِكِّير. MMAD 39 (1964) 365–737

Jussi Aro: Der *maṣdar al-mīmī* und seine Funktion im Arabischen (Studia Orientalia 28). Helsinki 1964

Peter Bachmann: Zwei Verse von Muḥyi d-dīn Ibn al-ʿArabī über den 'Plural der kleinen Menge'. In: Festschrift zum 60. Geburtstag von Gustav Ineichen, 1–11 (Stuttgart 1989) (Variatio Linguarum: Beiträge zu Sprachvergleich und Sprachentwicklung)

Michel Barbot: La Structure du mot en arabe littéral. Modèles Linguistiques 12 (1990) 7–32

E. Beck: Die Ausnahmepartikel *ʾillā* bei al-Farrāʾ und Sībawaih. Orientalia N.S. 25 (1956) 42–73

—: Die Partikel *ʾiḏan* bei al-Farrāʾ und Sībawaih. Orientalia N.S. 15 (1946) 432–438

V. Becker: A Transfer Grammar of the Verb Structure of Modern Literary Arabic and Lebanese Colloquial Arabic. Yale University diss. 1964

A. F. L. Beeston: Classical Arabic *Niʿma* and *Biʾsa*. The Arabist: Budapest Studies in Arabic 3–4 (1991) 101–105 (Proceedings of the Colloquium on Arabic Grammar, Budapest, 1–7 September 1991)

—: Parallelism in Arabic Prose. Journal of Arabic Literature V (1974) 134–146

Omar Bencheikh: *ʾinna*, outil grammatical. Emploi et fonction. MAS – Gellas (1983) 129–150

Gotthelf Bergsträßer: Verneinungs- und Fragepartikeln und Verwandtes im Kurʾan. Ein Beitrag zur historischen Grammatik des Arabischen. Leipzig 1914 (Leipziger semitistische Studien; Bd. 5, 4)

Monique Bernards: Except for a Few ... The Exception in Qurʾan 11.116. The Arabist: Budapest Studies in Arabic 15–16 (1995) 3–10 (Proceedings of the 14th Congress of the Union Européenne des Arabisants et Islamisants II Budapest 29. Aug.–3. Sept. 1988)

Harris Birkeland: Altarabische Pausalformen. Oslo 1940 (Skrifter utgitt av det Norske Videnskaps-Akademi i Oslo, Hist.-filos. Kl. 1940, no. 4)

W.B. Bishai: Form and Function in Arabic Syntax. Word 21 (1965) 265–269

J. Blau: Remarks on Some Syntactic Trends in Modern Standard Arabic. Israel Oriental Studies 3 (1973) 172–231

—: Some Additional Observations on Syntactic Trends in Modern Standard Arabic. Israel Oriental Studies 6 (1976) 158–190

Otto Blau: Altarabische Sprachstudien. ZDMG 25 (1871) 525–592

Alfred Bloch: Kleine Beiträge zur Arabistik, 1. Zur Herkunft der Partikel *qad*. 2. Zur Wortfolge Subjekt - Akkusativobjekt - Verbum. Anthropos 41–44 (1946–1949) 723–736

Ariel Bloch: Direct and Indirect Relative Clauses. ZAL 5 (1980) 8–34

—: Studies in Arabic Syntax and Semantics. 2nd rev. print. Wiesbaden 1991

—: The Vowels of the Imperfect Preformatives in the Old Dialects of Arabic. ZDMG 117 (1967) 22–29

(Meïr) Max Bravmann: The Arabic Elative: A new approach. Leiden 1968 (Studies in Semitic Languages and Linguistics 2)

Afif Bulos: The Arabic Triliteral Verb: A comparative study of grammatical concepts and processes. Beirut 1965

Marius Canard: La forme arabe "faʿāli". AJEO 1 (1934/35) 5–72

Jean Cantineau: Le pronom suffixe de 3e personne singulier masculin en arabe classique et dans les parlers arabes modernes. BSL 40 (1939) 89–100

Moustapha Chouémi: Le verbe dans le Coran: Racines et formes. Paris 1966 (Études arabes et islamiques 3)

David Cohen: Essai d'une analyse grammaticale de l'arabe. La Traduction Automatique 2 (1961) 48–70

Christoph Correll: ...'Ein Esel, welcher Bücher trägt ...': Zum Prädikativ im Klassisch-Arabischen. ZAL 26 (1993) 7–14

Federico Corriente: Problematica de la Pluralidad en Semitico: el Plural fracto. Madrid 1971

A. Denz: Zur Noetik des arabischen ʾ*in*-Satz–Hauptsatzgefüges. ZDMG 121 (1971) 37–45.

Hartwig Derenbourg: Essai sur les formes des pluriels arabes. Paris 1867

W. Diem: Divergenz und Konvergenz im Arabischen. Arabica 25 (1978) 128–147

L. Drozdík: Compounding as a Second-order Word-formational Procedure in Modern Written Arabic. Asian and African Studies 3 (1967) 60–97

—: The Loss of Relevancy of Some Grammatical Meanings in Modern Written Arabic. Jazykovědný Časopis 15 (1964) 109–115

Wilhelm Eilers: Zur Funktion von Nominalformen: Ein Grenzgang zwischen Morphologie und Semasiologie. Die Welt des Orients 3 (1964) 80–145

Abdelhamid Ibn El Farouk: La fiction du subjonctif en arabe littéral et la question du *muḍâriʿ*. La Linguistique: Revue de la Société Internationale de Linguistique Fonctionnelle 30 (1994) 121–130

Abdelkader Fassi Fehri: Issues in the Structure of Arabic Clauses and Words. Dordrecht; Boston 1993 (Studies in Natural Language and Linguistic Theory; v. 29)

August Fischer: Auflösung der Akkusativrektion des transitiven Verbs durch die Präposition *li* im Klassischen Arabisch. Berichte über die Verhandlungen der Kgl. Sächs. Gesellschaft d. Wissenschaften zu Leipzig, Phil.-hist. Kl. 62, 6. Leipzig 1910, 161–188

—: Arab. أيش. ZDMG 59 (1905) 807–818

—: Die weiblichen Demonstrativ-Pronomina *hāḏihī, ḏihī, tihī* und *hāḏihi, hāḏih, ḏih, tih*. Islamica 3 (1927) 44–52, 491

—: Grammatisch schwierige Schwur- und Beschwörungsformeln des Klassischen Arabisch. Der Islam 28 (1948) 1–105

-:Das Geschlecht der Infinitive im Arabischen. ZDMG 60 (1906) 839–859; 61 (1907) 241–243

—: Imra'alqais...Islamica 1 (1925) 1–40, 365–389; 4 (1931) 200

—: Grammatische arabische Miszellen (I), I. Allerlei Bemerkungen zum Verbindungsalif. II. Zum Wegfall der Nunation vor *bin, ibn, ibnah*. Islamica 4 (1931) 94–108

—: Grammatische arabische Miszellen (II), I. Arab. *ʾīјā* mit Suffix als Nominativ. II. Arab. *ʾīјāka* "nimm dich in acht". Islamica 5 (1932) 211–226, 363–375

—: Die Quantität des Vokals des arabischen Pronominalsuffixes *hu* (*hi*). In: Paul-Haupt-Festschrift (Baltimore 1926) 390–402

—: Zur Syntax der muslimischen Bekenntnisformel. Islamica 4 (1931) 512–521

—: Die Terminologie der arabischen Kollektivnomina. ZDMG 94 (1940) 12–24

Wolfdietrich Fischer: Die arabische Pluralbildung. ZAL 5 (1980) 70–88

—: Daß-Sätze mit *ʾan* und *ʾanna*. ZAL 1 (1978) 24–31

—: Zur Bestimmung der Funktionskategorien des arabischen Verbums. In: Gedenkschrift Wolfgang Reuschel: Akten des III. Arabistischen Kolloquiums, Leipzig, 21–22 November 1991 herausgeben von Dieter Bellmann. (Stuttgart 1994) 60–96.

Henri Fleisch: L'aspect lexical de la phrase arabe classique. Studia Biblica et Orientalia 3 (1959) 78–94

—: Études sur le verbe arabe. In: Mélanges Louis Massignon II (Dames 1957) 153–181

—: Le nom d'agent *faʿal*. MUSJ 32 (1955) 167–172

—: Les démonstratifs arabes *ʾulā ʾulāʾi, ʾulāʾika*. MUSJ 46 (1970) 469–478

Samuel Freund: Die Zeitsätze im Arabischen, mit Berücksichtigung verwandter Sprachen und moderner arabischer Dialekte. Kirchhain 1892

Barbara Freyer: Formen des geselligen Umgangs und Eigentümlichkeiten des Sprachgebrauchs in der frühislamischen Gesellschaft Arabiens. Der Islam 38 (1962) 51–105; 42 (1966) 25–57,179–234

Johann Fück: Taṣġīr al-ǧamʿ. ZDMG 90 (1936) 626–636

Helmut Gätje: Strukturen der Genitivverbindungen: Untersuchungen am arabischen Genetiv. Die Sprache 11 (1965) 61–73

—:Zur Syntax der Determinationsverhältnisse im Arabischen. Hamburg 1973 (Mitteilungen des Deutschen Orient-Instituts. Nr. 2.)

A. Gonegai: La syntaxe des constructions relatives restrictives arabe. BEO 43 (1991) 161–195

Yaakov Gruntfest: From the History of Semitic Linguistics in Europe: An early theory of redundancy of Arabic case-endings. The Arabist: Budapest Studies in Arabic, 3–4 (1991) 195–200 (Proceedings of the Colloquium on Arabic Grammar, Budapest, 1–7 September 1991)

Adrian Gully: Synonymy or not Synonymy: That is the question: The case of the particle in mediæval Arabic. ZAL 27 (1994) 36–46

A. Joly: Quelques mots sur les dérivations du trilitère et les origines du quatrilitère en arabe. Actes du XIVe Congrès International des Orientalistes, Alger 1905, IIIe Partie, 3e section, 394–436

P. Joüon: Études de sémantique arabe. MUSJ 11 (1926) 1–35

—: Remarques sur les 3me et 7me formes verbales *faʿala* et *infaʿala* de l'arabe. MUSJ 19 (1935) 97–116

Samar Afif Kadi: *Ḥattā idhā* in the Qurʾan: A linguistic study (Ph.D. Dissertation Columbia University, 1994)

E. Kahle: Studien zur Syntax des Adjektivs im vorklassischen Arabisch. Erlangen 1975

Naphtali Kinberg: Adverbial Clauses as Topics in Arabic: Adverbial clauses in frontal position separated from their main clauses. Jerusalem Studies in Arabic and Islam 6 (1985) 353–416

—: Some Temporal, Aspectual, and Modal Features of the Arabic Structure *la-qad* + Prefix Tense Verb. JAOS 108 (1988) 291–295

J. H. Kramers: La pause en arabe et en hébreu considérée au point de vue phonologique. Analecta Orientalia 2 (1953) 3–13

Jerzy Kuryłowicz: Le diptotisme et la construction des noms de nombre en arabe. Word 7 (1951) 222–226

—: La mimation et l'article en arabe. ArOr 18 (1950) 323–328

Pierre Larcher: Les Arabisants et la catégorie de *ʾinšāʾ*: Histoire d'une 'occultation'. Historiographia-Linguistica; 20 (1993) 259–282

—: La forme IV *ʾafʿala* de l'arabe classique: *faire faire* et *laisser faire*. ZAL 35 (1998) 14–28

—: D'une grammaire à l'autre: catégorie d'adverbe et catégorie de *mafʿūl muṭlaq*. BEO 43 (1991) 139–159

—: *Mā faʿala* vs. *lam yafʿal*: une hypothèse pragmatique. Arabica 41 (1994) 388–415

—: Les *mafʿûl muṭlaq* "a incidence enonciative" de l'arabe classique. In: L'adverbe dans tous ses états publication preparée par Claude Guimier et Pierre Larcher (Rennes 1991) 151–178 (Travaux-linguistiques-du-CERLICO; 4)

—: Où il est montré qu'en arabe classique la racine n'a pas de sens et qu'il n'y a pas de sens à dériver d'elle. Arabica 42 (1995) 291–314

—: Quand, en arabe, on parlait de l'arabe.. Essai sur la méthodologie de l'histoire des "métalangages arabes" (I) Arabica 35 (1988) 117–142

—: Quand, en arabe, on parlait de l'arabe ... (II) Essai sur la catégorie de '*ʾinšāʾ*' (vs *ḫabar*). Arabica 38 (1991) 246 273

—: Quand, en arabe, on parlait de l'arabe ... (III) Grammaire, logique, rhetorique dans l'Islam postclassique. Arabica 39 (1992) 358 384

—: Sur la valeur "expositive" de la forme *ʾafʿala* de l'arabe classique. ZAL 31 (1996) 7–26

—: Vous avez dit "délocutif"? Langages 20 (1985) 99–124

F. Leemhuis: The D and H Stems in Koranic Arabic. Leiden 1977

Bernhard Lewin: Non-conditional 'if'-clauses in Arabic. ZDMG 120 (1970) 264–270

N. K. Lewkowicz: Topic-Comment and Relative Clause in Arabic. Language 47 (1971) 810–825

Enno Littmann: Zwei seltenere arabische Nominalbildungen (*qaitūl* und *quttail*). ZS 4 (1926) 24–41

Ernst Mainz: Zur Grammatik des modernen Schriftarabisch. Hamburg 1931

Basim Majdi: Word Order and Proper Government in Classical Arabic. Perspectives on Arabic Linguistics I (1990) 127–153: Papers from First Annual Symposium on Arabic Linguistics (Amsterdam Studies in the Theory and History of Linguistic Science Series IV: Current Issues in Linguistic Theory 63)

Shinya Makino: Über die Verneinung durch *mā* im Arabischen: Ein Beitrag zur Affektsyntax der semitischen Sprachen. Gengo Kenkyu 38 (1960) 136–147

L. Matouš: Zum sog. inneren Plural im Arabischen. ArOr 24 (1956) 626–630

Adam Mez: Über einige sekundäre Verba im Arabischen. In: Orientalische Studien, Th. Nöldeke gewidmet, I (Gießen 1905) 249–254

André Miquel: La particule *innamā* dans le Coran. JA 248 (1960) 483–499

Sabatino Moscati: Il plurale esterno maschile nelle lingue semitiche. RSO 29 (1954) 28–52

—: Sulla flessione nominale dell'arabo classico. RSO 29 (1954) 171–182

Teufik Muftić: Infinitivi Trilitera u arabskom jeziku, odnos oblika i značenja (Orientalni Institut u Sarajevu, Posebna Izdanja 5). Sarajevo 1966

—: O intensifikaciji u arapskom, Sur l'intensification dans la langue arabe. Prilozi za Orientalnu Filologiju i Istoriju 6–7 (1956/57) 5–37

—: Trilitere u arapskom jeziku, Statisticko-fonetska studija. Prilozi za Orientalnu Filologiju I Istoriju 3–4 (1953) 509–551

A. Murtonen: Broken Plurals: Origin and development of the system. Leiden 1964

ʿĀrif an-Nakadī: مفاعيل - مفعول. MMAD 40 (1965) 109–116

Norbert Nebes: Funktionsanalyse von *kāna yafʿalu*: Ein Beitrag zur Verbalsyntax des Althocharabischen mit besonderer Berücksichtigung der Tempus- und Aspektproblematik. Hildesheim-Zürich-New York 1982 (Studier zur Sprachwissenschaft Bd. 1)

—: *ʾin al-muḫaffafa* und *al-lām al-fāriqa* ZAL 7 (1982) 7–22; 14 (1985) 7–44; 16 (1987) 7–30

Jonathan Owens: The Syntactic Basis of Arabic Word Classification. Arabica 36 (1989) 211–234

Yishai Peled: Conditional Structures in Classical Arabic. Wiesbaden 1992. (Studies in Arabic Language and Literature; v. 2)

—: 'Conditional Sentences without a Conditional Particle' in Classical Arabic Prose ZAL 16 (1987) 31–43

—: On the Obligatoriness of *fa-* in Classical Arabic *ʾin* Conditional Sentences. JSS 30 (1985) 213–225

Charles Pellat: *Allaḏī* et sa série dans un ouvrage d'al-Ǧāḥiz. In: Mélanges offerts au R. P. Henri Fleisch. Vol. I. Beirut 1976, 177–202

S. Pena: *Iʿrāb* as Syntax. ZAL 33 (1997) 100–104

Fabrizio A. Pennacchietti: La nature sintattica e semantica dei pronomi arabi *man*, *ma* e *ʾayyun*. Annali dell'Istituto Universitario Orientale di Napoli 14 (1966) 57–87

Karel Petráček: Morphologisches aus dem Dīwān des al-Aḥwaṣ al-Anṣārī - Syntaktisches aus dem Dīwān des al-Aḥwaṣ al-Anṣārī. ArOr 28 (1960) 67–71, 174–180

H. J. Polotsky: A Point of Arabic Syntax: The indirect attribute. Israel Oriental Studies 8 (1978) 159–173

Franz Praetorius: Über die aramäischen und arabischen Passivperfekta. ZS 2 (1924) 134–141

Stephan Prochazka: *Bayda ʾanna* 'weil' — Unwissen, Mißverstandnis oder Falschung? ZAL 29 (1995) 7–22

M. Rechad: Sur la syntaxe de la phrase nominale et la nature de pron arabe. Recherches linguistiques de Vincennes 23 (1994) 65–82

Hermann Reckendorff: Zum Gebrauch des Partizips im Altarabischen. In: Orientalistische Studien, Theodor Nöldeke gewidmet, I (1906) 255–265

Wolfgang Reuschel: Darstellung und Gebrauch der Form *yakūnu* (*qad*) *faʿala* im Arabischen. Asien in Vergangenheit und Gegenwart. Beiträge der Asienwissenschaftler der DDR zum XXIX. Orientalistenkongreß 1973 in Paris. (Berlin 1974) 355–370

—: *wa-kāna llāhu ʿāliman raḥīman*. Studia Orientalia in Memoriam Caroli Brockelmann, Halle (Saale) 1968, 147–153

André Roman: L'aspect en arabe. Langues Modernes 83 (1989) 135–141

—: Le hasard et la nécessité dans l'ordre des langues: L'illustration de l'arabe. BEO 43 (1991) 93–117

—: Les divers nombres de consonnes de la racine arabe. The Arabist: Budapest Studies in Arabic 3–4 (1991) 313–333 (Proceedings of the Colloquium on Arabic Grammar, Budapest, 1–7 Sept. 1991)

—: Genèse et typologie des unités de la langue arabe. Linguistique et sémiologie (Lyon) 1994 117–147

Frithjof Rundgren: Die Konstruktion der arabischen Kardinalzahlen: Zur historischen Würdigung der komplementären Distribution. Orientalia Suecana 17 (1968) 107–119

Ismaʿīl as-Sāmarrāʾī: The Plural in Arabic. Sumer 16 (1960) 25–37

—: تحقيق لغوي في الصّياغ والاستعمالات. MMAD 40 (1965) 215–233

Arthur Schaade: Attributive, appositionelle und anknüpfende Relativsätze im Arabischen und Syrischen. Islamica 2 (1926) 498–504

G. M. Schramm: An Outline of Classical Arabic Verb Structure. Language 38 (1962) 360–375

Michael A. Schub: The Expression of Panchronic Actions in Arabic. An exegetical clarification. JSS 27 (1982) 57–59

Friedrich Schulthess: Zurufe an Tiere im Arabischen. Berlin 1912

—: Noch einige Zurufe an Tiere. ZS 2 (1924) 14–19

Paul Schwarz: Der Diwan des ʿUmar ibn Abi Rebiʿa, IV: ʿUmars Leben, Dichtung, Sprache und Metrik. Leipzig 1909

—: Der sprachgeschichtliche Wert einiger älterer Wortschreibungen im Koran. ZA 30 (1915/16) 46–59

S. Sikirić: Sintakticke funkcije arapskich prijedloga. Prilozi za Orientalnu Filologiju i Istoriju 3-4 (1952/53) 553–574

E. A. Speiser: The "Elative" in West-Semitic and Akkadian. Journal of Cuneiform Studies 6 (1952) 81–92; In: Oriental and Biblical Studies, Collected Writings of E. A. Speiser (Philadelphia 1967) 465–493

Anton Spitaler: *Al-Ḥamdu lillāhi llaḏī* und Verwandtes: Ein Beitrag zur mittel- und neuarabischen Syntax. Oriens 15 (1962) 97-114

—: *Mā rāʿahū illā bi* und Verwandtes: Ein Beitrag zur arabischen Phraseologie. In: Serta Monacensia Franz Babinger dedicata (Leiden 1952) 171–183

—: *Šattāna*. In: Mélanges offerts au R. P. Henri Fleisch. Vol. I (Beirut 1976) 97–135

—: Zwei sekundäre arabische Nominaltypen aus der Affektsprache. In: Islamwissenschaftliche Abhandlungen Fritz Meier zum 60. Geburtstag (Wiesbaden 1974) 292–305

Saleh M. Suleiman: The Semantic Functions of Object Deletion in Classical Arabic. Language Sciences (Oxford) 12 (1990) 255–266

David Testen: On the Development of the Arabic Subjunctive. Perspectives on Arabic Linguistics VI (1994) 151–166: Papers from 6th Annual Symposium on Arabic Linguistics (Amsterdam Studies in the Theory and History of Linguistic Science Series IV: Current Issues in Linguistic Theory, 115)

—: On the Development of the Energic Suffixes. Perspectives on Arabic Linguistics V (1993) 293–311: Papers from the 5th Annual Symposium on Arabic Linguistics (Amsterdam Studies in the Theory and History of Linguistic Science Series IV: Current Issues in Linguistic Theory, 101)

Renate Tietz: Bedingungssatz und Bedingungsausdruck im Koran. Diss. Tübingen 1963

C. Touratier: Propositions pour une analyse morphématique du verbe arabe. Travaux – Cercle linguistique d'Aix-en-Provence 14 (1997) 121–134

G. L. Trager – F. A. Rice: The Personal Pronoun System of Classical Arabic. Language 30 (1954) 224–229

G. Troupeau: Le schème de pluriel "fuʿlan" en arabe classique. GLECS 7 (1955) 65–66

Ernst Trumpp: Der Bedingungssatz im Arabischen. Sitzungsberichte der Königl. bayer. Akademie der Wissenschaften zu München, Philos.-philol. Classe 1881. 337–448

—: Über den arabischen Satzbau nach der Anschauung der arabischen Grammatiker. Sitzungsberichte der Königl. bayer. Akademie der Wissenschaften zu München. Philos.-philol. Classe 1879, 309–398

—: Über den Zustandsausdruck in den semitischen Sprachen, speciell im Arabischen: Ein Beitrag zur vergleichenden Syntax der semitischen Sprachen. Sitzungsberichte der königl. bayer. Akademie der Wissenschaften zu München, Philos.-philol. Classe 1876, 119–170

—: Structure de la phrase simple en arabe. BSL 84 (1989) 345–359

Manfred Ullmann: Arabisch *ʿasā* "vielleicht": Syntax und Wortart. (Beiträge zur Lexikographie des Klassischen Arabisch Nr. 5). München 1984 (Bayer. Akad. der Wissenschaften, Philos.-histor. Klasse. Sitzungsberichte 1984, Heft 4)

—: Arabische Komparativsätze. Göttingen 1985 (Nachrichten der Akademie der Wissenschaften in Göttingen. I. Philologisch-Historische Klasse 1985, Nr. 7)

—: Nicht nur...sondern auch... Der Islam 60 (1980) 3–36

—: Das arabische Nomen generis. Göttingen 1989 (Abhandlungen der Akademie der Wissenschaften in Göttingen. Philologisch-Historische Klasse; 3. Folge, Nr. 176)

Werner Vycichl: Die Deklination im Arabischen. RSO 28 (1953) 71–78

—: Der Ursprung der diptotischen Flexion im Klassischen Arabischen. Le Muséon 82 (1969) 207–212

Hans Wehr: Die Besonderheiten des heutigen Hocharabischen mit Berücksichtigung der Einwirkung der europäischen Sprachen. MSOS 37 (1934), 2. Abtl., 1–64

—: Der arabische Elativ (Akademie der Wissenschaften und der Literatur in Mainz, Abhandlungen der Geistes- und Socialwissenschaftl. Klasse, 1952, Nr. 7). Wiesbaden 1953

—: Zur Funktion arabischer Negationen. ZDMG 103 (1953) 27–39

—: Starre syntaktische Schemata als affektische Ausdrucksformen im Arabischen. ZDMG 101 (1951) 107–124

Stefan Weninger: Satzgefüge mit *ʾillā ʾan* bzw. *ʾanna*. ZAL 27 (1994) 7–35

Stefan Wild: Die Konjunktion *ḥattā* mit dem Indikativ Imperfekt im klassischen Arabisch. In: Studien aus Arabistik und Semitistik, Anton Spitaler zum siebzigsten Geburtstag (Wiesbaden 1980) 204–223

W. H. Worrell: The Interrogative Particle *hal* in Arabic according to Native Sources and the Kurʾan. ZA 21 (1908) 116–150

Zafer Youssef: Das Partizip im Arabischen : die Aufassungen der arabischen Grammatiker und der Sprachgebrauch in klassisch-arabischen Texten. Thesis (Ph.D.) Friedrich-Alexander-Universität, 1990)

5. Lexicography

Arabic Lexicons

Abū Manṣūr al-Azharī: تهذيب اللّغة, ed. ʿAbdassalām M. Hārūn [et al.]. 15 Vol. Cairo 1964–1967

Abū ʿUbaid al-Bakrī: Das geographische Wörterbuch des Abu ʿObeid ʿAbdallah ben ʿAbd el ʿAzîz el-Bekri, ed. Ferdinand Wüstenfeld I. II. Göttingen/Paris 1876–1877

—: معجم ما استعجم من اسماء البلاد والمواضع, ed. Muṣṭafā as-Saqqā Bd. I-IV. Cairo 1945–1951

Buṭrus al-Bustānī: محيط المحيط. 2 Vol. Beirut 1867–1870 – Reprint 1983.

Muḥammad ibn Yaʿqūb al-Fīrūzābādī: القاموس المحيط. 2 vol. Bombay 1259/ 1817 – 4 vol. Cairo 1970

al-Jawharī: تاج اللّغة وصحاح العربيّة, ed. A. ʿAbd al-Ghafūr. 7 vol. Cairo 1956–1958

Ibn al-Athīr: النّهاية في غريب الحديث والاثر, ed. Maḥmūd M. at-Tanāḥī [et al.]. 4 vol. Cairo 1383/1963

Abū Bakr Ibn Durayd: كتاب جمهرة اللّغة. 4 vol. Hyderabad 1344/1925 (Publications of the Dairatu 'l-Ma'arif il-Osmania)

Abū l-Ḥusayn Ibn Fāris: معجم مقاييس اللّغة, ed. ʿAbd as-Salām Hārūn. 6 vol. Cairo 1366/1946-1371/1951

Muḥammad Ibn Mukarram Ibn al-Manẓur: لسان العرب. 20 vol. Būlāq 1308/ 1890 – 15 vol. Beirut 1955/56

—: لسان العرب؛ نسّقه وعلّق عليه ووضع فهارسه علي شيري. الطبعة ١، طبعة جديدة محقّقة. 18 vol. Beirut 1988

—: لسان العرب المحيط، اعداد وتصنيف يوسف حياه ونديم مرعشلي. 4 vol. Beirut 1970

Abū l-Ḥasan Ibn Sīdā: المخصّص في للّغة. 17 vol. Būlāq 1316–1321/1898–1903

—: المحكم والمحيط الاعظم, ed. As-Saqqā Ḥ. Naṣṣār, A. Farrāj. Cairo 1958–1960

al-Khalīl ibn Aḥmad: كتاب العين اوّل معجم في اللّغة العربيّة, ed. A. Darwīsh. Vol. I. Baghdad 1967

—: كتاب العين؛ تحقيق مهدي المخزومي، ابراهيم السامرّائي. الطبعة ١. في ايران. Qum 1405 [1984 or 1985] 7 vol.

—: مختصر العين لابي بكر محمّد ابن الحسن ابن عبد الله الزبيدي الاندلسي. الطبعة ١. بيروت، ١٩٩٦ 2 vol.

Lūyis Maʾlūf: المنجد في اللّغة والادب والعلوم. Beyrouth 1956

Nashwān b. Saʿīd al-Ḥimyarī: شمس العلوم ودواء كلام العرب من الكلوم, ed. K. V. Zetterstéen Tl. I. Leiden 1951–1953

Saʿīd al-Khūrī ash-Shartūnī: أقرب الموارد في فصح العربيّة والشّوارد Vol. I, II, 1 Supplement. Beirut 1889–1893

Yāqūt ar-Rūmī: Jacuts Geographisches Wörterbuch hrsg. von Ferdinand Wüstenfeld. 6 vol. Leipzig 1866–1873

—: معجم البلدان. 6 vol. Beirut 1955–1957

Murtaḍā az-Zabīdī: تاج العاروس من جواهر القاموس. 10 vol. Cairo 1306/1888 – Ed. ʿA. A. Farrāj. 21 vol. Kuwait 1385/1965 – 1404/1984

Abū l-Qāsim az-Zamakhsharī: اساس البلاغة. 2 vol. Cairo 1372/1953
—: كتاب الفائق في غريب الحديث. ed. M. Abū l-Faḍl Ibrāhīm. Vol. I–III. Cairo 1945–1948

Arab Lexicography

ʿAbd as-Samīʿ Muḥammad Aḥmad: المعاجم العربيّة، دراسة تحليليّة. Cairo: 1391/1974

Abdel Fatah el-Berkawy: Die arabischen Ibdāl-Monographien insbesondere Das Kitab al-Ibdāl des Abū ṭ-Ṭayyib al-Luġawī: Ein Beitrag zur arabischen Philologie und Sprachwissenschaft. Erlangen 1981

Georges Bohas: Matrices, étymons, racines : Éléments d'une théorie lexicologique du vocabulaire arabe. Leuven; Paris 1997. (Orbis/supplementa; 8)

ʿAbd Allāh Darwīsh: المعاجم العربيّة مع اعتناء خاصّ بمعجم العين للخليل ابن احمد. Cairo 1956

Werner Diem: Das Kitāb al-Ǧīm des Abū ʿAmr ash-Shaibānī. Dissertation München 1968

Helmut Gätje: Arabische Lexikographie: Ein historischer Überblick. Historiographia Linguistica 12 (1985) 105–147

Wajdī Rizq Ghālī: المعجمات العربيّة· ببليوغرافيّة شاملة مشروحة. Cairo 1391/ 1971

Wagdy Rizk Ghali: Arabic Dictionaries: An annotated comprehensive bibliography supplement. MIDEO 12 (1974) 243–287

A. Guillaume: Hebrew and Arabic Lexicography: A comparative study. Abr-Nahrain 1 (1959/60) 3–35; 2 (1960/61) 5–35; 3 (1961/62) 1–10; 4 (1963/64) 1–18. Reprint: Leiden 1965

John A. Haywood: Arabic Lexicography: Its history, and its place in the general history of lexicography. Leiden 1960. ^{2}1965

—: An Indian Contribution to the Study of Arabic Lexicography. The Bulgha of Ṣiddīq Ḥasan Khān Bahādur (1832–1890). JRAS 1956 165–180

Naphtali Kinberg: A Lexicon of al-Farrāʾ's Terminology in his Qurʾān Commentary: With full definitions, English summaries, and extensive citations. Leiden; New York 1996 (Handbuch der Orientalistik. Erste Abteilung, Nahe und der Mittlere Osten; 23. Bd.)

Lothar Kopf: Arabic Lexicography: Its origin, development, sources and problems. Ph.D. dissertation. Hebrew University of Jerusalem 1953

Jörg Kraemer: Studien zur altarabischen Lexikographie. Oriens 6 (1953) 202–238

Fritz Krenkow: The Beginnings of Arabic Lexicography until the Time of Jawharī: With special reference to the work of Ibn Duraid. JRAS 1924, 250–270

E. G. Lane: Über die Lexikographie der arabischen Sprache. ZDMG 3 (1849) 90–108

Ḥusayn Naṣṣār: المعجم العربي، نشأته وتطوّره. 2 vol. Cairo 1968

Stefan Wild: Das Kitāb al-ʿAin und die arabische Lexikographie. Wiesbaden 1965

Arabic-Foreign Language Lexicons

X. K. Baranov: Arabsko-russkij slovar' – al-qāmūs al-ʿarabī ar-rūsī. Moscow 1957

Jean-Bapt. Belot: Dictionnaire français-arabe à l'usage des étudiants, 17e éd. Beyrouth 1955

A. de Biberstein Kazimirski: Dictionnaire Arabe-Français contenant toutes les racines de la langue arabe... T. I, II. Paris 1860 – rev. et corr. par Ibn Gallab. Caire 1875. Reprint Paris 1960. Reprint Beirut [1970?]

Régis Blachère, Moustafa Chouémi, Claude Denizeau: Dictionnaire arabe-français-anglais (Langue classique et moderne). Paris 1964 [t. 1–4, fasc. 46, 1988]

Ellious Bocthor: Dictionnaire Français-Arabe, revu et augmenté par A. Caussin de Perceval, 4. éd. Paris 1869

Reinhart Dozy: Supplement aux dictionnaires arabes. 2 vol. Leide/Paris 1881. – Reprint: Beirut 1991

A. E. Elias and E. E. Elias: Elias' Modern Dictionary English-Arabic. 8th ed. Cairo 1951

—: القاموس العصري عربي - انجليزي – Modern Dictionary Arabic-English. Re-issue with several additions and alterations. Cairo 1983

Gerhard Endress and Dimitri Gutas: A Greek and Arabic Lexicon: Materials for a dictionary of the medieval translations from Greek into Arabic. Leiden; New York 1992– (Handbuch der Orientalistik. Erste Abteilung, Nahe und der Mittlere Osten; 11 Bd.)

Edmond Fagnan: Additions aux dictionnaires arabes. Alger 1923

Georg Wilh. Freytag: Lexicon Arabico-Latinum praesertim ex Djeuharii Firuzubadiique et aliorum libris confectum, 4 vol. Halle 1830–1837

Jacobus Golius: Lexicon Arabico-Latinum. Lugduni Batavorum 1653

J. G. Hava: Arabic-English Dictionary for the Use of Students – الفرائد الدرّيّة في اللّغتين العربيّة والانكلزيّة. Beirut 1951

Jörg Kraemer: Theodor Nöldeke's Belegwörterbuch zur klassischen arabischen Sprache, Fasz. 1. 2. Berlin 1952–1954

Günther Krahl: Deutsch-arabisches Wörterbuch. Leipzig 1964

Günther Krahl und Gharieb Muhamed Gharieb: Wörterbuch Arabisch-Deutsch. München 1984

Georg Krotkoff: Langenscheidts Taschenwörterbuch der Arabischen und Deutschen Sprache. 2 Vol. Berlin 1976–1977

Edward William Lane: Maddu-l-Kamoos: An Arabic-English lexicon derived from the best and the most copious eastern sources. . . , Part. 1-5. London 1863–1874: Part. 6–8. ed. Stanley Lane Poole. London 1877–1893. Reprints: New York 1955–56; Beirut 1980; Cambridge, England 1984; New Delhi 1985

Götz Schregle: Deutsch-Arabisches Wörterbuch: Unter Mitwirkung von Fahmi Abu l-Fadl, Mahmoud Hegazi, Tawfik Borg und Kamal Radwan. Wiesbaden 1977

—: Arabisch-Deutsches Wörterbuch: Unter Mitwirkung von Kamal Radwan und Sayed Mohammad Rizk. Wiesbaden 1981–. [Issued in fascicles]

Adolf Wahrmund: Handwörterbuch der neuarabischen und deutschen Sprache, 2 vol. Gießen 1887–1898 – Reprint 1980

Hans Wehr: Arabisches Wörterbuch für die Schriftsprache der Gegenwart, Arabisch-Deutsch. 5. Aufl. unter Mitwirkung von Lorenz Kropfitsch neu bearbeitet und erweitert. Wiesbaden 1985

—: A Dictionary of Modern Written Arabic (Arabic-English). Ed. J Milton Cowan. Fourth ed. considerably enlarged and amended by the author. Wiesbaden 1979

Wörterbuch der Klassischen Arabischen Sprache: Auf Grund der Sammlungen von August Fischer, Theodor Nöldeke, Hermann Reckendorf und anderer Quellen hrsg. durch die Deutsche Morgenländische Gesellschaft. Bd. I. (ك) Begründet von Jörg Kraemer und Helmut Gätje. In Verbindung mit Anton Spitaler bearbeitet von Manfred Ullmann. Wiesbaden 1970. - Band II. (ل) Bearbeitet von Manfred Ullmann. Wiesbaden 1972–.

Dictionaries of Dialects

Hermann Almquist: Kleine Beiträge zur Lexikographie des Vulgärarabischen 1. Actes du VIIIe Congrès International des Orientalistes 1889 à Stockholm et à Christiania Sect. I. Leiden 1891, 261–469; II. MO 19 (1925) 1–186

A. Barthélemy: Dictionnaire Arabe-Français, Dialectes de Syrie: Alep, Damas, Liban, Jérusalem. Paris 1935 – Fascicule complémentaire. Introduction générale publié sous les auspices de l'Institut de France. Paris 1969

Marcelin Beaussier: Dictionnaire pratique arabe-français contenant tous les mots dans l'arabe parlé en Algérie en en Tunisie, nouvelle édition par M. Mohamed Ben Cheneb. Alger 1931

Gilbert Boris: Lexique du parler des Marazig. Paris 1958 (Études arabes et islamiques)

B. E. Clarity, K. Stowasser, and R. G. Wolfe: A Dictionary of Iraqi Arabic: English-Arabic. Washington D.C. 1964

Federico Corriente. A Dictionary of Andalusi Arabic. New York 1997. (Handbuch der Orientalistik. Erste Abteilung, Nahe und der Mittlere Osten; 29. Bd.)

Jeffrey Deboo: Jemenitisches Wörterbuch: Arabisch-Deutsch-Englisch. Wiesbaden 1989

Claude Denizeau: Dictionnaire des Parlers arabes de Syrie, Liban et Palestine: Supplément au Dictionnaire arabe-français de A. Barthélemy Paris 1960 (Études Arabes et Islamiques)

Giovanni Battista Falzon: Dizionario Maltese-Italiano-Inglese. Seconda ed. Malta 1882

Th. Fox and M. Abu Talib: A Dictionary of Moroccan Arabic: Arabic-English. Washington D.C. 1966

Anis Frayha: A Dictionary of Non-Classical Vocables in the Spoken Arabic of Lebanon. Beirut 1947 (American University of Beirut, Publications of the Faculty of Arts and Sciences, Oriental Series 19)

Martin Hinds – El-Said Badawi: A Dictionary of Egyptian Arabic: Arabic-English. Beirut 1986

Alan S. Kaye: A Dictionary of Nigerian Arabic. Malibu, CA, 1982 (Bibliotheca Afroasiatica v. 1)

—: Nigerian Arabic-English Dictionary. Malibu, CA, 1986 (Bibliotheca Afroasiatica v. 2)

Carlo de Landberg: Glossaire daṯînois, I. II. III. Leiden 1920–1942

Albert Lentin: Supplément au Dictionnaire pratique arabe-français de Marcelin Beaussier. Alger 1959

William Marçais: Quelques Observations sur le Dictionnaire pratique arabe-français de Beaussier. Recueil de Mémoires et de Textes publié en l'honneur du XIVe Congrès des Orientalistes (Alger 1905) 409–503

—: et A. Guiga: Textes arabes de Takroûna II: Glossaire, Contribution à l'étude du vocabulaire arabe. Paris 1958–1961

Moshe Piamenta. A Dictionary of Post-classical Yemeni Arabic. Leiden; New York 1990–

Hamdi A. Qafisheh: A Glossary of Gulf Arabic: Gulf Arabic-English, English-Gulf Arabic. Beirut 1996.

—: NTC's Gulf Arabic-English Dictionary: In consultation with Tim Buckwalter and Ernest N. McCarus. Lincolnwood, Ill. 1997.

'Awn ash-Sharīf Qāsim: قاموس اللّهجة العامّيّة في السّودان. Beirut 1972. 2. ed. Cairo 1985

Aḥmad Riḍā: قاموس ردّ العامّي الى الفصيح. Beirut 1981

A. Roth-Laly: Lexique des parlers arabes tchado-soudanais. Paris 1969

Aḥmad ibn Muḥammad al-Ṣabīḥī al-Salāwī: معجم ارجاع الدارج في المغرب الى حظيرة اصله العربي؛ تقديم وتخريج محمّد حجّي. Salā, al-Maghrib [1990]

Zakia Iraqui Sinaceur (Zakīyah 'Irāqī Sīnāṣir) : Le Dictionnaire Colin d'arabe dialectal marocain = معجم كولان للعامّيّة المغربيّة. Rabat 1994

S. Spiro: Arabic-English Dictionary of the Modern Arabic of Egypt, second ed. Cairo 1923

E. V. Stace: An English-Arabic Vocabulary for the Use of Students of the Colloquial. London 1893

Karl Stowasser, Moukhtar Ani: A Dictionary of Syrian Arabic: English-Arabic. Washington, D.C. 1964. (Richard Slade Harrell Arabic series; no. 5)

Sibylle Vocke, Wolfram Waldner: Der Wortschatz des Anatolischen Arabisch. Erlangen 1982

D. R. Woodhead, W. Beene: A Dictionary of Iraqi Arabic, Arabic-English. Washington D.C. 1967

Detailed Treatises on the Lexicon

Soheil M. Afnan: Philosophical Terminology in Arabic and Persian. Leiden 1964

Dionisius A. Agius: Arabic Literary Works as a Source of Documentation for Technical Terms of the Material Culture. Berlin 1984. (Islamkundliche Untersuchungen; Bd. 98)

Khalid Ismail Ali: Studien über homonyme Wurzeln im Arabischen: Mit besonderer Berücksichtigung des Muʿǧam Maqāyīs al-Luġa von Aḥmad ibn Fāris (Diss. Heidelberg). Heidelberg 1964

Arne A. Ambros: Lexikostatistik des Verbs im Koran. WZKM 77 (1987) 9–36

Mohamed Ben Cheneb: Liste des abréviations employées par les auteurs arabes. Revue Africaine 61 (1920) 134–138

A. Benhamouda: Les noms arabes des étoiles: Essai d'identification. AJEO 9 (1951) 76–210

A. A. Bevan: Some Contributions to Arabic Lexicography: In: A Volume of Oriental Studies Presented to Eduard G. Browne (Cambridge 1922) 323–337

J. Bielawski: Deux périodes dans la formation de la terminology scientifique arabe. Rocznik Orientalistyczny 20 (1956) 262–320

Seeger A. Bonebakker: *Tanaḥḥala* and *Intaḥala*: A lexicographical puzzle. The Arabist: Budapest Studies in Arabic, 6–7 (1993) 105–123 (Proceedings of the Colloquium on Arabic Lexicology and Lexicography (C.A.L.L.), I, Budapest, 1–7 September 1993)

C. E. Bosworth: The Mediaeval Islamic Underworld: The Bānū Sāsān in Arabic Society and Literature. 2 vol. Leiden 1976

A. Boudot-Lamotte: Lexique de la poésie guerrière dans le Dīwān de ʿAntara b. Šaddad al-ʿAbsī. Arabica 11 (1964) 19–56

Ernst Bräunlich: The Well in Ancient Arabia. Islamica 1 (1925) 41–76, 228–343, 454–528

Pierre Cachia: العارف: معجم في مصطلحات النّحو العربي، عربي - انجليزي، انجليزي - عربي. Beirut 1973

Norman Calder: *Ḥinth, birr, tabarrur, taḥannuth*: An inquiry into the Arabic vocabulary of vows. BSOAS 51 (1988) 214–239

—: The *Qurrāʾ* and the Arabic Lexicographical Tradition. JSS 36 (1991) 297–307

David Cohen: Aḍdād et ambigüité linguistique en arabe. Arabica 8 (1961) 1–29

Abū Ḥanīfah ad-Dīnawarī: The Book of the Plants, Part of the Alphabetical Section. Ed. with an Introduction, Notes, Indices, and a Vocabulary of Selected Words by Bernhard Lewin. Uppsala/Wiesbaden 1953

Reinhart P. A. Dozy: Dictionnaire détaillé des noms des vêtements chez les Arabes. Amsterdam 1845

César E. Dubler: Los nombres arabes de materia médica en la obra del Doctor Laguna. Al-Andalus 16 (1951) 141–164

August Fischer: Ausdrücke per merismum im Arabischen. In: Streitberg-Festgabe (Leipzig 1924) 46–58

Wolfdietrich Fischer: Farb- und Formenbezeichnungen in der Sprache der altarabischen Dichtung: Untersuchungen zur Wortbedeutung und zur Wortbildung. Wiesbaden 1965.

A. Fonahn: Arabic and Latin Anatomical Terminology Chiefly from the Middle Ages. Kristiania 1922 (Videnskapsselskapets Skrifter, II. Histor.-Filos. Kl. 1921, No. 7)

Sigmund Fraenkel: Beiträge zur Erklärung der mehrlautigen Bildungen im Arabischen. Leiden 1878

Israel Friedländer: Der Sprachgebrauch des Maimonides, I. Lexikalischer Teil, Arabisch-Deutsches Lexikon zum Sprachgebrauch des Maimonides. Frankfurt a.M. 1902

Friedrich Giese: Untersuchungen über die Aḍdād auf Grund von Stellen in altarabischen Dichtern. Berlin 1894

A. M. Goichon: Lexique de la langue philosophique d'Ibn Sina (Avicenne). Paris 1938

Georg Graf: Verzeichnis arabischer kirchlicher Termini. Louvain 1954 (Corpus scriptorum christianorum orientalium, v. 147; Subsidia, Tome 8)

David A. Griffin: Los mozarabismos del "Vocabulista" atribuido Ramón Marti. Al-Andalus 23 (1958) 251–324 (1959) 333–380; 25 (1960) 93–169

Adolf Grohmann: Griechische und Lateinische Verwaltungstermini im Arabischen Ägypten. Chronique d'Égypte N°s 13–14 (Janvier 1932) 275–284

Nigel Groom: معجم الطّوبوغرافيّة واسماء الاماكن العربيّة. Dictionary of Arabic Topography and Placenames. London 1983

H. Grotzfeld: Das Bad im arabisch-islamischen Mittelalter. Wiesbaden 1970

Jaakko Markus Hameen-Anttila: Lexical Ibdal, I: Introduction; source studies, with a reconstruction of Abū Turāb's *K. al-Iʿtiqāb* (F. T. Dissertation: Helsingin Yliopisto, 1995)

H. H. Hirschberg: Some Additional Arabic Etymologies in Old Testament Lexicography. Vetus Testamentum 11 (1961) 373–385

Fritz Hommel: Die Namen der Säugetiere bei den südsemitischen Völkern. Leipzig 1879

Tamás Iványi: Laḥn and Luġa. The Arabist: Budapest Studies in Arabic 1 (1988) 67–86

Farid Jabre: Essai sur le lexique de Ghazali. Beirut 1970 (Publications de l'Université Libanaise. Section des Études Philosophiques et Sociales; No. 5)

L. Kopf: Arabische Etymologien und Parallelen zum Bibelwörterbuch. Vetus Testamentum 8 (1958) 161–215; 9 (1959) 247–287

—: Das arabische Wörterbuch als Hilfsmittel für die hebräische Lexikographie. Vetus Testamentum 6 (1956) 286–302

Alfred von Kremer: Beiträge zur arabischen Lexikographie. Wien 1883–1884 (Sitzungsberichte der Kaiserl. Akademie der Wissenschaften, Philos.-Hist. Cl. Bd. 103, S. 181 ff.; Bd. 105, S. 329 ff.)

Paul Kunitzsch: Arabische Sternnamen in Europa. Wiesbaden 1959

—: Untersuchungen zur Sternnomenklatur der Araber. Wiesbaden 1961

Aryeh Levin: The Category of ʾ*asmāʾ al-fiʿl* in Arabic Grammar. The Arabist: Budapest Studies in Arabic, 3–4 (1991) 247–256 (Proceedings of the Colloquium on Arabic Grammar, Budapest, 1–7 September 1991)

Immanuel Löw: Die Flora der Juden. 4 vol., Wien-Leipzig 1928

—: Semitische Färberpflanzen. ZS 1 (1922) 97–162

—: Aramäische Pflanzennamen. Leipzig 1881

Radwan S. Mahadin: Doublets in Arabic: Notes towards a diachronic phonological study. Language Sciences 11 (1989) 1–25

Louis Massignon: Essai sur les origines du lexique technique de la mystique musulmane. Paris 1968

R. Mielck: Terminologie und Technologie der Müller und Bäcker im islamischen Mittelalter. Glückstadt-Hamburg 1913

A. Morabia: Recherches sur quelques noms de couleur en arabe classique. SI 21 (1964) 61–99

Paul Nwyia: Exégèse coranique et langage mystique: Nouvel essai sur le lexique technique des mystiques musulmanes. Beirut 1970 (Recherches publiés sous la direction de l'Institut des Lettres Orientales de Beyrouth, 1e Série, vol. 49)

Ahmed Mokhtar Omer: Early Arabic Lexicons of Homophonic Words. The Arabist: Budapest Studies in Arabic, 6–7 (1993) 3–11 (Proceedings of the Colloquium on Arabic Lexicology and Lexicography (C.A.L.L.), I, Budapest, 1–7 September 1993)

Charles Pellat: Un fait d'expressivité en arabe: Iʾitbāʿ. Arabica 4 (1957) 131–173

D. C. Phillott: Vocabulary of Technical Falconry Terms in Urdu, Persian and Arabic. Journal and Proceedings of the Asiatic Society of Bengal, N. S. 6 (1910) 315–380

F. Pollak: Beiträge zum arabischen Lexikon. WZKM 32 (1925) 245–274; 38 (1932) 100–124

Fred Renfroe: Arabic-Ugaritic Lexical Studies. Münster 1992 (Abhandlungen zur Literatur Alt-Syrien-Palästinas; Bd. 5)

Frithjof Rundgren: La lexicographie arabe. In: Studies on Semitic Lexicography by James Barr ... [et al.] ; ed. by Pelio Fronzaroli (Firenze 1973) 145–159 (Quaderni di semitistica; 2)

—: Semitische Wortstudien. Orientalia Suecana 10 (1961) 99–136

J. Sadan: Le Mobilier au proche orient médiéval. Leiden 1976

Werner Schmucker: Die Pflanzliche und Mineralische Materia Medica im Firdaus al-Ḥikma des Ṭabarī Bonn 1969 (Bonner Orientalistische Studien N. S.; 18)

Marco Scholler: Die Palmen (*līna*) der Banū n-Naḍīr und die Interpretation von Koran 59:5: Eine Untersuchung zur Bedeutung des koranischen Wortlauts in den ersten Jahrhunderten islamischer Gelehrsamkeit. ZDMG 146 (1996) 317–380

Friedrich Schwally: Lexikalische Studien. ZDMG 52 (1898) 132–148

Friedrich Wilhelm Schwarzlose: Die Waffen der alten Araber aus ihren Dichtern dargestellt: Ein Beitrag zur arabischen Altertumskunde, Synonymik und Lexikographie nebst Registern. Leipzig 1886

Alfred Siggel: Arabisch-deutsches Wörterbuch der Stoffe aus den drei Naturbereichen, die in arabischen alchemistischen Handschriften vorkommen, nebst Anhang: Verzeichnis chemischer Geräte. Berlin 1950 (Institut für Orientforschung; Nr. 1)

—: Decknamen in der arabischen alchemistischen Literatur (Institut für Orientforschung; Nr. 5). Berlin 1951

Muṣṭafā a<u>sh</u>-<u>Sh</u>ihābī: المصطلحات العلميّة في اللّغة العربيّة في القديم والحديث. Dima<u>sh</u>q 1965

Mohamed Souissi: Langue de mathématique en arabe. Tunis 1968

Anton Spitaler: *al-qalamu aḥadu l-lisānaini*: Beiträge zur Lexikographie des Klassischen Arabisch; Nr. 8. München 1989 (Sitzungsberichte – Bayerische Akademie der Wissenschaften, Philosophisch-Historische Klasse; Jahrg. 1989, Heft 2)

—: Bemerkungen zu den Quellen des Lisān al-ʿArab. In: Festschrift Ewald Wagner zum 65. Geburtstag, I: Semitische Studien unter besonderer Berucksichtigung der Südsemitistik (Stuttgart 1994) 259–274 (Beiruter Texte und Studien; 54)

Jaroslav Stetkevych: Arabic Hermeneutical Terminology: Paradox and the production of meaning. JNES 48 (1989) 81–96

Peter Stocks: Edward William Lane and His Arabic-English 'Thesaurus'. The British Library Journal 15 (1989) 23–34

Charles Ambrose Storey: Lexicographical Jottings. In: A volume of Oriental studies presented to Edward G. Browne (Cambridge 1922) 445–456

Heidi Toelle: L'Étranger: Étude sémantique lexicale de quelques racines et de leur inter-relation. Arabica 36 (1989) 272–285

Charles C. Torrey: The Commercial-Theological Terms in the Koran. Leyden 1892

Manfred Ullmann: Aufs Wasser schreiben. Beiträge zur Lexikographie des klassischen Arabisch; nr. 7. München 1989 (Sitzungsberichte – Bayerische Akademie der Wissenschaften, Philosophisch-Historische Klasse; Jahrg. 1989, Heft 1.)

—: Flughühner und Tauben. Beiträge zur Lexikographie des klassischen Arabisch; Nr. 3. München 1982 (Sitzungsberichte – Bayerische Akademie der Wissenschaften. Philosophisch-historische Klasse; Jahrg. 1982, Heft 1)

—: Das Gespräch mit dem Wolf. Beiträge zur Lexikographie des klassischen Arabisch; Nr. 2. München 1981 (Sitzungsberichte – Bayerische Akademie der Wissenschaften, Philosophisch-Historische Klasse; Jahrg. 1981, Heft 2)

—: *Launuhū ilā l-ḥumrati mā huwa*. Beiträge zur Lexikographie des Klassischen Arabisch Nr. 11. München 1994 (Sitzungsberichte – Bayerische Akademie der Wissenschaften. Philosophisch-historische Klasse; 1994, no. 4, 338)

—: Das Motiv des Spiegels in der arabischen Literatur des Mittelalters. Göttingen 1992 (Abhandlungen der Akademie der Wissenschaften in Göttingen. Philologisch-Historische Klasse; 3. Folge, Nr. 198)

—: Sätze mit *lau*; vorgelegt von Anton Spitaler. Beiträge zur Lexikographie des Klassischen Arabisch; Nr. 14. München 1998 (Sitzungsberichte – Bayerische Akademie der Wissenschaften, Philosophisch-Historische Klasse; Jahrg. 1998 Heft 1)

—: *Wa-ḫairu l-ḥadīṯi ma kāna lahnan*; mit einem Anhang von Rainer Degen. Beiträge zur Lexikographie des Klassischen Arabisch ; Nr. 1. München 1979 (Sitzungsberichte – Bayerische Akademie der Wissenschaften. Philosophisch-Historische Klasse; Jahrg. 1979, Heft 9)

—: Zur Geschichte des Wortes *barīd* “Post”. Beiträge zur Lexikographie des klassischen Arabisch; nr. 13. München 1989 (Sitzungsberichte – Bayerische Akademie der Wissenschaften, Philosophisch-Historische Klasse, Jahrg. 1997, Heft)

Concepcion Vazquez de Benito: Adiciones a los diccionarios árabes, II. Al-Qanṭara: Revista de Estudios Árabes 9 (1988) 151–167

F. Viré: Falconaria Arabica, Glanures philologiques. Arabica 8 (1961) 273–293; 9 (1962) 37–60, 152–192

Marcus Wald: Die Arabischen Glossen in den Schriften der Gaonim. Abhandlung zur Erlangung der Doktorwürde ... Zürich. Oxford 1935

Concordances, Frequency Statistics

Muḥammad Fuʾād ʿAbd al-Bāqī: المعجم المفهرس لالفاظ القرآن الكريم. Cairo 1364/1945. Reprint: Cairo 1968

Marwān al-Bawwāb [et al.]: احصاء الافعال العربية في المعجم الحسوبي Beirut 1996. (المعجم الحسوبي ١)

Hartmut Bobzin: On the Frequency of Verbs in Modern Newspaper Arabic. al-Abḥāth 31 (1983) 45–63

—: Zur Häufigkeit von Verben im Neuhocharabischen. ZAL 5 (1980) 35–69

Moshe Brill, D. Neustadt, P. Schusser: The Basic Word-list of the Arabic Daily Newspaper. Jerusalem 1940

Concordance et Indices de la Tradition Musulmane, Organisés et commencés par A. J. Wensinck et J. P. Mensing. Continués par J. Brugman. 7 vol. Leiden 1936–1969. vol. 8: Indices. Leiden 1985. Reprint: Istanbul 1986 (7 vol.).

August Fischer – E. Bräunlich: Schawāhid Indices: Indices der Reimwörter und der Dichter der in den arabischen Schawāhid-Kommentaren und in verwandten Werken erläuterten Belegverse. Leipzig/Wien 1945

Gustav Flügel: Concordantiae Corani arabicae: Ad literarum ordinem et verborum radices diligenter disposuit... Leipzig 1842 [numerous reprints]

W. D. Fromm: Frequency Dictionary of Modern Newspaper Arabic: A skeleton vocabulary Arabic-German-English. Leipzig 1982

Hanna E. Kassis. A Concordance of the Qurʿan. Berkeley 1983.

Jacob M. Landau: A Word Count of Modern Arabic Prose. New York 1959 (American Council of Learned Societies)

مجمع اللّغة العربيّة، الادارة العامّة للمعجمات واحياء التراث. معجم الفاظ القرآن الكريم. الطبعة ٢، طبعة منقّحة. القاهرة ١٩٨٨-١٩٩٠

Abdulghafur Sabuni: Wörterbuch des arabischen Grundwortschatzes: Die 2000 häufigsten Wörter. Hamburg 1988.

Foreign Language Words in Arabic

Asya Asbaghi: Persische Lehnwörter im Arabischen. Wiesbaden 1988.

as-Sayyid Yaʿqūb Bakr: دراسات مقارنة في المعجم العربي. Beirut 1970

D. Guiseppe Barbera: Elementi Italo-Siculo-Veneziano-Genovesi nei linguaggi Arabo e Turco con una prefazione storico-filologica. Beirut 1940

Rudolf Dvořák: Über die Fremdwörter im Koran. Wien 1885

W. Eilers: Iranisches Lehngut im arabischen Lexikon: Über einige Berufsnamen und Titel. Indo-lranian Journal 5 (Festschrift H. W. Duda, 's-Gravenhage 1957) 203–232; Nachtrag: 308–309

—: Iranisches Lehngut im Arabischen. Actas IV congresso de estudos árabes e islâmicos (Leiden 1971) 581–656

Sigmund Fraenkel: Die aramäischen Fremdwörter im Arabischen. Leiden 1878

—: De Vocabulis in antiquis Arabum carminibus et in Corano peregrinis. Leiden 1880

Hubert Grimme: Über einige Klassen südarabischer Lehnwörter im Koran. ZA 20 (1912) 158–168

Gustav von Grünebaum: Persische Wörter in arabischen Gedichten. MO 31 (1937) 18–22

Fuʾād Ḥasanayn: الدّخيل في اللّغة العربيّة. BFA 10,2 (1948) 75–112; 11, 1 (1949) 27–56; 11, 2 (1949) 1–36; 12, 1 (1950) 37–74

Ahmed Irhayem Hebbo: Die Fremdwörter in der arabischen Prophetenbiographie des Ibn Hischam (gest. 218/834). Dissertation Heidelberg 1970

Abū Manṣūr al-Jawālīqī: المعرّب من الكلام الاعجمي على حروف المعجم, ed. A. Šākir. Cairo 1361/1942

Ǧawālīḳī's al-Muʿarrab: Nach der Leydener Handschrift mit Erläuterungen hrsg. von Eduard Sachau. Leipzig 1867

Arthur Jeffery: The Foreign Vocabulary of the Qur᾿an. Baroda 1938 (Gackwad's Oriental Series; vol. 79)

Murad Kamil: Persian Words in Ancient Arabic. BFA 19 (1957) 55–67

Ṣalāḥ ad-Dīn al-Kawākibī: الكلمات الدّخيلة على العربيّة الاصيلة· مجلّة مجمع اللّغة العربيّة بدمشق 48 (1973) 519–550; 50 (1975) 484–493, 737-758; 51 (1976) 23–32

L. Kopf: The Treatment of Foreign Words in Mediæval Arabic Lexicology. Scripta Hierosolymitana 9 (1961) 191–205

David Samuel Margoliouth: Some Additions to Professor Jeffery's Foreign Vocabulary of the Qu᾿an. JRAS 1939 53–61

Armas Salonen: Alte Substrat- und Kulturwörter im Arabischen. Helsinki 1952 (Studia Orientalia 17:2)

Ibrāhīm al-Sāmarrā᾿ī: الدخيل في الفارسيّة والعربيّة والتركيّة: معجم ودراسة· الطبعة ١. Beirut 1997

Ramazan Şeşen: Cāḥiẓ' in eserlerinde farsça kelimeler. Şarkiyat Mecmuası 7 (Istanbul 1972) 137–181

A. Siddiqi: Ibn Duraid and His Treatment of Loan-words. The Allahabad University Studies 6 (1930) 669–750

—: Studien über die persischen Fremdwörter im Klassischen Arabisch. Göttingen 1919

Addī Shīr: الالفاظ الفارسيّة المعرّبة. Beirut 1908 (Addi Shirr: Persian Arabicised Words in Arabic. Reprint. Teheran 1965)

Anton Spitaler: Materialien zur Erklärung von Fremdwörtern im Arabischen durch retrograde Ableitung. In: Corolla linguistica: Festschrift F. Sommer (Wiesbaden 1955) 211–220

Wilhelm Spitta: Die Lücken in Ǧawālīkī's Mu῾arrab. ZDMG 33 (1879) 208–224

Ṭubīyā al-῾Unaysī: تفسير الالفاظ الدّخيلة في اللّغة العربيّة. Cairo 1964

Heinrich Zimmern: Akkadische Fremdwörter als Beweis für Babylonischen Kultureinfluß. Leipzig [2]1917

Nomenclature

Y. ῾Abdallāh: Die Personennamen in al-Hamdānīs al-Iklīl und ihre Parallelen in den alt-südarabischen Inschriften. Dissertation Tübingen 1975

Adrien C. Barbier de Meynard: Surnomes et sobriquets dans la littérature arabe. JA X 9 (1907) 173–244, 365-428; 10 (1907) 55–118, 193–273

Ḥasan al-Bā<u>sh</u>ā: الالقاب الاسلاميّة في التّاريخ والوثائق والآثار. Cairo 1958

A. F. L. Beeston: Arabic Nomenclature: A summary guide for beginners. Oxford 1971.

C. E. Bosworth: Laḳab. Encyclopædia of Islam[2] vol. 5 618–631

—: A Note on *taʿarrub* in Early Islam. JSS 34 (1989) 355–362

H. H. Bräu: Die altnordarabischen kultischen Personennamen. WZKM 32 (1925) 31–59; 85–115

Leone Caetani – Giuseppe Gabrieli: Onomasticon Arabicum ossia Repertoire Alfabetico dei nomi di persona e di luogo contenuti nelle principali opere storiche ... vol. l. (Aʿābīl – ʿAbdallāh). Roma 1915 – Reprint 1975

Cahiers d'onomastique arabe. Responsable: Jacqueline Sublet. Éditions du Centre National de la Recherche Scientifique. [1979] (Paris 1979); 1981 (Paris 1982); 1982–1984 (Paris 1985)

Cahiers d'onomastique arabe, 1988–1992. ed. Denise Aigle ... [et al.] Responsable: Jacqueline Sublet. Paris 1993

Le dictionnaire des noms et prénoms arabes [sous la dir. de Dominique Penot]. Lyon 1996

Albrecht Dietrich: Zu den mit *ad-dīn* zusammengesetzten Personennamen. ZDMG 110 (1961) 43–53

August Fischer: Muḥammad und Aḥmad die Namen des arabischen Propheten. Leipzig 1932 (Berichte über die Verhandlungen der Sächsischen Akademie der Wiss. zu Leipzig Phil.-Hist. Kl.; 84, 3)

—: Vergöttlichung und Tabuisierung der Namen Muḥammad's bei den Muslimen. In: R. Hartmann u. H. Scheel [Hrsg.]: Beiträge zur Arabistik, Semitistik und Islamwissenschaft (Leipzig 1944) 307–339

Henri Fleisch: Ism. Encyclopædia of Islam[2] vol. 4 181–182

Emil Gratzl: Die altarabischen Frauennamen. Leipzig 1906

J. H. Kramers: Les noms musulmans composés avec Dīn. Acta Orientalia 5 (1927) 53–67

Manuela Marin: Onomástica árabe en al-Andalus: Ism ʿalam y Kunya. Al-Qanṭara 4 (1983) 131–149

M. Naimur-Rahman: The Kunya-names in Arabic. Allahabad University Studies 5 (1929) 341–442; 6 (1930) 751–883

Heinrich Ringel: Die Frauennamen in der arabisch-islamischen Liebesdichtung (Dissertation Erlangen). Leipzig 1938

Ibrāhīm as-Sāmarrā'ī: الاعلام العربيّة ، دراسة لغويّة اجتماعيّة. Baghdad 1964.

Annemarie Schimmel: Islamic names. Edinburgh 1989. (Islamic surveys)

Joachim Senfft: Beiträge zur frühislamischen Personennamenkunde. Berlin 1942 (Dissertation in Maschinenschrift)

Anton Spitaler: Beiträge zur Kunya-Namengebung. In: Festschrift Werner Caskel zum 70. Geburtstag gewidmet (Leiden 1968) 336–350

Jacqueline Sublet: Nisba. Encyclopædia of Islam[2] vol. 8 53–56

Ulrich Thilo: Die Ortsnamen in der altarabischen Poesie. Ein Beitrag zur vor- und frühislamischen Dichtung und zur historischen Topographie Nordarabiens. Wiesbaden 1958

Manfred Ullmann Das arabische Nomen generis. Göttingen 1989. (Abhandlungen der Akademie der Wissenschaften in Göttingen. Philologisch-Hist. Kl. 3. Folge; Nr. 176)

A. J. Wensinck: Kunya. Encyclopædia of Islam[2] vol. 5 395–396

Stefan Wild: Libanesische Ortsnamen. Typologie und Deutung. Beirut 1973 (Beiruter Texte und Studien; Bd. 9)

Journal Abbreviations

AIEO	Annales de l'Institut d'Études Orientales (Faculté des Lettres de l'Université d'Alger)
ArOr	Archiv Orientální (Československá Akademie věd: Orientální – Úststav, Praha)
BEO	Bulletin d'Études Orientales (Institut Français de Damas)
BFA	Bulletin of the Faculty of Arts, University of Cairo – Majallat Kulliyyat al-Ādāb
BSL	Bulletin de la Société de Linguistique de Paris
BSOAS	Bulletin of the School of Oriental and African Studies, London
JA	Journal Asiatique, Paris
JAOS	Journal of the American Oriental Society, New Haven/Ann Arbor
JNES	Journal of Near Eastern Studies, Chicago
JRAS	Journal of the Royal Asiatic Society, London
JSS	Journal of Semitic Studies, Manchester
MMAD	Majallat al-Majmaᶜ al-ʿIlmī al-ʿArabī bi-Dimashq (Revue de l'Academie Arab, Damas)
MMLA	Majallat Majmaᶜ al-Lughah al-ʿArabiyyah, al-Qāhirah
MO	Le Monde Oriental, Uppsala
MSOS	Mitteilungen des Seminars für Orientalische Sprachen, Berlin
MUSJ	Mélanges de l'Université Saint Joseph, Beyrouth
OLZ	Orientalistische Literaturzeitung, Leipzig/Berlin
RSO	Rivista degli Studi Orientali, Roma
SI	Studia Islamica, Paris
WZKM	Wiener Zeitschrift für die Kunde des Morgenlandes, Wien
ZA	Zeitschrift für Assyriologie und verwandte Gebiete, Berlin
ZAL	Zeitschrift für Arabische Linguistik, Wiesbaden
ZDMG	Zeitschrift der Deutschen Morgenländischen Gesellschaft, Leipzig/Wiesbaden
ZS	Zeitschrift für Semitistik, Leipzig

Index

All numbers refer to paragraphs (§).
Decimal numbers refer to paragraph notes.